THE NEW MEXICO GUIDE

The Definitive Guide to the Land of Enchantment

THE NEW MEXICO GUIDE

Third Edition

DON & BARBARA LAINE

Fulcrum Publishing
Golden, Colorado

This third edition of *The New Mexico Guide* is dedicated to our friend and colleague Charles L. Cadieux, the author of the first two editions and a man who loves New Mexico as much as we do.

Text and interior photographs copyright © 2005 Don and Barbara Laine

Every effort was made to make *The New Mexico Guide, Third Edition*, as accurate as possible. However, prices, hours of operation, addresses, phone numbers, Web sites, and other items change rapidly. If something in the book is incorrect, please write to the authors in care of Fulcrum Publishing, 16100 Table Mountain Parkway, Suite 300, Golden, Colorado 80403; fulcrum@fulcrum-books.com.

The New Mexico Guide provides many safety tips about weather and travel, but good decision-making and sound judgment are the responsibility of the individual. Neither the publisher nor the author assumes any liability for injury that may arise from the use of this book.

Library of Congress Cataloging-in-Publication Data

Laine, Don.
  The New Mexico guide : The Definitive Guide to the Land of Enchantment / Don and Barbara Laine.—3rd ed.
      p. cm.
  Includes index.
  ISBN 1-55591-318-0
  1. New Mexico—Guidebooks. I. Laine, Barbara. II. Title.
  F794.3.L353 2005
  917.8904'54—dc22

                              2004024230

Printed in the United States of America
0 9 8 7 6 5 4 3 2 1

Project Editor: Daniel Forrest-Bank
Editor: Faith Marcovecchio
Interior design: Trina Stahl
Page compositor: Patty Maher
Maps: Don and Barbara Laine
Cover image: San Francisco de Asis Church, Ranchos de Taos Plaza,
        © Melanie Stephens • www.melaniestephens.com

Fulcrum Publishing
16100 Table Mountain Parkway, Suite 300
Golden, Colorado 80403
(800) 992-2908 • (303) 277-1623
www.fulcrum-books.com

CONTENTS

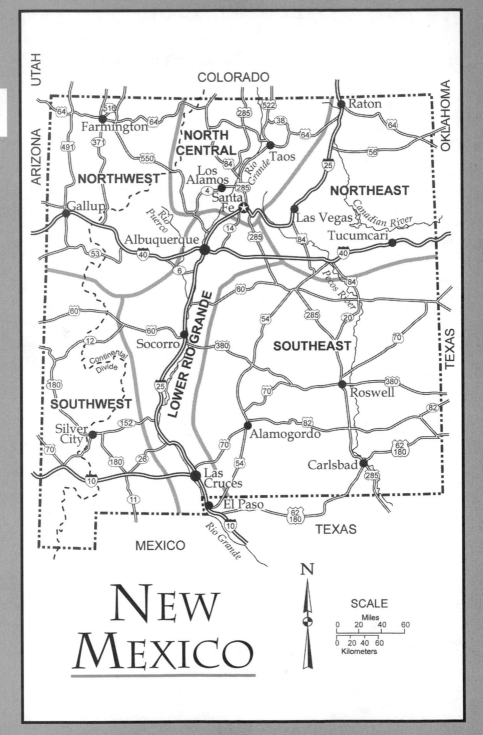

NEW MEXICO

Introduction

This Is New Mexico

A land of contrasts and contradictions, New Mexico is a mix of extremes— prickly pear cactus and tall evergreens, sun-baked desert and deep powder snow, modern America and ancient civilizations. Some come to New Mexico to see American Indians, wrapped in blankets in their centuries-old adobe pueblos. Others visit the state to follow the trail of legendary gunslinger Billy the Kid, or to explore crumbling ghost towns where sagebrush and cactus have taken over once-busy streets. Railroad depots from long-gone mining days dot the state, and visitors can climb aboard a historic steam train for a memorable trip into the past.

In many ways, a trip to New Mexico is an excursion to a foreign country, an exotic land of enchantment and excitement, yet no passport is needed. The state's three dominant cultures—American Indian, Hispanic, and Anglo—are unique but intertwined, each retaining its individual identity and culture while influencing each other in a sometimes-reluctant melting pot.

The state is an art center, with hundreds of galleries, studios, and museums. Art lovers can not only see and buy art from prehistoric petroglyphs to the most avant-garde modern mediums, but can also join classes, tour studios, and watch many of today's artists at work. Museums explore the cultural and historic, including beautiful American Indian pottery and blankets, artifacts from the state's Spanish colonial days, Civil War and Old West memorabilia, and events continuing right up to the atom bomb and the exploration of outer space.

This is a land of spectacular scenic beauty. New Mexicans brag about their towering Rocky Mountains, pristine desert sands, and vast underground caverns. Hunting, fishing, and camping are extremely popular, and hikers revel in the state's unspoiled wilderness. Winter snows turn New Mexico into a paradise for skiers and snowboarders, with deep powder and plenty of sunshine. In addition to world-class downhill ski resorts, there are plenty of opportunities for cross-country skiing, snowshoeing, and snowmobiling.

In short, there are many reasons to visit New Mexico, and a great variety of activities that are bound to satisfy most every taste and budget. We hope you will take time exploring the state's hidden treasures as well as its major attractions, seeing its mountains and deserts, enjoying its foods, and meeting its people. You won't find anything like New Mexico anywhere else in America.

History

Back in the old days, some 20,000 to 25,000 years ago, Sandia Man roamed into the area we now call New Mexico. These early people were following the mastodon, bison, and early forms of the camel and horse, sources of food and clothing for their nomadic life. The only shelters they knew were natural ones— caves or small indentations in rocks. As glaciers receded and the climate became drier, they became more dependent on plants, although hunting was still important.

Then in the first few centuries A.D. corn was introduced from Mexico. The

Introduction

people in the western two-thirds of what was to become New Mexico settled in permanent or semi-permanent villages, often located along rivers, while those in the eastern third remained primarily nomadic. Those who settled in the northwestern corner of New Mexico are known as Ancestral Puebloan (also called Anasazi), while those in the southwestern section are called Mogollon.

The Mogollon lived in pit houses and carried on a lively trade with the peoples to the south in the region we call Mexico. The Ancestral Puebloan were more urbanized, with complex houses, usually constructed aboveground. Discovering the increased strength of cluster-type construction, they eventually created complex stone buildings, with several stories and often hundreds of rooms, and ceremonial belowground structures called kivas. During this time, both groups started making pottery and baskets to transport and store their plants and grains.

The Ancestral Puebloan territory covered much of the Four Corners area—northwestern New Mexico and adjacent areas of Colorado, Utah, and Arizona—and one of the major centers of their civilization was Chaco Canyon, an extremely complex and highly developed settlement in northwestern New Mexico. For reasons we don't fully understand, the Ancestral Puebloans left the Four Corners area about A.D. 1200. The move probably was triggered by changes in climate, although there may have been other reasons as well. It's generally believed that most of them resettled in smaller communities, the pueblos.

When Spanish conquistadors arrived in the 1500s, they called the people they found "Pueblo" Indians, because their buildings resembled Spanish villages, or pueblos. Francisco Vasquez de Coronado set out from Mexico in 1540 to find the rumored "Seven Cities of Gold," exploring what is now Arizona, New Mexico, Texas,

Rafting on the Rio Grande.

Oklahoma, and Kansas, until turning back in disappointment. There were several other unsuccessful expeditions into the region in the late 1500s, and then in 1598 Don Juan de Oñate was appointed governor and directed to settle the area along the upper Rio Grande.

Oñate led an expedition of about 200 settlers—including soldiers, families, and priests—and 7,000 head of livestock and established the first Spanish colony along the Rio Grande near its confluence with the Rio Chama, close to Española, at present day San Juan Pueblo. The settlers began setting up farms, and the Franciscan priests began their job of converting the Indians to Christianity.

Spanish settlements appeared along the Rio Grande and its tributaries, from Taos in the north to Socorro in the south. Life was far from peaceful, however, with both civil and religious conflicts between settlers and Indians. In 1680, in an unprecedented demonstration of unity, the Pueblos revolted and drove the hated Spanish conquerors south to El Paso. Twelve years later, Capt. Gen. Diego de Vargas led the Spanish in a peaceful recapture of New Mexico.

Spain's influence came to an end in 1821 with the Mexican Revolution, and under Mexican control New Mexico was encouraged to trade with its American neighbors. That same year, the Santa Fe Trail was opened, an event that changed forever the course of New Mexican history. So many traders and settlers came over the Trail that you can still see the ruts from their wagon wheels in the northeastern part of the state. Santa Fe soon became a bustling hub of trade, through which caravans made their way to northern Mexico along the Camino Real (Royal Road) and to California via the Old Spanish Trail.

In 1841, the Mexican governor granted 1,714,764 acres of northeastern New Mexico, the largest grant in the state, to Carlos Beaubien, a French trapper, and Guadalupe Miranda of Taos. In 1849, Lucien B. Maxwell, a hunter and trapper who came to New Mexico from Illinois, married Beaubien's daughter Luz, and later bought out the remaining heirs, to become the largest single landholder in the Western Hemisphere.

New Mexicans felt isolated because their mother country, Mexico, was busy with its own problems. In 1841, the new Republic of Texas invaded New Mexico in an effort to capture control of the trade route through the state. The Texans were defeated, but the inability of Mexico to protect the northern province from attack led inevitably to the success of the United States.

In 1846, U.S. Brig. Gen. Stephen Watts Kearny led a peaceful takeover of New Mexico when he marched into Santa Fe, the capital, and took control without opposition. He did suffer a setback four months later when a group of New Mexicans rebelled and killed most of the new government officials, including the newly appointed governor, Charles Bent. The revolt was quickly suppressed, however, and the insurgents were tried for treason and executed.

The Treaty of Guadalupe Hidalgo ended the Mexican War in 1848, and the United States officially took possession of New Mexico, Arizona, and California. In 1853, the Gadsden Purchase set the present-day boundary between Mexico and the United States.

When the Civil War began in 1861, the South looked to the West for the gold of Colorado and California, and military supplies from centers such as

Fort Union, near Las Vegas, New Mexico. In July 1861, a Confederate army from Texas invaded New Mexico, and by early 1862 it had captured both Albuquerque and Santa Fe, thereby controlling the Santa Fe Trail. For two weeks, the Confederate flag flew over the territory's capital city. At the end of Mar. 1862, a force of Colorado volunteers and New Mexico militia engaged the Texans at the Battle of Glorieta, just east of Santa Fe, defeating them and ending any further threat to the Union in the West.

In 1880, the railroad arrived in New Mexico and within 10 years railroads reached into every corner of the territory, bringing new residents, new ideas, new goods, and faster communication. The Santa Fe Trail closed, and towns sprang up along the rails. It was during this period that New Mexico contributed to the folklore and myths that built the famed Wild West, with William (Billy the Kid) Bonney, Clay Allison, and other notorious outlaws among its more infamous residents. It was also during this era that the Indians were subdued and confined to reservations.

The Territory of New Mexico was granted statehood on Jan. 6, 1912, and became the 47th state in the Union. In the early part of the century, farming and ranching flourished alongside a rapidly expanding mining industry. In the 1920s, Taos and Santa Fe became recognized art colonies, and by the late 1930s, tourism was a new and important industry.

New Mexico has always assumed her share in the nation's wars, but World War II had the greatest impact on the state. A large number of New Mexicans were among American troops subjected to the infamous Bataan Death March in the Philippines, and Navajo code talkers used their native tongue to send secret radio messages for the military, confounding the Japanese throughout the war.

Finally, Los Alamos, a small town in the mountains northwest of Santa Fe, was chosen as a secret location to develop the atomic bomb. After two years of work, a team of scientists drove to the Trinity Test Site in the New Mexico desert, and in the early hours of July 16, 1945, the first atomic bomb was detonated. At the moment of the explosion, project director Robert J. Oppenheimer recalled a passage from the Hindu poem *Bhagavad Gita*, "I am become death. The destroyer of worlds." The atom bomb not only led to the end of the war in the Pacific, but also ushered in the Nuclear Age.

As New Mexico moves into the 21st century, it is seeing tremendous growth and change, moving from a reliance on oil, gas, and minerals to high technology and manufacturing. Still, New Mexico remains rooted in its past, from American Indians to Spanish colonists to cowboys. Alongside the computer wiz telecommuting to some big-city corporation, Chimayo weavers work at the looms their ancestors built a hundred years ago, and pueblo potters quietly release the beauty from a lump of clay. There's poetry in the wind through the aspens and in the rushing waters of the melting snows of spring. This is a land and a people of contrasts and similarities, traditions and innovations.

Geography and Climate

New Mexico is a big place—with 121,666 square miles it's America's fifth largest state, behind Alaska, Texas, California, and Montana. It's called the Land of Enchantment, but it could also be called the Land of Infinite Variety, as it includes brilliant red sandstone cliffs, beautiful pine-clad mountains, sparkling cold streams, and flat burning desert. This is the meeting ground for the Great Plains, the southern Rockies, and the Colorado Plateau. Elevations range from 2,800 to more than 13,000 feet, and encompass six of the seven life zones found in the United States: Arctic-Alpine, Hudsonian, Canadian, Transition, Upper Sonoran, and Lower Sonoran. (The one you won't find is Tropical.)

New Mexico's weather is dramatic, exciting, and capricious. You may not like what it's doing, but it will never bore you. The state is known for its spring winds—great for windsurfing, lousy for most other activities—and one prominent newspaper columnist has decreed that the state's four seasons should be called summer, fall, winter, and wind.

Visitor Information

General Information

For statewide information and a free copy of the official *State Guide to New Mexico*, contact the **New Mexico Department of Tourism, 491 Old Santa Fe Trail, Santa Fe, 87501; 505-827-7400; www.newmexico.org.**

There are nine state welcome centers where you can pick up brochures and maps: **In Santa Fe in the Lamy Building at 491 Old Santa Fe Trail, 505-827-7336; along the Texas border south of Las Cruces at I-10 exit 0, 505-882-2419; in Chama, 2372 NM 17, 505-756-2235; in Gallup, at I-40 exit 22, 505-863-4909; near Glenrio, just inside the state's eastern boundary on I-40; at Lordsburg at the I-10 exit 20 rest area, 505-542-8149; on I-25, 17 miles south of Santa Fe, 505-424-0823; in Raton at I-25 exit**

Average Temperatures

Average high and low monthly temperatures (in degrees Fahrenheit) and precipitation (in inches) for Albuquerque, Las Cruces, and Santa Fe:

| | Albuquerque | | Las Cruces | | Santa Fe | |
	Temp.	Precip.	Temp.	Precip.	Temp.	Precip.
January	47/22	0.41	57/26	0.39	40/19	0.69
February	53/26	0.40	63/29	0.45	44/22	0.69
March	61/32	0.51	69/35	0.30	51/28	0.71
April	71/40	0.40	77/42	0.14	60/35	0.83
May	80/49	0.46	85/49	0.24	69/43	1.37
June	91/58	0.51	94/59	0.63	79/52	1.14
July	93/65	1.30	94/65	1.50	82/57	2.19
August	89/63	1.51	92/63	1.84	80/56	2.27
September	83/55	0.85	87/56	1.15	74/49	1.44
October	72/43	0.86	78/44	0.83	63/38	1.05
November	57/31	0.38	66/32	0.40	50/27	0.60
December	48/23	0.52	57/26	0.44	41/20	0.70
Average, Total	71/42	8.11	77/44	8.31	61/37	13.68

451, 505-445-2761; and at Anthony (near Clovis), at the New Mexico–Texas border at the junction on US Hwys. 70, 60, and 84, 505-482-3321.

For road conditions and closure information, check the state **Transportation Department's Highway Hotline: 800-432-4269; www.nmshtd.state.nm.us.**

The telephone area code 505 covers the entire state. New Mexico is on Mountain Time, which is two hours earlier than Eastern Time (New York) and one hour later than Pacific Time (California). The state observes Daylight Saving Time.

Outdoor Recreation Information

With five national forests, dozens of state and national parks, and vast tracts of other public land, there is no excuse to stay indoors. Information on most of the state's public lands, both state and federal, is available from the **Public Lands Information Center (www.publiclands.org),** which has a visitor center located at **1474 Rodeo Rd., Santa Fe, 87505; 505-438-7542.**

There are a number of parks and monuments in New Mexico administered by the National Park Service. Information is available from the **Intermountain Region Support Office of the National Park Service, 2968 Rodeo Park Dr., Santa Fe, 87505; 505-988-6100; www.nps.gov.** Information on New Mexico's almost three dozen state parks can be obtained from **New Mexico State Parks, P.O. Box 1147, Santa Fe, 87504; 888-667-2757; 505-476-3355; www.nmparks.com.**

National forest and wilderness maps and information on recreation in the

national forests can be obtained from the **USDA Forest Service Office, 333 Broadway SE, Albuquerque, 87102; 505-842-3192; www.fs.fed.us/r3.** A variety of maps and other information is available from the **Bureau of Land Management, N.M. State Office, P.O. Box 27115, Santa Fe, 87502-0115; 505-438-7400; www.nm.blm.gov.**

New Mexico has numerous opportunities for fishing and hunting, particularly in the northern mountains. Licenses, information, and equipment can be obtained at sporting goods stores throughout the state. You can also contact the **New Mexico Department of Game and Fish, P.O. Box 25112, Santa Fe, 87504; 800-862-9310; 505-476-8000; www.gmfsh.state.nm.us.**

The state's mountains offer some of the best skiing and snowboarding in the country. For information on downhill and cross-country resorts, contact **Ski New Mexico, P.O. Box 1104, Santa Fe, 87504; 505-982-5300; www.skinewmexico.com.** Contact the USDA Forest Service (see above) for information on the numerous places to cross-country ski in the national forests.

With generally mild weather and dozens of golf courses, there are ample opportunities for golfers. Check with **Golf New Mexico, 308 Enchanted Valley Cir. NW, Albuquerque, 87107; 866-485-3661; 505-342-1563.**

Getting to and around New Mexico

A large state with many wide, open spaces, New Mexico is best explored by car or RV, unless you are planning to limit your trip to Santa Fe, Albuquerque, or one of the larger ski resorts. The state is crossed by major interstate highways—I-25 north to south, I-40 east to west, and I-10 in the southwest corner—and there is a network of U.S. and state highways. Major airports serving the state are in Albuquerque and El Paso, Texas. New Mexico is also served by Amtrak and several major bus lines.

Using This Book

This book is organized into six geographic regions: North Central Mountains, Northeast, Northwest, Lower Rio Grande, Southeast, and Southwest. Each region has a corresponding map pinpointing its location in the state. The regions are then broken down into communities, with discussions on the history, special events, outdoor activities, attractions, accommodations, and restaurants. Where appropriate there are also sections on shopping, scenic drives, and other things that might interest the visitor. Contact information, hours, and price ranges are also provided.

Choosing Accommodations

Travelers have a wide variety of lodging choices in most areas of the state, ranging from very basic motels to luxurious hotels and bed-and-breakfast inns. Rates vary considerably, both for the different lodging properties and by season, as well as for specific days. Rates in summer and during Christmas vacation times are usually the highest (especially at ski areas) and can be obscenely high during special events. In short, you'll always get the best rates by traveling when other people aren't.

Another way to save money, for those who don't want to make reservations, is by using discount coupons. Visitor centers and a variety of businesses (but not hotels) distribute free booklets that contain nothing but discount lodging coupons. These are usually for chains, and almost always are for walk-ins only, but if you can use one of these coupons you can often save 20–40 percent. The coupons are also available online: **www.hotelcoupons.com; www.roomsaver.com.**

Some of the best places to stay are at New Mexico's bed-and-breakfast inns. Many are discussed throughout this book; you can also get information from the **New Mexico Bed & Breakfast Association, P.O. Box 2925, Santa Fe, 87504-2925; 800-661-6649; www.nmbba.org.**

In the following chapters we have included local phone numbers for each property, including local toll-free phone numbers and Web sites when available. To conserve space, we have not included the major chains' national toll-free numbers and Web sites in each description. Following is that information for chains with a significant presence in the state:

Best Western,
  800-WESTERN;
  www.bestwestern.com
Choice Hotels (Comfort Inn, Comfort Suites, Econo Lodge, Quality Inn, Rodeway Inn, Sleep Inn),
  800-4CHOICE;
  www.choicehotels.com
Days Inn,
  800-DAYSINN; www.daysinn.com
Hampton Inn,
  800-HAMPTON;
  www.hamptoninn.com
Holiday Inn,
  800-HOLIDAY;
  www.holiday-inn.com
Motel 6,
  800-4MOTEL6; www.motel6.com
Ramada Inn,
  800-2RAMADA; www.ramada.com
Super 8,
  800-800-8000; www.super8.com

Travelodge,
 800-578-7878; www.travelodge.com

The reviews of lodging properties throughout this book contain price ranges, based on double occupancy. These are for rack rates—the official nightly rate before discounts, such as AAA or AARP, are applied:

$—less than $40
$$—$40 to $80
$$$—$80 to $130
$$$$—$130 and up

Choosing Restaurants

New Mexico is known for its excellent restaurants, and especially for its New Mexico–style Mexican food, which almost always contains spicy chile peppers. While many locals have so severely scorched their taste buds that they can gobble down the hottest chile peppers without screams of pain, people with more normal eating habits may want to proceed slowly with our food. Ask your server about the item's hotness, and if there's any doubt ask if the chile can be served on the side, so you can add it sparingly. Once you become accustomed to chile dishes you'll probably love them, but caution is definitely advisable. For more information, see the sidebar "Hot Stuff!" in the **Lower Rio Grande** chapter.

Lately, many restaurants have been expanding their menu choices—even most steak houses now have at least one vegetarian item—and many are also offering a broader range of prices. If you want to experience a fancy, expensive restaurant without spending so much, eat there at lunch. Very often slightly smaller portions of their dinner items are offered at much lower prices. Our restaurant reviews contain price ranges,

usually including both lunch and dinner items, based on the price of an entrée per person:

$—less than $5
$$—$5 to $10
$$$—$10 to $20
$$$$—$20 and up

Traveling with Pets

New Mexico is generally a pet-friendly state, and in our discussions of lodgings we have made a point of noting which accommodations accept pets and if there is an additional fee. We suggest that you confirm whether a particular property accepts pets before you arrive and whether or not there is a fee; these policies do change. Some properties state that only small pets are allowed, but we have not included this information for two reasons: there is no universally agreed upon definition of what size pet is small, and our experience has been that the majority of lodgings that claim to accept only small pets will take any size pet—and usually not even ask about size—if you simply tell them in advance that you have a pet.

Those of us who enjoy hiking with our dogs have plenty of opportunities to do so in New Mexico, but it's worth noting that facilities operated by the National Park Service—national parks, national historic sites, and many but not all national monuments—almost universally prohibit pets on the trails. On the other hand, U.S. Forest Service and Bureau of Land Management areas, as well as New Mexico's state parks, are much more agreeable, allowing leashed pets in most areas, including on trails.

It's also worth remembering that New Mexico can be hot and dry, and pets, just like humans, will need extra water. Pet stores sell handy non-spill travel water bowls. Also, closed cars heat up very quickly when parked in the sun, and pets should never be left in such a situation. Fleas carrying bubonic plague are found in many parts of New Mexico, so pets should be treated with a good flea and tick repellent. A good information source for those traveling with pets is **www.petswelcome.com.**

Here We Go

That's pretty much all you need to know about using this book. We love New Mexico and are happy to be able to share some of our special places with you. We hope you have as much fun exploring the Land of Enchantment as we did in preparing this book.

A blooming yucca greets the sunset.

NORTH CENTRAL
MOUNTAINS

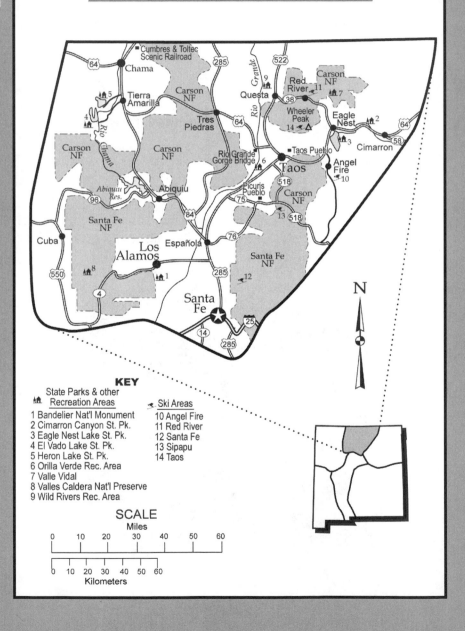

KEY

**State Parks & other
Recreation Areas**

1 Bandelier Nat'l Monument
2 Cimarron Canyon St. Pk.
3 Eagle Nest Lake St. Pk.
4 El Vado Lake St. Pk.
5 Heron Lake St. Pk.
6 Orilla Verde Rec. Area
7 Valle Vidal
8 Valles Caldera Nat'l Preserve
9 Wild Rivers Rec. Area

Ski Areas

10 Angel Fire
11 Red River
12 Santa Fe
13 Sipapu
14 Taos

SCALE

Miles

0   10   20   30   40   50   60

0   10   20   30   40   50   60
Kilometers

North Central Mountains

Nestled in this southern part of the Rocky Mountains are some of the most popular tourist destinations in the state. First there's Santa Fe, the artsy self-billed "City Different" that has become a favorite of Hollywood stars because of its many fine restaurants and hotels, excellent museums and historic sites, world-famous opera, and exciting shopping. About an hour and a half away is Taos, a world-renowned art colony and ski area that is also home to the centuries-old Taos Pueblo, without a doubt the most photogenic and appealing American Indian dwelling in the Southwest.

This region is also home to a number of smaller but equally interesting towns, such as Red River and Eagle Nest, born in the mining boom of the late 1800s and today staking their existence on skiing, fishing, and other types of outdoor recreation.

New Mexico's north central mountains include the state's highest mountain—Wheeler Peak, at 13,167 feet—and numerous stunningly beautiful mountain lakes and streams. There

Chili ristras can be found throughout New Mexico.

are scenic drives and an especially scenic tour in a historic steam train. And speaking of history, this region also contains prehistoric sites from the area's earliest residents as well as the city of Los Alamos, the birthplace of the atomic bomb.

SANTA FE

At 7,000 feet above sea level in the shadow of the Sangre de Cristo Mountains, Santa Fe—the New Mexico state capital—is the highest state capital in America. Also considered the oldest capital city in the United States, Santa Fe has been called one of the three most interesting cities in the country, along with Charleston, South Carolina, and New Orleans, Louisiana.

New Mexico's tricultural history is nowhere more evident than in Santa Fe, which was the seat of government in this portion of New Spain long before the United States of America existed. Santa Fe is situated among a grouping of eight Indian pueblos that share their past. It is the western terminus of the Santa Fe Trail, an important trade route and major player in the western expansion of the United States.

With a population of about 62,200, Santa Fe is the state's third-largest city, behind Albuquerque and Las Cruces. It boasts a thriving art colony and carefully nurtures its unique identity and look—preferring historic Pueblo-style and Spanish colonial architecture to more modern designs.

Calling itself the "City Different," Santa Fe is a city of narrow winding streets, of hundred-year-old shade trees, three-foot-thick adobe walls, red chile *ristras*, and a quiet serenity all too rare in our modern world. More than any other city in New Mexico, Santa Fe has an individuality of character—it is the *only* Santa Fe.

History

Santa Fe was founded in 1610 by Spanish explorers pushing up from Mexico into Indian country. The names of its streets (Paseo de Peralta, Guadalupe, Otero, De Vargas) attest to the Spanish influence. The Spaniards named it *La Ciudad de la Santa Fe de San Francisco de Assis*, or "The City of the Holy Faith of Saint Francis of Assisi."

The Spanish forced the peaceful Pueblo Indians to accept the Roman Catholic faith, and were cruel task masters, treating the Indians more like work animals than fellow human beings. In 1680, the Pueblo Indians rebelled, driving the Spanish out in a bloody uprising. It was 12 years before the Spanish reclaimed northern New Mexico.

The Santa Fe Trail was started by merchants and fur traders who became suppliers for Santa Fe. Despite bloody attacks by hostile Indians, American merchants kept open this route to the city, bringing in both goods and people to settle in this wide open space. Economic reasons were probably more important than political reasons, but during the first half of the 19th century, Anglos became the guiding forces in Santa Fe, completing the tricultural nature of Santa Fe's heritage—Indian, Hispanic, and Anglo.

Getting There

Santa Fe is located on Interstate 25, just 59 miles north of Albuquerque and 385 miles south of Denver, Colorado. US Hwys. 84 and 285 also pass through the capital city. Commuter airlines and shuttles connect Albuquerque's busy **Sunport (505-244-7700)** to **Santa Fe Municipal Airport,** at the end of Airport Rd. off Cerrillos Rd., **505-955-2908.**

Rental cars are available at both airports.

There are three shuttle services to take you from the airport to your hotel, and reservations are strongly recommended. Call **Sandia Shuttle Express, 888-775-5696; Twin Hearts, 800-654-9456;** or **Santa Fe Shuttle, 888-833-2300.**

TNM&O buses connect to **Greyhound** at the bus station, **858 St. Michael's Dr., 505-471-0008.**

Amtrak's Southwest Chief stops twice a day in Lamy, about 18 miles south of Santa Fe, once in each direction **(800-872-7245; www.amtrak.com).** The **Lamy Shuttle** brings passengers into the city by reservation **(505-982-8829).**

Festivals and Events

FLEA MARKET

Sat.–Sun. year-round plus Fri. in summer, 9 A.M.–4 P.M. People-watching is just as interesting as the vast sea of wares, ranging from the most predictable cast-offs to exquisite hand-made furniture to Guatemalan handbags and hats. North of town on US Hwys. 84/285 just past the Santa Fe Opera. Busiest in late spring, summer, and fall, of course.

EL RANCHO DE LAS GOLONDRINAS SPRING FESTIVAL

first weekend in June. People in Spanish colonial garb demonstrate spring tasks on an 18th-century New Mexico ranch, including such things as spinning, weaving, soap making, and other domestic chores of 1790. Food, music, dance, art, and entertainment. **505-471-2261.**

RODEO DE SANTA FE

third weekend in June. Since the mid-1940s, this PRCA (Professional Rodeo Cowboys Association) rodeo has attracted top riders, ropers, steer wrestlers, and bull riders from the United States and Canada. It lasts four nights, with a Sat. matinee, and pleases some 20,000 spectators annually. **505-471-4300.**

SPANISH MARKET

last full weekend in July. Spanish Market is a juried exhibit of traditional Hispanic arts and crafts held on the Plaza, including carving, painting, tinwork, embroidery, weaving, furniture, and more. **505-982-2226; www. spanishcolonial.org.**

INDIAN MARKET

third weekend in Aug. As it approaches its centenary, Indian Market draws more than 1,000 Indian artists to compete and show an incredible array of arts and crafts. It's held on the Plaza. **505-983-5220; www.swaia.org.**

LA FIESTA DE SANTA FE

weekend following Labor Day. One of the oldest festivals in the state, La Fiesta de Santa Fe commemorates the reconquest of the city by Don Diego de Vargas in 1692, after the Pueblo Revolt of 1680. The entire city turns out for this three-day celebration of Hispanic culture, with two parades, mariachi music, singing, dancing, and, of course, food. The burning in effigy of Zozobra, "Old Man Gloom," to dispel the sadness of the year and to make way for joy in the coming year, kicks things off on Thurs. night. Closing ceremonies are Sun. evening, with Plaza performances and a mass. **800-777-2489; 505-955-6200.**

SANTA FE

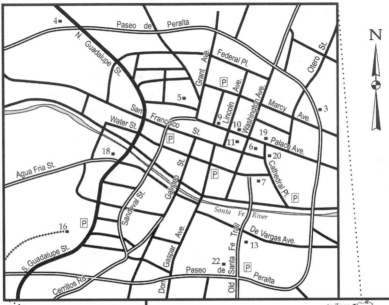

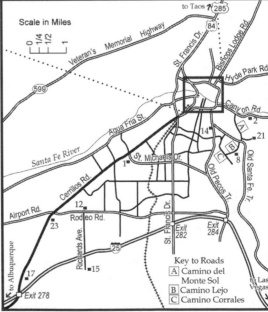

public parking lot P

■ KEY to POINTS of INTEREST
1 College of Santa Fe
2 Cristo Rey Church
3 Cross of the Martyrs
4 De Vargas Center
5 Georgia O'Keeffe Museum
6 Institute of American Indian Art
7 Loretto Chapel
8 Museum Hill - Museum of
   Indian Arts & Culture; Museum
   of International Folk Art;
   Museum of Spanish Colonial
   Art; Wheelwright Museum of the
   American Indian
9 Museum of Fine Arts
10 Palace of the Governors
11 Plaza
12 Rodeo & Fairgrounds
13 San Miguel Mission Church
14 Santa Fe Children's Museum
15 Santa Fe Community College
16 Santa Fe Depot
17 Santa Fe Premium Outlets
18 Santuario de Guadalupe
19 Sena Plaza
20 St. Francis Cathedral
21 St. John's College
22 State Capitol
23 Villa Linda Mall

EL RANCHO DE LAS GOLONDRINAS HARVEST FESTIVAL

first weekend in Oct. People in Spanish colonial garb go about their autumn tasks: crushing grapes for wine, stringing chile *ristras*, milling and threshing wheat, making sorghum molasses, and bringing in the harvest. Food, music, dancing, and fun for the entire family. 505-471-2261.

HOLIDAY EVENTS

mid-Dec. to Christmas Eve. The open house at the Palace of the Governors, Christmas at the Palace, includes a **Children's Art Show & Sale (505-476-5100).** The **Museum of Fine Arts (505-476-5072)** hosts a delightful Gustave Baumann Marionette Show. The traditional Spanish outdoor play, **Las Posadas,** takes place on the Plaza **(505-476-5100).** The **Santa Fe Southern Railroad, Inc. (505-989-8600)** offers several Special Holiday Trains. The Plaza is beautifully lit with lights and, on Christmas Eve, with *farolitos.*

Outdoor Activities

The **Santa Fe National Forest** wraps around the city on the east, and there you'll find plenty of outdoor opportunities, including **hiking, biking, camping, wildlife viewing, and horseback riding.** Other public lands are administered by the BLM. For maps and information stop at the **New Mexico Public Lands Information Center, 1474 Rodeo Rd., Santa Fe, 87505 (505-438-7542; www.publiclands.org).** At the same location are the offices of the **Santa Fe Ranger District (505-438-7877; www.fs.fed.us/r3)** and the **Bureau of Land Management (505-438-7400; www.nm.blm.gov).**

Bird-Watching

RANDALL DAVEY AUDUBON CENTER

Once home to renowned artist Randall Davey, this is now the headquarters for **Audubon New Mexico,** which operates an education and visitor center. Staffed with naturalists, this is a place where urbanites come to experience nature. Located on 135 acres about 10 miles from downtown. **Upper Canyon Rd., Santa Fe; 505-983-4609.**

Golf

The top golfing choice in Santa Fe is **Marty Sanchez Links de Santa Fe, 200 Lincoln Ave., Santa Fe, 505-955-4400,** a par-3, 18-hole public course that combines scenic beauty with shot-making tests. **The Santa Fe Country Club, Airport Rd. 87, Santa Fe, 505-471-2626,** opens its 18-hole course to the public but not its clubhouse. North of town in Pojoaque Pueblo is **Towa Golf Resort, 17746 US Hwys. 84/285, Santa Fe; 505-455-9000; www.towagolf.com,** with good teachers and a fine Hale Irwin/Bill Phillips-designed 18-hole course.

Hiking

DALE BALL FOOTHILL TRAIL SYSTEM

This trail system consists of about 20 miles of multiuse trails along the eastern edge of the city. It's open to both dogs and bicycles in addition to hikers, and it runs through the Santa Fe Canyon Preserve (see next page), connecting to hiking trails there.

HYDE MEMORIAL STATE PARK

This is a great winter playground, popular with cross-country skiers and snowshoers. In warmer weather it offers

5

several good hikes in addition to providing access to miles of hiking trails in the nearby Santa Fe National Forest. It encompasses 350 beautiful acres in the mountains above Santa Fe, about 8 miles northeast of the Plaza. Elevation starts at about 8,500 feet. There are 50 individual campsites (seven with electric hookups) and several group shelters set among Douglas fir, ponderosa pine, aspen, and juniper, with picnic tables and fire pits, water spigots scattered around, vault toilets, no showers, an RV dump station, a playground, and a volleyball court. Check in at ranger station. **740 Hyde Park Rd., Santa Fe, 87501; 505-983-7175; www.nmparks.com.**

SANTA FE CANYON PRESERVE

Covering some 190 acres just 2 miles from Santa Fe Plaza, this peaceful preserve has hiking trails and a grove of cottonwoods and willows. Some 140 species of birds call it home, and it's a great place to get away from city bustle. There's a 1.5-mile Interpretive Loop Trail meandering along the remains of the Two-Mile Dam to an overlook of the pond—all that's left of the reservoir that once served Santa Fe. Dogs and bicycles are not permitted in the preserve except on the Dale Ball Foothill Trail System (see page 5), which runs through the preserve. Parking lot gates are closed from sundown to sunrise. **Nature Conservancy, 505-988-3867; www.nature.org.**

Rafting and Kayaking

The Rio Grande offers everything from a smooth, calm float trip to exciting white water. The water is highest during spring and early summer. Contact the BLM Taos Field Office (see Whitewater Rafting in the Taos section) for information and a list of licensed operators.

Skiing

SKI SANTA FE

A good family skiing destination, Ski Santa Fe covers 660 acres with 45 well-groomed runs rated 20 percent beginner and 40 percent each intermediate and expert. It has a vertical drop of 1,703 feet from its peak elevation of 12,503 feet and snowmaking on half of its runs. Located 16 miles northeast of downtown Santa Fe via NM 475. **505-982-4429; 505-983-9155 (snow conditions); www.skisantafe.com.**

Seeing and Doing

Before you set out to explore Santa Fe, remember: you'll be walking much more than driving, so wear comfortable shoes. Back in the 17th century, life centered on the Plaza, and things gradually spread out from there. Consequently, the roads in the downtown area are narrow and don't easily accommodate parking. So find one of the paid parking lots, as close to the Plaza as possible, and then head out. Many of the attractions are within easy walking of the Plaza.

Historic Sites

CRISTO REY CHURCH

One of the largest modern adobe structures standing today, the church was built by its parishioners, using dirt from the site to form the adobe bricks. It commemorates the 400th anniversary of Coronado's exploration of the Southwest (and you thought Plymouth Rock was old!). It houses a magnificent carved stone altar screen, or *reredo*, a superb example of the art of New Mexico's Spanish colonial period. **1120 Canyon Rd., Santa Fe; 505-983-8528.**

CROSS OF THE MARTYRS

For a stupendous view of the city, follow the long brick walkway to the Cross of the Martyrs. Start at the **corner of Paseo de Peralta and Otero St.**, and read the plaques placed along the way to guide you up to the great white cross, which commemorates the Franciscan monks killed in the 1680 Pueblo Revolt.

EL RANCHO
DE LAS GOLONDRINAS

This 200-acre living history museum opened in 1972 after extensive restoration of existing ruins, reconstruction of authentic structures on old foundations, and relocation of additional buildings from other sites. It's a fascinating place to visit anytime, especially during their theme weekends in summer. There's an 18th-century *hacienda*, with the rooms surrounding a central *placita* where most day-to-day living and working took place, plus a 19th-century home complete with outbuildings. Numerous other buildings—molasses mill, blacksmith shop, wheelwright shop,

schoolhouse, several water-powered gristmills, a *morada, descansos, Campo Santo, oratorio*—complete the story of life in Spanish colonial and territorial New Mexico. This ranch was an important overnight stop on the 1,000-mile Camino Real, or Royal Road, between Mexico City and Santa Fe. Open June–Sept., Wed.–Sun. 10 A.M.–4 P.M.; Apr., May, and Oct. by appointment; closed rest of year. Fee charged. Located 15 miles south of Santa Fe Plaza off I-25 exit 276. **334 Los Pinos Rd., Santa Fe, 87507; 505-471-2261.**

LORETTO CHAPEL

The chapel was built in 1873 to house the Sisters of Our Lady of Light, who came to establish a school for young ladies in Santa Fe. (The Inn at Loretto was built on the site of the school, see Where to Stay.) Inside you can see what is referred to as the miraculous staircase: it contains two 360-degree turns, with no visible central support. Built in 1878 by a carpenter using only a T-square, hammer, and saw, he

The old mill at El Rancho de Las Golondrinas.

disappeared without even asking for his pay. A legend grew that St. Joseph the carpenter divinely guided the work. The chapel is occasionally closed for weddings or other liturgical ceremonies. Open Mon.–Sat. 9 A.M.–6 P.M.; Sun. 10:30 A.M.–5 P.M. Admission fee charged. **211 Old Santa Fe Trail, Santa Fe; 505-982-0092.**

PALACE OF THE GOVERNORS

This just may be the oldest seat of government in the United States: it housed the Spanish governor when it was first built in 1609–1610, 160-odd years before the Declaration of Independence was signed in the English part of North America. In 1909, it became the state's history museum, and the long, low adobe building with its massive walls is still *the* place to feel the ancient history of New Mexico. A part of the Museum of New Mexico, this facility has historical exhibits that clearly define New Mexico's colorful past—Spanish, Mexican, Indian, and territorial American. Be sure to stroll along the portal out front, where American Indian artisans display—and sell—an incredible array of turquoise and silver jewelry and other Indian artwork. Located on the north side of Santa Fe Plaza. **105 Palace Ave., Santa Fe; 505-476-5100.**

ST. FRANCIS CATHEDRAL

One block east of the Plaza at San Francisco St., the cathedral seems slightly out of place in this very Hispanic town, because its styling reflects the fact that it was built by French archbishop Jean-Baptiste Lamy in 1869. The archbishop and the church itself feature predominantly in Willa Cather's classic *Death Comes for the Archbishop*. Ask to see the wooden statue of St. Francis of Assisi and the famed *La Conquistadora* statue. On the Sun. after the feast of Corpus Christi, *La Conquistadora* is carried through the city to Our Lady of the Rosary Chapel. When visiting St. Francis Cathedral, please remember it is a church and treat it with respect. Open Mon.–Sat., 6 A.M.–6 P.M. **213 Cathedral Pl., Santa Fe; 505-982-5619.**

SAN MIGUEL MISSION CHURCH

Built in the 1600s by Tlaxcala Indians who came from Mexico as servants of the Spanish conquistadors, this is one of the oldest continuously used churches in America. The church was severely damaged in the Pueblo Revolt in 1680 and rebuilt in 1710. It displays the San Jose Bell, believed to have been cast in Spain in 1356 and eventually brought to Santa Fe by oxcart via Mexico. In addition to its historical and architectural interest, the church contains excellent examples of Hispanic religious art. **401 Old Santa Fe Trail at E. De Vargas St., Santa Fe; 505-983-3974.** Next door at **215 E. De Vargas St.** is the **oldest house in America,** according to Santa Fe folklore.

SANTA FE DEPOT

If you love trains as much as we do, check out the **excursion trains** offered by the Santa Fe Southern Railway. There are daily scenic rides—the schedules change with the seasons—in restored vintage passenger cars from downtown Santa Fe to Lamy, 17 miles south. Round-trip takes 3 to 5 hours. There are also cocktail trains, special BBQ trains, and a variety of special events scheduled year-round. Fees charged. **410 S. Guadalupe St., Santa Fe, 87501; 888-989-8600; 505-989-8600.**

SANTUARIO DE GUADALUPE

Built around 1796, the 3-foot-thick adobe walls house some of the largest and finest oil paintings of the

Southwest. The most famous rendering of Our Lady of Guadalupe was painted in Mexico City by Jose de Alzibar, who signed and dated it in 1783. This large work of art was brought a thousand miles up the Camino Real on muleback! **100 S. Guadalupe St., Santa Fe; 505-988-2027.**

SENA PLAZA

This small, enclosed area offers a spot of quiet serenity: exquisite gardens are encircled by delightful little shops and the well-known restaurant La Casa Sena (see the Where to Eat section). This historic spot was given to Alférez Diego Arias de Quiros in 1692 as a reward for helping with the reconquest of Santa Fe after the Pueblo Revolt. Major Sena, a friend of Kit Carson, bought it in 1867. The Sena family lived here until 1927, then deeded it to a group of Santa Feans. It is still private property but always open to the public. **On Palace Ave. across from St. Francis Cathedral.**

STATE CAPITOL

The New Mexico State Capitol building was built in the shape of a *zia*, the sun symbol from Zia Pueblo. At the center of the building on the ground floor is the rotunda, and if you stand in the center, directly under the dome high above, and speak in a normal tone, you will notice a unique, almost eerie echo. Take a self-guiding tour to see the house and senate and the offices of the governor and lieutenant governor. The capitol is decorated with a collection of art in a variety of media and subject matter. For one's work to hang in the capitol, the artist must be born in New Mexico or be a current resident of the state. Open

---

New Mexico's Flag

In the 1920s, the New Mexico chapter of the Daughters of the American Revolution held a flag design competition, and in Mar. 1925 the governor signed legislation proclaiming the winning design as the official state flag: a red *zia*—a sun symbol—on a field of yellow. These were the colors of Isabel of Castilla, brought to New Spain by the Spanish conquistadors.

The dimensions of the *zia* are also fixed by legislation: the four groups of rays are set at right angles, with the inner two being one-fifth longer than the outer two, and the circle's diameter is one-third the width of the symbol.

The *zia* as we know it is an interpretation of an ancient sun design found on a late 19th-century water jar from Zia Pueblo. Four is the sacred number of *zia*, so the figure is composed of a circle from which four points radiate. Each of the four  is itself made up of four: the four directions of earth (north, south, east, west); the four seasons of the year (spring, summer, autumn, winter); the four times of day (sunrise, noon, evening, night); and the four stages of life (childhood, youth, adulthood, old age). Everything is bound together in a circle of life, without beginning, without end.

Simple. Beautiful.

Mon.–Fri. 8 A.M.–5 P.M. year-round; also Sat. Memorial Day–Labor Day; closed major holidays. **Corner of Old Santa Fe Trail and Paseo de Peralta, Santa Fe; 505-986-4589.**

Horse Racing

The Downs at Santa Fe offers horse racing four days a week from late May through Labor Day. It's located a few miles south of town just off the interstate at **27742 W. Frontage Rd. #27475, Santa Fe, 87501; 505-471-3311.**

Indian Pueblos

There are about a half dozen American Indian pueblos north of Santa Fe in the Española area, and these islands of American Indian culture have done a remarkable job of preserving their language and traditions against great odds. Some welcome outsiders more than others, and not all the pueblos have a lot for visitors to see, although most do have casinos. Following are several of our favorites.

Pojoaque Pueblo is home to the Poeh Cultural Center Museum, which offers archeological and historical exhibits and Pueblo artwork. The pueblo is open to the public daily 9 A.M.–5 P.M.; the museum is open Mon.–Fri. only. Located 15 miles north of Santa Fe on US Hwys. 84/285. **505-455-3460.**

San Ildefonso Pueblo, one of the larger pueblos of the region, is famed for its black-on-black pottery, developed by famed potter Maria Martinez (1887–1980), whose family continues the tradition. Visitors can explore the ancient plaza, shop for pottery and other crafts, and visit a museum with exhibits on pottery making. The pueblo celebrates its feast day on Jan. 23. Usually open daily 8 A.M.–5 P.M. Admission and camera fees charged. Located 22 miles north of Santa Fe via US Hwy. 285 and NM 502. **505-455-3549.**

San Juan Pueblo is the headquarters for the eight northern pueblos and home to a handsome visitor center. The pueblo contains many structures dating back some 700 years and is known for the interesting designs incised into the brown and red clays of its pottery. Special feast days are June 23 and 24. Open daily dawn to dusk; camera fee. Located 25 miles north of Santa Fe via US Hwy. 285 and NM 68, then a mile west on NM 74. **505-852-4400.**

Museums

GEORGIA O'KEEFFE MUSEUM

This is the place to see the work of and learn about famed artist Georgia O'Keeffe (1887–1986), who spent many years living in isolated but nearby Abiquiu and is well known for her desert landscapes, often including bleached cattle skulls and colorful flowers. The museum, housed in a handsome pueblo revival–style building, has a permanent collection of more than 130 of O'Keeffe's paintings, drawings, and sculptures, with about 50 on display at any given time. It also presents changing exhibits on O'Keeffe and her work or her contemporaries' who also worked in the modernist style. Open Thurs.–Tues. 10 A.M.–5 P.M., plus Fri. until 8 P.M.; July–Oct. add Wed. 10 A.M.–5 P.M. Admission fee charged. **217 Johnson St., Santa Fe; 505-946-1000; www.okeeffemuseum.org.**

INSTITUTE OF AMERICAN INDIAN ART

The National Collection of Contemporary Indian Art is on display, plus works by the students, alumni, and faculty. Media include paintings, sculpture, pottery, ceramics, beadwork, and textiles, as well as new art forms from contemporary American Indians. Open daily June–Sept. 9 A.M.–5 P.M.; Oct.–May 10 A.M.–5 P.M.;

closed major holidays. Admission fee charged. **108 Cathedral Pl., Santa Fe; 505-983-8900; www.iaiancad.org/museum.**

MUSEUM OF FINE ARTS

Built in 1917, the museum displays traditional and contemporary American art from a collection of more than 8,000 pieces. Southwestern artists are the focus of changing exhibits, particularly artists from Santa Fe and Taos. Part of the Museum of New Mexico (see following). **107 W. Palace Ave., Santa Fe; 505-476-5072.**

MUSEUM OF INDIAN ARTS & CULTURE—LABORATORY OF ANTHROPOLOGY

This museum does a fine job of interpreting the American Indian cultures and southwestern artifacts extending from ancestral to contemporary times. Part of the Museum of New Mexico (see below). **Museum Hill, 708-710 Camino Lejo off Old Santa Fe Trail, Santa Fe; 505-476-1269; www.miaclab.org.**

MUSEUM OF INTERNATIONAL FOLK ART

This is one of the largest folk art museums in the world. Specializing in Hispanic arts, the museum houses a collection of 125,000 pieces, including the world-famous Alexander Girard collection. The Hispanic heritage wing offers a wonderful display of Mexican art. Part of the Museum of New Mexico (see below). **Museum Hill, 706 Camino Lejo off Old Santa Fe Trail, Santa Fe; 505-476-1200.**

MUSEUM OF NEW MEXICO

This huge complex is comprised of five museums: Palace of the Governors, Museum of Fine Arts, Museum of Indian Arts & Culture, Museum of International Folk Art, and Museum of Spanish Colonial Art. A visit to each will afford you a good overview of Indian and Hispanic culture in the Southwest and internationally. Open Tues.–Sun. 10 A.M.–5 P.M.; closed major holidays. Admission fee charged. **113 Lincoln Ave., Santa Fe; 505-476-5060; www.museumofnewmexico.org.**

MUSEUM OF SPANISH COLONIAL ART

Located in a home designed by well-known architect John Gaw Meem in 1930, this museum houses a fine collection that represents the heart and soul of Hispanic culture and history in New Mexico and the Southwest. Part of the Museum of New Mexico (see above). **Museum Hill, 750 Camino Lejo off Old Santa Fe Trail, Santa Fe; 505-982-2226; www.spanishcolonial.org.**

SANTA FE CHILDREN'S MUSEUM

The arts, humanities, and sciences are represented, with hands-on, interactive displays that allow children to learn by doing. There is a water and sensory climbing area for toddlers and for children up to age 12, a solar greenhouse, and a 16-foot climbing wall, among other enticing exhibits. Open Sept.–May, Thurs.–Sat. 10 A.M.–5 P.M. and Sun. noon–5 P.M.; June–Aug., Wed.–Sat. 10 A.M.–5 P.M. and Sun. noon–5 P.M. Admission fee charged. **1050 Old Pecos Trail, Santa Fe; 505-989-8359.**

WHEELWRIGHT MUSEUM OF THE AMERICAN INDIAN

Founded in 1937 by Bostonian Mary Cabot Wheelwright and Hastin Klah, a highly esteemed Navajo medicine man, this museum was established to preserve the ceremonial heritage of the Navajo people for future generations. In 1977, the scope was broadened to include all American Indian traditional and contemporary art, and the museum now hosts changing exhibits. It is housed in an eight-sided building designed in the tradition of a Navajo hogan or cribbed log home. Open Mon.–Sat. 10 A.M.– 5 P.M.; Sun. 1–5 P.M.; closed major holidays. **Museum Hill, 704 Camino Lejo off Old Santa Fe Trail, Santa Fe; 800-607-4636; 505-982-4636; www.wheelwright.org.**

Nightlife

There are numerous places in Santa Fe to relax, sip your favorite drink, and enjoy your choice of live music. There's anything from rhythm and blues to rock, jazz to

---

The Hills Are Alive with the Sound of ... Opera?

For more than 30 years, opera lovers have been leaving the big cities to come to the City Different to enjoy superb opera. Until recently, about half of the audience didn't even have a roof over their heads! But still they came—in droves. The opening gala each year is sold out far in advance, and people arrive early to enjoy a "picnic" dinner in the parking lot while watching the sun set in this clear mountain air. You'll see them gathered around the back of their vehicles in folding chairs, the men in black tie and the women in evening gowns, often sipping champagne from crystal and savoring an elegant repast. It's quite a sight.

Well before the curtain rises, everyone finds their seat in this stunning architectural enigma, and they breathlessly await the first notes from the orchestra, heralding the beginning of another grand set of operas. The staging and costumes are always stupendous, and the singers sublime. Five operas are presented each year, in repertory. Recent productions have included Mozart's *Cosi fan Tutte, Don Giovanni,* and *La Clemenza di Tito;* Verdi's *La Traviata* and *Simon Boccanegra;* Rossini's *The Italian Girl in Algiers;* Offenbach's *La Belle Helene;* and the world premiere of *Madam Mao* by Bright Sheng and Colin Graham. Near the end of the season, apprentice artists take the stage in two performances consisting of a scene from each of the operas. For anyone not already an opera buff, this can be a terrific introduction to this magical music.

A few years ago, the SFO underwent a major renovation, adding a roof so no one need get wet during one of the infrequent evening rainstorms. They also added an electronic libretto to each seat, so you can more easily follow what's happening in the story even if you don't understand German or Italian or whatever language they happen to be singing.

We've attended a number of operas here over the years, and in some ways we miss the lack of roof over the middle section of seats, which opened the building to the heavens. But as the sides have not been closed and you can still see the horizon out the back of the stage, one still has the feeling of nature soaring with music, especially during a lightning storm.

So if you're in Santa Fe from late June through Aug., try to take in one of these performances. It's a chance in a lifetime. Located on US 84/285 about 5 miles north of Santa Fe. **800-280-4654; 505-986-5900; www.santafeopera.org.**

Broadway, hillbilly to hip-hop, and even some locals performing their own compositions. Among the top venues here—all in Santa Fe—are **Cowgirl Hall of Fame BBQ and Western Grill (319 S. Guadalupe St.; 505-982-2565); Eldorado Hotel (309 W. San Francisco St.; 505-988-4455); El Farol (808 Canyon Rd.; 505-983-9912); Inn at Loretto (211 Old Santa Fe Trail; 505-988-5531); La Casa Sena (125 E. Palace Ave.; 505-988-9232); La Fonda (100 E. San Francisco St; 505-982-5511); The Ore House (50 Lincoln Ave.; 505-983-8687);** and **Second Street Brewery (1814 2nd St. at the railroad tracks; 505-982-3030).**

The **Catamount Bar & Grille (125 E. Water St.; 505-988-7222)** offers big screen sports, pool tables you can rent by the hour, and live music.

Performing Arts

SANTA FE CHAMBER MUSIC FESTIVAL

July and Aug. Performances of works by classical music greats. **505-983-2075. www.sfcmf.org.**

SANTA FE DESERT CHORALE

June–Aug. The professional Desert Chorale performs works from a global repertoire, including great cathedral music. **505-988-2282; www.desertchorale.org.**

Shopping and Gallery Hopping

Along every street downtown, spreading out from the Plaza like spokes on a wheel, are an incredible array of shops and galleries. There are ethnic handcrafts, wearable art, fine and costume jewelry, posters, prints, and fine art. Many of the fine art galleries are downtown, within a few blocks of the Plaza, and along Canyon Rd. The **Santa Fe Gallery Association**

(P.O. Box 9245, Santa Fe, 87504; 505-982-1648; www.santafegalleries.net) prints a very nice brochure with a gallery list of members and a map showing their locations.

ADIEB KHADOURE FINE ART

Contemporary paintings; traditional and contemporary sculpture in bronze, wood, and stainless steel; hand-blown glass; Navajo, Oriental, and other hand-woven rugs. **610 Canyon Rd., Santa Fe; 505-820-2666.**

ALEXANDRA STEVENS GALLERY OF FINE ART

Paintings and sculpture by traditional and contemporary artists, with emphasis on Taos and Santa Fe artists. **820 Canyon Rd., Santa Fe; 505-988-1311; www.alexandrastevens.com.**

ANDREA FISHER FINE POTTERY

Fine selection of traditionally made southwestern Indian pottery by master potters such as Maria Martinez, as well as contemporary potters, organized by pueblo. **100 W. San Francisco St., Santa Fe; 505-986-1234; www.andreafisherpottery.com.**

DEVARGAS CENTER

A neighborhood shopping center for more than 30 years, with a six-screen movie theater, post office, and some 43 stores. **564 N. Guadalupe St., Santa Fe; 505-982-2655.**

FRANK HOWELL GALLERY

Representing some of the best-known artists of the Southwest, including Frank Howell and Texas sculptors Bill Worrell and Gene and Rebecca Tobey. Large bronze sculptures grace the front. **103 Washington Ave., Santa Fe; 505-984-1074; www.frankhowellgallery.com.**

GERALD PETERS GALLERY
Wide range of very fine art. Classic western, Taos Society of Artists, Santa Fe Art Colony, Georgia O'Keeffe, 20th-century American modernism, contemporary, naturalism, sculpture, photography, and works on paper. **1011 Paseo de Peralta, Santa Fe; 505-954-5700; www.gpgallery.com.**

JACKALOPE
Mexican and other imports from toys to blankets, decor to furniture, pottery to glassware. A fun place to browse even if you don't plan to buy. **2820 Cerrillos Rd., Santa Fe; 505-471-8539; www.jackalope.com.**

KAREN MELFI COLLECTION
Contemporary jewelry, crafts, and textiles by local and regional artisans. Inlay, faceted gemstones, silver and turquoise, high-carat gold jewelry, handmade clothing. **225 Canyon Rd., Santa Fe; 800-884-7079; 505-982-3032; www.karenmelficollection.com.**

THE MAZE AT PLAZA MERCADO
Some 45 galleries, shops, and restaurants in a group of historic buildings connected by a delightful atrium. Ethnic handcrafts; southwestern jewelry, clothing, and pottery; home furnishings; contemporary art. **112 W. San Francisco St., Santa Fe; www.plazamercado.com.**

MCLARRY FINE ART
Features internationally known artists as well as emerging southwestern artists, with an emphasis on contemporary landscapes and sculpture. **225 Canyon Rd., Santa Fe; 877-983-2123; 505-988-1161; www.mclarryfineart.com.**

NAMBÉ
This soft metal alloy has been formed into beautiful shapes for the home, from tableware to cookware, plus decorative pieces such as candlesticks. Also full-lead crystal, jewelry, and porcelain. Two Santa Fe locations plus stores in Las Cruces and Taos. **924 Paseo de Peralta, Santa Fe; 505-988-5528; 104 W. San Francisco St., Santa Fe; 505-988-3574; www.nambe.com.**

NEDRA MATTEUCCI FINE ART
Traditional paintings, sculpture, jewelry, and decorative art by nationally and internationally recognized artists. **555 Canyon Rd., Santa Fe; 505-983-2731; www.nedramatteuccifineart.com.**

PHOTOGENESIS
Stunning, classic black-and-white photography—a real gem. **Inside La Fonda Hotel, 100 E. San Francisco St., Santa Fe; 505-989-9540; www.photogenesisgallery.com.**

POSTERS OF SANTA FE
Posters by Georgia O'Keeffe, R. C. Gorman, Tony Abeyta, and other well-known artists of New Mexico and the Southwest. Also cookbooks, art books, CDs, South American folk art, and more. **111 E. Palace Ave., Santa Fe; 800-827-6745; 505-982-6645; www.postersofsantafe.com.**

SANBUSCO MARKET CENTER
This former home to Santa Fe Builders Supply now houses several restaurants and fun boutiques plus two national chains: Borders and Cost Plus World Market. **500 Montezuma Ave., Santa Fe.**

SANTA FE OUTLETS
Laid out like a small adobe village, the shops meander along a pleasant walkway. Shops include Eddie Bauer, Bose, Brooks Brothers, Liz Claiborne, OshKosh B' Gosh, Leather Outlet, Samsonite, and more. **8380 Cerrillos**

Rd. at I-25 (9 miles south of Santa Fe Plaza), **Santa Fe; 505-474-4000.**

THIRTEEN MOONS GALLERY

Fine fiber art by known and emerging artists: basketry, tapestry weavings, art quilts, stitchery, and mixed media. **652 Canyon Rd., Santa Fe; 505-995-8513; www.thirteenmoonsgallery.com.**

WYETH HURD GALLERY

Original paintings, prints, and books; representing four generations from the Wyeth and Hurd families. **839 Paseo de Peralta, Santa Fe; 505-989-8380; www.wyethhurd.com.**

Scenic Drives

HIGH ROAD TO TAOS

The quick way to Taos from Santa Fe is about 70 miles on a route that partly follows the Rio Grande. It's a pretty drive and is especially scenic in summer when the river is dotted with colorful rafts. An alternate route, only about a dozen miles longer, winds through historic Spanish colonial villages known for beautiful weaving where you'll also see some of the most picturesque churches in the Southwest.

Both routes to Taos first go to Española via US Hwy. 285. The shorter route, following the Rio Grande, continues north on NM 68.

The High Road, however, takes off east from Española on NM 76, wandering through the mountains. Your first stop will be in the tiny village of Chimayo, settled in 1598. Be sure to stop at **Ortega's Weaving Shop (877-351-4215; 505-351-4215; www.ortegasdechimayo.com)**, where the eighth generation of weavers is still working at the looms. There are several other interesting shops here, as well as the excellent **Restaurante Rancho de**

Chimayo ($$$; 505-351-4444), serving lunch and dinner daily and breakfast Sat. and Sun. Nearby is the handsome and inspiring **Santuario de Chimayo,** built in the early 1800s, which is visited annually by thousands of people seeking relief from medical problems from what many consider the "miraculous dirt" found in a corner of the chapel.

Continuing east and north on NM 76, you soon come to the village of **Truchas,** one of the most isolated of the Spanish colonial towns, which was the scene for much of Robert Redford's movie *The Milagro Beanfield War.* There are also spectacular mountain views and some good art galleries. A short detour just south of Truchas leads to **Cordova,** a tiny village known for its woodcarvers. Back on NM 76, the next village to stop in is **Las Trampas,** home to the

Many believe that the Santuario de Chimayo has healing powers in the "miraculous dirt."

Church of San Jose de Grácia, one of the most beautiful built during the Spanish colonial period.

The road continues through the mountains, passing through the village of Chamisal before arriving in Peñasco. From here you can make a side trip to **Picuris Pueblo,** discussed in the Taos section later in this chapter, and then continue on toward Taos via NM 518. This particularly scenic route takes you into the Carson National Forest to the U.S. Hill Scenic Overlook and then to Ranchos de Taos, where you can turn right and follow the main drag into Taos or turn left and head back to Santa Fe following the Rio Grande via NM 68.

TURQUOISE TRAIL

This pleasant drive starts in Santa Fe and travels south on NM 14, passing through the historic towns of Cerrillos (which once boasted 21 saloons), Madrid (a coal-mining ghost town that now is home to a wide array of craftspeople and artists since its revival in the 1960s), and Golden (the site of the first gold rush west of the Mississippi). Below Golden the road skirts the eastern side of the Sandia Mountains, and when you reach San Antonito you can take a side trip to the top. From that 10,000-foot-high perch you have an incredible view of Albuquerque spread out below and all the way to Mount Taylor, 75 miles to the west. The trail then follows I-40 east to Moriarty where you pick up NM 41 north for the drive back to Santa Fe.

Where to Stay

Accommodations

Santa Fe has more than 100 lodging choices with some 4,500 rooms, so if you're thoroughly confused and in need of help, contact **Santa Fe Central Reservations, 800-776-7669; 505-983-8200.** They can also help with tickets to theater and musical performances and specialized outdoor trips.

Numerous chain motels are located along Cerrillos Rd. with dependably clean, comfortable lodgings, more reasonably priced than some of the historic properties closer to the Plaza.

BED-AND-BREAKFASTS

Most of the following bed-and-breakfasts do not permit smoking or have specific areas where guests may smoke.

Alexander's Inn—$$$–$$$$

Located in a quiet residential neighborhood, this elegant B&B offers classic comfort. Housed in a 1903 Victorian/New England–style building, the inn is filled with antiques. Fresh flowers grace the rooms, there's a whirlpool tub in the back garden, and guests have privileges at a nearby tennis club. Breakfast is expanded continental with homemade baked treats. Ten rooms, eight with private bath. **529 E. Palace Ave., Santa Fe, 87501; 888-321-5123; 505-986-1431; www.alexanders-inn.com.**

Bishop's Lodge—$$$–$$$$

Bishop's Lodge has it all: luxurious accommodations, delectable dining, and a variety of recreational activities. This is a full resort with its own stables and acres of trails, as well as tennis courts and a swimming pool, hiking trails, an exercise room, and a whirlpool tub. In summer, a children's program is offered for ages 4 to 12. The grounds boast displays of wildflowers spring through fall with a stream running through. A shuttle carries you into town for sightseeing and shopping. Located outside the downtown area. **P.O. Box 2367,**

Bishop's Lodge Rd., Santa Fe, 87501-2367; 800-419-0492; 505-983-6377; www.bishopslodge.com.

Dos Casas Viejas—$$$$

The name means "two old houses", and they are located in one of the most historic areas in Santa Fe, behind a weathered wooden security gate. Nonetheless, everything is impeccably cared for, with beautifully manicured grounds and richly decorated rooms. Each has its own patio and entrance off a private brick walkway. Breakfast is served either in the dining room or on the poolside patio. Or, you can pick it up and take it to your own private patio. Eight casitas. **610 Agua Fria St., Santa Fe, 87501; 505-983-1636; www.doscasasviejas.com.**

Galisteo Inn—$$$–$$$$

This 250-year-old country inn, done in southwestern decor, has 12 guest rooms, some of which share a bathroom. Horses and llamas can be seen grazing in the tree-shaded courtyard. The inn has a fine dining room, open Wed.–Sun., which is worth a visit even if you do not plan to spend the night. Outdoor heated pool, sauna, whirlpool, bicycles. Horseback riding and massage are available for a fee. From Santa Fe take I-25 north to exit 290 and head south on NM 41. **HC 75 Box 4, Galisteo, 87540; 505-466-4000.**

Hacienda Nicholas—$$$–$$$$

Thick adobe walls and massive vigas create a peaceful refuge from a busy world where you can relax and unwind in a southwestern-style atmosphere. The great room boasts a 20-foot ceiling and huge fireplace. In summer, enjoy your breakfast or afternoon tea in the garden courtyard, which also provides food for the soul as myriad singing birds sing flit among the roses, wisteria, iris, daisies, pansies, and geraniums. Guests have privileges at a nearby tennis club. Seven rooms. **320 East Marcy St., Santa Fe, 87501; 888-284-3170; 505-992-8385; www.haciendanicholas.com.**

Inn on the Paseo—$$$–$$$$

This elegant territorial-style building boasts a large raised fireplace just inside the front door. Decor is southwestern, with local artwork and handmade quilts on the walls. There are also beautiful heirloom-quality quilts on each bed. Breakfast buffet; afternoon refreshments. There are 20 rooms. **630 Pasco de Peralta, Santa Fe, 87501; 800-457-9045; 505-984-8200; www.innonthepaseo.com.**

The Madeleine—$$$–$$$$

This three-story building dates back to Santa Fe's territorial days. The two garden casitas continue the theme, with the same pitched roof of the main house. The decor is a lovely mix of Victorian and southwestern, with a modern emphasis on comfort. Guests have privileges at a nearby tennis club. Full, homemade breakfast. Six rooms, four with private bath; two casitas; pets welcome. **106 Faithway St., Santa Fe, 87501; 888-321-5123; 505-986-1431; www.madeleineinn.com.**

LARGE HOTELS
Eldorado Hotel—$$$$

This five-story pueblo revival–style hotel just a few blocks off Santa Fe Plaza dominates the downtown area. Even if you don't stay here, it's worth a visit just to see the marvelous collection of art displayed on the walls in the public areas. There are more than 200 rooms, all decorated in southwestern style, many with kiva fireplaces and balconies—request an east-facing room to have a view toward the Plaza. The list of amenities is a long one and includes a concierge, heated

17

rooftop swimming pool and whirlpool tub, a health club, massage therapists, and two saunas. Pets are accepted. **309 W. San Francisco St., Santa Fe, 87501; 800-286-6755; 505-988-4455; www.eldoradohotel.com.**

Hilton of Santa Fe—$$$–$$$$

This Hilton takes up a full city block not far from the Plaza and encompasses most of the 350-year-old Casa de Ortiz. Built around a central courtyard with a patio and heated swimming pool, it has approximately 155 rooms with balconies overlooking the courtyard. It beautifully blends the old and the new into warmth and comfort. There's also a whirlpool tub and health club, as well as a concierge and two restaurants. **100 Sandoval St., Santa Fe, 87501; 800-336-3676; 800-445-8667; 505-988-2811; www.hiltonofsantafe.com.**

Hotel Santa Fe—$$$–$$$$

Owned by Picuris Pueblo, this attractive three-story pueblo revival–style hotel is set on three acres just a few blocks south of the Plaza. Decor is southwestern with an emphasis on American Indians of the area, and in summer, Pueblo dancers perform on the patio. Its 131 rooms carry out the Pueblo Indian theme, but with modern comfort. There's an outdoor heated pool and a restaurant serving three meals daily. Pets accepted with prior approval (fee). **1501 Paseo de Peralta, Santa Fe, 87501; 800-825-9876; 505-982-1200; www.hotelsantafe.com.**

Hotel St. Francis—$$$–$$$$

Listed on the National Register of Historic Places, this elegant hotel was built in 1923 as the De Vargas Hotel, and in 1986 it was totally renovated and renamed. A lovely Victorian fireplace plus antiques and reproductions of period pieces contribute a European charm and style, and a pleasant southwestern ambience is added through the use of wrought iron chandeliers and tile floors. The 84 guestrooms continue the European/southwestern decor, yet each with its own special motif. Three meals are served daily in the casually elegant restaurant, and the lounge would make any Brit feel at home. Closed for one week in mid-Aug. Located just south of Santa Fe Plaza within easy walking distance of many area attractions, galleries, and shops. **210 Don Gaspar Ave., Santa Fe, 87501; 800-529-5700; 505-983-5700; www.hotelstfrancis.com.**

Inn and Spa at Loretto—$$$$

Built on the site of a school established by the Sisters of Loretto back in 1853, this five-story inn was designed to resemble the multistoried Taos Pueblo. The historic Loretto Chapel is next door (see Seeing and Doing section). The inn proclaims its nativity everywhere: design motifs found in petroglyphs, pottery, and weavings; fabric colors drawn from the blue of the sky and the reds of the earth; softly plastered light-colored walls; wrought iron; and carved pine furniture. But don't think this means you'll be roughing it—far from it. The Inn at Loretto is another way to spell luxury, with the TV tucked into an armoire, minibar and coffeemaker in every room, CD clock radios, your own climate control, and thick, soft bathrobes. The full-service **Spa Terre (505-984-7997)** offers individual and couples massages plus in-room massage; facials, manicures, and pedicures; and a Vichy shower—a massaging multijet shower. They offer a variety of room packages; a fine restaurant serves all three meals daily. **211 Old Santa Fe Trail, Santa Fe, 87501; 800-727-5531; 505-988-5531; www.innatloretto.com.**

La Fonda—$$$$

This is the "Inn at the End of the Santa Fe Trail" located on the southeast corner of Santa Fe Plaza. La Fonda was already there when Santa Fe was founded in 1610, but this hotel offers much more than history—it is the meeting place of the city. If you don't choose to stay at La Fonda, at least walk through its historic lobby and shops to savor the essence of Santa Fe.

The rooms at La Fonda are authentic to Old Spanish Santa Fe. Each is unique, fireplaces abound, and window sills are deep since adobe walls were made thick to keep the heat inside in winter and outside in summer. Furniture is heavy and massive but comfortable, and you'll see delightfully colorful hand-painted tinwork and woodwork scattered about. There's a concierge, in-room massage, outdoor heated pool, two indoor whirlpool tubs, a restaurant, and a lounge. **100 E. San Francisco St., Santa Fe, 87501; 800-523-5002; 505-982-5511; www.lafondasantafe.com.**

La Posada de Santa Fe—$$$$

This full-service resort and spa pampers guests from the moment they arrive— from valet parking to elegant dining to a wide range of spa treatments. Nestled on six beautifully landscaped acres, the 159 rooms and suites are decorated in a distinctly southwestern mix of Old World and Spanish colonial style. Many rooms have kiva fireplaces and patios, but don't expect any distant vistas—you're only three blocks from the Plaza. The **Avanyu Spa** features five massage rooms, two facial rooms, and one spa wet room for a comprehensive selection of treatments. There's also an outdoor heated pool and a cardiovascular workout and exercise room. The Fuego Restaurant serves innovative regional dishes from 7 A.M. daily. **330 E. Palace Ave., Santa Fe,** 87501; 888-FOR-ROCK; 505-986-0000; **www.laposada.rockresorts.com.**

SMALLER MOTELS AND INNS

Best Western Lamplighter Motel— $$–$$$

This comfortable motel has a heated indoor/outdoor pool and whirlpool, plus a restaurant and lounge. There are 79 rooms; continental breakfast included in the rates. **2405 Cerrillos Rd., Santa Fe, 87505; 800-528-1234; 505-471-8000; www. bwlamplighter.com.**

Comfort Suites—$$–$$$

Each of the 60 suites has a microwave, a refrigerator, and a coffeemaker. There's also an indoor pool, indoor and outdoor whirlpools, and coffee and tea available 24 hours. **1435 Avenida de las Americas, Santa Fe, 87505; 800-424-6423; 505-473-9004; www.choicehotels.com.**

El Rey Inn—$$$

This lovely, historic adobe inn is pure old Santa Fe. It opened in the 1930s and has the traditional thick adobe walls, corner kiva fireplaces, vigas, beautiful woodwork, and understated southwestern furnishings. Some suites have kitchenettes. There's an outdoor heated pool, a sauna, and sunken whirlpool in their own secluded courtyard plus delightful patio areas with umbrella tables, pots of flowers, and a fountain. There are 86 rooms. **1862 Cerrillos Rd., Santa Fe, 87505; 800-521-1349; 505-982-1931; www.elreyinnsantafe.com.**

Fairfield Inn by Marriott—$$–$$$

A small-scale hotel with a small indoor heated pool, fitness center (fee). There are 56 rooms with refrigerator, microwave, and coffeemaker. **4150 Cerrillos Rd., Santa Fe, 87505;**

800-758-1128; 505-474-4442;
www.fairfieldinnsantafe.com.

Hampton Inn—$$$

An attractive adobe-style lodging with a large indoor pool, fitness center, sauna, and whirlpool. There are 81 rooms; pets accepted. **3625 Cerrillos Rd., Santa Fe, 87507; 800-426-7866; 505-474-3900.**

Holiday Inn Santa Fe—$$$–$$$$

Heated indoor/outdoor pool, sauna, whirlpool, exercise room; restaurant serves breakfast and dinner; lounge; shuttle to Santa Fe Airport. There are 130 rooms. **4048 Cerrillos Rd., Santa Fe, 87507; 800-HOLIDAY; 505-473-4646.**

Sleep Inn—$$–$$$

Located next to the Santa Fe Outlets mall just off exit 278 of I-25, this is a very comfortable, reasonably priced option. Hot tub; 99 rooms. **8376 Cerrillos Rd., Santa Fe, 87505; 800-424-6423; 505-474-9500.**

Campgrounds

COMMERCIAL

Los Campos de Santa Fe RV Resort

Located on the east side of Cerrillos Rd., with city bus service to the Plaza area, this campground has all the usual amenities including full hookups, a seasonal swimming pool, a self-serve laundry, and restrooms with showers. Open year-round; 95 sites. Take I-25 exit 278 for Cerrillos Rd. north about 3.5 miles; resort is behind Los Campos de Santa Fe Commercial Center. **3574 Cerrillos Rd., Santa Fe, 87501; 800-852-8160; 505-473-1949; www. hometown.aol.com/loscampossf.**

Rancheros de Santa Fe

Some shaded sites, full hookups, limited groceries, RV dump station, pool, laundry, restrooms with showers. Open mid-Mar.–Oct; 91 RV sites, 37 tent sites. Take I-25 north to exit 290. **736 Old Las Vegas Hwy., Santa Fe, 87505; 800-426-9259; 505-466-3482; www.rancheros.com.**

Santa Fe KOA

Most sites set among trees; basketball, horseshoes, and game room; ten Kamping Kabins share the campground's bathhouse, fenced dog run, propane available; plus the usual KOA amenities except a swimming pool. Open Mar.–Oct.; 68 sites. Take I-25 north to exit 290 or 294 and follow the signs. **934 Old Las Vegas Hwy., Santa Fe, 87505; 800-562-1514; 505-466-1419; www.koa.com.**

Trailer Ranch RV Park

This RV park is senior oriented, with city bus service to the Plaza area, full hookups, a seasonal swimming pool, laundry, and restrooms with showers. Open year-round; 120 sites (no tents); reservations recommended. Take I-25 exit 278 and go about 3.5 miles north on Cerrillos Rd. **3471 Cerrillos Rd., Santa Fe, 87507; 505-471-9970; www.trailerranch.com.**

PUBLIC

In addition to the forest service campgrounds listed below, see also Hyde Memorial State Park in the Outdoor Activities section; the Bandelier National Monument section later in this chapter; and Cochiti Lake in the **Lower Rio Grande** chapter.

Aspen Basin

In the Santa Fe National Forest at 10,300 feet elevation; dispersed primitive camping, no developed sites, water, vault toilets, no showers. Open mid-May–Oct. About

12.5 miles northeast of town on NM 475. **P.O. Box 3307, Española, 87533; www.fs.fed.us/r3.**

Big Tesuque

In the Santa Fe National Forest at 9,700 feet elevation; dispersed primitive camping, no developed sites, no water, vault toilets. Open May–Oct. Located about 12 miles northeast of Santa Fe on NM 475. **P.O. Box 3307, Española, 87533; www.fs.fed.us/r3.**

Black Canyon

In the Santa Fe National Forest at 8,400 feet elevation; 43 mostly shaded sites, 38 with water hookups, vault toilets, no showers. Open May–Oct. Located 8 miles northeast of Santa Fe on NM 475. **P.O. Box 3307, Española, 87533; www.fs.fed.us/r3.**

Where to Eat

Santa Fe offers hundreds of eateries, running the gamut from familiar fast-food chains to elegant restaurants. Below are several of our favorites. In addition, the Santa Fe Restaurant Association's Web site is worth checking out: **www.santaferestaurants.net.**

The Blue Corn Cafe & Brewery— $$$–$$$$

A great choice for modern northern New Mexico cuisine or old favorites with new taste twists. The food is tasty and plentiful, and the service very good. You can't miss the huge beer vats in the middle of the restaurant, and of course they have several choices on tap at all times. There are also big-screen TVs for sports lovers and patio dining for fine weather. Nightly specials. Reservations suggested. Open Mon.–Thurs. 11 A.M.–10 P.M.; Fri.–Sat. 11 A.M.–11 P.M.

4056 Cerrillos Rd. at Rodeo Rd. (across from Villa Linda Mall), Santa Fe; 505-438-1800. Another location downtown at 133 Water St. in the Plaza Mercado; 505-984-1800.

Bumble Bee's Baja Grill—$$

This fast-food restaurant offers good Mexican food, some salads, and rotisserie chicken for hungry people in a hurry. Local favorite a few blocks northwest of the Plaza. Open Mon.–Sat. 11 A.M.–9 P.M. **301 Jefferson St., Santa Fe; 505-820-2862.**

Cafe Paris—$$$–$$$$

Casually elegant, friendly atmosphere with a French motif to set off the excellent French cuisine. Paris scenes grace the walls, French music fills the air, and fresh flowers adorn the tables. Open Tues.–Sun. 11:30 A.M.–2:30 P.M. and 5:30–9 P.M. **31 Burro Alley, Santa Fe; 505-986-9162.**

Cafe Pasqual's—$$–$$$

Pasqual's has been around for more than 20 years, serving food that combines the culinary traditions of New and Old Mexico with Asia. The emphasis is on fresh, seasonal, organic ingredients. The small, tightly packed restaurant is always busy, so you may have to wait for a table, but the service is good and the food worth the wait. Open daily 7 A.M.–3 P.M. and 5:30–10 P.M. **121 Don Gaspar Ave., Santa Fe; 505-983-9340.**

Chocolate Maven Bakery and Cafe— $$

This bakery built its reputation on sinfully delectable desserts accompanied by a good cup of coffee. After several changes in ownership and location, it's now an unpretentious but very good cafe offering a wide selection of wonderful breakfasts, plus sandwiches and salads. The omelettes are light and delectable, and the tasty sandwiches are served on excellent breads baked in house. For dessert try the carrot cake with cream cheese frosting, homemade cheesecake, or our personal favorite—Belgian chocolate fudge brownie with Chantilly cream and warm chocolate sauce. As the name indicates, this bakery knows how to do chocolate! Open Mon.–Fri. 7 A.M.–3 P.M.; Sat.–Sun. 9 A.M.–3 P.M. **821 W. San Mateo Rd., Santa Fe; 505-984-1980.**

The Compound—$$$$

Relaxed yet sophisticated elegance aptly describes The Compound, a fine-dining institution here for many years. The contemporary American cuisine has been creatively expanded with Spanish and Mediterranean flavors. The buttermilk roast chicken and grilled beef tenderloin practically melt in your mouth, but just about everything on the menu is a culinary treat. Open daily 6–9 P.M.; plus Mon.–Fri. noon–2 P.M. **653 Canyon Rd., Santa Fe; 505-982-4353.**

Cowgirl Hall of Fame BBQ and Western Grill—$$–$$$

Great food in a fun and funky atmosphere: low ceilings, photographs of cowgirls and other western memorabilia covering the adobe walls, and something sparkly in the wall paint. The service is good and the menu includes solid American fare plus some excellent—albeit hot—southwestern choices. Save room for their signature dessert: ice cream baked potato—a chunk of good vanilla ice cream molded into the shape of a potato, rolled in cocoa, placed in a pool of chocolate sauce (gravy?), and topped with whipped cream and shaved pistachios (sour cream and chives?) and a square of golden frosting tucked into it like a pat of butter. It's not only

delightful to look at but yummy to eat. Patio dining in warm weather. Open Mon.–Fri. 11 A.M.– midnight; Sat. 8:30 A.M.–midnight; Sun. 8:30 A.M.–11 P.M. **319 S. Guadalupe St., Santa Fe; 505-982-2565.**

Coyote Cafe—$$$–$$$$

One of the most consistently highly rated restaurants in town, with excellent food, premium tequilas, and an extensive wine list. Elegant decor in the dining room; casual rooftop dining in summer. The cuisine is southwestern with new-age twists. Open daily 6–9 P.M. **132 W. Water St., Santa Fe; 505-983-1615.**

Delectables—$–$$

Gourmet sandwiches plus soups, salads, and numerous old-style fountain choices such as malts and shakes, sundaes, and floats. Dine in or take out. Open Mon.–Sat. 11 A.M.–9 P.M.; Sun. noon–7 P.M. **720 St. Michael's Dr., in Plaza del Sol, Santa Fe; 505-438-8152.**

Joe's Diner and Pizza—$$–$$$

Both the atmosphere and menu define this as an old-style diner, with neon lights, red counters, a mirrored wall, heavy coffee cups with the restaurant's name emblazoned on them, and nightly specials handwritten on a blackboard. One entire page of the menu is devoted to pizzas, plus there are taste-tempting sandwiches, salads, and pasta offerings. Open Sun.–Thurs. 11 A.M.–8 P.M.; Fri.–Sat. 11 A.M.–9 P.M. **2801 Rodeo Rd. A5, in Rodeo Plaza, Santa Fe; 505-471-3800.**

La Casa Sena—$$$–$$$$

Located in historic and lovely Sena Plaza, the restaurant opens onto the delightful garden patio in warm weather. The food is southwestern gourmet, featuring such surprises as pollo mole—chicken in a chile-chocolate sauce that caresses your taste buds. Classy service, excellent food, and an extensive wine list. Reservations suggested; open Mon.–Sat. 11:30 A.M.–3 P.M. and 5:30–10 P.M.; Sun. 11 A.M.–3 P.M. **125 E. Palace Ave., Santa Fe; 505-988-9232.**

La Plazuela—$$–$$$$

Good food and excellent service make this a great place to relax and enjoy your meal. The menu includes northern New Mexico items such as chile rellenos and enchiladas, plus some exquisite chef's specialties that combine the familiar with the exotic, such as pork tenderloin with mango salsa. Located inside the famed La Fonda Hotel, at the corner of Central Plaza. Open daily 7 A.M.–10 P.M. **La Fonda Hotel, 100 E. San Francisco St., Santa Fe; 505-982-5511; www.lafondasantafe.com.**

New York Deli—$$

The Schwartzberg family opened their first deli in—you guessed it: New York City. That was a generation ago, and the family has finally brought it to Santa Fe. Tucked into a small storefront at the corner of Rodeo and Cerrillos Rds. (across from the Villa Linda Mall), you can eat in or get something to go. The small dining area holds about a dozen small tables, and the walls are literally covered with photographs: mostly old black and whites of New York City and Hollywood people. The food is fresh and tasty. They have bagels (of course), deli and grilled sandwiches, plus salads and specialty coffees. Breakfast—the omelettes are superb—is served all day. Open daily 6 A.M.–4 P.M.; shorter hours in winter. **4056 Cerrillos Rd., Santa Fe; 505-424-1200.**

The Ore House—$$$$

One of the best things about the Ore House is its location on the west side of the Plaza. If you're visiting in summer, snag a table on the upstairs balcony so you can do some serious people watching while sipping one of their popular margaritas. But don't think that's the only reason to come. The food is very good, too. There's beef, lamb, chicken, seafood, and a few vegetarian offerings, most with a southwestern flavor. Open daily 5:30–10 P.M.; Mon.–Sat. 11:30 A.M.–2:30 P.M.; Sun. noon–2:30 P.M. **50 Lincoln Ave., Santa Fe; 505-983-8687; www.orehouseontheplaza.com.**

Pink Adobe—$$$–$$$$

A Santa Fe institution since 1944, the Pink Adobe features a continental menu along with excellent New Mexican dishes. Occupying a number of small rooms in a very old adobe with walls several feet thick, the relaxed atmosphere has remained unchanged over the years. The food is dependably good, and the service is reliable. Its Dragon Room Bar is quite popular with locals. Open daily 5:30–9 P.M.; plus Mon.–Fri. 11:30 A.M.–2 P.M. **406 Old Santa Fe Trail, Santa Fe; 505-983-7712.**

Pranzo Italian Grill—$$–$$$$

The main dining room is relaxed elegance, with white tablecloths and cloth napkins setting the tone for a delicious Italian meal. In nice weather you might opt to dine on the upstairs covered deck overlooking a busy shopping mall–like area. The menu also includes fresh fish and grilled meat. Pasta is cooked to order so don't be in a hurry. Appetizers and pizza are available in the bar. An all-Italian wine list is offered. Reservations recommended. Open Mon.–Sun. 11:30 A.M.–3 P.M. and

5–11 P.M. **540 Montezuma Ave., Santa Fe; 505-984-2645.**

Ristra—$$$$

Locals choose Ristra for special occasions—the food is superb, service is attentive but never intrusive, and the surroundings are conducive to quiet conversation while soft jazz plays in the background. The presentation of each course is a song for the eyes, and the melding of French and southwestern flavors to New American cuisine must be tasted to be believed. The pear and watercress salad is garnished with dried apple slices, crisply fried, paper-thin potato slices, bits of smoked bacon, piñon nuts, and slices of Manchego cheese (a Spanish cheese made from sheep's milk). Popular entrées include crispy salmon with ancho-chile-and-honey glaze and mesquite-grilled filet mignon with green chile mashed potatoes. Nightly specials. Reservations recommended. Open daily 5:30–9:30 P.M. **548 Agua Fria St., Santa Fe; 505-982-8608.**

Santacafé—$$$–$$$$

Generally favored by locals over the Coyote Cafe; rated as one of America's top restaurants by the Zagat Survey; and recommended by *Condé Nast Traveler*, *Gourmet* magazine, and *The New York Times*. All of these kudos are well deserved—the menu is varied and unusual, combining contemporary American with Asian and southwestern flavors. Some of its most popular appetizers are tiger prawn tempura, lightly battered and served on a bed of slaw with sweet and sour dipping sauce; crispy calamari, lightly fried and served with a spicy lime sauce; and shiitake and cactus spring rolls with a green chile dipping sauce. If you have room for an entrée, you can choose from fresh fish, rack of lamb, or Black Angus beef—everything is tasty and tender. The

desserts defy description; suffice it to say they are scrumptious. The setting is four elegant rooms in a 150-plus-year-old hacienda built by a prominent defrocked priest-turned-politician in the late 1800s. Open daily 11:30 A.M.–2 P.M.; 6:00–9:30 P.M. **231 Washington Ave., Santa Fe; 505-984-1788; www.santacafe.com.**

Second Street Brewery—$$–$$$

This is a good, although sometimes noisy, brewpub with some really tasty appetizers, several good sandwiches, daily specials, and English-style brews made on-site. There are always several beers on tap and one specialty beer available. The India pale ale is tops. Unfortunately, the parking is limited. Open Mon.–Thurs. 11 A.M.–10 P.M.; Fri.–Sat. 11 A.M.–11 P.M.; Sun. noon–10 P.M. **1814 2nd St., at the railroad tracks, Santa Fe; 505-982-3030; www.secondstreetbrewery.com.**

The Shed—$$–$$$

Just east of the Plaza, The Shed has been pleasing hungry people for well over 50 years. Usually jammed in summer, you can wait for your table on the pleasant patio. A good start to your meal is the trademark mushroom soup: fresh mushrooms in light cream and delicately seasoned. Follow that up with one of the excellent northern New Mexican specialties The Shed is known for, such as chicken adobo—chunks of breast meat marinated in red chile—or blue corn red chile enchiladas. Reservations not accepted. Open Mon.–Sat. 11:30 A.M.–2 P.M., 5:30–9 P.M. **113 1/2 E. Palace Ave., Santa Fe; 505-982-9030.**

Tomasita's Santa Fe Station—$$–$$$

Located in the 1904 Santa Fe Railroad station, Tomasita's serves excellent northern New Mexico cuisine. There are a few non-chile offerings, but what Tomasita's does best is chile dishes, red or green: burritos, enchiladas, tacos, rellenos, and the like. You can dine in the main dining room, the bar, or the patio, weather permitting. Reservations not accepted. Open Mon.–Sat. 11 A.M.–10 P.M. **500 S. Guadalupe St., Santa Fe; 505-983-5721.**

Wok Chinese Cuisine—$$–$$$

Definitely a cut above the usual Chinese take-out joints, Wok's dining room is elegant, with well-appointed tables, attractive wall art, a fountain gently bubbling, and soft background music. Instead of a seemingly endless menu, Wok offers about a dozen vegetable dishes as well as a dozen meat or fish entrées and several specials nightly. You'll find traditional Peking duck, lo mein, and fried rice, soups, and appetizers. Take out is available. Reservations not accepted. Open Mon.–Sat. 11:30 A.M.–2 P.M.; 4–9:30 P.M. **2860 Cerrillos Rd., Santa Fe; 505-424-8126.**

Services

Visitor Information

Santa Fe Visitors and Convention Bureau—open Mon.–Fri. 8 A.M.–5:30 P.M.; **201 W. Marcy St., Santa Fe,** 87501; 800-777-2489; 505-955-6200; **www.santafe.org.**

New Mexico Department of Tourism, **Santa Fe Welcome Center**—open daily summer 8 A.M.–7 P.M., winter 8 A.M.–5 P.M.; **Lamy Building, 491 Old Santa Fe Trail, P.O. Box 20002, Santa Fe, 87503;** 800-545-2040; 505-827-7336; **www.newmexico.org.**

Santa Fe County Chamber of Commerce—Open Mon.–Fri. 8 A.M.–5 P.M.; **Santa Fe Outlets, 8380 Cerrillos Rd., Ste. 302, Santa Fe, 87507; 505-983-7317; www.santafechamber.com.** They operate a **visitor center**—open Mon.–Sat. 10 A.M.–8 P.M., Sun. 11 A.M.–6 P.M.—just inside the main entrance to the outlet mall, which is located just off I-25 exit 278. There's also a **Bienvenidos booth** that provides visitor information at the First National Bank branch on Santa Fe Plaza from mid-May to mid-Oct.

Public Lands Information Center, open Mon.–Fri. 8 A.M.–5 P.M.; **1474 Rodeo Rd. in the BLM building, Santa Fe, 87505; 505-438-7542; www.publiclands.org.** This is where you can get information about recreation on public lands statewide, plus hunting and fishing licenses, maps, and camping permits.

LOS ALAMOS

Perched on volcanic cliffs amid pine forests at a 7,355-foot elevation is Los Alamos, best known as the birthplace of the atomic bomb and what some may consider one of the state's most underrated tourist destinations. Possibly because Los Alamos is so close to Santa Fe—they're just 34 miles apart—most visitors to northern New Mexico consider Los Alamos little more than an afternoon excursion from Santa Fe. But it would be easy to spend several days in Los Alamos, seeing its two excellent museums and exploring Bandelier National Monument and other nearby sights. We assure you that this city of 18,000 is a lot less crowded than that "other" city to the southeast.

History

The human history of this area traces back at least to the 1300s, with the arrival of prehistoric peoples. There was a European settlement here by 1880, and Alamos Ranch was named for the cottonwood trees that grow here—*alamos* being Spanish for "cottonwoods." In 1917, the Los Alamos Ranch School was established as a place where well-to-do boys from the eastern United States "might become robust, learned men." Then in 1943, the U.S. Army took over the school for the top-secret Manhattan Project, bringing some of the world's best scientific minds to New Mexico to produce the world's first atomic bombs, which brought the end of World War II in two mighty explosions at Hiroshima and Nagasaki, Japan. The community remained completely in federal government ownership until the 1960s, when the residents were finally allowed to buy land and buildings, but

Los Alamos remains a government town in the fact that its main reason for being continues to be scientific research at Los Alamos National Laboratory.

Getting There

Located 34 miles west of Santa Fe via US Hwys. 84/285 and NM 502.

Major Attraction

Bandelier National Monument

This escape from 21st-century civilization offers an up-close look at prehistoric American Indian ruins, several hikes—including one trail that takes you to two picturesque waterfalls, plus opportunities to see a variety of wildlife and a delightful shady campground. Elevation here is 6,066 feet.

Bandelier takes its name from Adolph Bandelier, a self-taught anthropologist-historian who left his native Switzerland in 1880 to study the early peoples of the American Southwest. He was enthralled with the ruins that would someday bear his name, and used them and the canyon in which they were built as the setting for a novel, *The Delight Makers*, a story of American Indian life before the arrival of the Spanish in the 1500s.

SEEING THE RUINS
Bandelier is best known for its fascinating 13th-century Ancestral Puebloan ruins, including a large pueblo, cliff dwellings, and a variety of rock art. The Tyuonyi Trail, also called the Main Loop Trail, begins just outside the visitor

Prehistoric American Indian ruins at Bandelier National Monument.

center/museum and leads through the ruins of Tyuonyi Pueblo to a series of cliff dwellings. This paved 1.4-mile loop is relatively level and quite an easy hike to Tyuonyi Pueblo, the fascinating ruins of an almost perfectly round pueblo that once had about 400 rooms.

Anthropologists believe that Tyuonyi was a mix of one, two, and three stories, built around a large central plaza in which there were three small kivas—underground ceremonial chambers. There were probably no windows on the compound's exterior walls and only one ground-level exterior entrance. The pueblo was built in the 1300s and was likely occupied into the early 1500s, but by the time Spanish explorers arrived later that century it had been abandoned.

From Tyuonyi Pueblo the trail continues to a series of cliff dwellings, built into a south-facing canyon wall that caught the warming winter sun. From here you have a choice of a level, easy walk with views up at the cliff dwellings or a paved but somewhat steep and narrow trail along the cliff side, with ladders providing access to some of the dwellings.

Canyon walls here are composed of tuff, a soft, pinkish volcanic rock that weathers easily, producing holes that the prehistoric residents enlarged for storage and living quarters. These caves were often used as the back rooms of more formal houses, constructed on the cliff face from talus, the broken chunks of rock deposited at the cliff base. One talus home has been reconstructed.

Continuing along the trail you'll come to Long House, believed to have been a condominium-style community. Extending for about 800 feet along the side of the cliff are rows of holes dug into the rock to support roof beams, called vigas, which show clearly the outline of the multistoried cliff dwelling. Also along the cliff side are a number of petroglyphs and a large pictograph, likely created by people standing on roofs. (Petroglyphs are designs chipped or pecked into a rock surface, while pictographs are images painted onto a rock surface.) Above the pictograph is a tall, narrow cave that is the summer home to a colony of bats.

From the Long House cliff dwellings the path returns to the visitor center via a shady nature trail, with signs describing the area's plant and animal life. However, a side trail leads to another cliff dwelling called Ceremonial Cave, a natural cave that was enlarged by the prehistoric residents, who constructed clusters of rooms and a small kiva. Located about 150 feet above the canyon floor, it is accessed by a level dirt trail plus a steep 140-foot climb up a series of ladders and steps. This side trip adds about 1 mile round-trip to the Tyuonyi Trail.

In the Tsankawi section of the monument, about 11 miles north of the main entrance, the Tsankawi Trail is a 1.5-mile loop that is generally easy and fairly level, but does include some narrow passages between rocks and climbing a 12-foot ladder. Passing among juniper, piñon, brush, and yucca, the trail offers views of petroglyphs including images of birds, humans, and four-pointed stars, as well as the mounds of dirt and rock that mark the unexcavated ruins of a pueblo, probably built in the 1400s, that contained about 350 rooms.

HIKING

The easy-to-moderate Falls Trail hike offers wonderful scenery and the possibility of seeing wildlife. It follows the Frijole Canyon (named for the beans Ancestral Puebloans grew here) to two picturesque waterfalls, passing through a lush forest of juniper, ponderosa pine, and cottonwoods before dropping to the falls area, where yucca, cactus, and sagebrush predominate. The trail begins near the visitor center and crosses Frijoles Creek several times on wooden bridges. The dramatic Upper Falls plunges 70 feet, while the smaller Lower Falls has a more delicate appearance.

It's an easy 1.5 miles with a drop of 400 feet from the visitor center parking area to the Upper Falls viewing area. Then the trail becomes somewhat rocky as it continues another 0.25 mile to the Lower Falls, where most people turn around. For those who feel the need to work harder, from the Lower Falls it is 0.75 mile down a steep, rocky trail to the creek's confluence with the Rio Grande.

In addition to the park's main trails there are about 70 miles of backcountry trails, most of which are in the Bandelier Wilderness, a designated wilderness area that comprises more than 70 percent of the monument's 32,737 acres. The terrain is rugged, with steep canyons, but take hikers to relatively secluded sections of the monument where there are additional archeological sites and excellent chances of seeing wildlife. Detailed maps, additional information, and the required free permits for overnight trips can be obtained at the visitor center.

WILDLIFE VIEWING

Birds and a variety of other wildlife are seen throughout the monument. Observed year-round are Steller's jays, western scrub jays, northern flickers, common ravens, canyon wrens, pygmy nuthatches, and both spotted and canyon towhees. In the warmer months, look for western bluebirds, violet-green swallows, white-throated swifts, broad-tailed hummingbirds, and turkey vultures.

In wooded areas you're likely to see various squirrels, including Abert's, rock, golden-mantled ground, and red, plus their cousins the least and Colorado chipmunks. Also, watch for coyotes, raccoons, porcupines, mule deer, and elk. Numerous lizards inhabit the drier areas, plus a few snakes, including the poisonous western diamondback rattler.

CAMPING

The delightful Juniper Campground, in a forest of junipers, has 94 nicely spaced campsites, each with a picnic table and fireplace. There are no RV hookups or showers, but there are restrooms with flush toilets and an RV dump station. A relatively easy trail connects the campground with Tyuonyi Trail, which leads to the visitor center, about 2 miles away. Backcountry camping is also permitted.

VISITOR INFORMATION AND DIRECTIONS

The attractive visitor center/museum was built in the 1930s by the Civilian Conservation Corps, along with some adjacent buildings, the main road, and some of the monument's trails. The museum contains exhibits on both the prehistoric and more recent residents, including a series of sculptures of the people who inhabited the monument, in authentic dress, which show the continuity of the Puebloan culture from the mid-1100s to the early 1900s. During the summer, there are regularly scheduled guided walks and talks, and on summer weekends there are often craft demonstrations by members of local Indian tribes.

Parking is limited, and there can be waits of up to an hour for a parking space on summer weekends, with the busiest times from late morning through early afternoon. Holiday weekends get so packed that visitors may be turned away and told to come back later. Parking for RVs and other large vehicles is extremely limited. Trailers and towed vehicles are prohibited from the visitor center area, but can be left in the amphitheater parking lot near Juniper Campground. In addition to the main parking lot, visitors can park in the nearby picnic area, and a separate parking area is provided for backpackers.

Trails are open daily from dawn to dusk; the visitor center is open daily in summer from 8 A.M.–6 P.M. with shorter hours the rest of the year. The monument is closed New Year's Day and Christmas. There are both entrance and camping fees. The main section of the monument is located 10 miles south of Los Alamos via NM highways 501 and 4. **HCR 1, Box 1, Ste. 15, Los Alamos, 87544; 505-672-0343 (recording); 505-672-3861, ext. 517; www.nps.gov/band.**

Outdoor Activities

Golf

LOS ALAMOS GOLF COURSE

This 18-hole municipal golf course, right in town, offers great views and is open spring through fall only. **4250 Diamond Dr., Los Alamos; 505-662-8139.**

Hiking

VALLES CALDERA NATIONAL PRESERVE

Located in the Jemez Mountains west of Los Alamos, this rugged area of forests, meadows, peaks, and valleys has elk by the thousands, historic ranch buildings, and practically unlimited opportunities to hike, camp, fish, and hunt. Covering 88,900 acres, the preserve, part of an old ranch, was purchased by the federal government in 2000 and is gradually being opened to the public.

The name Valles Caldera refers to the numerous valleys (*valles* in Spanish) that occupy the caldera—a large crater formed by volcanic eruptions more than 1 million years ago. The caldera is more than a half-mile deep and 12 to 15 miles wide. Scientists say that eruptions from this volcano released some 50 cubic miles of ash and rock, more than 16 times the material that spewed from the Mount St. Helens's eruption in 1980. Elevations range from 8,400 to 8,900 feet.

After becoming a private ranch in 1860, the area remained off-limits to the public except for some guided elk hunts. Ranch owners also harvested timber, and there are miles of old logging roads that provide relatively easy access to much of the ranch's backcountry.

Considered to be one of America's most spectacular remaining private ranches until its purchase by the government, the Valles Caldera is known primarily for its magnificent herds of elk—estimated at more than 5,000 animals—but it is actually home to a wide range of wildlife, including mule deer, mountain lions, black bear, golden-mantled squirrels, chipmunks, and coyotes. Birds here include mourning doves, black-chinned hummingbirds, violet-green swallows, mountain bluebirds, and peregrine falcons.

The Valles Caldera includes the headwaters of two rivers and some 27 miles of streams where anglers catch rainbow and brown trout. In addition to fishing, there are opportunities for hiking, cross-country skiing, and exploring the historic sites. Access is limited to protect the natural environment, especially the wildlife. For current details on activities, including hours and fees, contact **Administrative Office for the Valles Caldera Trust, 2201 Trinity Dr., Los Alamos, 87544; 505-661-3333; www. vallescaldera.gov.**

Skiing

PAJARITO MOUNTAIN SKI AREA

This ski area began as a ski club for employees of Los Alamos National Laboratory and other locals. It has ungroomed mogul runs plus groomed runs. Seven lifts spread over 37 runs rated 20 percent beginner, 50 percent intermediate, and 30 percent advanced, with a vertical drop of 1,410 feet from the peak elevation of 10,441 feet. Pajarito gets an average of 125 inches of snow each year; it has no snowmaking. Located west of Los Alamos via NM 502. Usually open only several days a week; call for schedule. **397 Cape May Rd., Los Alamos; 505-662-5725; www.skipajarito.com.**

Seeing and Doing

Museums

ART CENTER AT FULLER LODGE

Built in 1928 as the dining hall for the Los Alamos Ranch School, this massive building was designed by prominent architect John Gaw Meem and constructed of vertical logs. It now displays the works of northern New Mexico artists in changing exhibits, has a good gallery shop, and presents classes, workshops, and talks. It hosts arts and crafts fairs in Aug. and Oct., and has a popular Affordable Art Sale each Dec. Open Mon.–Sat. 10 A.M.–4 P.M. Closed New Year's Day, Independence Day, Thanksgiving, and Christmas. **2132 Central Ave., Los Alamos; 505-662-9331; www.artfulnm.org.**

BRADBURY SCIENCE MUSEUM

This fine museum, operated by Los Alamos National Laboratory, has exhibits not only on the development of the atomic bomb, but also some fascinating science displays based on work done at the lab since World War II, including exhibits on some of the lab's current research on the human genome and biomagnetism. There is also a fascinating exhibit on lasers and displays on supercomputers, including the "historic" Cray 1A supercomputer, which was state-of-the-art way back in 1977. Open Tues.–Sat. 10 A.M.–5 P.M., Closed federal holidays. **1309 15th St. (at Central Ave.), Los Alamos; 505-667-4444; www.lanl.gov/museum.**

LOS ALAMOS HISTORICAL MUSEUM

We find the human history of Los Alamos and the Manhattan Project to be just as fascinating, or maybe more so, than the scientific milestones that occurred here, and this museum is the place to come for that. There are exhibits on area geology, the prehistoric peoples who lived in the area, the Los Alamos Ranch School, and a great exhibit dealing with the Manhattan Project entitled "Life in the Secret City." At the museum you can also pick up a free brochure that takes you on a self-guided walking tour of the town. Open summers Mon.–Sat. 9:30 A.M.–4:30 P.M. and Sun. 11 A.M.–4 P.M.; rest of the year Mon.–Sat. 10 A.M. 4 P.M. and Sun. 1–4 P.M. Closed major holidays. **1921 Juniper St., Los Alamos; 505-662-6272; www. losalamos.com/historicalsociety.**

Where to Stay

Accommodations

Best Western Hilltop House Hotel—$$$–$$$$

This attractive Best Western offers a restaurant and lounge and a great view of the Sangre de Cristo Mountains. There are 92 units, all with mini-refrigerators and microwaves, and the hotel has a heated indoor pool, sauna, and exercise room. **400 Trinity Dr. (at Central Ave.), Los Alamos, 87544; 800-462-0936; 505-662-2441; www.bestwesternlosalamos.com.**

Hampton Inn & Suites—$$$

This attractive new Hampton Inn, opened in 2003, has 72 nicely appointed units, all with high-speed modem hookups, mini-refrigerators, and microwaves. There is a sauna and exercise room. Located about 5 miles east of Los Alamos. **124 NM 4, White Rock, 87544; 888-813-0912; 505-672-3838; www. hamptoninnlosalamos.com.**

Los Alamos Inn—$$$

This small hotel and conference center offers attractive and very spacious rooms, decorated in western style. All 105 units have high-speed Internet connections and some also have coffeemakers, mini-refrigerators, and microwaves. There's also a heated outdoor swimming pool and a good restaurant and bar. Pets accepted. **2201 Trinity Dr., Los Alamos, 87544; 800-745-9910; 505-662-7211; www.losalamosinn.com.**

Where to Eat

The Blue Window—$$–$$$

A popular and busy restaurant, The Blue Window serves southwestern cuisine, sandwiches, and salads. Open Sun.–Fri. 11 A.M.–3 P.M., 5–9 P.M.; Sat. 8 A.M.– 3 P.M., 5–9 P.M. **813 Central Ave., Los Alamos; 505-662-6305.**

Hill Diner—$$–$$$

Located in a historic building, this cafe has a cabinlike atmosphere and offers American standards, including a variety of sandwiches and burgers, as well as full meals. Open daily 11 A.M.–8 P.M. **1315 Trinity Dr., Los Alamos; 505-662-9745.**

Services

Visitor Information

Los Alamos Chamber of Commerce, 109 Central Park Square, Los Alamos, 87544; 800-444-0707; 505-662-8105; www.visit.losalamos.com.

31

Pueblo Revolt

The residents of New Mexico's pueblos show how tenaciously a people can fight for the things that they hold dear. Although surrounded by English- and Spanish-speaking peoples, the Pueblo Indians have kept their own language and many of their customs throughout the centuries.

Raided and pillaged by Navajo, Apache, and Comanche for centuries before the Spanish came to add to their troubles, the Indians of the pueblos maintained their integrity in difficult circumstances. Many accepted the Roman Catholic faith, which came with the Spanish conquistadors, but they accepted it in addition to, not instead of, their own beliefs and customs. In some cases, the people of the pueblos bring statues of the Catholic saints out of the church and place them at a vantage point where the saints can observe the old beliefs as portrayed in the Corn Dance or other festivals.

But the rule of the Spanish conquerors was very hard. Indians were expected to work long hours for the Spanish and to give up large portions of their crops to tide the Spanish over in winter. In addition, the Spanish had brought European diseases for which the Pueblo people had no immunity, and those diseases, combined with a lack of food caused by both drought and demands by the Spanish settlers, resulted in the deaths of thousands of Indians. But there was a boiling point, even for such calm and peaceful peoples.

In 1675, the Spaniards, intolerant of native religious beliefs, burned kivas and other ceremonial sites and made the mistake of killing several Pueblo religious leaders and flogging almost 50 more, accusing them of being sorcerers and promoting idolatry. One of those beaten was Popé, a member of the San Juan Pueblo. After his punishment, he fled north to the biggest pueblo, Taos. There, Popé convinced the Pueblo leaders to rebel and worked with them to plan it. Then, on Aug. 10, 1680, the northern pueblos rose in unison against the intolerant Spaniards.

The rebels burned missions and killed priests, soldiers, and farmers alike, driving out or killing every Spaniard they found. The tattered survivors gathered in Santa Fe and withstood a siege by the Indians for nine days. Then they made a break for it, traveling downriver to El Paso. The Indians watched them go and then moved in to occupy Santa Fe. Once in the capital of New Spain, they ceremoniously eradicated signs of Spanish occupation.

The Indians held Santa Fe for 12 years, until Aug. 1692, when the Spanish began a systematic reconquest of the now-factionalized Pueblo Indians. Led by Don Diego de Vargas (his full name was Don Diego de Vargas Zapata Lujan Ponce de Leon), they marched up the Rio Grande and easily conquered the first pueblos they encountered. They then laid siege to Santa Fe, convincing the few Indians holed up there that they had no chance against De Vargas's soldiers. The Indians surrendered, and De Vargas moved back into his capital city. It took him four years, however, to quell the revolt in the northern pueblos.

Nowhere in North America did the native people rebel so long and so successfully against European occupation as in New Mexico. This stubbornness has served the Pueblo people well in their struggle to maintain their language and keep their old ways in addition to their devout Catholicism.

TAOS

To our way of thinking, Taos is the smallest metropolitan area in the world. No, there aren't any subways or skyscrapers—although the ancient Taos Pueblo, handmade of adobe mud, does stand five stories tall—but the community is surprisingly sophisticated, in a casual sort of way, and offers so much more than practically any other town its size. Taos is a major art center, oozes historic charm, and has a world-class ski resort. It also attracts interesting people and boasts part-time residents and full-time retirees from the world's major cities and professions, from scientists and politicians to writers and actors. These people (along with tourists) have created a market for excellent restaurants and shops. Not bad for an out-of-the-way little town of some 4,700 permanent residents.

The town sits at an elevation of 6,965 feet at the base of beautiful Taos Mountain, part of the Sangre de Cristo (Blood of Christ) Mountains. The mountain chain received its name when Spanish explorers saw the snow-clad slopes gleaming a dull red in the late-afternoon sun. By the way, local legend has it that Taos Mountain has magical powers and a mind of its own—if the mountain likes you, you're destined to return to Taos, but if you displease the mountain, it will banish you forever.

History

The Taos Valley has been inhabited for at least 1,000 years, and probably much longer. First came the ancestors of today's residents of Taos Pueblo. Then came the Spanish—they explored the area in 1540

and began to settle here about 1617, but they were not welcomed by the Indians. A missionary who had built a church on the outskirts of the pueblo was killed in 1631, and Taos Pueblo was the site of the beginning of the Pueblo Revolt of 1680, in which all the Pueblos joined forces to drive the Spanish out. The Spanish returned in 1692, and several years later the Taos Pueblo people attempted to once again drive them out, but this time the Spanish were too strong and the second revolt failed.

Starting back in the last decade of the 17th century and continuing into the 1900s, Taos trade fairs were important business and social events, for the Pueblo people, Utes, Comanches, Apaches, and even the Spanish. Even during the 1760s, when the Comanches raided the pueblos and drove away some of the settlers, the trade fairs grew in importance.

Trappers from both the United States and Canada discovered the Taos area in the early 1800s and often made the community their headquarters, where they gambled and consumed large quantities of Taos Lightning, the local whiskey. These included famed frontiersman Kit Carson, who made his home in Taos from 1826 until 1868. In 1847, during the American occupation of New Mexico, Pueblo Indians killed Governor Charles Bent in his home on what is now Bent St. in Taos.

Gold was discovered in the nearby mountains in 1866, which brought another influx of people. But the most lasting invasion started in 1898, when artists flocked to Taos, attracted by the clear light, majestic scenery, Taos Pueblo, and the picturesque adobe homes. That invasion is ongoing, and many famous artists live and work in Taos, making its galleries some of the most important in the entire art world. The latest invasion began in the 1950s, with the creation of Taos Ski Valley, and now skiers come by the thousands to enjoy New Mexico's top ski resort.

Getting There

Taos is located at the junction of US Hwy. 64, NM 68, and NM 522.

Major Attractions

Taos Plaza

Not so much an attraction as a starting point, Taos Plaza is not only where Taos began historically, but a geographical reference point today. Ask anyone where a certain downtown museum or restaurant or shop is, and you'll be given directions from the Plaza. It's both the geographic and spiritual center of Taos. The Plaza is also the best place to begin your exploration of this enchanting community.

Spanish settlers arrived in the Taos area in the early 1600s, but it was not until 1796 that the village of Don Fernando de Taos was officially established, with its central plaza the commercial, political, and social center of the community. Although today you'll find mostly tourist-related businesses—restaurants, galleries, and a few too many T-shirt shops—even into the 1970s Taos Plaza was where locals came for hardware, lumber, prescription drugs, and the other necessities of life.

The area's very first commercial lodging was on the south side of the Plaza, and the Taos County Courthouse was established on the Plaza in about 1830.

(Note that the building on the north side of the Plaza with a sign indicating that it was the county courthouse—make sure you stop in to see the old jail—was actually a "new" courthouse, built in 1932.)

You may notice that unlike most places, the American flag over Taos Plaza is never taken down. This isn't because the town doesn't know any better, it's because the U.S. government gave them permission. It seems that during the Civil War southern sympathizers kept tearing down the American flag that flew over Taos Plaza. In retaliation, Kit Carson, who was a Taos resident, and several other Union supporters got a tall cottonwood pole from the forest, nailed an American flag to it, erected it in the Plaza, and with guns in hand guarded it around the clock. In recognition of their loyalty, Congress then authorized Taos to fly its American flag day and night.

Many of Taos Plaza's earliest buildings have been destroyed by fires over the years—it was a devastating Taos Plaza fire that inspired the creation of the Taos Volunteer Fire Department in the 1930s—and so what we see today is a mix of the old and relatively new. Still, pausing on Taos Plaza to contemplate the adobe architecture, the flag, and even the businesses and people gives us a bit of the feeling of what Taos was like 200 years ago.

Taos Pueblo

Home to Taos Indians since long before Columbus arrived in the so-called New World, this awe-inspiring five-story adobe structure, the largest and most photogenic multistory pueblo in existence, remains a living community, where Taos Indians continue to live and work. The pueblo's main buildings—the living quarters and where you'll find a number of shops—are on each side of the Rio Pueblo de Taos, the pueblo's main source of drinking water.

The two sides are connected by footbridges, with a plaza along the riverbanks. Facing the Plaza is the San Geronimo Chapel, the pueblo's handsome Roman Catholic church, which remains in use today. Nearby are the ruins of an earlier mission church, built about 1598, and the pueblo's cemetery.

Throughout the pueblo are shops selling handmade pottery, jewelry, and other crafts plus traditional pueblo foods such as fry bread. Guided tours are available and are highly recommended. Some areas of the pueblo are completely off-limits to outsiders; these are usually well marked. About a dozen tribal ceremonial dances are open to the public each year; some are listed below under Festivals and Events. For others call or check the Web site for dates. Taos Pueblo has also opened **Taos Mountain Casino (888-946-8267; 505-737-0777; www.taosmountaincasino.com),** with slot machines and table games. The casino, open daily from 8 A.M. until after midnight, is on the main pueblo access road.

Approximate hours the pueblo is open to visitors are Mon.–Sat. 8 A.M.– 4:30 P.M. and Sun. 8:30 A.M. 4:30 P.M. Non-public tribal ceremonies will occasionally close the entire pueblo to outsiders, and it is also often closed for up to 10 weeks in late winter and early spring. Admission and camera fees charged. Located about 2.5 miles north of Taos Plaza via Paseo del Pueblo Norte and the Taos Pueblo access road. **Taos Pueblo Tourism, P.O. Box 1846, Taos, 87571; 505-758-1028; www.taospueblo.com.**

Festivals and Events

Unless noted otherwise, contact the **Taos Pueblo Tourism Dept. (505-758-1028; www.taospueblo.com)** for information about events at Taos Pueblo. Most of these are considered religious ceremonies and photography is not permitted. Contact the **Taos County Chamber of Commerce, 800-732-8267; 505-758-3873;**

Though here before the time of Columbus, Taos Pueblo remains a living community today.

www.taoschamber.com, for information about events elsewhere.

TURTLE DANCE

Jan. 1. A New Year's Day celebration at Taos Pueblo.

DEER OR BUFFALO DANCE

Jan. 6. At Taos Pueblo.

TAOS WINTER WINE FESTIVAL

late Jan. Lovers of fine wine, along with those who want to know more about wine, head to Taos Ski Valley for this wine festival, which features daily wine and food tastings, cooking demonstrations, a series of winemaker dinners, and wine seminars. Three to four dozen wineries are represented during the 10-day event, most from California, the rest from elsewhere in the United States and from Europe. Takes place at **Taos Ski Valley. 866-968-7386; 505-776-2291; www.skitaos.org.**

TAOS SPRING ARTS CELEBRATION

May. This monthlong festival includes special shows at area art galleries, studio tours, an arts and crafts fair, and numerous performing arts events.

TAOS PUEBLO POWWOW

mid-July. Tribes throughout America gather at Taos Pueblo to compete in traditional and contemporary dances. There are also arts and crafts sales and traditional Indian foods.

FIESTAS DE SANTIAGO Y DE SANTA ANNA

late July. A traditional Hispanic fiesta with the crowning of the fiesta queen, Roman Catholic masses at Our Lady of Guadalupe Church, a procession, several parades, live entertainment on Taos Plaza, arts and crafts sales, and too many

food booths. There are also Corn Dance ceremonies at Taos Pueblo.

TAOS FALL FESTIVALS

late Sept.–early Oct. A slew of activities take place over several weeks, including an arts festival with two major art exhibits, numerous gallery openings and special shows, an arts and crafts fair, a wool festival—everything from sheep to shawl—and the wonderful Old Taos Trade Fair, like trade fairs of the 1800s, at the historic La Hacienda de los Martinez.

SAN GERONIMO DAY

late Sept. Trade fair, dances, a pole climb, and foot races at Taos Pueblo.

TAOS MOUNTAIN BALLOON RALLY

late Oct. Limited to about 70 hot air balloons, this junior version of the Albuquerque International Balloon Fiesta includes mass ascensions at dawn, balloon glows, balloon rides for the public, and a parade.

Taos Mountain Balloon Rally is held in October.

BREW MASTER'S FESTIVAL

mid–Dec. About 20 microbreweries throughout the Southwest bring their best brews, local restaurants provide food, and live music performances make up this great party, which takes place at the Taos Ski Valley Resort Center. **866-968-7386; 505-776-2291; www.skitaos.org.**

PROCESSION OF THE VIRGIN

Christmas Eve at Taos Pueblo. Parishioners carry a statue of the Virgin Mary from the pueblo's Roman Catholic church through the pueblo, illuminated by tall bonfires.

DEER OR MATACHINES DANCE

Christmas Day. A Christmas celebration at Taos Pueblo with dancing.

TORCHLIGHT PROCESSION

New Year's Eve. After dark, a parade of skiers carrying torches snake their way down the mountain at Taos Ski Valley. **866-968-7386; 505-776-2291; www.skitaos.org.**

Outdoor Activities

Many outdoor recreational activities in northern New Mexico take place in the Carson National Forest and on land administered by the Bureau of Land Management. For maps, brochures, and other information contact **Carson National Forest Supervisor's Office, 208 Cruz Alta Rd., Taos, 87571; 505-758-6200; www.fs.fed.us/r3/carson.** Also, contact the **Bureau of Land Management (BLM), 226 Cruz Alta Rd., Taos, 87571; 505-758-8851; www.nm.blm.gov.**

Fishing

There are plenty of good spots to fish in the Taos area, including the Rio Grande, mostly under the jurisdiction of the Bureau of Land Management, and the many streams and lakes in the Carson National Forest. Contact the federal agencies above for information.

ORILLA VERDE RECREATION AREA

Located along the banks of the Rio Grande, this popular recreation area offers splendid scenery, ranging from rugged mesas to deep canyons carved by the river. Anglers catch native brown trout, German brown trout, rainbow trout, and northern pike, and there is an easy-to-moderate 1.25-mile (one-way) hiking trail that leads past prehistoric petroglyphs and offers wonderful scenic views. There are picnic tables, camping, and easy access to a relatively calm section of the Rio Grande, which makes it especially inviting to those with small inflatable boats. A visitor center offers a variety of exhibits. You'll find primitive and developed camping, including a limited number of campsites with RV electric hookups. Drinking water and restrooms are also available. Day use and camping fees are charged. The recreation area is located near the community of Pilar, 14 miles south of Taos via NM 68 and NM 570. **Bureau of Land Management; 505-758-8851; www.nm.blm.gov.**

Golf

TAOS COUNTRY CLUB

This 18-hole semiprivate links-style course is one of the state's top courses, with spectacular mountain views and beautiful greens and fairways set among rolling hills of sagebrush. There's also an especially good restaurant. **54 Golf Course Dr., Ranchos de Taos; 505-758-7300; www.americangolf.com.**

Hiking and Mountain Biking

The two federal agencies previously mentioned—Carson National Forest and the Bureau of Land Management—are your best sources for information on area hiking and mountain biking trails.

WHEELER PEAK

Hikers in excellent physical condition who want to experience one of New Mexico's premier hikes can tackle Wheeler Peak Trail, which, not surprisingly, takes you to the top of Wheeler Peak, the state's tallest mountain at 13,167 feet. This 16-mile round-trip hike (the trail enters a wilderness area so is off-limits to mountain bikes) gains almost 4,000 feet from its start at the far end of the Taos Ski Valley parking lot. The trail heads into the forest, passes a pasture, then climbs above timberline, following a ridge with spectacular panoramic views. It finally ends at the Wheeler Peak summit, where you'll be treated to wonderful and seemingly endless views of the Sangre de Cristo Mountains and beyond.

This hike, considered moderate to difficult, takes most hikers 10 to 12 hours round-trip and should be attempted in summer and early fall only. It can be done as a backpacking trip—contact Carson National Forest offices for camping information—but those planning to do the hike in one day should get a very early start, so they can be off the summit before the typical summer afternoon thunderstorms begin.

A much easier mountain hike, which starts at the same location as the Wheeler Peak Trail, is Williams Lake Trail. Considered easy to moderate, this 8-mile round-trip hike leads through the forest to pretty Williams Lake, at an elevation of about 11,000 feet.

To cut the length of this hike in half, you can drive a gravel road to a hiker parking area near Taos Ski Valley's Phoenix Restaurant, at an elevation of 10,300 feet.

For great views of the Wheeler Peak Wilderness, the town of Taos spread at your feet, and the more distant Rio Grande Gorge, drive east of Taos on US 64 about 3 miles to the El Nogal Picnic Area and the trailhead for the Devisadero Loop Trail, open to both hikers and mountain bikers. Rated moderate to difficult—especially difficult for bikers—the rocky and sometimes steep trail totals about 5 miles. It begins across the highway from the picnic area, at 7,200 feet elevation, and wanders through the forest, up onto a ridge, and then to Devisadero Peak, at 8,304 feet, before looping back down to its starting point.

This peak was once used as a lookout by Taos Pueblo Indians, seeking advance notice of raids by Apaches. Along the trail are several overlooks, offering views of the mountains, the town of Taos, and Taos Pueblo.

Skiing

For more information on skiing in nearby communities, check the Skiing sections in the Red River and Eagle Nest and Angel Fire listings, found later in this chapter.

SIPAPU SKI AND SUMMER RESORT

This family-oriented ski resort offers little glitz but plenty of beautiful mountain scenery and good skiing and snowboarding on 70 acres. It has 31 runs rated 20 percent beginner, 45 percent intermediate, and 35 percent expert, with snowmaking on 70 percent of the mountain. Vertical drop is 1,055 feet from a peak elevation of 9,255 feet. Sipapu is usually the least expensive downhill ski area in northern New Mexico. Located 22 miles southeast of Taos via NM 68 and NM 518. **Vadito; 800-587-2240; 505-587-2240; www.sipapunm.com.**

TAOS SKI VALLEY

Famous for its deep powder snow, bright sunshine, and challenging runs, Taos Ski Valley has one of the top-rated ski schools in the country. Although it has plenty of intermediate and beginner runs, Taos is known for its advanced terrain and takes its skiing very seriously. In fact, Taos is one of only four U.S. ski resorts that does not permit snowboarding. At a base elevation of 9,207 feet, Taos Ski Valley has 110 runs rated 51 percent expert, 25 percent intermediate, and 24 percent beginner, and a lift-served vertical drop of 2,612 feet, or 3,244 feet if you're willing to hike to the top of Kachina Peak at 12,481 feet elevation. All beginner and intermediate trails have snowmaking, even though the mountain gets an average of more than 300 inches of the real stuff each year, the most of any New Mexico ski area. Taos Ski Valley is located about 15 miles northeast of Taos Plaza via NM 522 and NM 150. **866-968-7386; 505-776-2291; www.skitaos.org.**

Whitewater Rafting and Kayaking

The Rio Grande is a river of many moods—south of Santa Fe it is mostly wide, shallow, and fairly placid, while north of Santa Fe the Rio Grande is primarily a fast-flowing, narrow river that dashes itself against the rocky sides of the Rio Grande Gorge, making it the perfect spot for whitewater boating. The whitewater boating season, which depends on the amount of snow received in the mountains whose streams feed the Rio Grande, usually lasts from late Apr. through Aug. or Sept. You can go on your own, if you have the proper equipment, or book a trip with a local rafting company.

Those planning to go on their own should first check in with the BLM (see contact information on page 37) as advance registration is required for some sections of the river, and it's also a good idea to discuss your experience and equipment with the BLM's river runners before setting out so they can direct you to the appropriate sections. The Rio Grande can be extremely rough in spots, definitely not the place for on-the-job training.

Unless you're an expert with a very good quality raft or kayak, we recommend that you go with an established company for your whitewater adventure. Trips vary from a few hours to a few days, but we especially like the full-day trip (lunch is almost always included) that includes the Taos Box, a whitewater roller coaster where you're guaranteed to get wet. You can get a list of the approved companies from the BLM office in Taos or on the Web at **www.nm.blm.gov/tafo/rafting/commercial.html.** Several reliable outfitters that have received BLM river-running permits in recent years are **Far Flung Adventures (800-359-2627; 505-758-2628; www. farflung.com); Known World Guide Service (800-983-7756; 505-852-3579; www. knownworldguides. com); Los Rios River Runners (800-544-1181;**

Whitewater kayaker on the Rio Grande.

505-776-8854;
www.losriosriverrunners.com);
Native Sons Adventures (800-753-
7559; 505-758-9342; www.nativesons
adventures. com); and New Wave
Rafting Company (800-984-1444;
505-984-1444;
www.newwaverafting.com).

40

Seeing and Doing

An American Indian Village

PICURIS PUEBLO

Believed to have been established by
1250, Picuris is home to close to 350
people. Although some parts of the

Taos Art Colony Begins with a Breakdown

Sept. 3, 1898, is without doubt the most significant day in the history of the Taos art colony. That afternoon a wheel broke on a wagon transporting artists Ernest Blumenschein and Bert Phillips on a painting trip from Denver to Mexico.

The breakdown occurred about 20 miles north of Taos, and a coin toss determined that Blumenschein would take the wheel by horseback into Taos for repairs. Blumenschein returned with the repaired wheel, but also with stories of a fantastically picturesque community. The artists rolled their wagon into town and soon both were enthralled. The Mexico trip was forgotten.

"When they got to Taos and saw the pueblo, the Indians, and the mountains, they realized that this was exactly what they had been seeking," says David Witt, a writer, art historian, and curator at the Harwood Museum in Taos. "They were looking for exotic subject matter, and they realized when they saw Taos that this was the place—this was why they had left New York."

Blumenschein stayed several months then visited Taos frequently before relocating there in 1919. Phillips, however, remained, after meeting and marrying Rose Martin, who was visiting a relative in Taos when Phillips arrived. Soon other artists followed, and the Taos Society of Artists was founded in 1915.

"If the artists had not discovered New Mexico when they did, we would have seen a very different history," Witt says. "Following that event is the development of New Mexico as a tourist destination center, changing the economy and demographics—nothing is the same after the artists discover New Mexico."

Although the story of the broken wagon wheel was well known, the exact location of the mishap had been forgotten. Then, in the early 1990s, several art historians headed into the forest, armed with three photographs that Phillips had taken, and after much searching found what they dubbed the "sacred site."

However, in May 1996, tragedy struck. Fanned by spring winds, a fire raced through the forest, devouring over 7,500 acres of trees and brush. Witt, who was a member of the group that had found the site, says that since it was directly in the path of the fire, they believed the site must have been burned beyond recognition.

"I went up there after the fire," he says, "and by chance, if chance is what it is, a slurry bomber had dropped one of its fire retardant loads right on top of the site. We'd always called it the 'sacred site,' and then miraculously, when thousands and thousands of acres of forest burned, this one little circle surrounding the place where their wagon wheel broke is not touched by the flames."

original structures are gone, there are some ancient mud and stone houses left, and you can't help but notice the striking above-ground ceremonial chamber called a roundhouse, which is believed to be at least 700 years old. The pueblo has also excavated some ancient kivas and storage rooms that it allows visitors to see. Also of note is the Mission of San Lorenzo, which has been in use for more than 200 years and was recently restored. There is also a tribal museum, and visitors often see the small herd of bison that roam freely on tribal lands. The Picuris people make pottery from micaceous clay that is similar to the pottery at Taos Pueblo. Open daily 9 A.M.– 6 P.M.; admission and camera fees charged. Located 21 miles south of Taos via NM 68, 518, and 75. **505-587-2519.**

Archeological Sites

POT CREEK CULTURAL SITE

For a peek into the very early human history of the Taos area, head south of town to Pot Creek Cultural Site, maintained by the Carson National Forest. The site includes a small reconstructed pueblo, with ladders providing access to the roof entrances, and a kiva—an underground ceremonial chamber that you can climb down into. Archeologists say that Pot Creek Pueblo, which was named for the large quantity of clay pots found here, was inhabited prior to 1350, and it is believed that residents of Taos and Picuris Pueblos, who built this reproduction for the forest service, are their descendents.

An easy-to-follow 1-mile loop trail winds through a piñon-juniper forest to the reconstruction, with signs discussing the people who lived here as well as the trees and other flora. There's also a shady picnic area.

The gate is usually open from late June through early Sept., Wed.–Sun.

9 A.M.–4 P.M. The site is accessible by walking in from NM 518 at other times. From its intersection with NM 68 at Ranchos de Taos, follow NM 518 south about 6 miles to a gate on the east (left) side of the road and a sign for the cultural site. Drive through to a parking lot if the gate is open, but if not park outside the gate and walk into the site. **505-758-6200; www.fs.fed.us/r3/carson.**

Art Galleries

It's said that there are more artists per capita in the Taos area than anywhere else in the world, and we don't doubt it. There are also close to 100 art galleries, with thousands upon thousands of paintings, drawings, sculptures, posters, and art of every sort. The galleries welcome browsers and generally offer payment plans for those tempted to buy. You can find original works ranging from $100 to more than $50,000, as well as relatively inexpensive prints and posters.

To explore the gallery scene here, start on Taos Plaza and work out. There are dozens of galleries on Kit Carson Rd., Bent St., Ledoux St., and Paseo del Pueblo Norte, all within easy walking distance of the Plaza. Following are a few of our favorites.

GALLERY A

Opened in 1960, Gallery A is quite likely the oldest continuously operating fine art gallery in the state. It offers an interesting mix of traditional southwestern works and very contemporary pieces, including sculptures and textiles. Gallery A also has the best selection anywhere of etchings by noted Taos artist Gene Kloss. **105-107 Kit Carson Rd., Taos; 505-758-2343; www.gallerya.com.**

MISSION GALLERY

Located in the historic home of early Taos artist Joseph Sharp, the Mission

Gallery opened in 1962 and specializes in historically important works, including paintings by the Taos Moderns, as well as significant contemporary works. **138 Kit Carson Rd., Taos; 505-758-2861.**

NAVAJO GALLERY

Taos's most famous living resident artist is undoubtedly R. C. Gorman, a Navajo best known for his freestyle paintings of Indian women. His gallery offers a fascinating cross section of Gorman's work, from his older and hard-to-find prints to his more recent bronzes and ceramics. **210 Ledoux St., Taos; 505-758-3250; http://rcgormangallery.com.**

PARKS GALLERY

Works by contemporary artists, such as Jim Wagner, Douglas Johnson, and Melissa Zink, plus bold political portraits and other subjects created from trash by Erin Currier, are the highlights at the hip Parks Gallery, where you'll see some particularly intriguing mixed-

D. H. Lawrence Memorial houses the ashes of the famous author.

media pieces. **127A Bent St., Taos; 505-751-0343; www.parksgallery.com.**

ROBERT L. PARSONS FINE ART

Those who might want to invest in museum-quality paintings, including works by founders of the Taos Society of Artists such as Oscar Berninghaus and Joseph Sharp, should head to Robert L. Parsons Fine Art. The gallery, which has a museum feel, also sells antique pueblo pottery and Navajo textiles. **131 Bent St., Taos; 800-613-5091; 505-751-0159; www.parsonsart.com.**

WALDEN FINE ART

Contemporary works are featured here, with an eclectic mix of styles from among about 20 artists. These include the dreamy oil paintings by Lynne Windsor, wildlife paintings by Charles Ewing, nudes by Ron Barsano, and some especially colorful and somewhat whimsical paintings by Arlene Ladell Hayes. **106 #A Paseo del Pueblo Norte, Taos; 505-758-4575; www.waldenfineart.com.**

Engineering Wonder

RIO GRANDE GORGE BRIDGE

A great view and maybe a touch of dizziness await you at Rio Grande Gorge Bridge, an impressive steel and concrete structure that spans a 650-foot-deep gorge carved by the Rio Grande. Completed in 1965, this is the third-highest bridge in the United States, behind Royal Gorge Bridge in Colorado and Glen Canyon Bridge in Arizona, and offers absolutely stunning views of the Rio Grande Gorge straight down to the river, where large rubber rafts filled with people look like tiny toys. The bridge is more than 1,200 feet long, contains more than 2,000 tons of steel, and was designed to withstand 90-m.p.h. winds. It has a 28-foot roadway, 4-foot-wide fenced sidewalks along each side, and four observation platforms. There are parking areas on each end of the bridge, so leave your car and walk out to the middle for a great view. Be prepared for some vibration, though, when large vehicles speed by; bridges like this need to be flexible to keep from breaking. The bridge is located about 12 miles northwest of Taos Plaza via US 64.

Historic Sites

D. H. LAWRENCE MEMORIAL

This small chapel houses the ashes of D. H. Lawrence, the famous and controversial English author of the then-scandalous *Lady Chatterly's Lover*, among other well-known works, who spent much of his time from 1922 to 1925 writing at a ranch on the property. The memorial is the only part of the ranch, owned by the University of New Mexico, that is open to the public. It's open daily 8 A.M.–5 P.M., and is located off NM 522 in San Cristobal, about 15 miles north of Taos. **505-776-2245.**

SAN FRANCISCO DE ASIS CHURCH

Built during the 1770s, the church of San Francisco de Asis (St. Francis of Assisi) in Ranchos de Taos provides a glimpse into the religious past and present of northern New Mexico. It contains a variety of historic religious objects, and the massive adobe buttresses along the back facing the road are a familiar sight to many people from numerous paintings and photographs, such as those done by artist Georgia O'Keeffe and photographer Ansel Adams.

Although open to the public, please remember that the church is not a museum but a place of worship. Photography is not permitted inside the church or nearby parish hall, where a video presentation on the church is shown and you can see a Mystery Painting—an image of Christ that mysteriously glows in the dark. The church and parish hall are open to the public Mon.–Sat. 9 A.M.–4 P.M. (call for the schedule of masses). Admission to the church is free, but donations are welcome; a small admission fee is charged to see the video and Mystery Painting. Located about 4 miles south of Taos Plaza. NM 68, **Ranchos de Taos; 505-758-2754.**

Museums

Two of the following museums are part of of Taos Historic Museums, which offers combination tickets for those visiting both of them. The Museum Association of Taos (**www.taosmuseums.org**) offers a combo ticket for most local museums that is good for up to a year and is transferable.

E. L. BLUMENSCHEIN HOME AND MUSEUM

After his first visit to Taos in 1898, artist Ernest Blumenschein made frequent trips here from his home in New York until 1919, when Blumenschein (Blumy to his friends), his wife, Mary (an accomplished artist in her own right), and their nine-year-old daughter, Helen, moved permanently to Taos. Their home—portions of which date to 1797—is now a unit of Taos Historic Museums.

The house, filled with French and English antiques, handmade New Mexican furnishings, and memorabilia from the 1930s and '40s, shows how relatively well-to-do Taos artists lived in the early to mid-1900s. Throughout the house are paintings by both Ernest and Mary, some from daughter Helen, as well as works by other prominent Taos artists of the day. Open daily 9 A.M.–5 P.M.

(shorter hours in winter); admission fee charged. Located a short walk off the southwest corner of Taos Plaza. **222 Ledoux St., Taos; 505-758-0505; www.taoshistoricmuseums.com.**

HARWOOD MUSEUM OF ART

A good first stop for your adventure into the Taos art scene is the Harwood Museum of Art, affiliated with the University of New Mexico. The museum features a beautifully displayed collection of works by a "Who's Who" of Taos art in the 20th century, plus Hispanic religious paintings and wood carvings. Open Tues.–Sun. 10 A.M.–5 P.M., Sun. noon–5 P.M. Admission fee charged. Located a short walk off the southwest corner of Taos Plaza. **238 Ledoux St., Taos; 505-758-9826; www.harwoodmuseum.org.**

LA HACIENDA DE LOS MARTINEZ

One of the few remaining Spanish colonial haciendas in northern New Mexico, parts of La Hacienda de los Martinez date to 1804. Part of Taos Historic Museums, the hacienda has a fortlike appearance, with thick adobe walls and 21 rooms surrounding two large courtyards. It contains exhibits on frontier life in the early 19th century, especially on the prominent Martinez family, including Padre Antonio Jose Martinez, who is credited with starting the region's first newspaper.

In its day the hacienda was a showplace and gathering spot where visiting dignitaries would be entertained. While practically all homes of the era had mud floors, the hacienda contained one large room with a wood floor—constructed specifically for dancing. The hacienda also contains a working blacksmith shop, and demonstrations of blacksmithing, weaving, and other Spanish colonial activities are regularly scheduled. Open daily 9 A.M.–5 P.M. (shorter hours in winter); admission fee charged. Located 2 miles southwest of Taos Plaza on Ranchitos Rd. (NM 240). **505-758-0505; 505-758-1000; www.taoshistoricmuseums.com.**

San Francisco de Asis Church, as see from the back, was built during the 1770s.

44

MILLICENT ROGERS MUSEUM

You won't find a better collection of northern New Mexico Hispanic and American Indian art than at Millicent Rogers Museum. Opened in 1956 to display items collected by Millicent Rogers (1902–1953), the granddaughter of a founder of Standard Oil, the collection has grown tremendously, and contains not only the American Indian jewelry and textiles Millicent Rogers so loved, but also Hispanic weavings and embroidery, religious art, Indian baskets, and pottery. Although many of the items displayed are 19th and early 20th century, the museum also contains contemporary art and presents changing exhibits. Open daily 10 A.M.–5 P.M.; closed Mon., Nov.–Mar. Closed New Year's Day, Thanksgiving, and Christmas. Admission fee charged. Located 4 miles north of Taos Plaza off US Hwy. 64/NM 522. **1504 Millicent Rogers Museum Rd., Taos; 505-758-2462; www.millicentrogers.org.**

TAOS ART MUSEUM

This relative newcomer to the Taos museum scene displays works by members of the Taos Society of Artists—its collection contains at least one work by every member artist, such as Bert Phillips, Oscar Berninghaus, and the group's only woman member, Catharine Critcher—plus other important 20th-century Taos artists. The art is wonderful, but equally wonderful is the building in which the museum is located—the home of renowned Russian artist Nicolai Fechin. Fechin lived here from 1927 until 1933, transforming a small adobe house into a magnificent showpiece in the style of a Russian country home, with beautiful hand-carved doors, posts, windows, and cabinets. Also open to the public is Fechin's studio, located behind the main house. Fechin was known for his portraits, and among those displayed is the striking and somewhat seductive *Manicure Lady*. In summer open Tues.–Sun. 10 A.M.–5 P.M.; call for hours in other seasons. Admission fee charged. **227 Paseo del Pueblo Norte, Taos; 505-758-2690; www.taosartmuseum.org.**

TAOS FIREHOUSE COLLECTION

It might be an odd place for an exhibit of fine art, but buried at the back of the Taos Fire Station, behind the fire trucks, hoses, and pool tables, are more than 100 paintings representing practically every style imaginable. Among the most eclectic collections in Taos, the works have only two things in common: the artists lived and worked in the Taos area and each piece was donated to the fire department. The somewhat haphazardly hung exhibit covers practically every square inch of wall space in the fire station's recreation hall. Although no one claims that these are each artist's best work—they are, after all, donations—it's a fascinating collection. Look for the delightfully whimsical painting by Eugene Dobos that shows a man dressed in a tuxedo and firefighter's helmet. There are also works by members of the Taos Society of Artists. Open Mon.–Fri. 9 A.M.–4:30 P.M. Located several blocks north of Taos Plaza, off the Plaza's northwest corner. **323 Camino de la Placita, Taos; 505-758-3386.**

Nightlife

Most of the action takes place at local hotels and restaurants; check the Tempo section of the weekly *Taos News*, published Thurs. The Adobe Bar at the Historic Taos Inn and the large lobby bar at Sagebrush Inn have been the locals' favorites for decades, and to our way of thinking they're still the best nightspots around. You'll also often find live music

at Momentitos de la Vida, Ramada Inn,
and El Taoseño Restaurant & Lounge. All
of the above are discussed below. Other
good bets for a lively and noisy good time
are **Alley Cantina, 121 Teresina Ln.**
(off the north side of Taos Plaza), **505-
758-2121; Eske's Brew Pub, 106 Des
Georges Ln.** (just southeast of Taos
Plaza), **505-758-1517; The Old Blink-
ing Light, at Mile Marker 1 on Taos
Ski Valley Rd. (NM 150), 505-776-
8787;** and **Ogelvie's Grill & Bar, 103
E. Plaza Place, 505-758-8866.**

Performing Arts

In addition to the following, check the
schedule at the area's main performing
arts venue: **Taos Community
Auditorium, 133 Paseo del Pueblo
Norte, Taos; 505-758-4677.** Also
check the Tempo section of the weekly
Taos News, published Thurs.

TAOS SUMMER
CHAMBER MUSIC FESTIVAL

late June–early Aug. Several internationally renowned string quartets, a
pianist, and often guest soloists present
chamber music as part of the Taos School
of Music's annual summer program,
which also has programs by the school's
extremely talented students. Concerts
take place at the Taos Community Auditorium in downtown Taos and Hotel St.
Bernard at Taos Ski Valley. **505-776-2388;
www.taosschoolofmusic.com.**

TAOS CHAMBER MUSIC GROUP

fall through spring. Led by Taos flutist
Nancy Laupheimer, Taos Chamber Music
Group presents a varied series of chamber music concerts—from Baroque to
contemporary—in several locations,
with local professional musicians as well
as nationally recognized guest performers. **505-758-0150;
www.taoswebb.com/tcmg.**

Scenic Drive

THE ENCHANTED CIRCLE

This just might be the perfect driving
tour. The 84-mile Enchanted Circle loop
winds through some of northern New
Mexico's most spectacular mountain
scenery—including views of 13,167-
foot Wheeler Peak, the state's highest
point—with stops at towns rich in history and culture and opportunities to
hike and fish. Allow a minimum of four
hours for the drive, or plan to spend the
night in Red River or Eagle Nest for a
two-day excursion.

Beginning our journey in Taos, we'll
go clockwise around the Enchanted
Circle. Of course, you can actually start
anywhere and go in either direction.
You'll find details on the attractions
discussed here elsewhere in this Taos
section, as well as in the Red River and
Eagle Nest and Angel Fire sections.
Much of this route runs through Carson
National Forest, and you can get
additional information about its numerous outdoor recreation possibilities from
the forest service office in Taos.

Taos is an internationally recognized
art colony where visitors can explore
close to 100 art galleries and several
world-class museums with exhibits on
both the art and history of the area.
Before leaving Taos, it's well worth taking a side trip a few miles south to see
the church of San Francisco de Asis.
Built in the 1770s, this striking adobe
church provides a glimpse into the religious past and present of northern New
Mexico. Just north of the town of Taos,
Taos Pueblo, home to Taos Indians long
before Columbus arrived in America, is
the largest and most photogenic multistory pueblo in existence.

Going north, you can't miss seeing
Taos Mountain, a majestic and
domineering peak that has been the

subject of many artists and photographers. Continuing north, it's an easy side trip to the west to see the Rio Grande Gorge Bridge, one of the nation's highest suspension bridges, at 650 feet above the Rio Grande.

Back on NM 522 and continuing north, our route passes through the community of Arroyo Hondo and enters the Carson National Forest. Just ahead is the turnoff for the community of San Cristobal and the D. H. Lawrence Memorial, a small chapel that houses the English author's ashes. Next stop is the Red River Hatchery, a state trout hatchery that annually produces more than 300,000 pounds of trout and some kokanee salmon.

Continuing north on NM 522 is the town of Questa, with several restaurants and motels. Questa began as a ranching community about 200 years ago and today continues as a ranching center and as a base for outdoor recreationists. It is also a bedroom community for a local molybdenum mine as well as businesses in Red River and Taos. Here, at the only traffic light in town, leave NM 522 and turn east onto NM 38, which leads past the Molycorp molybdenum mine—you'll see the tailings on the hillside—to the town of Red River.

Originally a turn-of-the-20th-century mining camp, Red River helps keep its Wild West image alive with false-front buildings, staged shoot-outs on the streets, and several saloons where you can dance the Texas two-step 'til you drop. There are a number of good restaurants and motels in Red River, as well as plenty of shopping opportunities along Main St.

Heading east from Red River, NM 38 climbs to the Enchanted Forest Cross Country Ski & Snowshoe Area and then tops scenic Bobcat Pass at 9,820 feet elevation.

From the pass it's just under 8 miles to the towering stone ruins of the community of Elizabethtown, which was the first incorporated town in New Mexico when it was founded in 1870, just after the discovery of gold. In its heyday it was a wild place, with thousands of residents, at least a half-dozen saloons, and three dance halls. Remains visible include the Elizabethtown Cemetery and the stone shell of what must have once been a handsome hotel.

The road now delivers us to the village of Eagle Nest, which lies at the junction of NM 38 and US Hwy. 64. The village is primarily a base for anglers trying their luck for rainbow trout and kokanee salmon at Eagle Nest Lake, and other outdoor activities in the nearby Carson National Forest. However, Eagle Nest is also a charming little place, with an Old West feeling, some good restaurants and motels, and a number of interesting shops.

Heading south from Eagle Nest, there are good views to the southwest of Wheeler Peak and the Wheeler Peak Wilderness Area. This is also where you'll find the Vietnam Veterans National Memorial, which presents a dramatic, soaring image along the west side of US Hwy. 64. Continuing south, this drive passes the turnoff to Angel Fire, a popular ski and golf resort, and then reenters the Carson National Forest for a slow, winding mountain drive through a forest of firs and pines.

The road seems to point straight up to Palo Flechado Pass at 9,101 feet elevation. Its name is Spanish for "tree pierced with arrows," and in the 18th and 19th centuries the pass was used by American Indians, Spaniards, and Anglo Americans traveling from the eastern plains to the trading center of Taos.

From here it's mostly downhill, passing a number of U.S. Forest Service recreation sites, including some good spots for picnicking, camping, hiking, cross-country skiing, and snowshoeing. Finally, we arrive back in Taos via Kit Carson Rd., which delivers us to the historic Taos Plaza.

Where to Stay

Accommodations

Following are some of our picks for lodging in the Taos area, but there are numerous other choices. Reservations companies you might want to check with include **Reservations of Taos, www.reservationstaos.com; Ski Central Reservations, 800-238-2829; www.taosskicentral.com; and Taos Valley Resort Association, 800-776-2233; www.visitnewmexico.com.**

If you're planning a ski vacation you should inquire about packages that will include lodging, lift tickets, possibly ski lessons, and at least some meals. A tip, though: don't be persuaded to book all your meals at one hotel—there are plenty of really good restaurants in the Taos area, and you'll want to experience at least a few of them.

BED-AND-BREAKFASTS AND HISTORIC HOTELS

Casa Benavides Bed-and-Breakfast Inn—$$$–$$$$

Romantic Taos elegance just a block from Taos Plaza. This extremely handsome and well-run bed-and-breakfast contains 31 rooms spread through five individual homes on a shared property in downtown Taos. The Southwest-style rooms are all unique—many with fireplaces, refrigerators, and/or original art—and all have private bathrooms (a few with showers only), handmade furniture, and antiques. Wonderful art is also displayed in the public areas, and it's

an excellent and eclectic collection of regional works. There are also two outdoor hot tubs (no swimming pool), and the property is on the National Registry of Historical Houses. Rates include an excellent homemade full breakfast. Smoking is not permitted indoors. **137 Kit Carson Rd., Taos, 87571; 800-552-1772; 505-758-1772; www.taos-casabenavides.com.**

Casa de las Chimeneas—$$$$

The most luxurious bed-and-breakfast inn in the Taos area, Casa de las Chimeneas (house of chimneys) offers eight beautifully decorated rooms—some with whirlpool tubs—and all with stocked refrigerators, fireplaces, hair dryers, and robes. Decor is southwestern with beamed ceilings, and the well-appointed bathrooms have hand-painted tiles. There are private patios, an outdoor whirlpool tub, on-site spa with a full program of spa and massage treatments, and a well-equipped exercise room and sauna. The room rates include a wonderful three-course breakfast and an evening buffet supper. Located on a quiet residential road several blocks southeast of Taos Plaza. The entire property is non-smoking. **405 Cordoba Rd., 5303 NDCBU, Taos, 87571; 877-758-4777; 505-758-4777; www.visittaos.com.**

The Historic Taos Inn—$$–$$$$

Just steps north of Taos Plaza, the Taos Inn offers a convenient location, lots of historic charm, delightful rooms, and an excellent restaurant, Doc Martin's (see Where to Eat section). This small hotel, which dates to the 1800s, has 36 unique units, all decorated in southwestern style with handmade furniture, original art, and touches such as hand-loomed Indian bedspreads. Many of the rooms have fireplaces and all have hair dryers, irons, and ironing boards. Guests share the use of a whirlpool tub. The hotel's Adobe Bar, a noisy and popular gathering spot for locals, often spills over into the delightful lobby, which is built around a wishing well that at one time was the actual water source for the community. If you crave quiet evenings, request a room away from the lobby (and Adobe Bar) in the back of the hotel. On the other hand, the rooms above the bar are usually the least expensive rooms in the hotel, so if you're a party person anyway, one of these rooms can be a bargain. **125 Paseo del Pueblo Norte, Taos, 87571; 888-518-8267; 505-758-2233; www.taosinn.com.**

Hotel La Fonda de Taos—$$$–$$$$

The oldest hotel in Taos—there has been a lodging establishment at this location since 1820—is also the only accommodation right on Taos Plaza. A recent extensive renovation has maintained the hotel's historic southwestern charm, while providing everything modern travelers want, from air-conditioning to cable TV to high-speed Internet access. Rooms also have handsome tiled bathrooms, and many have gas-burning fireplaces; suites also have refrigerators and most also include wet bars and sleeper sofas. There are 24 units—our favorites overlook Taos Plaza—and an on-site restaurant. Fans of early 20th-century writer D. H. Lawrence—who lived in the Taos area for a while—will want to see his nine paintings that in 1929 were deemed obscene by British authorities and removed by police from an exhibit in London. Mild by today's standards, the paintings are on display in La Fonda. The entire property is nonsmoking. **108 S. Plaza, Taos, 87571; 800-833-2211; 505-758-2211; www.hotellafonda.com.**

Sagebrush Inn—$$$–$$$$

A landmark in Taos since it opened in 1929, the Sagebrush Inn offers both historic ambiance—especially in the units in the original building—as well as all the amenities you would expect in a good small hotel. Of the 100 units, 68 have their own wood-burning fireplaces, and all units have lots of southwestern charm, handmade furniture from Mexico, and local artwork. There is a small outdoor heated pool, two whirlpool tubs, two restaurants, and an upbeat bar with live entertainment. Rates include a full cooked-to-order breakfast. Pets accepted. Located 2.5 miles south of Taos Plaza. **1508 Paseo del Pueblo Sur, Taos, 87571; 800-428-3626; 505-758-2254; www.sagebrushinn.com.**

HOSTEL
Abominable Snow Mansion—$

This member of Hostelling International offers very economical lodging in a picturesque little community roughly halfway between the town of Taos and Taos Ski Valley. Facilities here are clean and well maintained and, surprising for a hostel, pets are allowed. It has 38 dorm beds plus five private rooms, and guests have access to a kitchen and the Internet. The hostel is open year-round, and reservations are essential during the Christmas season and July and Aug. Guests have access to the hostel around the clock, but the office is open only from 8 A.M.–noon and 4–10 P.M. **476 Taos Ski Valley Rd. (NM 150), Arroyo Seco (P.O. Box GG, Taos, 87571); 505-776-8298; www.taoswebb.com/hotel/snowmansion.**

HOTELS AND MOTELS
Best Western Kachina Lodge—$$–$$$

A nicely appointed Best Western with lots of southwestern charm, the Kachina Lodge has 122 spacious rooms, an outdoor heated pool, and a whirlpool behind the motel away from the highway. A restaurant and bar are also on the premises. From May through Oct. there are nightly performances by American Indian dancers. Located five blocks north of Taos Plaza. **413 Paseo del Pueblo Norte, Taos, 87571; 800-522-4462; 505-758-2275.**

Comanche Inn—$$–$$$

One mile from Taos Plaza, this attractive motel has 124 rooms, an indoor heated pool, a whirlpool, and a game room. There is also a good restaurant and bar. Refrigerators and microwaves are available (fee). Pets accepted (fee). **615 Paseo del Pueblo Sur, Box 6257 NDCBU, Taos, 87571; 800-659-8267; 505-758-2900.**

Comfort Suites—$$–$$$$

An attractive all-suite hotel, the Comfort Suites has 60 units decorated in a southwestern style, an outdoor heated pool, and hot tub. All suites have microwave ovens, small refrigerators, and two TVs. **1500 Paseo del Pueblo Sur, Taos, 87571; 877-424-6423; 505-751-1555.**

Days Inn—$$

Good basic lodging at reasonable rates is what you'll find at this chain motel. **1333 Paseo del Publo Sur, Taos, 87571; 800-329-7466; 505-758-2230.**

Don Fernando de Taos Hotel & Suites— $$$–$$$$

This attractive motel has 126 spacious units, nicely decorated with southwestern decor. It has a very good restaurant serving three meals daily, a locally popular bar, a heated indoor-outdoor pool, whirlpool, and tennis courts. It offers valet laundry and local transportation and accepts pets. Located 1.8 miles south of Taos Plaza. **1005 Paseo del**

Pueblo Sur, P.O. Drawer V, Taos, 87571; 800-759-2736; 505-758-4444.

Fechin Inn—$$$–$$$$

This handsome southwestern-style hotel offers 84 beautifully appointed units, well back from the highway but within easy walking distance of Taos Plaza. Located behind the historic home of noted Russian artist and woodcarver Nicolai Fechin, the Fechin Inn contains handmade furniture and wood accents in a style inspired by Fechin's work. All rooms and suites here have mini-refrigerators, dataports, and plush robes. Many also have fireplaces and/or balconies or patios. There's a whirlpool and exercise room. Pets accepted (fee). **227 Paseo del Pueblo Norte, Taos, 87571; 800-746-2791; 505-751-1000; www.fechininn.com.**

Quality Inn—$$–$$$

A well-maintained motel with an attractive lobby, indoor corridors, indoor whirlpool, and outdoor heated pool, this Quality Inn has 99 rooms and a good restaurant and bar. Rates include a full cooked-to-order breakfast, and pets are accepted. Located 2 miles south of Taos Plaza on NM 68. **1043 Paseo del Pueblo Sur S., P.O. Box 2319, Taos, 87571; 800-845-0648; 505-758-2200.**

Campgrounds

Camping opportunities on public land abound in the Taos area. There are nice campsites along the Rio Grande at Orilla Verde Recreation Area, discussed under Outdoor Activities. There are also U.S. Forest Service campgrounds throughout the area; contact **Carson National Forest Supervisor's Office, 208 Cruz Alta Rd., Taos, 87571; 505-758-6200; www.fs.fed.us/r3/carson.** Camping information and reservations for national forest and some of the other public lands campgrounds is also available through the **National Recreation Reservation Service, 877-444-6777; www.reserveusa.com.**

TAOS RV PARK
Offers all the usual amenities except a swimming pool, although it does have a horseshoe pit and a recreation room with a kitchen. Full hookups include satellite TV, and a central modem hookup is available. The park is open all year with 29 RV sites and 6 tent sites. Located a few miles south of Taos along NM 68. **1798 Paseo del Pueblo Sur, Highway 68, P.O. Box 729, Ranchos de Taos, 87557; 800-323-6009; 505-758-1667.**

TAOS VALLEY RV PARK AND CAMPGROUND
Set back from the main highway with plenty of mature trees, this well-established park—it has been here since 1970—has all the usual amenities except a pool, with 90 sites, including more than two dozen tent sites. There's a playground and horseshoes, and the park is open all year. About 2.5 miles south of Taos, just east of NM 68. **120 Este Es Rd., Box 7204 NDCBU, Taos, 87571; 800-999-7571; 505-758-4469; www.camptaos.com/rv.**

Where to Eat

Apple Tree Restaurant—$$–$$$
In a historic home about one block north of Taos Plaza, the Apple Tree offers upscale dining at affordable prices, a delightful patio shaded by an apple tree (what else?), and an eclectic menu that offers American and international items, often with innovative twists.

Lunch includes good burgers, sandwiches, and salads, such as grilled salmon and asparagus salad, and New Mexican specialties, such as the mango chicken enchilada. Some of these items are also offered on the dinner menu, along with dishes such as the very popular grilled filet mignon topped with a brandy shiitake mushroom cream sauce, barbecued duck fajitas, and fresh grilled rainbow trout. The Apple Tree boasts an excellent wine list. Open Mon.–Sat. 11:30 A.M.–3 P.M., Sun. 11 A.M.–3 P.M., daily 5–9 P.M. **123 Bent St., Taos; 505-758-1900; www.appletreerestaurant.com.**

The Bavarian—$$$–$$$$
For a trip to the Alps head to Taos Ski Valley and this fine-dining restaurant in a handsome mountain lodge, where servers dressed in traditional Bavarian attire serve excellent Bavarian-Austrian cuisine. The menu changes periodically, but usually includes a variety of sausages such as the Kalbsbratwurst-veal brats served with sauerkraut, garlic mashed potatoes, and a dark beer sauce. There are also usually several steaks and dishes such as roasted rosemary-marinated duck breast with a port and cranberry sauce or homemade Bavarian pasta. A good selection of European beers are on tap, and there is also a well-stocked wine cellar. During ski season open daily 11:30 A.M.–close. Dinner reservations required. Located mid-mountain at the bottom of Lift #4 (call for directions). **Taos Ski Valley; 505-776-8020; www.thebavarian.net.**

Bent Street Cafe & Deli—$$–$$$
Among our top choices in Taos for an overstuffed deli-style sandwich, this cafe offers close to two dozen specialty sandwiches, from a traditional Reuben to

51

The Taos—turkey, green chiles, bacon, salsa, and guacamole rolled in a flour tortilla. Or you can create your own from numerous meats, cheeses, and breads. Sandwiches are available at any time. Breakfasts, served until 11 A.M., include a variety of egg dishes; dinner items, served from 5 P.M., include items such as herb-roasted chicken, spicy Greek pasta, and curried pork loin chop. The cafe is located in a historic building about a block north of Taos Plaza and has a pleasant patio open year-round. Open Mon.–Sat. 8 A.M.–9 P.M. Closed Thanksgiving and Christmas. **120 Bent St., Ste. M, Taos; 505-758-5787.**

Bravo—$$–$$$

This restaurant and package store combo—it has the best selection of fine wine and microbrewed and imported beer in Taos, plus a good choice of spirits—offers well-prepared and reasonably priced bistro-style food in a dining room surrounded by wine racks and beer coolers. The lunch menu includes big sandwiches such as the turkey club and BLT, plus some more unusual choices like the Cajun catfish sandwich. Dinner selections include wild mushroom pasta—fettuccine with wild mushrooms in a creamy black peppercorn sauce—roast duck, or chicken, plus pizza and some interesting salads. Open Mon.–Sat. 11 A.M.–8:45 P.M. **1353-A Paseo del Pueblo Sur, Taos; 505-758-8100.**

Doc Martin's Restaurant—$$–$$$$

A charming and romantic setting—a friend of ours became engaged here one New Year's Eve—Doc Martin's is located in the Historic Taos Inn, which has been a favorite gathering spot for locals for well over 50 years. This is strictly fine dining, with a menu that includes exciting variations on American standards. Dinner selections might include maple-cured venison with quinoa cake, carrot fries, and mango ketchup; prickly pear–glazed salmon; or grilled tenderloin of beef. Lunch items might include sautéed crab cakes or huevos rancheros, and the Taos Inn's green chile cheeseburger has been a local favorite for years. Dinner and Sun. brunch reservations recommended. Open Mon.–Sat. 7:30–11 A.M., 11:30 A.M.–2:30 P.M., 5:30–9:30 P.M.; Sun. 7:30 A.M.–2:30 P.M., 5:30–9:30 P.M. **125 Paseo del Pueblo Norte, Taos; 505-758-1977; www.taosinn.com.**

El Taoseño Restaurant & Lounge—$–$$

Favored by locals for good New Mexico–style Mexican food at reasonable prices, El Taoseño specializes in what many of us consider the state's best breakfast burrito—two scrambled eggs, plenty of bacon, and hash browns, wrapped in a flour tortilla and smothered with red or green chile. And it's available at all hours. Other recommended items here are the huevos rancheros, burgers, homemade French fries, and Mexican plates. Good choices from the dinner menu include grilled rainbow trout. The restaurant also has a fairly large children's and seniors' menu, with very reasonable prices. El Taoseño is located in a former bowling alley and consists of a large, simply decorated, and somewhat noisy dining room and bar. It has been owned and operated by the Archuleta family since 1983 and is one of the best spots in Taos to see a complete cross-section of the community. Open Mon.–Thurs. 6 A.M.–9 P.M., Fri.–Sat. 6:30 A.M.–10 P.M., Sun. 6:30 A.M.–2 P.M. **819 Paseo del Pueblo Sur, Taos; 505-758-4142; www.taoseno.com.**

Lambert's—$$$–$$$$

This upscale restaurant, located in a rambling historic adobe home, offers a mostly American menu, and although some selections use complex sauces, you'll always recognize what you're eating. The restaurant's signature dish is pepper-crusted lamb loin, grilled, with a red wine demi-glace and served on linguini with garlic and butter. Lambert's also features several fresh seafood specials daily, and the chile dusted rock shrimp from the appetizer menu is delicious. Game, such as wild caribou from northern Canada, is also often on the menu. The restaurant has a good wine cellar. Open Mon.–Sat. 5 P.M.–closing. **309 Paseo del Pueblo Sur, Taos; 505-758-1009; www. taoswebb.com/menu/lamberts.**

Mantes Chowcart—$

Mantes opened in 1972 in a converted delivery truck, and although it is now in a real building, complete with tables and chairs, its heritage remains with a painted wooden image of the familiar old brown truck. You can get items to eat in or take out, and there is a drive-up window. Mantes offers a dozen varieties of burritos—the locals' favorite is the Trujillo, which contains a green chile relleno, ground beef, salsa, guacamole, cheese, and sour cream. We also like the smothered burrito, which is a basic bean, meat, and cheese burrito swimming in a thick pool of green chile sauce, served with rice, lettuce, and tomatoes. The menu also includes burgers, hot dogs, fajitas, and a number of Mexican plates. Open Mon.–Thurs. and Sat. 7 A.M.–9 P.M., Fri. 7 A.M.–10 P.M. **402 Paseo del Pueblo Sur, Taos; 505-758-3632.**

Michael's Kitchen—$$–$$$

A favorite among both locals and tourists, Michael's Kitchen has been owned and operated by Michael Ninneman and his family since the early 1970s. It's a busy and noisy place, with a casual cafe atmosphere. Expect a waiting line during the busiest tourist seasons. Michael's is especially known for its breakfasts, with the most popular choices being the huevos rancheros and the build-your-own omelettes, but there are literally dozens of breakfast choices, including pancakes, waffles, and French toast. Burgers and Mexican combo plates are among lunch and dinner favorites, and Michael's Kitchen's homemade chile (red, green, or vegetarian) and salsa can be a bit spicy for those not accustomed to New Mexico's fiery cuisine. Those not sure if their taste buds can handle real chile can have it served on the side. The entire menu is served at all hours, and there is an excellent in-house bakery. Open daily 7 A.M.–8:30 P.M. **304 Paseo del Pueblo Norte, Taos; 505-758-4178; www.michaelskitchen.com.**

Momentitos de la Vida—$$$–$$$$

A casually elegant, charming setting, superb food, and attentive service make Momentitos de la Vida among our top choices in northern New Mexico for a special meal. Not the place to come if you're on an especially tight budget or in a hurry, this upscale restaurant is an excellent choice when you want to savor not only your food but also the service and ambiance of this old adobe home, set among the trees back from the road. Chef-owner Chris Maher prepares new American cuisine, using organic produce when available, dry-aged Nebraska beef, and New Mexico and Colorado lamb. Although the menu changes frequently, popular entrées often include pistachio-encrusted Colorado rack of lamb, a blackened filet mignon, roasted Cornish game hen, oven-roasted, plum-glazed duckling, fresh Atlantic salmon, and vegan shepherd's pie. The less formal bar (open Tues.–Sun. from 4:30 P.M. to close) offers a bistro menu that includes excellent burgers, Greek salads, fish and chips, and grilled barbecue baby back ribs. Reservations recommended for the main dining rooms. Open daily 5:30 P.M.–close. Located on the Taos Ski Valley Rd., southwest of Arroyo Seco. **474 NM 150, Arroyo Seco; 505-776-3333; www.vidarest.com.**

Orlando's New Mexican Cafe—$$

This small, busy restaurant, one of the best values you'll find in Taos, is alive with recorded Mexican music and decorated with bright colors, giving it a fiesta atmosphere. Owned and operated by Orlando and Yvette Ortega, the restaurant uses tried-and-true family recipes to concoct what Orlando calls, "plain, basic, nothing fancy authentic northern New Mexico cuisine." The same menu is served for lunch and dinner, and enchiladas, made with blue corn tortillas and chicken, beef, or shrimp, are among the most popular items. Orlando's also serves most other New Mexican standards, plus Baja-style fish tacos, burgers, and a chicken sandwich. Open Mon.–Sat. 10:30 A.M.–3 P.M. and 5–9 P.M. Located along NM 522 (Paseo del Pueblo Norte) about 1.8 miles north of Taos Plaza. **1114 Don Juan Valdez Ln., Taos; 505-751-1450.**

Stakeout Grill & Bar—$$$–$$$$

The best view of any Taos restaurant, with food and service to match. Resting in the foothills south of Taos, this handsome restaurant has refined western decor, with stained glass and dark polished wood. But who would notice? At least not if you're there at sunset, when you'll be busy watching the sun setting over Taos Valley while the lights of the town begin to sparkle below. Beef and seafood are the specialties here—we especially recommend the New York strip steak topped with herb butter, the filet mignon with béarnaise sauce, and the grilled salmon with a balsamic glaze. However, you won't be disappointed with the Alaskan king crab legs or the chicken, pork, or lamb for that matter. Reservations strongly recommended. Open daily 5 P.M.–close. Located 9 miles south of Taos via NM 68; turn east at the cowboy sign. **Outlaw Hill, 101 Stakeout Dr., Ranchos de Taos; 505-758-2042; www.stakeoutrestaurant.com.**

Services

Visitor Information

Taos County Chamber of Commerce, P.O. Drawer I, Taos 87571; 800-732-8267; 505-758-3873; www.taoschamber.com, operates a visitor center on the south edge of town at **1139 Paseo del Pueblo Sur,** at the intersection with Paseo del Cañon East, open daily 9 A.M.–5 P.M.

EAGLE NEST AND ANGEL FIRE

These small communities in the mountains northeast of Taos offer a base camp for almost unlimited outdoor recreation opportunities. Eagle Nest is home to Eagle Nest Lake, a prime trout-fishing destination, and Angel Fire is a year-round resort offering golf and skiing. Nearby is the Carson National Forest, the Vietnam Veterans National Memorial, and the ruins of a historic mining town.

Getting There

Eagle Nest is located about 31 miles northeast of Taos via US Hwy. 64; Angel Fire is about 27 miles east of Taos via US Hwy. 64 and NM 434.

Festivals and Events

MEMORIAL WEEKEND CEREMONIES
late May. These moving ceremonies each Memorial Day take place at the Vietnam Veterans National Memorial. **877-613-6900; 505-377-6900; www.angelfirememorial.com.**

FIREWORKS
Independence Day. One of the state's best Fourth of July fireworks displays takes place over Eagle Nest Lake, producing two fireworks shows—one in the air and another one reflected in the lake. **800-494-9117; 505-377-2420; www.eaglenest.org.**

MUSIC FROM ANGEL FIRE
mid-Aug.–early Sept. Top-notch professionals present classical music and jazz performances in Angel Fire, Taos, and Las Vegas. **888-377-3300; www.musicfromangelfire.org.**

Outdoor Activities

ANGEL FIRE RESORT
This all-season resort offers golf, skiing, tennis, hiking, and mountain biking, plus lodging and dining. Located in a beautiful mountain setting at 8,600 feet elevation, Angel Fire is one of the country's highest PGA-rated 18-hole golf courses. Open in warm weather only, it boasts a par-72, 6,600-yard course, a full-service pro shop, and club and cart rentals. The resort also has more than 30 miles of hiking and mountain biking trails (bike rentals available), plus a climbing wall, private fishing lake, and a scenic chairlift ride.

Come winter, Angel Fire becomes a family-oriented ski resort, with a good

July Fourth fireworks over Eagle Nest Lake.

range of terrain and some great snowboarding. From the peak elevation of 10,677 feet there is a vertical drop of 2,077 feet. The 450-acre ski area has four terrain parks totaling 67 runs rated 31 percent beginner, 48 percent intermediate, and 21 percent expert. Snowmaking equipment covers 52 percent of the area, and it gets an average of 210 inches of snow each year. Nordic skiing is also available. **10 Miller Ln., Angel Fire; 800-633-7463; www.angelfireresort.com.**

CIMARRON CANYON STATE PARK

Part of the Colin Neblett Wildlife Area, managed by the New Mexico Department of Game and Fish, Cimarron Canyon State Park runs for 8 miles along the Cimarron River through a spectacularly scenic stretch of Cimarron Canyon known for a majestic rock formation of crenellated granite called the Palisades. At an elevation of 8,000 feet, the park covers about 3,600 acres of the 33,000-acre wildlife area and attracts a large number of anglers, hikers, campers, and wildlife watchers.

This is a prime fishing destination. The Cimarron River is stocked with brown and rainbow trout from May through Sept., and there is fishing in Gravel Pit Lakes, a series of small ponds created by diverting water from Cimarron River into several former gravel pits.

Since this is part of a designated wildlife area, it comes as no surprise that the state park is a good place to spot wildlife. Black bears are sometimes seen in the campgrounds and along the trails, and the park is home to mule deer, elk, bobcats, badgers, and golden-mantled ground squirrels. Birds here include wild turkeys, red-tailed hawks, golden eagles, great horned owls, mourning doves, song sparrows, black-

chinned hummingbirds, and violet-green swallows.

The most popular hike is the moderately rated Clear Creek Canyon Trail, which follows aptly named Clear Creek through a forest of ponderosa pine and fir and leads past several picturesque waterfalls. It's about 7 miles round-trip.

Rock climbers are fascinated by the dramatic Palisades, but the rock is not stable and requires advanced skills. Beginners are directed to a safer section near the east end of the canyon, and all rock climbers should obtain free special-use permits from park officials.

There are 88 sites in the park's three somewhat cramped campgrounds, with no showers or RV hookups. The park is open for day-use from 6 A.M.–9 P.M. and around the clock for camping. Camping fees charged. It's located 3 miles east of Eagle Nest via US Hwy. 64. **P.O. Box 185, Eagle Nest, 87718; 505-377-6271; 877-664-7787 (campsite reservations); www.nmparks.com.**

The Palisades granite formation in Cimarron Canyon.

EAGLE NEST LAKE STATE PARK

Purchased by the state in 2002 with efforts underway to develop it into a New Mexico state park, Eagle Nest Lake has a history going back before statehood. The C. S. Cattle Company, founded in 1873, asked the New Mexico territorial government in 1907 for permission to build a dam across the river. The territorial engineer agreed, and within 10 years the dam was built, creating a lake covering more than 2,000 acres.

Although originally built to store water for irrigation, the lake soon attracted tourists, especially Texans escaping the sweltering summer heat. Eventually the lake was leased to the state for public use and stocked with rainbow and cutthroat trout and kokanee salmon.

The main activity here is fishing, from the bank or boat, plus ice fishing in winter, and windsurfers sometimes brave the chilly water. The lake is also the site of one of the best Fourth of July fireworks displays in the state. At the time of this writing, facilities are limited to public restrooms and a dock, but improvements to the existing facilities and construction of additional amenities, including a visitor center, are planned.

For fees, hours, and other information contact Cimarron Canyon State Park (see page 56) or the **New Mexico Department of Game and Fish: 505-445-2311; www.wildlife.state.nm.us.**

Seeing and Doing

ELIZABETHTOWN GHOST TOWN

To see more of the area's history, take the short drive out to the ruins of Elizabethtown, the first incorporated town in New Mexico when it was founded in 1870, just after the discovery of gold. In its heyday it was a wild place, with thousands of residents, at least a half-dozen saloons, and three dance halls. Remains visible today include the Elizabethtown Cemetery and the stone shell of what must have once been a handsome hotel. Nearby is the Elizabethtown Museum, with memorabilia from the late 1800s and early 1900s, which is open in summer only, daily 10 A.M.–5 P.M. Located along the south side of NM 38, about 5 miles west of its junction with US Hwy. 64 in Eagle Nest. **505-377-3420** (museum).

VIETNAM VETERANS NATIONAL MEMORIAL

This very moving memorial, which presents a dramatic, soaring image along the west side of US Hwy. 64, honors America's Vietnam veterans. It was built by the family of Dr. Victor Westphall in memory of his son, David, who was killed along with 12 others in an enemy ambush during the Vietnam War. There's a visitor center with exhibits on the war, and computers provide access to information about Vietnam veterans. There's also a gift shop. Chapel is open 24 hours daily. The visitor center is open daily 9 A.M.–7 P.M. in summer; closes at 5 P.M. the rest of the year. Located on US Hwy. 64, 8 miles south of Eagle Nest. **877-613-6900; 505-377-6900; www.angelfirememorial.com.**

Where to Stay and Eat

To book one of the practically countless condominiums in the Angel Fire–Eagle Nest area, as well as complete houses or hotel rooms, contact **Angel Fire Central Reservations, 800-323-5793; 505-377-3072; www.angelfirenm.com/cenres.**

Looking for a good, basic motel in Eagle Nest? Try the **Moore Rest Inn** ($$–$$$) on the highway at the east edge of town. Pets accepted. **715 US Hwy. 64, P.O. Box 138, Eagle Nest, 87718; 505-377-6813; www.moorerestinn.com.**

Another recommended choice is the **Laguna Vista Lodge** ($$$) in downtown Eagle Nest, which has spacious rooms and cabins, decorated in a southwestern style, with available refrigerators. **51 Therma Dr., P.O. Box 65, Eagle Nest, 87718; 800-821-2093; 505-377-6522; www.lagunavistalodge.com.**

Campers can head to Cimarron Canyon State Park (see page 56) or, for those who want RV hookups, go to **Golden Eagle RV Park,** right in town and close to everything. It's open Apr. through Oct. only, with 53 RV sites and sites for tents. **540 Therma Dr., Box 458, Eagle Nest, 87718; 505-377-6188.**

Among our top restaurant choices here is the **Laguna Vista Lodge** (see above), with the dining room in the former lobby of a historic hotel from the 1890s. It's open for lunch and dinner and serves southwestern cuisine ($$–$$$).

Services

Visitor Information

Eagle Nest Chamber of Commerce, 54 Therma Dr., P.O. Box 322, Eagle Nest, 87718; 800-494-9117; 505-377-2420; www.eaglenest.org.

Angel Fire Chamber of Commerce, P.O. Box 547, Angel Fire, 87710; 800-446-8117; 505-377-6661; www.angelfirechamber.org.

Bison at Philmont Scout Ranch near Cimarron.

A Side Trip to Cimarron

Located just 24 miles east of Eagle Nest on US Hwy. 64 is the tiny town of Cimarron. Look beyond the gas stations and modern motels of this little community and you'll see the real Cimarron, one of New Mexico's few genuine historic towns left relatively intact. In the 1800s, Cimarron was a stop on the Santa Fe Trail and well known for its land wars and gunfights, with an "honor role" of resident bad guys that included Billy the Kid, Clay Allison, and Black Jack Ketchum (who is said to have worn a white bow tie to his hanging).

Attractions here include the handsome three-story stone Old Mill Museum, which supplied flour to local soldiers and American Indians from 1864 until 1886. Today the museum shows off the milling equipment plus has displays on the area's turbulent history and local personalities, with artifacts, photographs, and documents. Open Mon.–Sat. 9 A.M.–5 P.M. and Sun. 1–5 P.M., Memorial Day to Labor Day. Open the same hours on weekends the rest of May and Sept.; closed Oct.–Apr. Small admission fee charged. Located just west of NM 21. **17th St., Cimarron; 505-376-2913.**

Be sure to drop by the St. James Hotel, built in 1880, for a glimpse into a simpler, albeit rougher time. Although the restored hotel is peaceful today (and a wonderful place to stay and eat), back in its heyday it attracted a rowdy and violent crowd. Infamous gunfighter Clay Allison is said to have danced on the bar, and in the dining room you'll see century-old bullet holes in the pressed-tin ceiling.

In all, 26 men died violently within the hotel's adobe walls, and it's said to be home to several ghosts. A short video on the hotel's history is shown in the lobby. Feel free to stop in, look around, and view the video; rooms and meals $$ to $$$. Located on NM 21. **Route 1, Box 2, Cimarron, 87714; 866-472-5019; 505-376-2664; www.stjamescimarron.com.**

Nearby, Philmont Scout Ranch is a national camping and hiking area owned by the Boy Scouts of America. The ranch covers some 215 square miles of rugged mountain wilderness and hosts close to 30,000 scouts for camping and training programs. Philmont began as a ranch developed in the 1920s by Oklahoma oil millionaire Waite Phillips, who built a lavish Spanish Mediterranean vacation home he called Villa Philmonte. Phillips later donated the property to the Boy Scouts, along with commercial real estate in Oklahoma, to provide an endowment for maintenance of the ranch.

Although the primary purpose of the ranch is scouting, the general public is welcome to visit the ranch's 150-head bison herd and its several museums, including an art museum and a restored 19th-century trading post started by famed scout Kit Carson. A highlight of a visit to the ranch is to take a guided tour of Villa Philmonte, to see what wealthy oil men of the early 1900s considered "roughing it." Museums open daily in summer 8 A.M.–5 P.M. (the same hours Mon.–Fri. the rest of the year). Located 5 miles south of Cimarron, off NM 21. **Route 1, Box 35, Cimarron, 87714; 505-376-2281, ext. 256; www.philmont.com.**

For additional information, contact the **Cimarron Chamber of Commerce, 104 N. Lincoln Ave., P.O. Box 604, Cimarron, 87714; 505-376-2417; www.cimarronnm.com.**

RED RIVER

Red River is only two and a half blocks wide, but it stretches for 2 miles along the edge of the river for which it is named. The town is walled in by mountains on both sides, and is cool in the summer and snow-clad in the winter. Among New Mexico's top ski areas, Red River has worked hard to promote itself as a summer destination—the ski slopes take care of winter visitation. Square dancing is a favorite pastime year-round. Begun in the late 1800s as a mining camp, Red River helps keep its Wild West image alive with false-front buildings, staged shoot-outs, and several genuine old saloons. There are a number of good restaurants and motels in Red River, as well as plenty of shopping opportunities along Main St.

History

It's believed that Apaches and Navajos traveled through the scenic Red River Canyon for at least a hundred years before the first white trappers arrived in the 1820s. The trappers were followed by miners in about 1860, spurred on by small gold strikes. Gold fever brought a lot of colorful characters, including the infamous Black Jack Ketchum, who relieved several miners of their gold pokes.

In 1905, Red River boasted 3,000 residents with 15 saloons, 4 hotels, 2 newspapers, a barbershop, hospital, sawmill, and an active red-light district. Gold, silver, and copper mines operated here until 1925; now molybdenum is still mined west of the town. Later, the real treasures of Red River were appreciated: wonderful ski slopes, more than

250 inches of snowfall annually, cool mountain air, and beautiful scenery.

Getting There

Red River is located along NM 38, which is accessed from the village of Eagle Nest and US Hwy. 64 to the southeast (this route is scenic but can be icy in winter) or from the village of Questa and NM 522 to the west.

Outdoor Activities

Much of the outdoor recreation in this area—from great fishing to hiking to cross-country skiing and snowshoeing—takes place in the Carson National Forest, which is just outside the door practically everywhere in Red River. The forest service has an office/visitor center, where you can obtain maps, brochures, and other information, on NM 38 about 2 miles east of Questa (on the way to Red River). **Questa Ranger District, P.O. Box 110, Questa, 87556; 505–586–0520; 505–758–6230; www.fs.fed.us/r3.**

Chairlift Ride

Ride the Red River Ski Area chairlift in the summer to the top of the mountain, where you can see for miles. It's a one-hour round-trip, but you can stay on top of the world (10,350 feet above sea level) for as long as you like. There's a fast-food restaurant on top of the mountain. The chairlift operates from Memorial Day through Labor Day, 9 A.M.–4 P.M. Take your camera along. Pick up a leaflet that guides you on the nature walk. Contact Red River Ski Area (see page 63).

Fish Hatchery

RED RIVER HATCHERY

This state trout hatchery annually produces more than 300,000 pounds of trout—mostly rainbow but some German browns—plus some kokanee salmon. Start a self-guided tour at the visitor center, with displays on the trout-rearing process, and see the fish in various stages of growth. A show pond contains huge rainbow trout, and machines dispense fish food (fee). There are picnic tables and campsites (free) along the hatchery entry road. The hatchery is open daily 8 A.M.–5 P.M., and is located on NM 515, 2 miles west of its intersection with NM 522, 2.5 miles south of Questa. **505-586-0222; www.wildlife.state. nm.us.**

Public Lands

VALLE VIDAL

Once the site of pioneer logging and ranching communities, this 100,000-acre area north of Red River and part of the Carson National Forest offers plenty of wide open spaces, sparkling lakes, tall pines, snowcapped peaks, historic sites, and some of the best wildlife viewing in the region. Although far from pristine after years of ranching and logging, the Valle Vidal offers a rugged beauty, with opportunities for hiking, camping, fishing, and all sorts of outdoor adventures. There's a feeling here, enhanced by the remains of pioneer ranch houses and railroad beds, that this is the genuine Old West.

The scenery is spectacular—it's sometimes compared to Yellowstone National Park in its richness and diversity of wildlife. More than 1,500 elk, several hundred mule deer, wild turkeys, hawks, bobcats, cougar, beaver, coyotes, and

black bear inhabit Valle Vidal. Abert squirrels are often seen on the east side, and bald eagles occasionally pass through.

The Valle Vidal also contains one of the largest pure stands of bristlecone pines in the Southwest, a species considered the world's oldest living tree. Located northwest of Clayton Corral, about a half mile off the roadway, the stand includes what is believed to be the world's largest bristlecone, a healthy 76-footer with a trunk almost 4 feet across.

The region's pioneer days are in evidence throughout the Valle Vidal, especially at the imposing Ring Ranch House. In the 1890s, this two-story log building was headquarters for a 320-acre ranch and home to Irish immigrant Timothy Ring, his wife, Catherine, and seven daughters. An interpretive trail leads about 0.5 mile from McCrystal Campground to the ranch house, with photo exhibits that describe the history of the ranch.

There are few marked hiking trails in the Valle Vidal, but numerous old logging

An old grave marker in Valle Vidal.

roads lead to pioneer homesteads, railroad buildings, and cemeteries. In fact, of about 350 miles of dirt roads open when Valle Vidal was donated to the forest service in 1982, all but 42 miles are now closed to motor vehicles and available for hiking, mountain biking, and horseback riding.

Anglers catch Rio Grande cutthroat trout in the unit's 67 miles of streams, with the best luck usually in Costilla Creek and Middle Ponil Creek, plus the Shuree Ponds, which also contain rainbow trout. All streams are catch-and-release, and a number of other special regulations apply. One of the two Shuree Ponds is open for fishing only for children under 12. Valle Vidal is also a popular hunting destination during the fall elk season.

There are 92 campsites in two shady campgrounds, with grills, picnic tables, vault toilets, and horse corrals, but no showers or RV hookups. Cimarron Campground, at 9,400 feet elevation, has drinking water available. McCrystal Campground, at 8,100 feet, does not. Camping fees are charged.

Access is via US Hwy. 64 and the communities of Eagle Nest and Cimarron to the east or from NM 522 and the towns of Questa and Costilla to the west. For information, contact the Carson National Forest's Questa Ranger District (see page 60).

WILD RIVERS RECREATION AREA

Sitting on a plateau on the edge of the Rio Grande Gorge, this recreation area, operated by the Bureau of Land Management, offers dramatic views down some 800 feet to the Rio Grande and its confluence with the Red River. It is a rugged area, carved by the two rampaging rivers, but the level mesa top provides a point from which you can look down into the awesome canyons. There are also opportunities for hiking and fishing, as well as viewing prehistoric American Indian petroglyphs.

There are 22 miles of hiking trails, including several that lead down from the mesa campgrounds to the Rio Grande, which is the only way to get down to the river. The recreation area

Prehistoric American Indian petrogoyphs found in the Wild Rivers Recreation Area.

also has several mountain biking trails and fishing for northern pike and brown and rainbow trout.

Although there are numerous petroglyphs here, one especially good spot to look is accessed by hiking into the gorge from the Big Arsenic Springs Campground. The hike is a little over 1 mile each way and rated moderate to difficult because of the 1,000-foot elevation change—not bad going down, but a little rough coming back up. A big, round rock near the river, which stands about 7 feet high, is covered with a variety of petroglyphs, including numerous animal images, that are believed to have been created between A.D. 1000 and 1600. Because there are no signs pointing to this rock, it's best to ask for directions at the visitor center before you start the hike.

If you are lucky, you may see eagles and red-tailed hawks soaring on the updrafts along the canyon walls, and if you camp here, you probably will hear the eerie night song of the coyote and possibly see a mule deer. There are river-view campsites along the canyon rim, with water and toilets but no showers or RV hookups. The recreation area is open 24 hours year-round; the visitor center is open in summer daily 10 A.M.–4 P.M., and additional times depending on staff availability. Small day-use and camping fees are charged. The recreation area is located about 25 miles west of Red River. Follow NM 38 west to Questa, then north on NM 522 to NM 378, which takes you west to the recreation area visitor center. **505-758-8851; 505-770-1600; www.nm.blm.gov.**

Skiing

ENCHANTED FOREST

This delightful cross-country ski area offers more than 16 miles of groomed trails that meander through the forest at elevations from 9,800 feet to 10,030 feet. Trails are rated 30 percent beginner, 40 percent intermediate, and 30 percent expert, with set track and skating lanes, plus snowshoe terrain. This full-service center has equipment for rent, professional instruction, and special race clinics. Located along NM 38 about 3.5 miles east of Red River. **505-754-2374; www.enchantedforestxc.com.**

RED RIVER SKI AREA

Located right in the middle of downtown Red River, this family-oriented resort is one of New Mexico's most beautiful ski areas. With 252 inches of annual snowfall, it is second only to Taos Ski Valley in the amount of natural snow it receives. Ski lifts begin right in town, within walking distance of most accommodations. From its peak elevation of 10,350 feet there's a vertical drop of 1,600 feet. Of the 57 trails, 32 percent are rated beginner, 38 percent intermediate, and 30 percent expert. Snowmaking covers 85 percent of the area. **505-754-2223; 505-754-2220 (snow report); www.redriverskiarea.com.**

Seeing and Doing

Family Entertainment

FRYE'S OLD TOWN

Don't miss the staged bank robberies and Wild West shoot-outs at Frye's Old Town every Tues., Thurs., and Sat. at 4 P.M. from late June through mid-Aug. **100 W. Main St., Red River; 505-754-6165; www.fryesoldtown.com.**

THE MINE SHAFT THEATER

The Mine Shaft Theater in the Red River

Inn presents a real old-time melodrama theater on summer evenings. Boo the villain, cheer for the hero—have fun, and put yourself into the act! Reserved seating, fee. **300 W. Main St., Red River; 505-754-2930.**

RED RIVER
COMMUNITY HOUSE

Red River considers itself the square-dancing capital of the Southwest, and if you don't know how they'll teach you. **Red River Community House, 116 E. Main St., Red River; 505-754-2349** or contact the chamber of commerce (see Services).

Museum

LITTLE RED SCHOOLHOUSE

Built in 1917, the schoolhouse has been preserved and now serves as a community museum with a re-created historic classroom, historic photos, and assorted memorabilia from Red River's past. Located at the south edge of town, behind the Red River Library, **702 E. Main St., Red River.** Call the Red River Library, **505-754-6564,** for hours.

Where to Stay and Eat

There are plenty of good lodging choices in Red River, including the **Best Western Rivers Edge** ($$–$$$), which has reasonable rates, 30 rooms, a whirlpool tub, and accepts pets (fee). **301 W. River St., Red River, 87558; 877-600-9990; 505-754-1766; www. redrivernm.com/bestwestern.**

The more upscale **Lifts West Condominium Resort Hotel** ($$–$$$$) offers 83 units with fully equipped kitchens and fireplaces. It has a restaurant, a heated outdoor swimming pool, two whirlpools, and a sauna. **201 W.**

Main St., P.O. Box 330, Red River 87558; 800-221-1859; 505-754-2778; www. redrivernm.com/liftswest.

Campground choices are numerous, including some very nice forest service campgrounds along the Red River (contact the Questa Ranger District, information on page 60) and at Wild Rivers Recreation Area (see page 62). For commercial campgrounds, try the **Roadrunner RV Resort,** with 150 sites (no tents), with all the usual amenities except a swimming pool. Open May–Sept. **1371 E. Main St., P.O. Box 588, Red River, 87558; 800-243-2286; 505-754-2286; www. redrivernm.com/roadrunnerrv.**

Our favorite Red River restaurant for years has been **Texas Reds Steakhouse** ($$–$$$$), a casual and fun Wild West sort of place where the beer has always been cold and the steaks were thick and juicy. Unfortunately, a fire in late 2004 burned the restaurant to the ground. However, the owner is in the process of rebuilding and hopes to reopen by summer 2005. In addition to steaks, the restaurant will serve buffalo, chicken, and fish. Open daily 5–9:30 P.M. **111 E. Main St., Red River; 505-754-2964; 505-754-2922 (hostess hotline, to put your name on a waiting list); www.texasreds.com.**

Services

Visitor Information
Red River Chamber of Commerce, P.O. Box 870, Red River, 87558, operates a visitor center, open Mon.–Sat. 8 A.M.–5 P.M., in Town Hall, 100 E. Main St., Red River; 800-348-6444; 505-754-2366; www.redrivernewmex.com.

CHAMA

This town of about 1,200 people has a wonderful location—at the base of 11,403-foot Brazos Mountain and surrounded by some of the most beautiful mountain scenery in the West. At 7,850 feet above sea level, it is one of New Mexico's highest communities, which helps explain its heavy winter snow and the chilly nights that are the rule even in the middle of summer. It's primarily a tourist town, the base for year-round outdoor recreation as well as the absolutely wonderful Cumbres & Toltec Scenic Railroad.

History

Chama was once an important mining town, which accounts for the narrow-gauge railroad winding its scenic way from Antonito, Colorado. The Denver and Rio Grande Western Railroad began construction on a rail extension in 1880, which ran from Alamosa, Colorado, to Durango, Colorado, by way of Chama. The first rail travel began in Feb. 1881, and for the next 30 years, Chama was a wild little place, complete with honest-to-goodness hold-ups of the payroll train, lots of saloons, and a great influx of good and bad individuals. The Charles Allison gang robbed and stole at will for a time.

At about the same time, loggers clear-cut the dense forests, forming the grasslands you see today—they did not replant trees. Because of the grasslands, sheep and cattle ranching flourished and are still important here. The catastrophic winter of 1932 almost wiped out all the livestock in the Chama Valley, a blow from which the town never really recovered, and now tourism and outdoor recreation are key elements in the community's economy.

Getting There

Just 8 miles below the Colorado border and about a dozen miles east of the Continental Divide, Chama is on US Hwys. 64/84 at its junction with NM 17.

Major Attraction

Cumbres & Toltec Scenic Railroad

Begun in 1880 to serve the area's remote mining camps, the Cumbres & Toltec Scenic Railroad follows a spectacular 64-mile path through the San Juan Mountains between Chama and Antonito, Colorado, crossing the state line 11 times. Along the way the narrow-gauge steam train weaves through forests of pine and aspen, climbing through tunnels and over trestles to the summit of 10,015-foot Cumbres Pass and through the spectacular Toltec Gorge of the Los Piños River. At the rail-junction community of Osier, passengers picnic or buy a catered lunch. Passengers can make the trip either from Chama to Antonito or from Antonito to Chama, with return transportation by bus; shorter trips and other options may also be available. The train usually runs from late May to mid-Oct. Call for the current schedule. Admission fee charged. **500 S. Terrace Ave., P.O. Box 789, Chama, 87520; 888-286-2737; 505-756-2151; www.cumbresandtoltec.com.**

Outdoor Activities

In addition to the two state parks discussed below, the Carson National Forest has plenty of room to roam and practically unlimited opportunities for hiking, mountain biking, cross-country skiing, snowshoeing, snowmobiling, camping, fishing, and hunting. Information is available at the state visitor center in Chama (see Services in this chapter), and at Carson's Canjilon Ranger Station, located in the community of Canjilon, about 33 miles south of Chama via US Hwy. 84 and NM 115. **P.O. Box 469, Canjilon, 87515; 505-684-2489; www.fs.fed.us/r3.**

EL VADO LAKE STATE PARK
Waterskiing and fishing are among the major activities at this 3,200-acre lake, where you'll see all varieties of boats, from high-powered speedboats to sailboats and even some canoes and small inflatables. At an elevation of 6,900 feet, the park also offers hiking, fishing, camping, wildlife viewing, cross-country skiing, and snowshoeing. Swimming is permitted, although there are no designated swimming areas and water temperatures are somewhat chilly.

A highlight of the park and nearby Heron Lake State Park, discussed below, is the 5.5-mile Rio Chama Trail, which connects El Vado Lake with Heron Lake. The trail follows the Rio Chama, rising gently from the El Vado Lake trailhead to a mesa on the south side of the river, which offers tree-framed views of both El Vado and Heron Lakes. The trail then winds down the side of the canyon, through a piñon-juniper forest. It crosses the Rio Chama on a cable footbridge and leads up a steep set of redwood stairs to the Heron Lake trailhead. The trail, open to foot travel only, is relatively flat and easy for the first 5

miles from El Vado Lake, and then moderately strenuous for the last 0.5 mile.

The Rio Chama Trail offers an excellent chance of seeing wildlife. The lake is a major wintering area for the bald eagle, which is easily recognized by its white head and tail, the flat appearance of its wings during flight, and its size—bald eagles wingspans can reach 8 feet. Also watch for wild turkeys, peregrine falcons, red-tailed hawks, Clark's nutcrackers, white-throated swifts, scrub jays, and mountain bluebirds. Elk and mule deer are often seen, especially in winter.

Anglers catch rainbow and German brown trout, kokanee salmon, and channel catfish, and ice fishing is popular in winter. Also during winter there is some cross-country skiing and snowshoeing when there is enough snow.

The park has 80 campsites (19 with electric hookups) that offer good views and easy access to the lake, but little shade except for the picnic table shelters. The campground rarely fills, although the electric hookup sites are usually taken first. There are restrooms with showers and an RV dump station. Located 27 miles south of Chama via US Hwys. 64/84 and NM 112. **P.O. Box 367, Tierra Amarilla, 87575; 505-588-7247; www.nmparks.com.**

HERON LAKE STATE PARK
A haven for sailboats—power boats are permitted but a no-wake policy keeps the speeds down—Heron Lake offers a seemingly endless lake tucked away in a mountain forest of ponderosa pines, piñons, and junipers. The park also offers fishing, wildlife viewing, cross-country skiing, snowshoeing, and camping. There's also that great hiking trail it shares with El Vado Lake State Park (discussed above).

Mostly seen on the lake are sailboats, plus some small fishing boats with trolling motors, a few canoes, and occasional windsurfers. The New Mexico Sailing Club sponsors a series of races throughout the summer, including Fourth of July and Labor Day regattas. The sailing season is Apr. through Oct., and conditions are often ideal, with mild afternoon breezes and clear skies.

The lake, which covers 5,900 acres at an elevation of 7,200 feet, is roughly 4 miles long and 3 miles wide, a broad expanse that gives sailors plenty of tacking room. A marina has a dock and slips for rent on a nightly basis, but no boat rentals or supplies. Businesses within a few miles of the park have canoe, fishing, and pontoon boat rentals, plus groceries and camping and fishing supplies. Swimming is permitted anywhere in the lake.

Anglers catch kokanee salmon and several species of trout. The lake does not freeze and is open for fishing year-round. However, Willow Creek, which leads into the lake, does freeze and is a popular ice fishing spot. Snagging is popular in the winter, and runs from Nov. through Dec. when the kokanee salmon are spawning.

Although there are no established trails, cross-country skiers have numerous opportunities, including some of the lesser-used roads that are not plowed. Snowshoers can traipse along the hiking trails or just head out across the fields and through the woods. The wildlife here is mostly the same as at neighboring El Vado Lake.

There are 250 developed campsites, including 54 with electric hookups, plus primitive camping. The park also has restrooms with showers and an RV dump station. Located 20 miles south of Chama via US Hwys. 64/84 and NM 95. **P.O. Box 159, Los Ojos, 87551; 505-588-7470; www.nmparks.com.**

Where to Stay

Accommodations
Branding Iron Motel—$$–$$$
Attractive, well-maintained property offering 41 basic motel rooms. Pets accepted (fee). On the west side of the highway, southern edge of Chama. **1511 W. Main St., Chama, 87520; 505-756-2162.**

Elkhorn Lodge—$$
A log cabin–style facility with 22 motel rooms and 11 cabins with kitchens, the Elkhorn sits next to a pretty stream. Units have knotty pine walls and comfortable seating, and the cabins have covered porches. Pets accepted. Located on the main highway near the south end of Chama. **2663 S. US Hwy. 64/84, Rte. 1, Box 45, Chama, 87520; 800-532-8874 (reservations); 505-756-2105; www.elkhornlodge.net.**

Gandy Dancer Bed & Breakfast—$$$
Built in 1913, this handsome Victorian inn offers seven unique and well-appointed rooms, each with a TV and VCR. There's a whirlpool and exercise equipment, and the full hot breakfasts will keep you going all day. Rooms are named for railroad themes; the name *gandy dancer* is a slang term for railroad laborer. Smoking is not permitted indoors. Located one block west of NM 17 via 3rd St. **299 Maple Ave., P.O. Box 810, Chama, 87520; 800-424-6702; 505-756-2191.**

River Bend Lodge—$$–$$$
This attractive motel offers quiet, reasonably priced rooms, including some with kitchens, and has an outdoor hot tub. There are 21 rooms and pets are accepted (fee). **2625 US Hwys. 64/84, P.O. Box 593, Chama, 87520; 800-288-1371; 505-756-2264.**

Campgrounds

Camping is offered at both Heron and El Vado Lakes and in the nearby Carson National Forest (see Outdoor Activities). There are several commercial campgrounds in Chama including the Rio Chama RV Park, a shady campground along the river that's open from early May to mid-Oct. It has 78 RV sites with hookups and 14 tent sites, horseshoes, and other games, but no swimming pool. It's within walking distance of the train depot. Located on NM 17, 2 miles north of its junction with US Hwys. 64/84. **P.O. Box 706, Chama, 87520; 505-756-2303; www.coloradodirectory.com/ riochamarv.**

Where to Eat

Branding Iron Restaurant—$$–$$$

Good, basic American grub and some southwestern favorites, all at reasonable prices, make this a favorite of locals. Open daily 6 A.M.–10 P.M. On the west side of the highway, southern edge of Chama. **1511 W. Main St., Chama; 505-756-9195.**

Elkhorn Cafe—$$

Home-style American and Mexican standards are the fare at this comfy, relaxed old-style cafe. Breakfasts are especially good. We also like the burgers and chicken-fried steak with gravy. Open daily 7 A.M.–8 P.M. (closed Tues. in winter). Located on the main highway near the south end of Chama. **2663 S. US Hwy. 64/84, Chama; 505-756-2229; www.elkhornlodge.net.**

High Country Steakhouse and Lounge—$$–$$$

Among the more upscale restaurants in laid-back Chama, the High Country has an Old West saloon atmosphere. It serves steak, seafood, and Mexican specialties. Open daily 11 A.M.–10 P.M. Closed Thanksgiving and Christmas. Located north of the junction of NM 17 and US Hwys. 64/84. **2299 NM 17, Chama; 505-756-2384.**

Viva Vera's Mexican Kitchen—$$–$$$

Turning out authentic New Mexico–style Mexican food since 1963, Viva Vera's is a good choice if you're looking for spicy chile rellenos, burritos, or enchiladas. It also serves a variety of sandwiches and salads. The decor is festive, with colorful Mexican and Indian rugs, Mexican sombreros, and chile *ristras*. Open Thurs.–Tues. 8 A.M.–8 P.M. It's just north of the junction of NM 17 and US 64/84. **2202 NM 17, Chama; 505-756-2557.**

Services

Visitor Information

Chama Valley Chamber of Commerce, 463 Terrace Ave., P.O. Box 306-RB, Chama, 87520; 800-477-0149; 505-756-2306; www.chamavalley.com. The state operates a visitor information center, with information on the entire state as well as Chama, at the northwest corner at the junction of US Hwy. 64 and NM 17. **2372 NM 17, Chama, 87520; 505-756-2235.**

NORTHEAST REGION

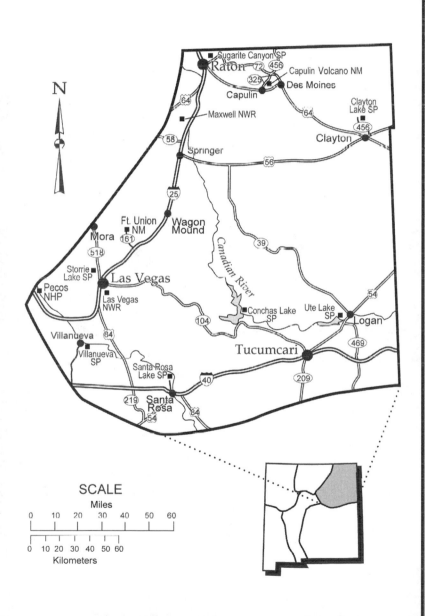

N

Sugarite Canyon SP
Raton
72 456
Capulin Volcano NM
325
Des Moines
Capulin
64
Clayton Lake SP
Maxwell NWR
64
456
58
Clayton
Springer
56
25
Ft. Union NM
Wagon Mound
Mora
161
39
518
Storrie Lake SP
Las Vegas
54
Pecos NHP
Las Vegas NWR
Canadian River
Conchas Lake SP
Ute Lake SP
Logan
104
Villanueva
84
469
Villanueva SP
Tucumcari
Santa Rosa Lake SP
209
40
219 Santa Rosa
84
54

SCALE

Miles

0 10 20 30 40 50 60

0 10 20 30 40 50 60
Kilometers

Northeast Region

Separated from the rest of the state by interstate highways I-25 and I-40, northeastern New Mexico offers a mix of mountains and plains where you'll find a healthy dose of 1950s nostalgia, a variety of historic sites, an abundance of scenic wonders, various outdoor recreational possibilities, and even some dinosaurs. Communities along the interstates are popular overnight stops for those just passing through, and the region's numerous lakes make good destinations for anglers and boaters. This is also an excellent area of the state for bird-watchers, especially during the spring and fall migrations.

The Santa Fe Trail brought wagon trains through this area in the mid-1800s until the railroad took its place later in that century, and both modes of transportation impacted the region. You'll see ruts from the wagon wheels and stately railroad depots; the main role of several of the towns here during the 19th century was as a stopover for travelers. New Mexico's territorial history comes alive at museums and sites such as Fort Union National Monument, and those who want to really step back in time can explore the dinosaur tracks at Clayton Lake State Park.

Boating in Sugarite Canyon State Park.

RATON

The first New Mexico town travelers hit as they come south from Colorado on I-25, Raton boasts a small but well-preserved historic district and makes a good base for the area's outdoor recreational opportunities. *Raton* is the Spanish word for rat, and both the town and Raton Pass just north of the town were named for the numerous rodents that thrive on piñon nuts growing in the area. The piñon nuts are still around; most of the rats are gone.

History

The community began as a water stop along the Santa Fe Trail, which followed American Indian footpaths over Raton Pass. The rugged trail through the mountains was a nightmare, though, resulting in countless wagon breakdowns, until 1866, when an enterprising rancher called Uncle Dick Wootton dynamited the worst sections and smoothed out the route. Wootton then set up a toll station to collect $1.50 per wagon from anyone who wanted to go through and on to Santa Fe. The only alternative to paying the toll was a detour around the mountains, which added about 125 miles to the trip. In 1879, the Santa Fe Railroad bought the toll road from Wootton and pushed the rails through. Raton quickly flourished as a railroad, coal-mining, and ranching center. Today Raton is a fascinating place, with lots of pioneer history still visible and much restoration work underway.

Major Attractions

Capulin Volcano National Monument

If you've ever wanted to walk down to the bottom of a volcanic crater, here's your chance. A beautifully symmetrical, almost perfectly shaped cinder cone, Capulin Volcano was created some 60,000 years ago on the grassy high plain of what would eventually become northeastern New Mexico. The eruption began with a split in the earth, followed by black smoke, ash, and glowing cinders, until finally the earth erupted in a river of hot lava. By the time it was over, a new mountain had been born, rising more than 1,200 feet. Named *capulin* by early Spanish explorers for the wild chokecherries that grow on its slopes, this is one of the most easily accessible volcanoes in the world, offering a close-up view of a volcanic crater. There are also several easy hiking trails and seemingly endless panoramic views.

SEEING THE CRATER

A paved 2-mile road leads from the visitor center to a parking area at the crater's rim, where there is an overlook down into the volcano. The 1-mile Crater Rim Trail loops around the crater's edge, offering good views into the volcano's depths as it passes jet black volcanic boulders, plus an assortment of wildflowers such as Indian paintbrush, bluebells, lupine, verbena, and sunflowers. The views from several spots along the trail are magnificent—on a clear day you can see parts of five states—and the trail also provides distant views of dozens of other extinct volcanoes. Although paved and generally easy, the trail has a few steep grades as it climbs about 300 feet to the monument's highest point at 8,182 feet.

Also from the rim parking area, the 0.2-mile (one-way) Crater Vent Trail drops into the crater. It leads to the vent—the spot on the earth's surface from which the volcano was born. The paved trail drops a bit more than 100 feet. Another trail, near the monument's picnic area, loops 1 mile through a piñon-juniper forest at the base of the volcano.

VISITOR INFORMATION AND DIRECTIONS

The monument's visitor center has exhibits on the volcano's creation, local geology, the region's plants and animals, and its human history. Worth seeing is the 10-minute video on the volcano's creation, which includes fascinating footage from a 1943 volcanic eruption in Mexico that scientists believe was similar to the birth of Capulin. There is no camping at the monument. Open 7:30 A.M.–6:30 P.M. Memorial Day to Labor Day, 8 A.M.–4 P.M. the rest of the year. Closed Thanksgiving, Christmas, and New Year's Day. Small admission fee. Capulin Volcano is located 33 miles east of Raton, via US Hwys. 64/87 to the town of Capulin, and north on NM 325. **Capulin Volcano National Monument, P.O. Box 40, Capulin, 88414; 505-278-2201; www.nps.gov/cavo.**

Sugarite Canyon State Park

One of our favorite New Mexico state parks, Sugarite Canyon truly has something for everyone. Located at 7,800 feet elevation in the heavily wooded mountains northeast of Raton, Sugarite (pronounced sugar-reet) is in a rugged forest of pine, fir, and aspen. The park contains two lakes, including the 120-acre Lake Maloya, plus campgrounds,

multiuse trails, an abundance of wildlife, and the ruins of a historic coal town. It is believed that Folsom man hunted here some 10,000 years ago and nomadic American Indian tribes, including the Apaches, Utes, and Comanches, stopped here in later times. The Santa Fe Trail passed nearby in the 1800s, and the Sugarite Coal Camp flourished from 1910 to 1941. The name Sugarite is believed to be a corruption of the Comanche word *chicorica*, which translates to "an abundance of birds," an appropriate title for a park that is home to more than 60 bird species.

BOATING AND FISHING

Lake Maloya is open to oar, paddle, sail, and electric-powered boats, but off-limits to gasoline engines because it is a source of Raton's drinking water. Both Lake Maloya and the park's 6-acre Lake Alice are stocked with rainbow trout and are popular with anglers fishing from shore or boats. Swimming is prohibited.

CAMPING

The park has two developed campgrounds. Those with RVs will find electric, water, and sewer hookups at the small **Lake Alice Campground,** in a protected area along the main park road. The shady campground has plenty of trees, but some sites are a bit too close to each other for our liking. Campers who prefer panoramic vistas and lots of elbow room should head up the hill to the larger **Soda Pocket Campground,** which offers easy access to hiking trails but has no RV hookups. Throughout the summer there are campfire programs Fri. and Sat. evenings at the park's amphitheater, near Soda Pocket Campground.

HIKING

About 10 miles of trails are open to hikers, mountain bikers, horseback riders, and cross-country skiers, offering great views of rugged mountain scenery and opportunities to see wildlife. Among them is the 0.5-mile round-trip Little Horse Mesa Trail. From its trailhead on Soda Pocket Rd., north of Soda Pocket Campground, the steep trail leads up onto Little Horse Mesa, the highest point in the park, where hikers have panoramic views from a delightful meadow spread with wildflowers.

HISTORIC SITES

Just outside the visitor center is a trail that leads to the ruins of Sugarite Coal Camp, which flourished here during the first half of the 20th century. This fairly easy 3-mile round-trip walk wanders through the remains of the coal camp, a substantial town in its heyday, when it had a population of about 1,000, a two-story schoolhouse, company store, social hall, and a resident doctor. Rows of solid concrete and rock houses line the hillsides, originally grouped by the ethnic makeup of the residents. Although some of the ruins are little more than rock walls or crumbling foundations, interpretive signs and historic photos help us visualize life in this once bustling town.

WILDLIFE VIEWING

Summer and fall are especially good times for wildlife viewing, when park visitors often see black bears as well as turkeys, mule deer, muskrats, beaver, and even a few mountain lions. Elk are sometimes seen, usually in herds of 25 or more, in the northern part of the park along the Colorado border. Tassel-eared Abert squirrels are plentiful year-round. The park's bears have learned that humans often have food. To avoid confrontations, campers should store food out of sight in airtight containers in locked vehicles.

VISITOR INFORMATION AND DIRECTIONS

The park's **visitor center/museum,** just inside the park entrance, is a good place to get information on recent wildlife sightings and also learn about the animals and history of the area. There are several hands-on exhibits popular with kids, including a "Guess Whose Hair" display to help learn about the park's mammals. The park remains open 24 hours. Visitor center open 8 A.M.–5 P.M. daily in summer; hours vary at other times. Day-use and camping fees. From I-25 exit 452 at Raton, follow NM 72 east for 3.5 miles and then go north on NM 526 about 2 miles to the visitor center. **Sugarite Canyon State Park, HCR 63, Box 386, Raton, 87740, 505-445-5607; www.nmparks.com.**

Festivals and Events

RATON RODEO

late June. Held at the Raton Rodeo Grounds on York Canyon Rd., this rodeo has bucking broncos, bulldogging, bull riding, and all the other traditional rodeo thrills. For dates and other information, check with the **Raton Chamber & Economic Development Council, 800-638-6161; 505-445-3689; www.raton.com.**

POOR MAN'S YACHT RACE

late July. A colorful and entertaining water show, this race on 120-acre Lake Maloya at Sugarite Canyon State Park is open only to homemade muscle-powered boats and usually attracts a varied assortment of unusual and sometimes bizarre craft. Past entrants have included boats constructed of old oil drums and vessels powered by bicycle parts. Contact **Sugarite Canyon State Park, 505-445-5607; nmparks.com.**

Outdoor Activities

Bird-Watching

MAXWELL NATIONAL WILDLIFE REFUGE

In the fall and winter, large numbers of ducks and geese congregate at the lakes of the refuge, but you'll see a variety of migrating birds year-round. During winter the refuge is home to Canada geese, snow geese, pintail ducks, and mallards, among others. At various times throughout the year, you might see bald eagles, peregrine falcons, willow flycatchers, warbling vireos, and burrowing owls. Trout fishing is limited, and free primitive camping is available Mar.–Oct. The refuge is open around the clock; a small visitor center is open 7:30 A.M.–4 P.M. Mon.–Fri. Located near the town of Maxwell, 25 miles south of Raton via I-25. **P.O. Box 276, Maxwell, 87728; 505-375-2331; http://southwest.fws. gov/refuges/newmex/maxwell.html.**

Sport Shooting

NRA WHITTINGTON CENTER

Operated by the National Rifle Association, this 33,300-acre recreation site offers a variety of shooting ranges for various firearms, from pistols to high power rifles to black powder. Individuals, who need not belong to the NRA, can use the ranges for practice on a daily basis, and numerous competitions and other events are scheduled. There is also an interesting visitor center and gift shop, wildlife and bird-watching opportunities, and hunting. Undisturbed tracks from the Santa Fe Trail cross the property, and visitors can view the tracks and even walk along them. The center also offers camping and various lodging. Open 8 A.M.–5 P.M. daily.

Admission to the visitor center and to see the Santa Fe Trail tracks is free; there are fees for use of the shooting ranges, for camping, and for hunting. Located 10 miles south of Raton along US Hwy. 64 (take I-25 to exit 446). **P.O. Box 700, Raton, 87740; 505-445-3615; www.nrawc.org.**

Seeing and Doing

Art Gallery

OLD PASS GALLERY

Home of the Raton Arts and Humanities Council, this attractive gallery is housed in a restored mission-style building, constructed in 1910 and located next to the railroad station. Works by a number of regional artists in a variety of media are displayed for sale. The council also sponsors art workshops, lecture series, children's programs and performing arts events (many at the historic Shuler Theater; see below). Open 10 A.M.–5 P.M. Tues.–Sat. in summer and 10 A.M.–4 P.M. Wed.–Sat. the rest of the year. **145 S. 1st St., P.O. Box 774, Raton, 87740; 505-445-2052; www.ratonarts.com.**

Museums and Historic Buildings

Pick up a copy of the chamber of commerce **visitor's guide**, which contains the detailed and interesting **Historic Downtown Walking Tour,** with stops at more than two dozen buildings, each one an exhibit of Raton's checkered past. The guide also contains details for about a half dozen **driving tours.** We especially recommend the tour along US Hwys. 64/84 to Folsom and Capulin Volcano National Monument. If you want to see deer, elk, and antelope along the road start early—preferably right after sunrise. Then kill some time so you get to the hamlet of Folsom about 10 A.M. to visit the interesting **Folsom Museum,** which contains exhibits of pioneer days and the area's archeology. (This is where the Folsom point was found. Its discovery pushed back the presence of humans on the North American continent by 10,000 years.) The museum is open 10 A.M.–5 P.M. daily from Memorial Day to Labor Day, weekends only in May and Sept., and by appointment the rest of the year. It is located on the main street of Folsom in a historic stone hotel built in 1896. After Folsom, head to the national monument. **P.O. Box 385, Folsom, 88419; 505-278-2122; www.folsommuseum.nctfirms.com.**

RATON MUSEUM

Exhibits on the Santa Fe Trail and Uncle Dick Wootton's famous toll road over Raton Pass are key displays here, plus there is also memorabilia of railroading, ranching, and coal-mining days, including historic photos and documents. The museum is located in Raton's historic district in a building constructed in 1906 by Coors Brewery. Open 10 A.M.–4 P.M. Tues.–Sat. in summer; 10 A.M.–3 P.M. Thurs.–Sat. the rest of the year. **216 S. 1st St., Raton; 505-445-8979.**

SHULER THEATER

Opened in 1915, the Shuler was one of the finest opera houses in the region, decorated in the ornate European rococo style of the era. It fell into disrepair in the 1950s but was restored in the early 1970s and today serves as a handsome community auditorium with wonderful acoustics. It hosts a varied calendar of events, ranging from local theater and music productions to nationally known touring performers. For the current schedule and to inquire about guided tours of the theater, call the Shuler or contact the **Raton Arts and Humanities Council** at the Old Pass Gallery (see page 74). The Shuler is in the historic district. **131 N. 2nd St., Raton; 505-445-5523.**

Where to Stay

Accommodations

Typical of towns along an interstate highway, Raton has a variety of lodging choices, including a good selection of basic and relatively inexpensive motels. We especially like the **Budget Host Melody Lane Motel** ($–$$), located three blocks north of downtown. It doesn't look like much from the outside, but inside offers spacious, well-maintained rooms—many with steam showers—in a Southwest decor with knotty pine ceilings. It includes a continental breakfast and accepts small pets (fee). The motel is closed for the month of Feb. **136 Canyon Dr. (I-25, exit 454), Raton, 87740; 800-BUD-HOST; 505-445-3655.**

You also won't go wrong with the **Best Western Sands** ($$–$$$), which boasts some of the more luxurious facilities in Raton, with well-appointed modern motel rooms, an outdoor heated swimming pool, and a hot tub. **300 Clayton Rd. (I-25 exit 451), Raton, 87740; 800-518-2581; 505-445-2737.** Pretty much on a par with the Sands and possibly a notch above is the **Holiday Inn Express** ($$$), which includes in its rates evening snacks and an upscale continental breakfast. There is an indoor heated pool and hot tub, rooms have two phone lines, and all the other usual amenities one expects in a motel of this level. **101 Card Ave. (I-25 exit 450), Raton, 87740; 800-HOLIDAY; 505-445-1500.**

Camping

Nearby camping can be found at **Sugarite Canyon State Park, Maxwell National Wildlife Refuge,** and the **NRA Whittington Center** (see pages 72 and 74), in addition to the following commercial campgrounds:

RATON KOA

Conveniently located off I-25 exit 450, this well-maintained campground sits in a quiet area and is still within walking distance of restaurants and shopping. There are good tent sites and long, level pull-throughs for RVs, plus game rooms, horseshoes, a laundry, and a store, but no swimming pool. **1330 S. 2nd St., Raton, 87740; 800-562-9033 (reservations); 505-445-3488.**

SUMMERLAN PARK

Another well-maintained commercial campground with all the usual amenities (except a swimming pool), the Summerlan also offers on-site RV repairs. Located near the junction of I-25 (exit 451) and US Hwys. 64/87. **1900 S. Cedar St., Raton, 87740; 505-445-9536.**

Where to Eat

All Seasons—$$-$$$

Good, basic American food in a casual, family restaurant setting is what you'll find here. Breakfast is served until 5 P.M. and there is a good salad bar. Open 6 A.M.–10 P.M. daily in summer, until 9 P.M. the rest of the year. Located at the junction of US Hwys. 64/87 and I-25. **1616 Cedar St., Raton; 505-445-9889.**

Pappas Sweet Shop Restaurant— $$-$$$$

Begun as a candy and ice cream shop by Greek immigrant Jim Pappas (short for Dimitrios Papadomanolakis) in the 1920s, this restaurant still has sweets— you won't go wrong with the fudge— but now offers a whole lot more, ranging from excellent steaks and prime rib to burgers, chicken, and fish. The restaurant continues to be run by the Pappas family and is decorated with antiques, collectibles, and historic photos, including displays on the history of the restaurant. Open 11 A.M.–2 P.M. and 5–9 P.M. daily in summer, Mon.–Sat. the rest of the year. **1201 S. 2nd St., Raton; 505-445-9811.**

Services

Visitor Information

Raton Chamber & Economic Development Council, 100 Clayton Rd., P.O. Box 1211, Raton, 87740; 800-638-6161; 505-445-3689; www.raton.com. Located in the same building as the chamber is a **New Mexico Visitor Information Center**, with brochures, maps, and other information on the entire state; **505-445-2761.**

SPRINGER

Forty miles south of Raton on I-25 is the sleepy little town of Springer, begun as a ranching center in 1879 with the arrival of the railroad. Springer was the county seat until some unprincipled rascals came with guns in the night, stole the courthouse records, and took them away to Raton, which is the present county seat. This is also where you can pick up US Hwy. 56, which runs east for an interminable 83 miles to Clayton, a stretch of road that crosses the flattest, driest, most featureless part of New Mexico. Although boring to look at, this part of New Mexico has some of the best cattle pastures in the nation. This is the ranch country of the Land of Enchantment, and fortunes have been made and lost on these broad plains.

Festivals and Events

BEAN DAY
Labor Day Weekend. Held in the tiny community of Wagon Mound, 24 miles south of Springer on I-25, this popular event began in 1910 as a harvest festival by local bean farmers. It includes several rodeos, a parade up the main street of town and then back again (hey, Wagon Mound is a very small town!), sack races and similar activities, plus a free barbecue. **505-666-2408.**

Outdoor Activities

Fishing
Springer is regionally famous for its fishing opportunities, with **Springer Lake**

ranked among the state's best fishing holes for big northern pike and rainbow trout. It's just 5 miles west of Springer, on the road that goes past the State Reform School for Boys. Fishing from the shore is productive here, especially in early spring and late fall, when aquatic weed growth is lowest.

Eight miles south of Springer on I-25, turn to the west on NM 569 to **Charette Lakes,** a prime out-of-the-way trout-fishing destination. The State Department of Game and Fish leases access to the lake for fishing. There are toilets at the lake and camping is free, but there is little else, except trout and privacy. From I-25, NM 569 runs 14 miles out to the lake and back again, no place else. **Springer Chamber of Commerce** (see next page) has additional information.

Seeing and Doing

Museums and Historic Buildings

DORSEY MANSION
This imposing log-and-stone Victorian mansion, just off the Santa Fe Trail in isolated rolling grasslands, was built by Stephen Dorsey, a Union Army officer, U.S. senator from Arkansas, and rancher who made a fortune but died in poverty. Dorsey built this fabulous 36-room home in 1878, using oiled logs and red sandstone, for his beloved and lovely wife, Helen. The mansion included a rose garden that spelled out her name, a swimming pool with three islands, and angry gargoyles carved from stone glaring out at all comers. Perennially

involved in questionable schemes, Dorsey left New Mexico in 1892, leaving bad debts and unhappy partners. Since then, the mansion has been a tuberculosis sanatorium, a post office, a private residence, and a bed-and-breakfast. Considerable renovation has been completed and more is planned.

Guided tours take you through the rooms, where you'll see the hand-carved cherry staircase, Italian marble fireplaces, a variety of artwork, animal trophies, and other features that made it a showplace of its day. Don't just drive out to see the Dorsey Mansion, though, because the road may be impassable in wet weather or the gate might be locked. Always call ahead for reservations. Usually open 10 A.M.–4 P.M. Mon.–Sat.; 1–5 P.M. Sun. A fee is charged. From Raton, take I-25 about 40 miles to Springer, then US Hwy. 56 east for 24 miles. A large sign shows where to turn north onto a dirt road, which leads 12 miles to the mansion. **HCR 62, Box 42, Raton, 87740; 505-375-2222; www.dorseymansion.com.**

SANTA FE TRAIL INTERPRETATIVE CENTER & MUSEUM

The historic Santa Fe Trail, which brought important trade goods from the eastern United States to New Mexico and the West, passed by Springer and here's where you can learn about it.

Located in the 1882 Colfax County Courthouse—which looks more like a church than a government building to us—the first floor is dedicated to the Santa Fe Trail, with a variety of exhibits and artifacts. Upstairs is an eclectic collection of memorabilia, mostly from Springer's early days, which includes a model of the Dorsey Mansion (see above). Here you can also see the state's only electric chair, which was used from the 1930s into the 1950s to execute seven convicted murderers. Open 10 A.M.–4 P.M. Tues.–Sat. in summer, Mon.–Fri. the same hours the rest of the year. A small admission fee is charged. **606 Maxwell Ave., Springer, 87747; 505-483-5554.**

Services

Springer offers gasoline, several restaurants, good grocery stores, and a couple of motels. Be aware that the State Reform School for Boys is located near Springer, so do not pick up hitchhikers in the vicinity.

Visitor Information

Springer Chamber of Commerce, 516 Maxwell Ave., P.O. Box 323, Springer, 87747; 505-483-2998. The chamber of commerce operates a visitor center in the Santa Fe Trail Interpretative Center & Museum (see above).

LAS VEGAS

Las Vegas—New Mexico, not Nevada—is a city of paradoxes. It's a sleepy little village of 15,000 souls, steeped in Spanish and pioneer lore, but it is also the home of Highlands University and the place chosen by magnate Armand Hammer for the United States campus of his United World College. A stopover on the Santa Fe Trail in the mid-1800s, Las Vegas boomed in 1879 with the arrival of the railroad, and by the beginning of the 20th century it was the largest city in the New Mexico Territory. Lavish Victorian homes were erected, many of which remain today with more than 900 buildings listed on the National Register of Historic Places.

Las Vegas sits on the edge of the eastern plains, a semiarid land of hot winds and driving snows, but it also perches at the edge of the Sangre de Cristo Mountains and looks up at snow-clad peaks about eight months of the year. Las Vegas's eastern horizon stretches flat all the way into Texas; its western horizon soars abruptly upward to the sparkling tips of the Rockies.

History

Las Vegas got its start in 1822, when Capt. William Becknell rode into Arrow Rock, Missouri, with tales of riches to be made by trading with the Spanish in faraway Santa Fe. The Santa Fe Trail was pushed through 900 miles of hostile American Indian territory so American traders could connect with the Camino Real. This "Royal Road" stretched more than 2,000 miles from gold and silver rich Mexico, along the banks of the Rio Grande, to the capital of New Spain at Santa Fe.

Despite Indian attacks, thousands of merchants undertook the three months of toil that was the Trail, and in 1835, Las Vegas was on its way to becoming an important way station. It thrived as a center for Spanish pioneers, but in 1860 the Anglos started coming in numbers, including many French Canadians and German Jews. The French influence was strong from 1849 through 1894, when the Des Marias family lived in a big house on the east side of the plaza.

In 1846, the United States declared war on Mexico, and American armies led by Gen. S. W. Kearney moved west to consolidate the new territories. Las Vegas was the first town of any size encountered by Kearney in what had been Mexican territory. There was little or no opposition to the American invasion of Las Vegas; after all, it was a long, long way to Mexico City. Another reason for the lack of resistance was General Kearney's promise: "I shall not expect you to take up arms and help me fight against your countrymen. But he who is found in arms against me, I will hang."

By the late 1800s, Las Vegas had become a notoriously wild town. Outlaws Jesse James and Billy the Kid spent time here and dentist-turned-gunfighter Doc Holliday practiced dentistry for a while. This was also a favorite filming location for actor Tom Mix in the early 20th century, Mix reportedly stating that he would love to live in the Las Vegas area forever, if only he could escape Hollywood.

Getting There

It's easy to find Las Vegas. Just stay on I-25 for 110 miles north from

Albuquerque or stay on I-25 for 110 miles south from the Colorado border.

Major Attraction

Fort Union National Monument

Once the largest fort in the Southwest and easily the most important fort in New Mexico, Fort Union was established to protect settlers and traders using the Santa Fe Trail, as well as local residents from attacks by American Indians, who were quite unhappy about the white man's "discovery" of the West. At first, army troops were stationed in Santa Fe, but fort commander Col. Edwin Sumner opted to move army headquarters away from the town, which he called "that sink of vice and extravagance," to a place where his men would be closer to the trouble spots but farther from temptation.

There have been three forts here, starting with one in 1851 of which nothing visible remains. The second fort, built in 1861, was intended to defend the Union against an expected Confederate invasion during the Civil War. They did invade in 1862 and were repulsed by the Colorado volunteers from Fort Union at the Battle of Glorieta Pass, 25 miles southeast of Santa Fe. That was the last Confederate attack on New Mexico. Very little remains of the hastily constructed second fort, which was built partly underground and where living conditions were so bad that most troopers preferred to sleep outside in tents.

The third Fort Union, however, was something to brag about. Construction was begun in 1863 and completed in 1869, at a cost of more than $1 million. It was an impressive structure of adobe bricks on a foundation of stone, neatly plastered, and included large glass windows, porches, fences, and even streetlights. The fort had all the usual military facilities, with numerous offices, barracks, workshops, a prison, guardhouse, and a parade ground. In addition, partly because of its role as the Southwest's primary military supply depot, the fort had large storehouses, corrals, and the region's largest hospital. Although it was abandoned in 1891 as no longer militarily necessary, Fort Union is a reminder of the days of both the Indian Wars and the Civil War.

EXPLORING THE MONUMENT

The **visitor center/museum** should be your first stop. It contains exhibits on the construction of all three forts, life at Fort Union, the Civil War in New Mexico, and the Santa Fe Trail. There is an audiovisual program and a well-stocked bookstore with titles on the history of New Mexico and the Southwest.

A 1.6-mile self-guided walking trail leads through the ruins of the third fort, as well as some of the remains from the second fort. You can stand in the central plaza of the crumbling third fort ruins, and thanks to modern electronics, hear the sound of a bugle, officers barking commands, and the horses hooves pounding the parade ground. Meanwhile, your mind can re-create the sights of long ago. Along the edge of the ruins, you'll find the ruts of the Santa Fe Trail—still visible after more than 175 years!

SPECIAL EVENTS

Living history talks and demonstrations are presented periodically during the summer. Special events include one guided tour each year (in June) to the site of the first fort. Cultural Encounters on the Santa Fe Trail, scheduled in July, is a living history camp with talks and demonstrations, presented in period dress. Contact monument offices for specific dates and times.

VISITOR INFORMATION, DIRECTIONS, AND FACTS

No camping is available. Open 8 A.M.–5 P.M. daily; closed New Year's Day, Thanksgiving, and Christmas. Small admission fee. To get to Fort Union, go 26 miles north of Las Vegas on I-25 to exit 366 and follow NM 161 for 8 miles west to the monument. **P.O. Box 127, Watrous, 87753; 505-425-8025; www.nps.gov/foun.**

Festivals and Events

LAS VEGAS FIESTA

early July. This traditional Hispanic fiesta, with the coronation of the fiesta queen, parades, northern New Mexico music, arts and crafts, and food, also celebrates the Fourth of July.

PLACES WITH A PAST HISTORIC BUILDINGS TOUR

early Aug. Get a look inside some of Las Vegas's fascinating Victorian buildings. **505-425-8803.**

PEOPLE'S FAIRE

late Aug. Sponsored by the Las Vegas Arts Council, this outdoor event includes original crafts and works of art, storytelling, food, and a variety of entertainment. **505-425-1085.**

CLEVELAND ROLLER MILLFEST

Labor Day weekend. This annual event, which takes place at the historic Cleveland Roller Mill (see page 85) includes live music, arts and crafts, and plenty of food. **505-387-2645.**

ELECTRIC LIGHT PARADE

early Dec. The Christmas season begins in earnest with this colorful parade through the streets of Las Vegas. **505-425-8631.**

Outdoor Activities

Fishing and Water Sports

There are plenty of opportunities for anglers in these parts. **McAllister Lake,** 8 miles east on NM 104, has a well-deserved reputation for both northern pike and trout, and **Storrie Lake** (see below) offers good fishing practically within walking distance of downtown Las Vegas. Stream anglers will find action with rainbow trout in the **Gallinas** and **El Porvenir Rivers** in the canyon above Montezuma, which is reached by driving north of Las Vegas on NM 65.

Above Mora, north of Las Vegas on NM 518, both the **Rio La Casa** and **Coyote Creek** offer rainbow and brown trout. Forty miles west on I-25, you'll come to the **Rio Pecos,** which offers a different kind of trout fishing, with a much larger stream but the same rainbows. Work your way up into the wilderness area along the Pecos, and you'll see excellent populations of trout in beautiful surroundings.

STORRIE LAKE STATE PARK

Created in 1916 when Robert Storrie built a 1,400-foot earth-filled dam across the Gallinas River to provide water for vegetable farms, Storrie Lake is a water playground serving Las Vegas and much of northern New Mexico. The lake is open to all types of boats, with no horsepower restrictions, and is popular with water-skiers, those with personal watercraft, and even canoeists, who can usually find a quiet corner of the lake in which to escape the high-powered boats. Windsurfers begin arriving in early spring, sometimes wearing wet suits, and can be seen whenever the winds are blowing. Swimming is permitted in most parts of the lake, although there are no designated swimming beaches and the water tends to be a bit cool.

Fishing is good year-round, although the lake may freeze over for several weeks in winter. The ice is seldom thick enough to support ice fishing, just thick enough to prevent boat and shore fishing. The lake is periodically stocked with rainbow trout, and anglers also catch German browns, crappie, and catfish. There is one wheelchair-accessible fishing dock.

There are no designated hiking trails, although walkers can stretch their legs on the several miles of gravel road that circle the lake or go cross-country skiing anywhere in the park.

Storrie Lake attracts waterfowl, especially in late fall and winter, when you are apt to see Canada geese and a variety of ducks. Winter is also the best time to catch a glimpse of a bald eagle or sandhill crane. Also seen in the park are falcons, burrowing owls, doves, and red-winged blackbirds. Mammals you might see include cottontail rabbits, ground squirrels, and an occasional mule deer.

At the visitor center there are exhibits on the history of the Santa Fe Trail and the community of Las Vegas in the 19th century.

There are developed tent and RV sites (without RV hookups) within several feet of the lake and a large lakeshore area for primitive camping that practically allows anglers to fish from the comfort of their RVs or tents. RV sites with electric hookups are back a bit from the lake, but they offer good views of the lake and are within easy walking distance. Many of the developed sites have cabana-style shelters and are also shaded by cottonwoods. Primitive camping is available along the grassy shoreline.

The campground is open year-round, although showers and some of the water spigots are shut off in winter. The park gates are open daily 7 A.M.–sunset Oct.–Mar. and 9 A.M.–sunset Apr.–Sept. (campers can get out, but not back in, when gates are locked). Day use and camping fees are charged. The park is 4 miles north of Las Vegas via NM 518. **HC 33, Box 109-2, Las Vegas, 87701; 505-425-7278; www.nmparks.com.**

Golf

NEW MEXICO HIGHLANDS UNIVERSITY GOLF COURSE
A public 9-hole course with narrow fairways and small greens. Open year-round, weather permitting. **E. Mills Ave., Las Vegas; 505-425-7711.**

PENDARIES GOLF & COUNTRY CLUB
This challenging high-mountain 18-hole resort golf course is set among tall pines about 25 miles northwest of Las Vegas. Open mid-Apr.–Sept. **1 Country Club Ln., Rociada; 800-733-5267; 505-425-6018; www.pendaries.net.**

Hiking

The **Santa Fe National Forest** to the west of Las Vegas provides the best hiking in the area, and two good hikes begin at the national forest El Porvenir Campground. The **Porvenir Canyon Trail** (Trail 247) is a one-way moderately rated trek that ambles for more than a dozen miles into the forest, offering good views of steep canyon walls and 10,263-foot Hermit's Peak. More adventurous hikers might opt to tackle the difficult **Hermit's Peak Trail,** which climbs almost 3,000 feet in 4 miles to the top of Hermit's Peak. The trailheads for both trails are at El Porvenir Campground, located about 17 miles northwest of Las Vegas via NM 65. **Las Vegas Ranger District, 1926 N. 7th St., Las Vegas, 87701; 505-425-3534; www.fs.fed.us/r3.**

Wildlife Viewing

LAS VEGAS NATIONAL WILDLIFE REFUGE

Strategically located along the line where the Great Plains meets the Rocky Mountains, this national wildlife refuge makes wildlife viewing easy, especially bird-watching. From late fall through early spring a multitude of our feathered friends make their way here. You'll have an excellent chance of seeing a variety of birds, including bald eagles, Canada and snow geese, sandhill cranes, and almost two dozen species of ducks, from mallard to ruddy. Also at this time of year watch for northern harriers, American coots, American kestrels, common snipes, horned larks, several species of juncos, red-winged blackbirds, and mountain bluebirds.

The most commonly seen mammal at the refuge is the pronghorn, but also keep an eye out for coyotes, mule deer, and the occasional black bear.

There is an 8-mile auto loop tour open year-round. On Sundays during Nov. the 4.5-mile Fall Flight Wildlife Drive loop leads you into areas of the preserve normally closed to the public, and volunteers with spotting scopes and field guides are stationed at strategic spots along the drive to help to find and identify the various species.

The refuge's 0.5-mile self-guided Gallinas Walking Trail is a terrific opportunity to escape the noise and exhaust fumes of motor vehicles and venture into a pretty canyon inhabited by cliff swallows and canyon wrens. But the trail is in a sensitive area that is open only when refuge offices are open and

requires a free permit. The trail also passes the remains of several rock homes built in the 1920s. Binoculars are recommended, and hikers are advised to watch out for rattlesnakes.

The auto tour loop is open daily 24 hours; the headquarters/visitor center and Gallinas Walking Trail are open Mon.–Fri. 8 A.M. 4:30 P.M. The refuge is 6 miles southeast of Las Vegas: from I-25 exit 345, go east on NM 104 for 1 mile and then south on NM 281 for 4 miles. **Route 1, Box 399, Las Vegas, 87701; 505-425-3581; http://southwest.fws.gov.**

Seeing and Doing

Historic Sites and Museums

The historic **Las Vegas Plaza** is a good place to begin a visit to this genuine Old West town. Although a number of the historic buildings here are in dire need of restoration, many have been restored and the overall feel is that you have stepped back to the 1890s. Free **walking tour brochures** to the plaza and the city's other historic districts are available from the chamber of commerce, leading you past numerous elegant stone homes created by carvers often brought to Las Vegas from Italy.

While checking out the architecture—which ranges from Spanish colonial adobe to luxurious Victorian mansions—be sure to step inside some of the shops and galleries, such as Art and Stones, on the south side of the plaza, which has unique northern New Mexico fine art plus rocks and minerals.

The attractively restored 1882 **Plaza Hotel,** on the northwest corner of the plaza, is a good place to stay for those who want to better experience Las Vegas's historic charm and a fun place to

The Plaza Hotel.

visit even if you don't need a room for the night.

The **Castañeda Hotel,** an excellent example of Spanish mission architecture, stands at the side of the railroad tracks, just three blocks from the town square. Once a luxury stopover on the railroad, it was the scene of Teddy Roosevelt's reunion with his famed Rough Riders, heroes of the Spanish-American War. Today, there's a beer parlor on the main floor. Visitors can walk the spacious veranda and look at it from the outside, but there is nothing left of the glory that was yesteryear.

THE CITY OF LAS VEGAS MUSEUM AND ROUGH RIDER MEMORIAL COLLECTION

To delve into the history of Las Vegas, stop at this fine little museum with the way-too-long name, which houses the largest public collection of Spanish-American War memorabilia in the United States.

A cavalry troop that became known as the Rough Riders and led by future president Theodore Roosevelt achieved fame during the Spanish-American War in the battle for San Juan Hill in Puerto Rico. The troop was largely made up of cowboys from the New Mexico Territory, and after the war the soldiers began holding annual reunions in Las Vegas. The museum displays the Rough Riders' flags, uniforms, medals, guns, and historic photos.

The museum also has exhibits on the area's history—from American Indian pottery to Spanish colonial shawls to railroad artifacts—and be sure to explore La Casita, a full-size replica of a typical 19th-century northern New Mexico home. There is also a well-stocked gift shop, with locally made crafts, educational toys, and books on the region's history. The museum is open Mon.–Fri. 9 A.M.–noon and 1–4 P.M.; Sat. 10 A.M.–3 P.M.; closed major holidays. **727 Grand Ave., Las Vegas, 87701; 505-454-1401.**

CLEVELAND ROLLER MILL

Located about 32 miles north of Las Vegas on NM 518 between the tiny villages of Mora and Cleveland, this handsome stone flour mill was built in 1900, in a long-gone era when this part of New Mexico was the state's leading wheat-growing area. Standing three stories high, the water-powered mill has been restored by Dan Cassidy, the great-grandson of an early owner. Inside you'll see the gigantic gears and the other milling equipment, plus exhibits on the mill and area history. The annual Millfest, held on Labor Day weekend, is loads of fun. Open Sat.–Sun. only, Memorial Day Oct., 10 A.M –3 P.M. and by appointment. A small admission fee is charged. **P.O. Box 287, Cleveland, 87715; 505-387-2645.**

MONTEZUMA CASTLE

On a hillside just outside Las Vegas, Montezuma Castle is a fantastic sight to see— a handsome, towering castle that looks very much out of place in this land of adobe fortresses and Victorian elegance.

Built in 1882 as the Montezuma Hotel, this was the first building in New Mexico to have electric lights, but that turned out to be a bad move—faulty wiring caused a fire that destroyed the hotel in 1884. It was rebuilt but burned again, and the third hotel—this time a handsome stone structure called Montezuma Castle—was opened in 1886.

Located close to natural hot springs, this luxurious resort hotel covered 90,000 square feet, contained a casino, bowling alley, and other amenities, and attracted such guests as Theodore Roosevelt, Ulysses S. Grant, and Jesse James.

The resort closed in 1903, went through several owners, and was in very bad condition when it was purchased by the Armand Hammer Foundation in 1981 to become part of the United World College, which operates an international pre-university program, with 10 schools around the world. The New Mexico campus hosts about 200 students from more than 75 countries. A $10.5 million renovation project was completed in late 2001, and it's well worth a visit to see this fascinating building and its splendid woodwork and spiral staircase.

The castle is not open to the public on a daily basis, but students lead tours to show off the magnificent building and tell visitors about the United World College program. Tours are offered some Saturdays at 2 P.M. It is located 6 miles northwest of Las Vegas via NM 65. **P.O. Box 248, Montezuma, 87731-0248; 505-454-4221; www.uwc-usa.org.**

85

Montezuma Castle was built in stone the third time, after burning twice before.

Other Area Attractions

AIR-LOCK LOG HOMES

This lumber mill and manufacturing facility just outside of Las Vegas creates kits for people who want to build log homes, either themselves or with the help of a builder. The logs are hollowed out to facilitate even drying, and a variety of house plans are available. At the mill you can see the equipment used to shape the logs and learn about the process. The Air-Lock people would also be very happy to sell you a log home kit. Free tours are available Mon.–Fri. 8 A.M.– 5 P.M. (reservations recommended). From I-25 exit 343, go south on Frontage Rd. 2 miles, then left onto Air-Lock Service Rd. and north 300 feet. **P.O. Box 2506, Las Vegas, 87701; 800-786-0525; 505-425-8888; www.air-lock.com.**

MADISON VINEYARDS & WINERY

Northeastern New Mexico may not be Napa Valley, but it does possess good growing conditions for grapes and for vintners who know what to do with those grapes. A good example can be found in this small family-owned winery,

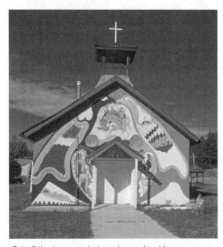

Colorfully decorated chapel near Las Vegas.

which has been in operation since 1980 and produces some 5,000 gallons of wine annually. Bill and Elise Madison produce both dry and semisweet wines, many using French hybrids. Especially popular is the semisweet "Pecos Wildflower," a blend of Riesling, Muscat, and Seyval Blanc. The tasting room is open 10 A.M.–4 P.M. Mon.–Tues. and Thurs.–Sat., noon–4 P.M. Sun., and by appointment. From Las Vegas drive south on I-25 for 20 miles, then 6.5 miles south on NM 3. **HC 72, Box 490, Ribera, 87560; 505-421-8028.**

VICTORY RANCH

You'll think you took a wrong turn and ended up in Peru when you arrive at Victory Ranch, which claims to be the largest alpaca ranch in the American Southwest, with about 100 alpacas on its 1,100 acres. Alpacas, which are somewhat smaller cousins of llamas, are usually found in the South American Andes, but have been brought to this northern New Mexico ranch for breeding, packing, and their soft, fine wool. Tours are offered, or you can watch a video on alpacas and browse in the visitor center/gift shop, where the alpacas will likely look in the windows at you as you gaze out the windows at them. The shop contains numerous items featuring alpaca wool, and the ranch will also sell you an alpaca (wouldn't that make a nifty souvenir?). Open Thurs.–Mon. 10 A.M.–4 P.M. (ranch tours 11 A.M., 1 P.M., 3 P.M.). Free admission to visitor center/gift shop; fee for guided tours (including alpaca feed—they'll eat right out of your hand). Victory Ranch is located 30 miles north of Las Vegas via NM 518, then 1 mile north of Mora via NM 434. **P.O. Box 680, Mora, 87732; 505-387-2254; www.victoryranch.com.**

Where to Stay

Accommodations

Most of the lodging is on N. Grand Ave., off I-25 exit 347. This is where you'll find a **Comfort Inn, Days Inn,** and **Super 8,** plus several inexpensive independents.

Inn on the Santa Fe Trail—$$–$$$

This 1920s-era motel has been extensively remodeled, but still retains much of its historic charm. Guest rooms overlook a central courtyard in hacienda style. Rooms are furnished with handmade wood furniture, and there is an outdoor heated swimming pool and hot tub. Also on-site is a restaurant—Blackjack's Grill—discussed on page 88. Pets accepted (fee). **1133 N. Grand Ave. (I-25 exit 345), Las Vegas, 87701; 888-448-8438; 505-425-6791; www.innonthesantafetrail.com.**

Plaza Hotel—$$–$$$$

Our top choice for lodging in Las Vegas, the Plaza Hotel, located right on the Las Vegas Plaza, provides an opportunity to experience the town's history firsthand. Elegant by northern New Mexico standards—not at the level (or cost) of the fabulous Brown Palace in Denver—the Plaza Hotel was built in 1882, and for many years hosted practically all the rich and mighty who made their way to the area. Standard rooms are a bit small by today's standards (premium rooms and suites are larger), but all combine Victorian decor with private bathrooms, televisions, telephones, and even Internet access. Some guests also claim visits by the hotel's resident ghost, Byron T. Mills (a former owner of the hotel). The Landmark Grill serves three meals daily (see page 88), plus there is an Old West–style saloon. A continental breakfast is included in the rates. Pets accepted (fee). **230 Old Town Plaza, Las Vegas, 87701; 800-328-1882; 505-425-3591; www.plazahotel-nm.com.**

Campgrounds

The closest public campground to Las Vegas is **Storrie Lake State Park,** which is discussed above and is open year-round. It has 41 developed sites, including 21 with electricity, plus primitive camping along the lake. There is also camping in the Santa Fe National Forest, including the 14-site **El Porvenir Campground,** which offers a somewhat primitive forest camping experience and is open from May through Oct. It's located about 17 miles northwest of Las Vegas via NM 65. **Las Vegas Ranger District, 1926 N. 7th St., Las Vegas, 87701; 505-425-3534; www.fs.fed.us/r3.**

LAS VEGAS KOA

Visible on the east side of I-25, south of Las Vegas, this member of the well-respected KOA chain offers almost everything you might want in a commercial campground: large, level sites, well-maintained bathhouses, a store, and even a swimming pool. The campground is open from Mar.–Nov. 15 only, with 65 sites. Located at I-25 (exit 339) and US Hwy. 84. **HCR 31, Box 16, Las Vegas, 87701; 800-562-3423 (reservations); 505-454-0180.**

VEGAS RV PARK

There are 33 full hookup sites, with cable TV included, plus tent sites at this open campground, which has all the usual amenities (no swimming pool). It's located between I-25 exits 343 and 347. **504 Harris Rd., Las Vegas, 87701; 505-425-5640.**

Where to Eat

Blackjack's Grill—$$-$$$
A top spot for a romantic dinner, Blackjack's offers an intimate and sophisticated setting, with a somewhat eclectic menu that ranges from Italian specialties to Old Mexico dishes to grilled steaks. Open 5–9 P.M. daily. Located in the Inn on the Santa Fe Trail. **1133 N. Grand Ave., Las Vegas; 888-448-8438; 505-425-6791; www.innonthesantafetrail.com.**

Charlie's Spic and Span Bakery and Cafe—$-$$
This locals favorite gets our vote for the best breakfast in Las Vegas. Lunch and dinner are pretty good, too. The atmosphere here is casual, with simple decor and friendly service. The menu is New Mexico–style Mexican food and American basics—many items with a southwestern twist. The omelettes and breakfast burritos are especially good, and you won't go wrong with enchiladas, burritos, Navajo tacos (the usual taco fillings on a hunk of Navajo fry bread), all-American burgers, or hot roast beef. Open Sun.–Thurs. 6:30 A.M.–5:30 P.M. **715 Douglas Ave., Las Vegas; 505-426-1921.**

Landmark Grill—$$-$$$
Located in the historic Plaza Hotel, this elegant restaurant oozes historic charm, with Victorian-style furnishings and attractive artwork. It has a varied menu offering American items including steak and seafood, plus an excellent burger, but specializes in very good northern New Mexico–style Mexican dishes, such as chile rellenos, fajitas, and burritos. Across the hotel lobby from the restaurant is a lively saloon. Open 7 A.M.–9 P.M. daily. **230 Old Town Plaza, Las Vegas; 800-328-1882; 505-425-3591; www.plazahotel-nm.com.**

The Mexican Kitchen de los Aragons—$-$$$
There are several good cafe-style eateries specializing in homemade northern New Mexico food in Las Vegas, and we think this is the best. It's a simple, family-run operation, offering generous portions of well-prepared items, including tacos, burritos and quesadillas, at reasonable prices. The open dining room is decorated with cowbells, lanterns, and other pioneer memorabilia, plus sombreros, posters, photos, and some paintings on velvet. Open daily 11 A.M.–7 P.M. **717 Grand Ave., Las Vegas; 505-454-1769.**

Services

Visitor Information
Las Vegas/San Miguel County Chamber of Commerce, 701 Grand Ave., P.O. Box 128, Las Vegas 87701 operates a visitor center, off I-25 exit 347, on S. Grand Ave. next to the red caboose. **800-832-5947; 505-425-8631; www.lasvegasnm.org.**

PECOS NATIONAL HISTORICAL PARK

As most of us know, the treatment of America's native Indian people by European colonizers was in most cases quite disgraceful, and nowhere is that more evident than at Pecos National Historical Park. Here you can see more than 1,000 years of human history, from prehistoric times through Spanish colonization to the early 20th century. The park includes prehistoric American Indian ruins, a mission church built by Spanish conquistadors, a Santa Fe Trail trading post, the site of New Mexico's most decisive Civil War battle, and an early 20th-century cattle ranch.

Although not all of these sites are open to the public on a daily basis, guided tours to many of the park's remote sites are offered by reservation of up to two weeks. There's also plenty to see for those who drop in without calling for tour reservations. The main activities here are exploring the ruins of Pecos Pueblo and the Spanish mission and viewing the excellent museum exhibits.

History

Nomadic hunter-gatherers had been attracted to this area for thousands of years before pit houses began to appear in the 9th century. Then in the 12th century, the pueblo of Pecos began taking shape. It started small, but by 1450, Pecos Pueblo had grown into a walled compound standing five stories high and housing some 2,000 people, making it one of the largest and most important pueblos in the Southwest.

The people of Pecos grew corn, beans, squash, and cotton and traded with Apaches and other Plains tribes, as well as other Pueblos. By the late 1500s, they were also trading with the Spanish, who visited Pecos in 1540 on their first foray into New Mexico in search of the fabled cities of gold.

Although the Spanish conquistadors did not find gold, they did discover what they believed were souls that needed saving, and by the late 1500s, they began setting up missions to convert the Pueblo people to Christianity. In all, four mission churches were built at Pecos, including the last one, built in 1717, whose ruins remain today.

The Pueblo people of New Mexico, including those at Pecos, did not appreciate being told by the Franciscan missionaries that their religious views and ceremonies, which they had practiced for centuries, were wrong. That insult, combined with the demand that they pay tribute to this new religion, plus the introduction of European diseases, a drought, and the resultant famine, led to the Pueblo Revolt of 1680, in which the scattered Pueblos joined together to force the Spanish back to Mexico. At Pecos, the priest was killed and the mission church, which had been the most impressive in the region, was destroyed. On the site of the mission's living quarters, the Pecos people built a kiva, their own traditional ceremonial chamber, that had been forbidden under Spanish rule.

The Spaniards returned 12 years later to retake New Mexico. Although their reconquest required bloodshed at some pueblos, the takeover of Pecos Pueblo was peaceful, and a new Pecos mission, built on the ruins of the old one, was the first mission reestablished after the revolt.

By this time, Pecos was an imposing pueblo and the trade hub for the Indians of the plains, who brought meat, hides, and other goods to exchange for the more sophisticated wares of the Indian pueblos along the Rio Grande.

In 1821, enterprising Yankee trader William Becknell opened the Santa Fe Trail, and merchandise from the young United States arrived in Pecos on its way to Santa Fe, where the Trail connected with the Camino Real. The "Royal Road" stretched, somewhat tenuously, all the way to Mexico City.

Although the Franciscans now treated the Indians better, disease, raids by other Indian tribes, and other problems led to the decline of Pecos. In 1838, its few final tribal members abandoned Pecos to join Jemez Pueblo, about 80 miles to the west. Pecos Pueblo was dead.

Here at Pecos National Historical Park, you can see all that remains from these peaceful Pueblo Indians, whose city was once the most magnificent of all the pueblos. You can walk into the ruins of the Spanish mission church and learn of the history of Spanish rule, which failed to succeed, by reason of its cruelty. You can see the ruts of the old Santa Fe Trail, one of the most important trade routes of the American frontier West. In the excellent visitor center, you can see the story of American victory over Spain and the conversion of New Spain into the Land of Enchantment.

Facts about the Park

The visitor center's museum contains exhibits on the pueblo, missions, and other aspects of the park, including a number of prehistoric Indian and Spanish colonial artifacts discovered during excavations. A 10-minute introductory video program is shown and there is a bookstore. During summer, craft demonstrations by local American Indian and Hispanic artisans are presented on several weekends each month. Both the park and the visitor center are open 8 A.M.–6 P.M. daily Memorial Day through Labor Day; 8 A.M.– 4:30 P.M. daily the rest of the year. Closed Christmas and New Year's Day. A small per person admission fee is charged.

Getting There

Pecos National Historical Park is 25 miles southeast of Santa Fe via I-25 and NM 63. Those traveling northbound on I-25 take exit 299 to Pecos Village; those traveling southbound on I-25 take exit 307.

Seeing and Doing

A 1.25-mile round-trip self-guiding trail leads from the visitor center through the ruins of Pecos Pueblo and the Spanish mission church. The two reconstructed kivas in the pueblo may also be entered. Trail guides are available at the visitor center.

In addition to the ruins of the pueblo and mission, the park has a number of nearby sites that can be seen only on guided tours. The free tours are offered year-round but fill quickly in summer. Calling for reservations at least two weeks in advance is recommended.

These nearby sites include several early Puebloan ruins, the remains of a 19th-century Spanish settlement, a section of the Santa Fe Trail (complete with wagon wheel ruts) and a stage station along the Trail. Also, the Forked Lightning Ranch, a working cattle ranch in the early 1900s that became known as a dude ranch and tourist attraction, has a main ranch house designed by famed architect John Gaw Meem. Nearby are two sites from the Battle of Glorieta Pass, which occurred in Mar. of 1862 and is considered the decisive battle of the Civil War for New Mexico, in that it

prevented the Confederates from over-running the Southwest.

Services

Visitor Information

Pecos National Historical Park, P.O. Box 418, Pecos, 87552-0418; 505-757-6414; www.nps.gov/peco.

A reenactment of the Battle of Glorieta Pass, a decisive victory that prevented the Confederation of the Southwest.

VILLANUEVA

The Spanish colonial village of Villanueva is located on the Pecos River, about a dozen miles south of I-25 on NM 3. It's a picturesque little community with quaint adobe houses and a well-preserved mission church, **Nuestra Señora de Guadalupe,** built in 1818. Settled in the 1790s at a time when American Indian attacks were frequent, the village was built around a central plaza, with the backs of its buildings forming a high wall, parts of which can be seen today.

Major Attraction

Villanueva State Park

This inviting park along the banks of the Pecos River offers enchanting scenery plus hiking, fishing, wildlife viewing, camping, and historic sites. Sandstone cliffs in shades of tan and reddish brown stand 400 feet high, providing a scenic backdrop to the green of the piñon and juniper trees that grow among the rocks and tall cottonwoods that shade the Pecos River. In the days of the Spanish conquistadors this was one of the routes of conquest, following the Pecos River north, and old Spanish ruins can be found in the park.

The park has two maintained hiking trails. The moderately rated Canyon Trail is a 2.5-mile loop from the river up to the top of the canyon and then back down again, offering good views of the river and surrounding mountains. Also along this trail are two interpretive signs: one discusses ruins of a 19th-century Spanish colonial ranch and a threshing floor on which horses trampled sheaves of grain. The other describes a conflict in 1841 in which members of an invading Texas group were captured.

The El Cerro Trail climbs from El Cerro Upper Campground to the top of the canyon, providing superb panoramic views of the river valley. The moderately difficult trail is rocky, with several steep sections, as it meanders through hillsides of piñon and juniper. There is also scrub oak and some ponderosa pine. The length out and back is about 1 mile.

The park's visitor center has exhibits on the area's geology, human history, fauna, and wildlife. Just outside the visitor center there is an interpretative garden, with signs identifying the plants of the area, including yucca, various species of cactus, and wildflowers.

Fishing in the Pecos is best from fall through spring, when the river is stocked and anglers catch rainbow trout, German brown trout, and channel catfish. The river is open to canoeing whenever the water level is high enough, usually only from early May through mid-June. Swimming is also permitted for those hardy enough to brave the chilly water, which seldom gets warmer than the upper 40s.

Wildlife to watch for include mule deer, coyotes, fox, bobcats, cottontail rabbits, jackrabbits, skunks, ground squirrels, and an occasional mountain lion. The park also has bull snakes, water snakes, and diamondback rattlers. Golden eagles have been known to nest in the park or nearby, and roadrunners are frequently spotted. Other birds that might be seen in the park include red-tailed hawks, western kingbirds, mountain bluebirds, northern flickers, mourning doves, summer tanagers, great horned owls, and rufous hummingbirds. Bird-watching is best in spring and summer; mule deer and other larger mammals are more likely to be seen in fall and winter.

There are 31 developed campsites here, including 12 with electric hookups. Campers can choose between sites along the river, which are shaded by tall cottonwoods, or sites on a hill above the river among piñon and juniper trees, which provide great views of the river and down the valley. The electric hookup sites are along the river, near the park's only showers, where there is also an RV dump station. Nearby is a historical marker that commemorates the route followed by the Spanish conquistadors, starting with Francisco Vasquez Coronado in 1540.

The park is open 24 hours; visitor center hours vary. Day-use and camping fees are required. Located just east of the village of Villanueva. **P.O. Box 40, Villanueva, 87583; 505-421-2957; www.nmparks.com.**

The roadrunner is the state bird of New Mexico.

CLAYTON

Nine miles from Texas on US Hwy. 87 and 10 miles from Oklahoma on US Hwys. 56/64 is Clayton, founded as a railroad town and rest stop for cattle drives in the 1880s. In some ways it hasn't changed all that much. Clayton remains a cattle ranching and feedlot center, and although it's isolated and quiet today, its Wild West heritage is remembered in the 1901 hanging (and accidental decapitation) of notorious train robber Black Jack Ketchum, captured while attempting to single-handedly stop and rob a moving train. Clayton is the trade center of a large and sparsely populated area, and it's fair to say that the town has more in common with Texas or Oklahoma than with New Mexico.

and west, beyond the railheads, and sold them to mining communities and the U.S. Army forts that dotted the new frontier. The Goodnight-Loving Trail brought thousands of longhorns north to New Mexico and Colorado. The herds were so large that one drive lost nearly 1,000 cattle to raiding Comanches, and the drive still showed a handsome profit for the long trip and the hard work. The trail drivers used several different routes because of the necessity of avoiding Indian ambushes. Goodnight said that he preferred the trail that led him across the endless grasslands to Chicosa Lake, southwest of Clayton, because it was a certain supply of water for his thirsty herds. He would have to change his route today, for Chicosa Lake is often dry now.

History

This tremendous expanse of grassland was the scene of historic travels. The Santa Fe Trail passed to the west of present-day Clayton during the time that most of the traffic used the original path over Raton Pass. Rabbit Ear—a distinctive rock formation—was one of the most sought-for landmarks on the Trail, for it meant that two more days' travel would bring the security and comfort of Fort Union. When most of the traffic began using the Cimarron cutoff, the new trail again was within easy reach of present-day Clayton.

When this nation was building westward, the cattle herds of Texas pastures were taken by trail drive to railheads in the north for eventual delivery to eastern markets. But enterprising trail drivers also brought great herds north

Major Attraction

Clayton Lake State Park

The number-one point of interest in these parts is Clayton Lake State Park, 12 miles north of town, where one of the world's best collections of dinosaur tracks is found. Created in 1955 as a fishing lake and winter stop for migrating waterfowl, the park's focus expanded greatly some 30 years later with the discovery of hundreds of dinosaur footprints. Paleontologists have catalogued more than 500 footprints, left in the mud by at least eight different types of dinosaurs more than 100 million years ago. At that time, this area was along the western coast of a large sea, with a warm and humid climate and an abundance of plant life.

Tracks are from both carnivores and herbivores, although the majority of the tracks are from large plant-eating dinosaurs. These prints have three toes, squared-off heels, and no claw marks. Herbivore footprints are also easily identified because of the long middle toe, often about twice the length of the two side toes. Those of the meat-eaters are smaller and birdlike, with thin toes, sharp claws, and pointed heels.

Among the more interesting tracks are those of a web-footed dinosaur, a baby dinosaur, and a winged pterodactyl, which looks as though it was taxiing for a takeoff because it left a series of prints where its wings' knuckle hit the mud as it struggled to get airborne. There is one set of tracks that appears to show a dinosaur slipping in the mud and dragging its tail to help keep it from falling.

The tracks are on the dam spillway, at the end of an easy 0.5-mile trail along the lake's east side. A boardwalk meanders among the tracks, and a gazebo contains information on the trackway. The tracks are easiest to see and photograph when the sun is low in the sky, early morning and late afternoon, when shadows throw them into relief.

Covering some 170 acres, Clayton Lake is open to all types of boats, although a no-wake speed limit is enforced. The lake is popular with canoeists and those with small inflatable boats and for windsurfing in the spring, but because it offers excellent fishing the lake is dominated by small fishing boats. The fishing season usually runs from Apr. through Oct. Cold water species include rainbow trout, walleye, and bluegill; warm water species include channel catfish and largemouth bass. Swimming is permitted, but there are no designated swimming areas.

From Nov. through Mar. the lake is off-limits to boats and anglers and becomes a virtual paradise for birdwatchers, as a variety of migrating waterfowl make their home here. They spend their nights at the lake, but each morning fly across the state line to feed in the fields north of Dalhart, Texas. They return to the lake by 10 A.M.—you can practically set your watch by it—and then go off for supper about 4 P.M., returning by sunset.

Species you're apt to see include great blue herons, white pelicans, double-crested cormorants, osprey, common loons, and lots of ducks; the lake is also a winter home for Canada geese. The best time to see waterfowl is usually from mid-Dec. through mid-Jan., although there likely will be some there throughout the winter.

Winter visitors should also be on the watch for bald eagles, which can usually be seen from mid-Nov. through Feb. Pronghorn antelope are often spotted just outside the park's entrance, and visitors might also see mule deer, coyotes, badgers, gray foxes, porcupines, and maybe a bobcat.

The park's North Trail meanders for about 0.75 mile through grasslands and woods to the top of a ridge, providing panoramic views across the lake. It crosses a seepage that feeds the lake, skirts rock pens built by pioneer sheepherders, and passes through a canyon with numerous picturesque rock formations. The trail is rated moderate at the beginning but soon becomes flat and easy. It offers a good chance of seeing a variety of birds and wildlife, plus wildflowers in late spring and summer, and can usually be hiked year-round.

Kids especially like the Rock Garden, a much smaller and somewhat less dramatic version of Bryce Canyon National Park in southern Utah. Wind and water erosion has sculpted sandstone in shades of orange, tan, and brown into a variety of stone sculptures, similar to the hoodoos of Bryce, but shorter and fatter.

The year-round campground has spacious and sunny sites, some with views of the lake and some surrounding the Rock Garden. There are 37 developed sites, including 7 with electric and water hookups. The park also has restrooms with showers, a boat ramp, a visitor center, and a playground.

The park is open 6 A.M.–9 P.M.; visitor center open 8 A.M.–4 P.M. daily. Clayton Lake State Park has both day-use and camping fees. Located 12 miles north of Clayton via NM 370. **141 Clayton Lake Rd., Clayton, 88415; 505-374-8808; www.nmparks.com.**

Seeing and Doing

To see some of the history of this genuine Wild West town, stop at the **Herzstein Memorial Museum,** located in a former church, built in 1891. The museum contains exhibits on the Santa Fe Trail, American Indians, the ranching history of Clayton, the area's dinosaurs, and some fascinating historic toys. There is also a model railroad depicting Clayton's railroading days and furnishings from a 1930s doctor's office. But the museum isn't just about the Clayton area. Two local residents who left town, made a pile of money, and traveled the world have donated their personal collections of art and craft items. Especially beautiful is the Italian porcelain. There is also a gift shop with a good selection of books on northeast New Mexico history. Open Tues.–Sun. 1–5 P.M. except major holidays. Free admission (donations welcome). Corner of S. 2nd and Walnut Sts. Operated by the **Union County Historical**

Society, P.O. Box 75, Clayton, 88415-0075; 505-374-2977.

A tourist attraction as well as a good place to eat and drink, the **Eklund Dining Room & Saloon** is on the first floor of the Eklund Hotel, a three-story stone hotel that in the late 1800s and early 1900s was one of the finest and most modern lodgings in the area. Check out the elaborately carved bar, still in use, that Carl Eklund installed in 1894. The guest rooms on the second and third floors are not open to the public at this time, but are being restored, so it is worth checking on their progress. The restaurant menu is discussed below, but you don't have to eat there to see the place. Just walk in and say hello; they're used to it.

Other attractions here include the grave of **Black Jack Ketchum,** which is in the local cemetery. When this notorious train robber was being put to death by hanging in 1901, the executioner accidentally ripped his head off, a gruesome sight for the spectators. Reportedly a local doctor sewed it back on before he was buried. The cemetery is located on the east side of town, off Water St. The chamber of commerce visitor center can provide a map and directions to the cemetery, as well as a map to the nearby ruts from the **Santa Fe Trail.**

Where to Stay and Eat

There are several chain motels located on S. 1st St. These include the Best **Western Kokopelli Inn** ($$–$$$), **702 S. 1st St., Clayton, 88415; 800-392-6691; 505-374-2589,** which has large, quiet rooms and accepts pets (fee). There is also a **Days Inn & Suites** ($$–$$$), **1120 S. 1st St., Clayton, 88415; 800-329-7466;**

505-374-0133, with an attractive indoor heated pool, and a slightly less expensive **Super 8** ($$), **1425 S. 1st St., Clayton, 88415; 800-800-8000; 505-374-8127.**

In addition to the campground at **Clayton Lake State Park,** there is a **KOA campground** here, with shaded tent sites, long pull-through RV sites, and all the usual amenities you would expect at a good commercial campground (no pool). Open Mar.–Oct. From 1st St., take Spruce or Aspen Sts. east 4 blocks. **903 S. 5th St., Clayton, 88415; 800-562-9507 (reservations); 505-374-9508.**

First St. is where you'll also find a lot of restaurants—both national chains and independents—but if you've got a hankering for really good food in a wonderful historic building, skip the fast-food joints and head to the **Eklund Dining Room & Saloon** ($–$$$) for lunch or dinner. It offers a surprisingly large menu, including an excellent half-pound burger (with or without chile), beef and vegetable stew, chicken-fried steak with cream gravy, enchiladas, tamales, steaks, grilled chicken breast, broiled or fried rainbow trout, and lobster tail. Open 10 A.M.–9 P.M. daily. **15 Main St., Clayton; 505-374-2551; www.theeklund.com.**

Services

Visitor Information

Clayton/Union County Chamber of Commerce, 1103 S. 1st St., P.O. Box 476, Clayton, 88415; 800-390-7858; 505-374-9253; www.claytonnewmexico.org. The chamber operates a visitor center at this address.

Prairie dogs are social creatures and can be found in rural as well as wild areas.

TUCUMCARI

Back in the days when Nat King Cole urged America to "get your kicks on Route 66," Tucumcari was a major stopping point on this Chicago-to-Los Angeles route. Because it was halfway between Amarillo, Texas, and Albuquerque, Tucumcari became a popular place to spend the night for auto travelers who felt that 250 miles per day was a long run. The creation of I-40, along with better cars, has enabled motorists to drive farther. The new interstate sent shock waves through Tucumcari as travelers zipped right by the town.

But Tucumcari has fought back, and promotes itself as *the* place to spend the night, with billboards screaming "Tucumcari Tonight!" It also tries to persuade travelers to extend their stay beyond their sleeping hours, with various special events, several attractive museums, and two nearby lakes.

Festivals and Events

For details on all of the following, check with the **Tucumcari Chamber of Commerce** (see Services).

TUCUMCARI CHAMBER OF COMMERCE RODEO
mid-June. Barrel racing, bull riding, and all the usual rodeo thrills and spills.

ROUTE 66 CELEBRATION
mid-July. Among Tucumcari's top annual events, this tribute to Route 66 includes a car show, parade, kids' games, a ranch rodeo, a dance, and plenty of food.

QUAY COUNTY FAIR
Aug. All the usual county fair activities, with demonstrations, contests, and food.

ROTARY CLUB AIR SHOW
early Oct. A spectacular show of modern and historic airplanes.

Outdoor Activities

Boating and Fishing
The main outdoor activities in this area—water sports and fishing—take place primarily at two nearby lakes—Conchas and Ute—both of which are state parks.

CONCHAS LAKE STATE PARK
This big lake offers plenty of opportunities for boating, water-skiing, fishing, and

---

Tucumcari

Wonder where the name Tucumcari came from? One story is that it's an American Indian name for the flat-topped "mountain" that is the big landmark in the vicinity. The Indians also claimed that Tucumcari meant "land of the buffalo hunts," and there is plenty of evidence that they did hunt great herds of buffalo in the area. You'll also hear the silly tale about the name coming from the murders and suicides of a quartet of Indians named Tucum, Kari, Tonopath, and so on. However, Tucumcari is only the latest name. It was once called Liberty, because soldiers from nearby Fort Bascom came here on liberty. It was also called Cactus Flats and for a while Six-Shooter Siding, for obvious reasons.

swimming. The park also has good camping and wildlife viewing. Created as a flood control and irrigation project in the late 1930s at a cost of $15.8 million, Conchas Lake became a state park in 1943. The dam is 200 feet high and 1,250 feet long, and when full the lake covers about 15 square miles.

As one would expect at one of the state's largest lakes, boating and fishing are the main activities. Conchas Lake is particularly popular with families and retirees, and boats here range from canoes to sailboats to large cabin cruisers and houseboats. Waterskiing and the use of personal watercraft are popular in summer, and because the wind blows at 15 m.p.h. more than half the time, the lake is being discovered by windsurfers. Those with canoes usually head for one of the many protected coves, but even there the water is often choppy. A system of flashing white lights warns boaters to stay out of open water when winds exceed 15 m.p.h.

There are about 60 miles of shoreline, with numerous little coves, inlets, and secluded beaches that make it easy for boaters to get away from the crowds. Although there are no designated swimming beaches, swimming, snorkeling, and scuba diving in the clear water are permitted in most areas. Swimmers usually prefer the beaches in the Central Recreation Area and near Cove Campground, where drop-offs are more gradual than in other parts of the lake.

The lake is regularly stocked by the New Mexico Department of Game and Fish. Spring and fall are the best time to catch walleye and crappie. Anglers catch channel catfish, bluegill, and largemouth bass year-round. Spearfishing is also gaining in popularity. In winter the lake occasionally has a light skim of ice, but does not freeze sufficiently for ice fishing.

The full-service **Conchas North Dock Marina** has boat docks, mechanics, a bait shop, store, restaurant and bar, overnight lodging (in mobile homes), and pontoon boat rentals.

Throughout the park are piñon and juniper trees, with elms and cottonwoods dotting the shore. Wildflowers are abundant in Apr. and May, and there are several species of cacti.

Conchas Lake is growing in popularity as a bird-watching destination, especially in winter, when the lake attracts an abundance of waterfowl, including Canada and snow geese, ring-necked ducks, green-winged teal, pintails, mallards, canvasbacks, and redheads. There are also American robins, swallows, golden and bald eagles, and sandhill cranes.

Tarantulas live in the park and are often seen in Aug. and Sept. Signs along the roads warn motorists to use extra care at tarantula crossings. Despite their rather unsavory reputations, most tarantulas are not poisonous—although their bite may sting a bit. Tarantulas will go to great lengths to avoid confrontations with people. Just don't step on them. Other park wildlife includes mule deer, which are sometimes spotted walking along the dam, along with coyotes, cottontail rabbits, jackrabbits, beaver, porcupines, muskrats, raccoons, chipmunks, and turtles. Snakes include rattlers, bull snakes, and racers, and the park is home to a variety of lizards.

A state park visitor center in the North Recreation Area has a few exhibits on the park's plants and animals and provides information on state park facilities and activities. The Army Corps of Engineers has offices and an information center north of the Central Recreation Area. Park officials warn that although the entire lake is open to the public, parts of the shoreline are on private property, and boaters should be careful to avoid trespassing.

Campgrounds offer a variety of facilities, from unlimited primitive camping along the shore to more than 100 developed sites, including 40 with water and electric hookups. All the developed sites have shelters, picnic tables, and fire grills. There are restrooms with showers and an RV dump station.

The park is open 24 hours, but call for other hours. Day-use and camping fees are required. Located 34 miles northwest of Tucumcari via NM 104. **P.O. Box 976, Conchas Dam, 88416; 505-868-2270; 505-868-2251 (marina); www.nmparks.com.**

UTE LAKE STATE PARK

A popular family camping and boating destination, this park also has excellent fishing, good swimming and scuba diving, and lots of migratory birds. Known for its numerous little coves and inlets, this deep-blue 8,200-acre lake is among the state's longest—almost 13 miles—but it is also skinny, less than 1 mile across at its widest point.

The lake was created in 1963 with construction of a 5,750-foot-long earth-filled dam to provide water for nearby communities. However, a lawsuit claimed that New Mexico was taking too much water from the Canadian River, which eventually flows into Texas and Oklahoma, and the U.S. Supreme Court ruled against the New Mexico towns. Bad news for the communities that wanted the drinking water, but good news for boaters and anglers, because a side effect of the ruling is that unlike most other reservoirs, Ute Lake's water level fluctuates very little.

Ute Lake attracts a variety of boaters, and during summer you are apt to see a mix of fishing boats, ski boats, personal watercraft, and sailboats. Windsurfing is popular in spring. The only restricted area is Ute Creek, where waterskiing is prohibited. **Ute Lake Marina** rents small fishing boats and boat slips, fills scuba tanks, and sells fuel, food, and other supplies. Although there are no designated swimming areas, there are a number of sandy beaches, especially in the North Area. Water temperatures during summer are usually in the 70s. One potential hazard is sand burrs, which stick to clothing and skin and can be quite painful to humans and pets.

The best fishing is in spring and fall, although anglers fish here year-round. The lake has excellent walleye fishing and has produced record-breaking small-mouth bass. Anglers also catch crappie, bluegill, and channel catfish.

Visitors looking for wildlife will see migratory birds, including ducks and geese, from late fall through early spring. Bald and golden eagles often roost in the northern sections of the park from Jan. through early Mar., and there are doves, quail, and pheasant. Roadrunners often are spotted in the campgrounds. Deer are sometimes seen in the Rogers Park area, plus the park is home to raccoons, rabbits, squirrels, and a variety of snakes, including bull snakes and rattlesnakes. Tarantulas are present in spring and fall as the males make their stately trek in search of a mate.

The park has practically unlimited camping with 142 developed sites, including 77 with electric hookups, plus plenty of space for primitive camping. Most camping areas have good views and easy access to the lake. There are restrooms with showers and an RV dump station. A small visitor center has exhibits and provides information on park activities.

The park is open 24 hours; the visitor center is open 8 A.M.–5 P.M. Day-use and camping fees are required. Located 3 miles west of Logan on NM 540 (Logan is 24 miles northeast of Tucumcari via US Hwy. 54). **P.O. Box 52,**

Logan, 88426; 505-487-2284; 505-487-2349 (marina); www.nmparks.com.

Seeing and Doing

Museums

MESALANDS DINOSAUR MUSEUM

Two hundred million years ago, dinosaurs began exploring eastern New Mexico, and they stayed right through the three geologic ages of dinosaurs—Triassic, Jurassic, and Cretaceous. To meet these huge beasts in person (or at least reasonable facsimiles of them), this museum is the place to come. Operated by Mesalands Community College, the museum takes visitors on a journey through geologic time, from the earliest dinosaurs up to the origins of mammals. Exhibits include the casting of a full-size skeleton of a *Torvosaurus* (which looks similar to a *Tyrannosaurus rex*), the first of its kind displayed anywhere, and a reconstruction of a unique *Struthiomimus*, an ostrichlike dinosaur. There are also models of dinosaurs, fossils from around the world, including dinosaur eggs from China, and the world's largest collection of life-size dinosaur skeletons cast in bronze. These bronze skeletons are beautiful works of art, and the museum people tell us that bronze also shows more detail than the composite materials that are usually used. The museum has a children's section with hands-on exhibits, and large windows let museum visitors see paleontologists and students at work in the adjacent research laboratory. Open Tues.–Sat. 10 A.M.–6 P.M. Mar. 1–Labor Day; noon–5 P.M. the rest of the year. Closed major holidays. Admission fee charged. **222 E. Laughlin Ave., Tucumcari, 88401;**

505-451-3466; www.mesalands.edu/museum/museum.htm

TUCUMCARI HISTORICAL MUSEUM

Housed in a three-story brick schoolhouse built in 1903, this interesting museum contains thousands of items from the area's past, most dealing with pioneer days and the American Indians. Here you'll see an authentic western schoolroom, a sheriff's office, a pioneer kitchen, a scary 1920s hospital room, plenty of Old West artifacts, a 1926 fire engine, and Route 66 memorabilia that includes a mural depicting travel through the area on Route 66. Open 9 A.M.–6 P.M. Mon.–Sat. in summer, 8 A.M.–5 P.M. Tues.–Sat. the rest of the year. Closed major holidays. Admission fee charged. **416 S. Adams St., Tucumcari, 88401; 505-461-4201; www.cityoftucumcari.com/museum/index.html.**

Where to Stay

Accommodations

As you might expect in a town that bills itself as *the* place for cross-country travelers to spend the night, there are dozens of motels here. Because of the competition, rates are often quite reasonable. Just about every mid- and low-price chain is represented, and there are a number of independents, although no historic bed-and-breakfast inns or fancy old hotels.

There are, however, some nostalgic roadside motels from the heyday of Route 66 that are being restored to their neon splendor. Built in 1939, **The Blue Swallow Motel** ($–$$) offers a step back in time, with 11 cozy (that means small) rooms that are simply decorated in the style of the 1950s. It has rooms with either one queen bed or two double beds. There are also suites—two rooms with a connecting hallway and bathroom; each room has a queen-size bed, one also has a daybed and the other has a refrigerator and microwave oven (and we thought this was the 1950s!). **815 E. Route 66 Blvd., Tucumcari, 88401; 505-461-9849; www.blueswallowmotel.com.**

Those opting for more modern accommodations have plenty of choices, most of them on E. Tucumcari Blvd., the main drag through town. Chains include two **Best Westerns,** a **Comfort Inn, Days Inn, Econo Lodge, Hampton Inn, Holiday Inn, Howard Johnson Express, Microtel Inn, Rodeway Inn, Super 8,** and **Travelodge,** as well as some independents. All offer pretty much what you would expect from these usually reliable chains, and most accept pets.

For really low-priced lodging, head to **Redwood Lodge Hostel** ($), affiliated with Hostelling International, which has 20 dorm beds and four private rooms, plus use of a kitchen and laundry. The office is open 7–10 A.M. and 4–10 P.M. **1502 W. Tucumcari Blvd., Tucumcari, 88401; 505-461-3635; www.hiayh.org.**

Campgrounds

In addition to camping at Conchas and Ute Lakes State Parks (see above), there are several commercial campgrounds in Tucumcari.

TUCUMCARI KOA

Located on Historic Route 66, on the east edge of Tucumcari, this is a lovely park with shade trees and scenic views of Tucumcari Mountain and nearby mesas. It is open year-round, welcomes tenters as well as RVers, and has all the usual commercial campground amenities including a heated swimming pool (open mid-May to mid-Sept.). **6299A Quay Rd. AL (I-40 exit 335), Tucumcari, 88401; 800-562-1871 (reservations); 505-461-1841.**

Where to Eat

There are good restaurants at several of the chain motels, including both **Best Westerns** and the **Holiday Inn,** plus fast-food chains and some independents along Tucumcari Blvd.

Del's Restaurant—$$–$$$

It would be hard to miss this Route 66 landmark—just watch for a big cow standing on top of the neon sign that announces "Del's Restaurant Since 1956." Inside you'll discover a comfortable, casual family restaurant with three spacious dining rooms decorated in southwestern style and large windows offering views of the historic street. The menu features American and Mexican standards, including a lot of diner-style comfort food such as roast beef with brown gravy and mashed potatoes. The steaks are top notch, and there's a good salad bar. On the Mexican side of the menu try the chicken quesadilla— shredded chicken with cheddar cheese, tomatoes, and green chile stuffed in a grilled flour tortilla and served with lettuce, tomato, and sour cream. Open Mon.–Sat. 7 A.M.–9 P.M. **1202 E. Tucumcari Blvd., 505-461-1740; www.delsrestaurant.com.**

Services

Visitor Information

Tucumcari Chamber of Commerce, 404 W. Route 66, P.O. Drawer E, Tucumcari, 88401; 888-664-7255; 505-461-1694; www.tucumcarinm.com.

The Road to Adventure

US Hwy. 66, better known simply as Route 66 or the Mother Road, was the road west for countless Americans from its beginning in 1926, when only 800 of its 2,400-plus miles were paved, before it was mostly buried by Interstate 40 in 1984. Although it may be officially dead and gone, sections of Route 66 still remain, and the memories and memorabilia of the famous road's glory days live on across New Mexico in Tucumcari, Santa Rosa, Albuquerque, Grants, and Gallup, as well as numerous stops in between.

Route 66 ran from Chicago to Los Angeles (actually Santa Monica), crossing eight states over a relatively flat course that made it the preferred route for many people heading to California. This was especially true during the depression, when Route 66 carried innumerable Dust Bowl victims to hopes of a new life. During World War II, the highway helped move troops and equipment, and after the war Route 66 carried returning servicemen back to their homes. In the prosperous postwar years, Route 66 became the road of choice for many Americans heading out to "See the USA in Your Chevrolet," as Dinah Shore sang to the country each week on that new phenomenon called television.

New Mexico boasted some 465 miles of Route 66 in two different alignments. Although both alignments entered New Mexico from the east following the general route of present-day I-40, the first Route 66 wandered north, beginning just west of Santa Rosa, to Santa Fe, and then turned south to Albuquerque. Later the detour to Santa Fe was dropped, resulting in a relatively straight east-west run across the state. The change was made in 1937 and resulted in the only place on the entire road where Route 66 crossed itself—in downtown Albuquerque.

Most people who think of Route 66 today conjure up images from the 1940s and 1950s of neon lights luring us to roadside motels and diners, the wonderful cars of that era, and the gas stations and billboards that sprang up along the road. Much of that actually remains—some restored and some in ruin—and a whole new tourism industry has appeared to help us remember the good old days.

Primarily along I-40, in towns from Tucumcari to Gallup, you'll find reminders of old Route 66, and even some stretches of the highway you can drive—watch for signs designated Historic Route 66. We'll be discussing many of them in the sections on the individual towns.

The nonprofit **New Mexico Route 66 Association** has been active in helping to secure grant money for preservation and renovation projects along New Mexico's section of Route 66. It also sponsors events commemorating the Mother Road and publishes a magazine. **1415 Central Ave. NE, Albuquerque, 87106; 505-224-2802; www.rt66nm.org.**

SANTA ROSA

This overnight stop along Historic Route 66, and more recently I-40, is a pleasant little town with at least a few reasons to pull off the highway. Like most of eastern New Mexico, Santa Rosa is semi-desert, but it's practically surrounded by lakes, including one warm water spring popular with scuba divers.

Although American Indians had known about the Blue Hole and the natural lakes of this city for centuries before the white man arrived, Santa Rosa was not really on the map until 1879, when one of the earliest Spanish settlers, Don Celso Baca, built a small chapel in honor of his mother. He named the chapel for Saint Rose of Lima, which accounts for the town's name. The remains of the chapel still stand along NM 91, which leads out of the city toward Puerto de Luna.

Festivals and Events

For details on all of the following, check with the **Santa Rosa City Hall** (see Services).

SANTA ROSA DAYS
Memorial Day weekend. This three-day celebration includes a softball tournament that attracts more than 40 teams, an arts and crafts fair, amusement rides, games, and goat roping.

NUESTRA SEÑORA DE REFUGIO FIESTAS
Fourth of July. Celebrate with games, entertainment, food, and a fiesta dance in Puerto de Luna (10 miles south of Santa Rosa).

GUADALUPE COUNTY FAIR
early Aug. The entire family will enjoy this fair, which includes a rodeo, exhibits, a flower show, pet parade, horseshoe throwing contest, and chili cook-off.

SANTA ROSA DE LIMA FIESTAS
late Aug. Features entertainment, food booths, mariachi singers, a dance, and crowning of the fiesta queen.

ROUTE 66 FESTIVAL
Sept. This event brags that it has something for everyone: live entertainment, exhibits, food booths, a street dance, a parade, and a car show.

Outdoor Activities

Cattle Drives

ROCKING J RANCH
Located about 20 minutes west of Santa Rosa, Rocking J Ranch is a genuine working cattle ranch where you can join cowboys on cattle drives, branding, and other ranch activities. Working ranch vacations range from 3 to 14 days and both adults and children are welcome. Or you can stay overnight and explore the ranch on your own or on a wagon ride, with chuckwagon-style meals. Costs vary, and reservations should be made at least two weeks in advance. **HCR 69, Box 842, Santa Rosa, 88435; 505-472-5127; www.rocking-j.com.**

Water Sports and Fishing

BLUE HOLE
Don't think of Santa Rosa as just another

wide spot on the fabled road. It is now a vacation destination, and there are many things going on here. For starters there are seven natural lakes in the area, the Pecos River flows through the city almost unnoticed, and it is one of the Southwest's most interesting **scuba diving** destinations.

Scuba diving? No, we're not kidding. Five minutes from downtown Santa Rosa is the famous Blue Hole, an artesian-fed hole in the sandstone. The water, a constant 64° F, is clear as bathtub gin, and visibility extends down to 80 feet. Divers come here all year long, but they need wet suits in the winter. The bell-shaped pool is about 80 feet in diameter at the surface and 130 feet at the bottom, and it's more than 80 feet deep. The city of Santa Rosa, which manages the pool, has provided steps and platforms for easier entry, and expert divers know that they must change the calibrations on their equipment to compensate for the fact that the surface of Blue Hole is 4,600 feet above sea level. A privately operated diving shop near the Blue Hole provides tank refills and equipment rentals. Permits (fee) are required, available at the diving shop and city hall, and divers must have the proper certification.

SANTA ROSA LAKE STATE PARK
This pretty lake, surrounded by low, rocky hills, is a great spot for fishing and water sports. The park also offers wildlife viewing, hiking, horseback riding, and camping. Created to provide irrigation water and flood control along the Pecos River, the level of the large lake varies considerably depending on irrigation needs. Built in 1981, the dam is 212 feet high and 1,950 feet long. The park is managed jointly by New Mexico State Parks and the U.S. Army Corps of Engineers.

Most of the boats here are of the fishing and skiing variety, 20 to 25 feet long, and are hauled over to the park's paved four-lane boat ramp. Those with canoes enjoy circling the lake's several islands and exploring its secluded coves. Occasionally you will see a sailboat gliding across the water. Although swimming is permitted, there are no designated swimming areas and most of the beaches are rocky or covered with brush and other vegetation. The lake has no marinas.

Anglers catch channel catfish, largemouth and smallmouth bass, walleye, and crappie, and the lake also produces sunfish, yellow perch, and an occasional trout.

There are two short, easy paved hiking trails. **Scenic Trail** is a loop of about 0.5 mile that offers good panoramic views of the lake and picturesque rock outcroppings at its beginning and end, and in between meanders through a low forest of piñon, juniper, prairie grasses, and cholla and prickly pear cacti. **Handicap Trail** is a loop of about 0.75 mile through similar terrain. It has one fairly long incline and offers good views of the rocky lakeshore through piñon and juniper trees. Both trails have wildflowers in spring and early summer.

There are also trails leading from Rocky Point Campground down a rocky slope to the lake, a distance of about 0.25 mile, although the distance varies depending on the lake level. This is a good area in which to catch a glimpse of mule deer, raccoons, squirrels, foxes, and coyotes as they come for water. Bobcats and mountain lions are also spotted occasionally, and pronghorn are sometimes seen along the road near the park entrance.

The lake attracts Canada geese, pelicans, ring-billed gulls, and a variety of ducks; in recent years bald eagles have had winter roosts on snags on the islands and along the lakeshore. Other birds observed in the park include barn swallows, mourning doves, scaled quails, and ospreys. Visitors climbing around the rocks should watch where they put their hands and feet to avoid disturbing rattlesnakes. There are also nonpoisonous bull snakes and racers, and tarantulas are often seen in late summer and fall.

Those who thought to bring their horses will find a pleasant equestrian trail, more than 20 miles long, that runs along the northeast side of the lake. The park also has a few stables available for overnight use.

There are two campgrounds, both in rocky terrain of piñon, juniper, and cactus, with a total of 76 sites, including 25 sites with electric hookups. Rocky Point has showers and is open year-round, and Juniper Park does not have showers and closes in winter. There is also a primitive camping area that is used primarily as an overflow. Both the state park and U.S. Army Corps of Engineers have offices at the lake. The Corps of Engineers office contains an information center with exhibits on the lake's plants, wildlife, and recreational opportunities. It also has displays on the dam's construction, including archeological artifacts discovered during the work.

The park is open 24 hours; call for office hours. Day-use and camping fees are required. Located 7 miles north of Santa Rosa via NM 91. **P.O. Box 384, Santa Rosa, 88433; 505-472-3110; www.nmparks.com.**

Seeing and Doing

PUERTO DE LUNA
Located 10 miles south of Santa Rosa via NM 91, Puerto de Luna (Spanish for "door of the moon") is a delightfully scenic and historic village where tiny irrigated farms and adobe homes reflect the New Mexico of 200 years ago. The road is good, and the red rock formations along the way contrast beautifully with the emerald green of irrigated crops, including an excellent strain of chile that has been grown here for more than 100 years. According to local legend, Spanish conquistadors camped here and built a bridge over the Pecos River, and today there is a marker at the spot. Worth a look are the lovely Catholic church, the original county courthouse building, and the nearby Grzelachowski Territorial House, a store and home built in 1800 by a retired Civil War chaplain who was reportedly a friend of outlaw Billy the Kid. The house is open for tours; call for current hours. **505-472-5320.**

ROCK LAKE FISH HATCHERY
Come to this trout rearing station to see how the New Mexico Department of Game and Fish raises fish to stock the area's lakes and rivers. Vending machines supply fish food. Open 8 A.M.–5 P.M. daily. Located 2 miles south of Santa Rosa off I-40. **River Rd.; 505-472-3690.**

ROUTE 66 AUTO MUSEUM
Perhaps the best car museum in the region, this facility displays close to three dozen classic and custom cars, such as an absolutely beautiful white 1958 Chevy Impala convertible and a red 1957 Chevy convertible, both of which were popular during the glory years of Route 66. There are custom street rods from the 1920s and 1930s, and vehicles all the way up to the muscle cars of the 1960s and 1970s. Most of the cars are for sale (bring your wallet), so the collection changes frequently. The museum is owned and operated by

James "Bozo" and Anna Cordova and is located across the street from Bozo's Garage, where all the beautiful restoration work has been done. Also on display are gas station pumps and signs, various highway signs, and other Route 66 memorabilia. There's a gift shop and snack bar. Open 8 A.M.–8 P.M. spring and summer and 8 A.M.–6 P.M. fall and winter. Admission fee charged. **2766 Historic Route 66, Santa Rosa, 88435; 505-472-1966.**

Where to Stay

Accommodations

Just as in Tucumcari, numerous motels invite cross-country travelers to spend the night and leave a bit of cash. Most of the major mid and low-priced chains are represented, along with some independents. Practically all of them are on the I-40 Business Loop, also known as Historic Route 66 (and formerly called Will Rogers Dr. and Parker Ave.). Santa

Rosa has two **Best Westerns**, a **Comfort Inn**, a **Days Inn**, a **Holiday Inn Express**, a **La Quinta**, a **Motel 6**, a **Super 8,** and a **Travelodge**—all in the $$ category.

Those looking for a hit of Route 66 nostalgia should check out the **La Loma Motel** ($), which dates from the 1930s and has clean, comfortable rooms simply decorated in 1950s' style, with new tile bathrooms, double or queen beds, and solid oak furniture. Rooms even include TVs with that new-fangled cable connection offering ESPN and Showtime. **761 Historic Route 66, Santa Rosa, 88435; 505-472-4379.**

Campgrounds

In addition to camping at **Santa Rosa Lake State Park** (see page 105) there are several commercial campgrounds in Santa Rosa.

SANTA ROSA KOA

This modern commercial campground has all the amenities, including a heated swimming pool (summer only) and even

The auto collection at the Route 66 Auto Museum is always changing, as many of the vehicles are for sale. The museum also has a gift shop and snack bar.

campsite phone/modem hookups. There are about 12 tent sites and 83 RV sites, many shaded. There's a large gift shop and convenience store, plus a barbecue restaurant, with meal delivery to your campsite available. Located on I-40 Business Loop between exits 275 and 277. **2136 Historic Route 66, Santa Rosa, 88435; 888-898-1999 (reservations); 505-472-3126.**

Where to Eat

Joseph's Restaurant and Cantina— $$-$$$

In business since 1956, Joseph's (Joe's to the locals) serves excellent Mexican meals, plus burgers, sandwiches, and seafood. The place is furnished and decorated in nostalgic Route 66 style, with old advertising signs and license plates and linoleum tables and booths. Breakfast selections run the gamut from ham and eggs to Belgian waffles to huevos rancheros. Lunch includes seven hamburger options and a variety of sandwiches, and the dinner menu includes chile rellenos, fajitas, enchiladas, trout, and salads including the tomato volcano. Joseph's serves good milkshakes and malts, plus killer margaritas. There's also an on-site bakery and gift shop. Open daily 6 A.M.–10 P.M. in summer, 6

A.M.–9 P.M. the rest of the year. **865 Historic Route 66; 505-472-3361.**

Route 66 Restaurant—$-$$

This fun step back to the 1950s (it has been a restaurant since 1947) serves good diner food at reasonable prices, in a setting that just might produce nostalgia overload. Throughout the diner-style restaurant you'll see memorabilia from Route 66's days of glory, from car photos to road signs and lots of pictures of Elvis. A seven-seat counter plus tables and booths are nicely done in red leatherette. The menu includes burgers, sandwiches, steaks, and fish, plus Mexican items such as enchiladas, burritos, and tacos. A small gift shop sells Route 66 souvenirs. Open daily 6 A.M.–10 P.M. in summer, 6 A.M.–9 P.M. the rest of the year. **1819 Historic Route 66; 505-472-9925.**

Services

Visitor Information

A visitor information center is located at **486 Historic Route 66; 505-472-3763.** You can also get information by contacting the **Santa Rosa City Hall, 141 S. 5th St., Santa Rosa, 88435; 505-472-3404; www.srnm.org.**

Northwest Region

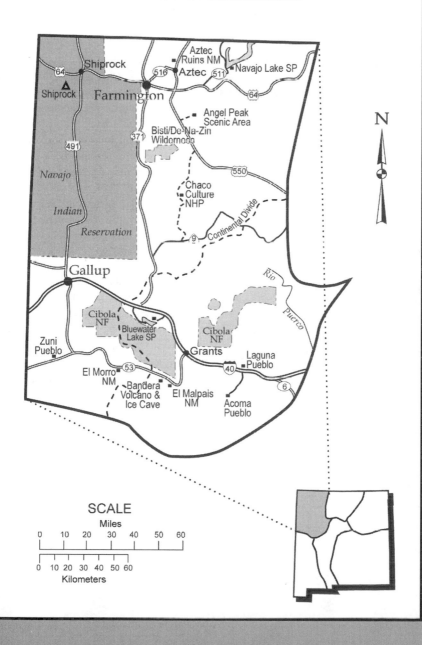

SCALE

Miles

0 10 20 30 40 50 60

0 10 20 30 40 50 60
Kilometers

Northwest Region

The northwest region is bordered on the south by Interstate 40, which bisects New Mexico east to west. The Navajo Dam and Navajo Reservoir impound the waters of the San Juan and Los Piños Rivers downstream of the state of Colorado and turn them into New Mexico's third largest water area and best water recreation area. The waters provide irrigation for thousands of acres of Navajo land, and the miracle of irrigation paints a great green stripe along the river valley below the dam. The stretch of the San Juan River fed by the cold waters from the Navajo Reservoir makes for wonderful trout fishing, and it is considered one of the 10 best trout streams in America.

The history of New Mexico's northwest corner is really the history of the Ancestral Puebloan people (also called Anasazi) and the Navajo.

It's believed that nomadic Paleo-Indians visited the area some 10,000 years ago, and by about 1000 B.C. Ancestral Puebloan peoples were living here, digging pit houses or finding shelter in shallow caves. By the time of Christ they were cultivating corn and squash, and soon after that they began making pottery and using a bow and arrow for hunting. The ancient cities you'll see here, such as the massive stone ruins at Chaco Culture National Historical Park and the smaller but equally impressive ruins at Aztec Ruins National Monument, were constructed between A.D. 800 and 1100, but by the mid-1300s they had been abandoned.

The reasons for this mass exodus are not entirely clear, but it is quite possible that a severe drought during that period was a major factor. It is generally accepted that these are the ancestors of today's Pueblo Indians, whose villages are found throughout much of New Mexico, and the Hopis, who live in northeastern Arizona, surrounded by the Navajo Nation.

The Navajo, meanwhile, are relative newcomers to the area. Relatives of the Apaches, the Navajos are believed to have migrated to the Southwest from western Canada and Alaska sometime in the 1400s. After repeated problems between the Navajos and Anglo settlers in the 1800s, the Navajos were hunted down and imprisoned at Fort Sumner, in southern New Mexico. A treaty in 1868 established the Navajo Reservation. Now the huge Navajo Nation covers some 27,000 square miles in Arizona, New Mexico, and Utah.

FARMINGTON & AZTEC

These two adjacent communities comprise the largest population center in the northwest corner of the state and serve as the supply depot for the oil and gas industry, which has many operations in this part of New Mexico and on into Arizona and Utah. This is also the major trading center for the huge Navajo Nation, and the business center for the irrigated farming area nourished by the Navajo Reservoir. The area sits atop large coal deposits, and its Four Corners Power Plant is one of the nation's biggest users of soft coal for power generation. Farmington has about 38,000 residents, while Aztec is home to about 6,400 people. Elevation for both is about 5,600 feet.

History

The earliest white settlers arrived in the 1870s, bringing cattle and establishing farms where they grew fruits and vegetables—and so the largest community here acquired the appropriate name of Farmington, or farming town. The town of Aztec, on the other hand, has a completely inappropriate name. Also a farming and ranching center, it was misnamed by settlers who mistakenly believed that the ancient American Indian ruins here were built by the Aztec Indians of central Mexico, who actually lived after these structures were constructed by the Ancestral Puebloans.

Getting There

Farmington straddles US Hwy. 64, which runs east and west across the north edge of New Mexico, and US Hwy. 491, which runs north and south through the Navajo Nation from Colorado down to Gallup. Aztec, along US Hwy. 550, lies 14 miles northeast of Farmington.

Major Attraction

Aztec Ruins National Monument

One of the largest Ancestral Puebloan communities in the Southwest, this pueblo is especially interesting because it appears that it was designed as a single unit and didn't simply expand in response to a growing population, as is the case at many other prehistoric sites. This kind of planning obviously shows that the builders were part of a highly organized society. The ruins include a large excavated pueblo and an impressive reconstructed great kiva that date from the early 12th century. The name, however, is wrong. Early Anglo settlers, convinced that the ruins were of Aztec origin, named the site, but it's now known that the structures here

Ancestral Pueblo ruins at Aztec Ruins National Monument.

were built long before the Aztecs of central Mexico lived.

Anthropologists believe that two different groups of Ancestral Puebloans, or are least people with two different influences, lived here. The fine stone masonry, open plaza, and other features indicate that the site was built and initially used by people either from Chaco, 55 miles to the south, or a group strongly influenced by the Chacoans. These people built the West Ruin and some of the other structures but apparently only lived in them for a few generations in the 1100s. A later occupation, however, occurred from about 1200 to 1275. It shows signs of influence from Mesa Verde, about 40 miles northwest. This second group, which may have been a new people or simply descendents of the first group with strong influence from Mesa Verde, remodeled the old pueblo and built other structures nearby using less elaborate techniques than the Chacoans.

Aztec was deserted by 1300, and archeologists are not certain why the people left or where they went. Tree rings show that there was a drought in the late 1200s, and their farmland and other natural resources may have been depleted. Another theory is that the people here were driven out by some enemy. Legends of the Hopis and other modern tribes, however, say that these prehistoric people periodically embarked on mass migrations for spiritual reasons, and their departure from Aztec may have simply meant that it was time for them to move on. It's likely that some of the people of Aztec moved southeast and may have established or joined existing pueblos along the Rio Grande, while others went to what is now Zuni Pueblo to the south or possibly to the Hopi villages to the west.

EXPLORING THE MONUMENT

Begin at the visitor center/museum, where you'll see a 25-minute video that documents the history of prehistoric cultures in the area, as well as some outstanding examples of Ancestral Puebloan pots and baskets, with exhibits that show the differences in styles among various groups.

From there, follow the 0.25-mile trail through the West Ruin for a unique perspective on the people who lived here centuries ago, providing a peek into their daily lives. The trail is easy and partly paved, but there are some stairs and low doorways. A trail guide is available at the visitor center/museum.

The buildings here were constructed primarily of sandstone, hauled from at least a mile away, which was squared off and finished using stone tools. Ceiling beams of spruce, fir, and pine were brought from the mountains at least 20 miles away. They were covered with posts of local cottonwood and juniper, then grasses, and finally a coating of mud.

Rooms in the West Ruin are small, and some of the rooms contain wood from the original ceilings. Some rooms were entered through openings in the roof, which also let light in, while others had traditional doorways that would be covered with mats, animals skins, or blankets. Covering one doorway is an original mat made of willows stitched together with strands of yucca.

The rooms surround a courtyard that contains a great kiva, a large, circular ceremonial room. The only completely reconstructed great kiva in existence, it measures about 50 feet in diameter and its main floor is 8 feet below the outside ground level. Four huge columns support the roof, there is a raised fireplace in the center, and what may have been an altar stands in an alcove. The kiva is surrounded, at ground level, by

15 rooms, which open into the courtyard.

Because of the tremendous size of the West Ruin, archeologists at first believed that it may have been home to 1,000 people. However, some archeologists now theorize that only 200 to 300 people actually lived in the pueblo at any given time and that the pueblo's main function was as a ceremonial center. In addition, excavations have shown that many of the pueblo's 450 rooms were not living quarters per se but were used for trash dumps, storage, toilets, work areas, and burial chambers.

Located along the Animas River, with a pond just outside the national monument boundaries, Aztec is a good spot for birding. Year-round, watch for mourning doves, ring-necked pheasants, piñon jays, American robins, red-winged blackbirds, and western meadowlarks. In addition, in winter and spring you might see mallards, dark-eyed juncos, and mountain bluebirds, while in summer you're likely to spot black-chinned hummingbirds.

VISITOR INFORMATION, DIRECTIONS, AND FACTS

No camping is available. Open 8 A.M.–6 P.M. daily Memorial Day through Labor Day; 8 A.M.–5 P.M. daily the rest of the year. Closed Thanksgiving, Christmas, and New Year's Day. Small admission fee. Located 0.5 mile north of US Hwy. 516 on Ruins Rd. (CR 2900) on the north edge of the city of Aztec. **84 CR 2900, Aztec, 87410; 505-334-6174; www.nps.gov/azru.**

Festivals and Events

UFO SYMPOSIUM

mid-March. Taking place in Aztec and sponsored by the Friends of the Aztec Public Library, this weeklong event includes programs on the purported crash of a UFO north of Aztec in 1948 (nine months after the purported UFO crash in Roswell, New Mexico), plus discussions on other UFO sightings, alien abductions and encounters, and possible government cover-ups. **505-334-9890; www.aztecufo.com.**

SHIPROCK MARATHON

early May. Marathon and relay races, sanctioned by the U.S. Athletic Congress, take place on the Navajo Nation near Shiprock. **800-448-1240; 505-368-6306.**

FARMINGTON INVITATIONAL BALLOON FESTIVAL

late May. Hot air balloons launch from the banks of Farmington Lake at 6 A.M. Sat. and Sun. **800-448-1240.**

RIVERFEST

late May. This festival to celebrate the Animas Rivers includes live music, arts and crafts, river raft rides, food, riverside trail walks, and a 10K and 5K walk and run at Animas Park. **800-448-1240.**

FIESTA DAYS

early June. Taking place the weekend after Memorial Day, this festival in Aztec celebrates the arrival of summer with live music, games, lots of food, arts and crafts sales, parades, a carnival, the burning of Old Man Gloom, and sprint car races at Aztec Speedway. Most activities take place in Aztec's Pioneer Park. **888-838-9551 or 505-334-9551.**

SAN JUAN COUNTY SHERIFF'S POSSE RODEO

early June. The largest open rodeo in the state, this event includes bronc busting, bull riding, and all the usual rodeo thrills and spills. It takes place at the County Rodeo Grounds on US Hwy. 550, east of Farmington. **800-448-1240** or **505-326-4007**.

FREEDOM DAYS CELEBRATION

Fourth of July weekend. Fireworks, an outdoor concert, a food fair, street dancing, a parade, a triathlon, and other activities celebrate Independence Day. **800-448-1240**.

NATIONAL HIGH SCHOOL FINALS RODEO AND AZTEC RODEO DAY

late July. Billed as the "World's Largest Rodeo," this rodeo at McGee Park (east of Farmington) includes participants from the United States, Canada, and Australia. The town of Aztec celebrates the rodeo with live entertainment, music, dancing, children's activities, rides, food, and, of course, a rousing game of "cow patty bingo." **888-838-9551** or **505-334-9551**.

CONNIE MACK WORLD SERIES BASEBALL TOURNAMENT

early Aug. This is the big one, a full week of baseball featuring top amateur players from all over the United States and Puerto Rico. It takes place Rickett's Park in Farmington, and the pro scouts are always there. **800-448-1240** or **505-327-9673**.

SAN JUAN COUNTY FAIR

mid-Aug. Loyal boosters call this the biggest county fair in New Mexico, and they just might be right. It has exhibits, livestock shows, a parade, arts and crafts booths, a fiddlers contest, food, and more, all taking place at McGee Park, east of Farmington. **800-448-1240** or **505-325-5385**.

TOTAH FESTIVAL

late Aug. This event at the Farmington

Civic Center features a juried fine arts and craft show and sale, highlighted with an Indian rug auction and powwow. **800-448-1240**.

NATIVE AMERICAN DAYS

late Sept. A celebration of the area's history and culture with American Indian dances, music, arts and crafts, and exhibits, held at the Animas Valley Mall in Farmington. **800-448-1240** or **505-326-5465**.

ROAD APPLE RALLY

early Oct. Mountain bikers from all over the country assemble for this annual mountain-bike race and tour, which follows a 30-mile single and double loop course though the rugged but beautiful countryside near Farmington. There's also a junior version for kids and novice riders. **800-448-1240**.

SHIPROCK FAIR

early Oct. The top annual celebration for the northern half of the Navajo Nation, this event at the fairgrounds in Shiprock features a parade, rodeo, arts and crafts, a powwow, along with traditional songs and dances. **800-448-1240**.

FANTASY OF LIGHTS HOLIDAY SHOW

late Nov.–Dec. Lighted sculptures depicting holiday scenes, animals, flowers, and other displays can be seen at Riverside Park in Aztec. You can walk, drive, or take a horse-drawn carriage ride through the park. **505-334-1111**.

SAN JUAN COLLEGE LUMINARIAS

early Dec. The San Juan College campus is illuminated by 50,000 luminarias, also called *farolitos* (brown paper bags weighted down with sand and containing a candle). **800-448-1240** or **505-566-3403**.

FESTIVAL DE LOS FAROLITOS

mid-Dec. A display of traditional New Mexico lanterns lights up the Aztec Museum, Pioneer Village, Pioneer Park, and the Aztec City Complex. There is also a parade of lights along Aztec's Main Ave., plus activities including visits with Santa, horse-drawn carriage rides, and live music. **888-838-9551** or **505-334-9551**.

LIVING NATIVITY

late Dec. Native Navajo costumes and live animals are the centerpiece of the living nativity, presented by the children of the Four Corners Home for Children in Farmington. **800-448-1240** or **505-325-0255**.

Outdoor Activities

Boating and Fishing

The main outdoor activities in this area—water sports and fishing—take place primarily at an especially scenic state park.

NAVAJO LAKE STATE PARK

This large, pretty lake, with a surface area of 13,000 to 15,000 acres, is one of northwestern New Mexico's prime boating and fishing destinations, and an excellent spot for waterskiing, swimming, scuba diving, and camping. It's one of the state's most attractive lakes, with numerous narrow channels and prominent rock formations. Hillsides covered with piñon and juniper trees create a forest atmosphere, and along with the cottonwoods and willows closer to the water, provide the right habitat to attract a variety of wildlife. Just below Navajo Dam, the San Juan River is one of America's best trout fishing waters.

Located at the base of the San Juan Mountains at an elevation of 6,100 feet,

the lake has almost 150 miles of shoreline, and at full capacity is 35 miles long. It is the only major lake shared by New Mexico and Colorado, with New Mexico claiming 80 percent of its surface area. Fed primarily by mountain snowmelt, the lake was born in 1962 with the construction of the earth- and rock-filled Navajo Dam that stands 400 feet high and is almost 0.75 mile long.

There are four recreation sites on the lake and one along the San Juan River. Two of the lake sites—Pine and Sims Mesa—and the San Juan River site comprise New Mexico's developed sections of Navajo Lake State Park. Another site in New Mexico, near the Colorado border—Miller/Sambrito—is operated by a concessionaire and offers primitive camping only. The one site in Colorado is in a different Navajo State Park, operated by the Colorado State Park system.

All types of boats are welcome on the lake, and there are several no-wake and no skiing sections. The upper end, near the state line, is particularly popular for sailing. The lake's two marinas offer boat rentals—mostly ski boats, personal watercraft, and houseboats—and there are boat ramps and courtesy docks.

The lake's clear water is especially good for swimming and scuba diving, and the water temperature usually warms into the 70s by mid-July. Although there are no designated swimming areas and much of the shoreline is rocky, there are a number of sandy beaches, particularly when the lake level is low. Some of the small beaches accessible only by boat are especially pleasant.

Anglers catch huge kokanee salmon, plus rainbow and brown trout, channel catfish, crappie, northern pike, bluegill, and both largemouth and smallmouth bass. The lake does not freeze, and fishing is good year-round. The San Juan River is considered one of America's top

115

10 trout-fishing waters. A section of the river for 6 miles south of the dam is in the state park, flowing through a scenic sandstone canyon. The river's first 3.75 miles from the dam is listed as a "special trout water," with stringent requirements and limits, including only one trout, at least 20 inches, in possession at any time. There is also a 0.25-mile section of the river that is catch-and-release only. There are four wheelchair-accessible fishing piers along the river.

An easy hiking trail runs for about 1.5 miles (one-way) along the north side of the San Juan River, and a number of paths lead to popular fishing spots along the river and the lake.

The best wildlife viewing is in the San Juan River section of the park. This is where you'll have a good chance of seeing bald eagles, as well as mallards, cinnamon teal, blue-winged teal, osprey, common mergansers, piñon jays, and violet-green swallows. Canada geese

All types of boats are welcome on Navajo Lake.

sometimes nest in the rocks above the river. Late fall through early spring offers the best bird-watching. Seen throughout the park are Colorado chipmunks, recognized by the white stripes on their faces and backs, black-tailed jackrabbits, and deer mice. The park is also home to mule deer, elk, bobcats, muskrats, beaver, raccoons, rock squirrels, and porcupines. Southern plateau lizards—about 2 inches long, brown, with striped markings along their flanks—are seen in summer, perched on sandstone ledges in the canyons.

The park's two lake camping areas—Sims Mesa and Pine—are forested, offering a bit of shade plus good views of the lake. Primitive lakeshore camping is also permitted, and you can also sleep on your boat or rent a houseboat. The Cottonwood Campground, on the San Juan River, is set in a large cottonwood grove, and is within easy walking distance of several good fishing spots. All told there are 248 campsites, including 89 with electric hookups and 9 with electric, water, and sewer hookups. There are restrooms with showers and a RV dump station.

Navajo Lake State Park is roughly located 25 miles east of Bloomfield via US Hwy. 64 and New Mexico 511, but its developed areas are spread out around the lake. The Pine site is the most developed, with a visitor center and park offices, and is located 0.5-mile north of the dam on New Mexico 511. The more remote Sims Mesa site is within sight of Pine across the lake, but its road access takes you about 42 miles, heading first east of the dam about 25 miles on NM 511 and NM 539 and US Hwy. 64, and then northwest for another 17 miles on NM 527 to Sims Mesa. The San Juan River site runs for about 6 miles along the river below the dam, and is accessed from NM 511 and

173. Day-use and camping fees are charged. **1448 NM 511, #1, Navajo Dam, 87419; 505-632-2278; www.nmparks.com.**

Golf

HIDDEN VALLEY GOLF CLUB

The area's newest course—opened in 2001—Hidden Valley is a regulation 18-hole public course with lovely rolling hills. It is best known for having fairly easy fairways but unforgiving greens. Open year-round, weather permitting. **29 CR 3025, Aztec; 888-323-9444; 505-334-3248.**

PIÑON HILLS GOLF COURSE

Considered one of the best municipal golf courses in the United States, this challenging and reasonably priced 18-hole course makes excellent use of the natural terrain and has beautifully manicured greens. Open year-round, weather permitting. **2101 Sunrise Pkwy., Farmington; 505-326-6066.**

Hiking

ANGEL PEAK SCENIC AREA

Sitting at the base of 6,998-foot Angel Peak, this scenic recreation area offers a variety of unusual and colorful rock formations, with opportunities for hiking among the formations and through several canyons. There is one short designated hiking trail, but plenty of other hiking opportunities and an especially scenic designated overlook. There is also a picnic area, with tables and grills, vault toilets, and a small, free primitive campground. There is no drinking water. Located about 30 miles southeast of Farmington via US Hwy. 64, NM 550, and a 6-mile dirt access road. **Bureau of Land Management, 1235 La Plata Hwy., Ste. A,** Farmington, 87401; 505-599-8900; www.nm.blm.gov.

BISTI/DE-NA-ZIN WILDERNESS

This badlands, south of Farmington in the middle of nowhere, is a good example of the power of erosion, and depending on your point of view is either a desolate and unfriendly lunar landscape or a fanciful land of unique geologic features. Either way, you'll discover a remote and primitive area where you're almost guaranteed to be alone, with no roads or designated trails, no visitor centers, no fees, and no drinking water. Activities here are primarily hiking and backpacking. Horseback riding is also permitted. The Bisti section is fairly easy to get to and receives the most visitors. It has fairly easy hiking by following the washes and is the best place to see hoodoos—those often colorful statues carved from stone by wind and water erosion. The De-Na-Zin section is more of a challenge to access   don't even think of going in rainy weather—and receives far fewer visitors. It is also more rugged, so your hike will involve more climbing and you'll need to be more careful not to get lost here. Throughout the 45,000-acre wilderness, watch for petrified wood and fossils that date from the Age of Dinosaurs.

As a designated wilderness area, all vehicles, including mountain bikes, are prohibited. Also forbidden are fires of any kind, climbing on the geologic formations, collecting fossils and petrified wood, or hiking in groups of more than eight people. Summers here are hot, and there is practically no shade, so spring and fall are the most popular times to hike. Hikers should carry plenty of water at any time.

To get to the Bisti section from Farmington, go south on NM 371 for about 37 miles, then turn left (east) onto CR

7297, a dirt road that you follow 2 miles to a parking area. To get to the De-Na-Zin section, continue south about 8 more miles from the Bisti turnoff to CR 7500, a dirt road that is often impassable in wet weather. Follow this road east about a dozen or so miles to a parking area; the road then continues about a dozen more miles to intersect with NM 550. **Bureau of Land Management, 1235 La Plata Hwy., Ste. A, Farmington, 87401; 505-599-8900; www.nm.blm.gov.**

Seeing and Doing

Archeological Site

SALMON RUINS AND HERITAGE PARK

Here you can see the remains of a large structure built by the Chaco people in the 11th century, and a museum displays prehistoric Ancestral Puebloan pottery, arrows, shell and turquoise beads, macaw feathers, plus Navajo and Spanish colonial items. Heritage Park contains reconstructed dwellings from the period of human habitation in the area, including a pit house from the Basketmaker period, a Jicarilla Apache teepee, Navajo hogan, and a historic trading post. Also on the grounds are the remains of the pioneer homestead of George Salmon, for whom the site is named. Open 8 A.M.–5 P.M. daily, noon–5 P.M. Sun. Nov.–Mar. A small admission fee is charged. Located about 12 miles east of Farmington. **6131 US Hwy. 64, P.O. Box 125, Bloomfield, 87413; 505-632-2013.**

Auto Racing

AZTEC SPEEDWAY

Races take place most Saturdays from Apr. through Sept. and feature street stocks, hobby stocks, modifieds, sprints, and various other types of race cars. To really see them get down and dirty, check the schedule for the mud bogs. An admission fee is charged. **Located 1 mile south of Aztec on NM 544; 505-334-2023; www.aztecspeedway.com.**

Museums and Historic Buildings

AZTEC MUSEUM AND PIONEER VILLAGE

The best place for an introduction of northwestern New Mexico history, this fine museum presents a wide variety of displays, ranging from fossils and minerals to ladies' fashions of the early 20th century. There are American Indian and pioneer artifacts, Aztec's first barbershop—with bathing facilities, of course—plus sleighs and wagons and an extensive exhibit on the region's oil drilling history, which dates to 1911. The complex also includes a pioneer village consisting of about a dozen structures, most furnished with antiques, either relocated from surrounding areas or reproductions of typical buildings from the area's past. It includes the community church, built in 1906, complete with the original pulpit, pews, piano, and hymnals; a log cabin built in 1880; the Aztec jail, constructed in 1912; and reproductions of a one-room schoolhouse, a farmhouse, doctor's office, and a blacksmith shop.

From mid-June through mid-Sept., local residents dress up in pioneer garb to perform a somewhat light-hearted shoot-out, based on a real gunfight that occurred between the local law and an outlaw gang back in Aztec's wilder days. Called the "High Noon Shoot-out," the performances take place at the museum Mon. through Sat. at noon. The museum also has a gift shop and is a good place to begin a walking tour of historic Aztec; ask for a copy of the Aztec Historical Walking Tour Guide. The museum is open 9 A.M.–5 P.M. Mon.–Sat. in summer, 10 A.M.–4 P.M. Mon.–Sat. the rest of the year. A small admission fee is charged. **125 N. Main Ave., Aztec, 87410; 505-334-9829; www.aztecnm.com/ museum/museum_index.htm.**

BOLACK MUSEUM OF FISH AND WILDLIFE AND BOLACK ELECTROMECHANICAL MUSEUM

The Museum of Fish and Wildlife displays a large collection of mounted animals from around the world, while the Electromechanical Museum contains a collection of items relating to electric power, communications, oil field equipment, and farming. Tours by appointment, on the hour, 9 A.M.–3 P.M. Mon.–Sat. **3901 Bloomfield Hwy. (US Hwy. 64), Farmington, 87401; 505-325-4275.**

E3 CHILDREN'S MUSEUM & SCIENCE CENTER

Lots of hands-on activities involving scientific subjects such as dinosaurs, magnetism, kaleidoscopes, sound and light, as well as art, make this a favorite of kids of all ages. One room—Tot's Turf—is designed especially for children 5 and younger. Special activities, such as an afternoon of creating paper airplanes and performances, are scheduled periodically. E3 is open noon–5 P.M. Tues.–Sat. **302 N. Orchard Ave., Farmington, 87401; 505-599-1425; www.farmingtonmuseum.org.**

FARMINGTON MUSEUM

Operated by and housed in the same building as the Farmington Convention & Visitors Bureau, this museum has permanent exhibits on local history and culture, including historic photographs and some great-looking cowboy garb, plus changing exhibits and art shows. It also schedules lectures, demonstrations, and other special events and has a good museum store. Open 8 A.M.–5 P.M. Mon.–Sat. **3041 E. Main St., Farmington, 87402; 505-599-1174; www.farmingtonmuseum.org.**

Other Sites

FOUR CORNERS MONUMENT

The only spot in the United States where you can physically be in four states at once, this Navajo Tribal Park, with the Colorado section owned by the Ute Mountain tribe, contains a flat monument that marks the exact spot where New Mexico, Colorado, Utah, and Arizona meet. The official seals of the four states are displayed, along with the motto "Four states here meet in freedom under God," and around the monument are the flags of the four states, the Navajo Nation and Ute tribes, and the United States. Pose the kids with one foot in Colorado, another in Utah, and their hands in Arizona and New Mexico.

There's a Navajo Nation visitor center, a variety of American Indian crafts for

Four Corners Monument, where you can be in four states at the same time.

sale, and frequent craft demonstrations. In addition, traditional Navajo food is sold, such as fry bread. Open daily 7 A.M.–7 P.M. in summer, shorter hours at other times. A small admission fee is charged. The monument is located 0.5 mile northwest of US Hwy. 160, about 60 miles northwest of Farmington. **Navajo Parks and Recreation Department, P.O. Box 2520, Window Rock, AZ 86515; 928-871-6647; www.navajonationparks.org.**

SHIPROCK PEAK

Visible for miles in all directions, this huge rock formation—igneous rock flanked by long walls of solidified lava—resembles, you guessed it, a ship. (At least it did to the Anglo settlers who named it.) On the other hand, its Navajo name of *Tse Bitai* translates to "rock with wings." The formation towers 1,700 feet above the plain (7,178 feet above sea level) southwest of the town of Shiprock, which is about 30 miles west of Farmington via US Hwy. 64. There are viewpoints along US Hwy. 491.

Where to Stay

Accommodations

INNS AND BED-AND-BREAKFASTS

Casa Blanca Inn—$$–$$$$

This bed-and-breakfast inn provides a touch of elegance and luxury you might not expect to find in this rugged section of New Mexico. Located in a quiet residential neighborhood in a mission-style home dating from the 1950s, Casa Blanca has three guest rooms and a suite in the main house, ranging from a small room with queen-size four-poster bed, a bathroom with shower only, and a

pleasant garden view to a suite that includes the entire second story of the building, with a king-size bed with an ornate wrought-iron headboard, a private sun porch, a large full bathroom, and a sitting room with two sofa sleepers. There is also a casita, which has two rooms (one with a jetted tub) that can be rented together or separately, and a separate cottage that accommodates up to six with two bedrooms, a living room, a full kitchen, a laundry room, a sun porch, and a patio. A full homemade breakfast is included in the rates. **505 E. La Plata St., Farmington 87401; 800-550-6503; 505-327-6503; www.4cornersbandb.com.**

Step Back Inn—$$$

An attractive, modern hotel built in the style of 100-year-old Victorian inns, the Step Back Inn has very successfully blended modern amenities and comfort with historic ambiance. The 39 rooms are large and quiet, and each is named for an early pioneer of the area. Each room has a queen-size bed, recliner, telephone, TV hidden in an armoire, and sauna shower in the bathroom (no tub). Included in the rates is a breakfast of hot and cold beverages and a huge fresh-baked cinnamon roll. **103 W. Aztec Blvd., Aztec, 87410; 505-334-1200.**

MOTELS

Anasazi Inn—$$

This is a well-maintained, older independent motel with a 1950s' feel but no swimming pool; 68 units. **903 W. Main St., Farmington, 87401; 505-325-4564.**

Best Western Inn & Suites—$$$

Attractive, modern motel with an indoor heated pool, sauna, and whirlpool. Small pets accepted (fee). An on-site restaurant serves three meals daily; 192 units. **700 Scott Ave.,**

Farmington, 87401; 800-528-1234;
505-327-5221.

Comfort Inn—$$

There's a heated outdoor pool and pets
are accepted (fee); 79 units. **555 Scott
Ave., Farmington, 87401; 800-228-
5150; 505-325-2626.**

Days Inn—$$

A basic, well-maintained motel that accepts
pets (deposit) but does not have a pool; 63
units. **1901 E. Broadway, Farmington,
87401; 800-329-7466; 505-325-3700.**

Enchantment Lodge—$$

This small, independent roadside motel
dates to the 1950s. It is well maintained and
has been updated without losing its nostalgic 1950s' charm. There's a small, heated
outdoor swimming pool; 20 units. **1800 W.
Aztec Blvd., Aztec, 87410; 800-847-
2194 (reservations); 505-334-6143.**

Holiday Inn—$$$

An upscale property with a heated outdoor pool, sauna, and whirlpool; pets
accepted (fee). 148 units. **600 E.
Broadway, Farmington, 87401; 800-
HOLIDAY; 505-327-9811.**

121

Visiting the Navajo Nation

On a 27,000-square-mile reservation stretching across Arizona and New Mexico
with a bit of Utah thrown in lives the nation's largest American Indian tribe—the
Navajo Nation, with a population of more than 250,000. Famed photographer
Laura Gilpin, one of the earliest to write about and photograph the Navajo
people, called them "enduring Navajo," and they certainly are that.

In many ways, the Navajo Nation government resembles the U.S. federal
government. Navajos govern themselves from their reservation headquarters in
Window Rock, Arizona. Most of their chapter houses—along with much of their
past—are based in New Mexico. Their land is beautiful, from the harsh rock
canyons to the cool pines, from the dry arroyos to the trout streams.

It is believed that the Navajo people came across the Bering Land Bridge
from Asia. At that time the Apache and Navajo were one tribe. As they moved
down to warmer climes, the two tribes became separated, and there are now
great differences between them.

Across the Navajo Nation are a variety of tribal parks and monuments,
historical sites, and good fishing lakes. Many Navajo are expert weavers, and
Navajo blankets and rugs are not only sold in trading posts and shops, but are displayed in the country's finest museums. The Navajo people are also skilled silversmiths, creating excellent silver and turquoise jewelry, and fairly recently have also
become well known as potters, turning out excellent jugs, jars, and trays.

The Navajo language is beyond comprehension for most outsiders, and this
made it indispensable during World War II. Navajo Code Talkers in the Pacific used
their native language as the basis for a code in talking by radio with other Navajos,
and the Japanese could never figure it out.

If you want to learn more about the Navajo Nation before you visit, contact
**Navajo Tourism, P.O. Box 663, Window Rock, AZ 86515; 928-871-6436;
www.discovernavajo.com.**

Northwest Region

La Quinta—$$–$$$

A small outdoor heated pool and video rental make this a good choice for those traveling with kids. Small pets accepted; 106 units. **675 Scott Ave., Farmington, 87401; 800-531-5900 or 505-327-4706.**

Super 8—$$

A reliable chain motel with a game room but no pool. Pets are accepted (fee); 60 units. **1601 E. Broadway, Farmington, 87401; 800-800-8000; 505-325-1813.**

Travelodge—$$–$$$

Outdoor heated pool and a 24-hour restaurant next door; 98 rooms. **510 Scott Ave., Farmington, 87401; 800-578-7878 or 505-327-0242.**

Campgrounds

In addition to the commercial campgrounds discussed below, you'll find several delightful, shady campgrounds at Navajo Lake State Park and a small primitive campground at Angel Peak Scenic Area. Both of these public lands are discussed above, under Outdoor Activities.

DOWNS RV PARK

No pool, but everything else you expect at a modern commercial campground, including clean bathhouses and a coin-op laundry. There are also some shade trees. Thirty-three sites have full hookups, and there are tent/no hookup RV sites. **5701 US Hwy. 64, Farmington, 87401; 800-582-6427; 505-325-7094.**

KOA KAMPGROUND

In the town of Bloomfield, about 15 miles east of Farmington along US Hwy. 64, this member of the well-respected KOA chain offers 75 spaces with full hookups, a heated outdoor swimming pool, whirlpool, game room, coin-operated laundry, clean bathhouse, store, and

cable TV and modem hookups. Convenient to Navajo Lake and to the stream fishing below Navajo Dam, it also has Kamping Kabins, which share the campground's bathhouses. Open year-round. **1900 E. Blanco Blvd., Bloomfield, 87413; 800-562-8513; 505-632-8339.**

MOM & POPS RV PARK

Located right in Farmington, there are all the usual commercial campground amenities except a swimming pool, but you will find a large-scale outdoor electric train layout. There are 35 paved sites with full hookups, and tent sites are also available. No shade trees. **901 Illinois Ave., Farmington, 87401; 505-327-3200.**

RIVER GROVE TRAILER PARK

Twenty-nine spaces with full hookups, located in town along the Animas River, with some nice shade trees. No pool. **801 E. Broadway, Farmington, 87401; 505-327-0974.**

Where to Eat

The Hiway Grill—$–$$

Want to fill up the kids (and yourself) at something other than a fast-food joint without breaking the bank? This full-service restaurant has been a favorite of the Aztec locals since 1951 and offers all the usual American favorites. There's a good kids menu and also a bar and package store. Open Mon.–Thurs. 11 A.M.–9 P.M.; Fri.–Sat. 11 A.M.–10 P.M. **401 NE Aztec Blvd., Aztec; 505-334-6533.**

K.B. Dillons—$$–$$$

A noisy, fun spot where you won't go away hungry, this restaurant and bar features an American menu with southwestern touches, such as the chicken with green chile. You'll also find plenty of sandwiches, burgers, steaks, and seafood on the menu. The atmosphere is rustic, dark, and sometimes smoky—quite appropriate for an Old West saloon. Open Mon.–Fri. 11 A.M.–10 P.M.; Sat. 5–10 P.M. Closed major holidays. **101 W. Broadway, Farmington; 505-325-0222.**

Los Hermanitos Restaurant—$$-$$$

Probably the best Mexican restaurant in this part of the state—serving New Mexico–style Mexican dishes—Los Hermanitos is owned and operated by Sam and Cathy Gonzales, who serve some of their favorite family recipes as well as a wide selection of other spicy dishes, from tacos to burritos to fajitas. Among house specialties is the carne adobada—thin slices of pork marinated in a hot red chile sauce—and the chile rellenos, smothered with either red or green chile and served with rice and beans. The dining room is furnished with hand-carved Southwest–style furniture and decorated with a large, colorful mural showing Farmington's southwestern heritage. Open Mon.–Sat. 7 A.M.–9 P.M. **3501 E. Main St., Middle Fork Square, Farmington; 505-326-5664; www.loshermanitos.com.**

River's Edge Café—$$$

An upscale restaurant that specializes in fine continental cuisine, the River's Edge offers a good selection of steaks, pasta, Mexican dishes, and seafood; especially noteworthy is the pan-seared salmon.

There's also a very good breakfast buffet. Smoking is not permitted. Open daily 6:30–10 A.M., 11 A.M.–2 P.M., 5–7 P.M. Located in the Courtyard by Marriott. **560 Scott Ave., Farmington; 505-325-5111.**

Three Rivers Brewhouse & Eatery—$$-$$$

Located in a building that dates to 1912, this brewery offers all the usual brewpub standards—great burgers, steaks, fish and chips, and the like—plus about a dozen handcrafted beers and seven homemade sodas. There's also a patio for dining outside, but we like being inside where we can read all the old advertising posters while waiting for our grub. Open daily 10 A.M.–9 P.M. **101 E. Main St., Farmington; 505-324-2187.**

Services

Visitor Information

Farmington Convention & Visitors Bureau, 3041 E. Main St., Farmington, 87402; 505-326-7602; 800-448-1240; www.farmingtonnm.org. It operates a visitor center in the Farmington Museum (see page 119).

Aztec Chamber of Commerce & Visitors Center, 110 N. Ash St., Aztec, 87410; 505-334-9551; 888-838-9551; www.aztecnm.com.

CHACO CULTURE NATIONAL HISTORICAL PARK

A trip to Chaco Culture National Historical Park is a journey to another time and place, to the prehistoric world of the Ancestral Puebloans, the people who dominated the Four Corners area more than 1,000 years ago. This remote park offers not just another ruin, but a feeling for the immensity of what we now call the Chacoan culture, a link with a distant past that provides an awe-inspiring look into the very center of a remarkable civilization.

Some 1,200 years ago, the Ancestral Puebloans of Chaco began a massive building project. Instead of simply starting with a few small rooms and adding more as the need arose, as was usual at the time, the Chacoans constructed massive stone buildings of multiple stories. More significant, though, is that these buildings show evidence of skillful planning. Obviously, a central government was in charge.

Within a century, six large pre-planned public buildings, or "great houses," were underway. New communities, each consisting of a large central building surrounded by smaller villages, sprang up, and established villages followed the trend by adding large public and ceremonial buildings. Eventually there were more than 150 such communities, most of them closely tied to Chaco by an extensive system of roads and shared culture.

By A.D. 1000, Chaco had become the center of commerce, ceremony, and culture for the area, with as many as 5,000 people living in some 400 settlements. As masonry techniques advanced, walls rose more than four stories high. Some of these remain standing today and are among the most impressive structures you'll see at Chaco. Artifacts found at Chaco, including shell necklaces, turquoise, copper bells, and the remains of Mexican parrots, indicate that Chacoan trade routes stretched from the California coast to Texas and south into Mexico.

You can't see them from the ground, but get up in a plane and you'll spot hundreds of miles of roads connecting the outlying settlements with the large buildings at Chaco. These communities appear to have been established along the roads at travel intervals of one day. Not simply trails worn into the stone by foot travel, these were carefully engineered roadways 30 feet wide, with a low wall of rock to contain the fill. Where the road went over flat rock, walls were built along the edges. This road network leads some scholars to believe that Chaco was the center of a widespread but unified society.

The decline and abandonment of Chaco in the 12th century coincided with a drought in the area, although archeologists are not certain that this was the only or even the major reason that the site was eventually abandoned. Some argue that an influx of outsiders may have brought new rituals to the region, causing a schism among tribal members. A relatively recent (and controversial) theory maintains that cannibalism existed at Chaco, practiced either by the Ancestral Puebloans themselves or by invaders, such as the Toltecs of Mexico.

Even though archeologists do not agree on why Chaco Canyon was abandoned, they generally concur that the Chacoans descendants live among today's

Pueblo people of the Four Corners region who consider Chaco a sacred area.

Exploring the Park

A paved one-way loop road of about 9 miles winds from the visitor center through Chaco Canyon, providing access to five self-guiding trails that lead into Chaco's major sites, and there is also one trail from the visitor center. Trail guides are available at the visitor center and at the sites; allow about an hour for each trail. The park also has four longer backcountry trails. Elevation is about 6,200 feet.

A must-see for every Chaco visitor is impressive Pueblo Bonito (Spanish for "beautiful town"), which is believed to have been the largest structure in the Chacoan system, as well as the largest prehistoric dwelling ever excavated in the Southwest. Covering more than 3 acres, it contains about 800 rooms surrounding two plazas, in which there were over two dozen kivas. The easy trail through Pueblo Bonito is 0.6 mile round-trip.

Other ruin sites accessible directly from the loop road include Chetro Ketl, which had about 500 rooms, 16 kivas, and an impressive enclosed plaza. It's accessed via an easy 0.6-mile round-trip trail with a few steep portions.

Pueblo del Arroyo was a four-story, D-shaped structure with about 280 rooms and 20 kivas, which is seen on an easy 0.25-mile round-trip walk. Casa Rinconada is reached on a 0.5-mile round-trip trail that has loose gravel and a few steep sections. The largest Great Kiva in the park, Casa Rinconada is astronomically aligned to the four compass points and the summer solstice. It may have been a center for the community at large, used for major religious observances.

Una Vida, a short walk from the visitor center, was one of the first of the Chacoan buildings to be built and has been only partially excavated. Considered a "great house," it had 150 rooms and five kivas, including a Great Kiva. A 1-mile round-trip walk, rocky with steep sections, includes a stop at Una Vida and a side trip to several petroglyph sites.

Hungo Pavi, which is just off the roadway via a short walk, is another of Chaco's "great houses." It contained about 150 rooms, and rose up three stories in places.

The following backcountry trails lead to a number of additional archeological sites. Those hiking into the backcountry should first obtain free permits at the visitor center and should also wear good hiking boots and take drinking water.

The 5.4-mile round-trip Pueblo Alto Trail climbs up the canyon rim and offers panoramic views of Pueblo Bonito and other sites as it leads to several prehistoric structures. This moderate trail gains about 350 feet. The easy to moderate Penasco Blanco Trail gains 150 feet elevation in its 6.4 miles round-trip. It leads to some of the oldest structures at

Chaco Culture National Historical Park, originally settled by Ancestral Puebloans more than 1,000 years ago.

Chaco and also affords views of a large number of petroglyphs, with a side trail to a pictograph.

South Mesa Trail, which leads to Tsin Kletsin, is moderate to difficult, climbing 450 feet over its 4.1-mile loop. With the highest elevation of any Chaco Canyon trails, it provides panoramic vistas as well as myriad spring and summer wildflowers.

Wijiji, which is open to both hikers and bikers, is fairly easy, with virtually no elevation change over its 3 miles round-trip. This route follows an old ranch road to ruins of a pueblo built about A.D. 1100 and a small pictograph panel. A longer excursion for those with bikes is the Kin Klizhin Trail, a 23.8-mile round-trip ride that follows a dirt road (occasionally used by motor vehicles) to the ruins of one of Chaco's outlying sites. The name is Navajo for "black house," so-called because of the dark stones that were used in this building's construction.

There is a surprising amount of wildlife at Chaco, considering its harsh landscape and lack of water. You are quite likely to see white-tailed antelope squirrels, and watch for desert cottontails, black-tailed jackrabbits, prairie dogs, gray foxes, deer, coyotes, and bobcats. Birds often seen here include western meadowlarks, mountain chickadees, western bluebirds, white-crowned sparrows, canyon towhees, killdeer, scaled quail, rock and canyon wrens, Say's phoebes, turkey vultures, and golden eagles.

Those visiting Pueblo Alto and Chetro Ketl have a good chance of spotting collared lizards, which can grow to more than a foot long and are named for their black-and-white collars over their mostly yellowish or yellow-green bodies. Harmless bull snakes are commonly seen in and near the ruins, but hikers should be especially careful to avoid the poisonous prairie rattlesnake, which frequents the backcountry.

Camping

Because the park is big and not really close to anything, you may want to spend a few days. Like most of the park, Gallo Campground is out in the open with little shade. Its 48 campsites have fire grates (bring your own wood or charcoal) and tables. Central toilets are available, but there is no drinking water in the campground—the visitor center is the only place in the park to obtain water. The campground cannot accommodate trailers and motor homes longer than 30 feet.

Visitor Information, Directions, and Facts

The visitor center has exhibits on the Chacoan culture and construction of this prehistoric city, in addition to artifacts discovered here during excavations. A video program tells about the Ancestral Puebloans. During the summer, rangers lead guided hikes and walks and also present evening campfire programs and astronomy programs. Both entrance and camping fees are charged. The visitor center is open 8 A.M.–6 P.M. in summer, with shorter hours the rest of the year; trails and archeological sites open daily sunrise to sunset. To get to the park from Farmington, take US Hwy. 550 south about 55 miles, then follow signs the remaining 21 miles (5 miles paved, 16 miles graded dirt). The park is 148 miles northwest of Albuquerque. Take I-25 north to Bernalillo exit 242, follow US Hwy. 550 northwest about 112 miles to the signed turnoff (left), and head south about 21 miles (5 miles paved, 16 miles dirt). **P.O. Box 220, Nageezi, 87037-0220; 505-786-7014; www.nps.gov/chcu.**

GALLUP

The first major community in New Mexico that travelers from the west get to after crossing the Arizona–New Mexico border, Gallup sits along Interstate 40 Historic Route 66 and even gained some national attention when the town was mentioned in the popular song "(Get Your Kicks on) Route 66," made famous by Nat King Cole and other singers from the late 1940s into the 1960s. Gallup's main claim to fame today, though, is as the site of the annual Inter-Tribal Indian Ceremonial, which takes place each Aug., attracting tribes from throughout North America. The town is also a shopping center for the Navajo Nation to the north and the Zuni Pueblo to the south, and it is a good spot to buy silver and turquoise jewelry and other American Indian crafts.

Gallup, at 6,468 feet elevation, offers a good home base for fishing in the vast Navajo Indian Reservation. With Grants, Gallup shares the privilege of being the gateway to Zuni Pueblo, El Morro and El Malpais National Monuments, as well as Bandera Volcano and the Ice Caves.

History

A fairly young city, Gallup was the pay station for construction workers on the Atlantic and Pacific Railroad, and it took its name from the paymaster, David L. Gallup. People talked about going to Gallup to get paid, and the name stuck. It was organized as a village in 1881, but the Western Overland Stage stopped here even before 1880. In this quiet frontier village, most residents wore their "shooting irons"—until a municipal ordinance stopped that in 1896.

The railroad was a mainstay of the economy for decades, along with the mining of the huge coal deposits that underlay so much of this country. Today, a big sheep-processing facility, oil refineries, and lumbering provide a solid base for Gallup, in addition to the growing tourism industry.

Getting There

Gallup sits along I-40, 22 miles east of the New Mexico–Arizona line. NM 264 goes north and then west for those heading to Window Rock, Arizona, the government seat of the huge Navajo Nation. NM 264 also connects with US Hwy. 491, which leads north to Shiprock—both the large rock formation and the town—with access via US Hwy. 64 to Farmington, and then into Colorado and Utah.

Major Attraction

Zuni Pueblo

The earliest Spanish explorers found their way to Zuni Pueblo, first thinking it was one of the fabled (but nonexistent) Seven Cities of Gold and then tried to bring the Zunis Christianity. The Zuni people were not impressed with this new religion, and two Spanish missionary priests were killed. Eventually the Zunis came to tolerate the newcomers, but even to this day they remain somewhat apart from the white man's ways and zealously guard their own religious rites. In a brochure published by the tribal government, the Zunis state: "We are considered the most traditional of all the New Mexico pueblos, with a unique language, culture, and history that resulted in part from our geographic isolation."

The largest of New Mexico's 19 Indian pueblos, Zuni covers more than 600 square miles with more than 11,000 residents. They have long been famed for their ability to fashion lovely jewelry from turquoise and silver, and their jewelry and other crafts are for sale to an ever-increasing flow of tourists. It is estimated by tribal authorities that 80 percent of Zuni households are involved some way in arts and crafts.

Start your visit to Zuni Pueblo at the Visitor Information Center, located in the Pueblo of Zuni Arts and Crafts Building, 1222 E. NM 53, as you enter the pueblo from the east. Here you'll learn about the pueblo's history, what you can see and do here, where to go for pueblo crafts, and the rules for visiting the pueblo, such as not photographing religious ceremonies.

Your visit will likely include stopping in the oldest part of the town, where the distinctive mission church faces a courtyard crowded with the crosses of Zunis who died in the church. This is also where you can see inspiring murals of Zuni ceremonial figures. There is also a community museum and numerous shops and galleries where you'll often find silversmiths, jewelry makers, pottery makers, and other artists busy at their crafts.

Several lakes have good fishing. Zuni permits, in addition to New Mexico State fishing licenses, are required; contact the **Pueblo of Zuni Fish and Wildlife Office; 505-782-5851.**

Open daily 9 A.M.–5:30 P.M.; closed New Year's Day, Thanksgiving, Christmas, and tribal holidays. Located about 30 miles south of Gallup via NM 602 and NM 53. **P.O. Box 339, Zuni, 87327; 505-782-7238; www.experiencezuni.com.**

The Devil Made Them Do It

If you're cruising northwestern New Mexico with an older map—probably anything published before 2004—you might be a bit confused. It seems that one of the major U.S. highways in this region, which runs from Gallup north through the Navajo Nation into Colorado and then into Utah, has had a sudden name change. On June 2, 2003, US Hwy. 666 officially became US Hwy. 491.

Why did the federal government, three states, and the Navajo Nation conspire to mess up thousands upon thousands of maps and help countless motorists lose their way? The Devil made them do it.

The road, which covers 190 miles, has been known as the "Devil's Highway" because, according to the Bible, the number 666 is the number of the Beast or the Antichrist. In addition, for years it has been one of the most dangerous roads in New Mexico. State highway department officials say the road has a high number of accidents because of poor design and a high rate of drunk driving in the area, but some people insist that the blame was with its number.

Whatever the cause of the traffic accidents, there is no doubt that the satanic implications of US Hwy. 666 frightened some residents living along the road and also made the road signs a target of thieves.

Festivals and Events

GALLUP LIONS CLUB RODEO

mid-June. No doubt this is cowboy country. This event, which began in the late 1940s and takes place at Red Rock State Park, includes all the usual rodeo thrills and spills, plus a parade, old-time fiddlers' contest, and a barbecue. **800-242-4282; 505-863-3841; www.gallupnm.org.**

INTER-TRIBAL
INDIAN CEREMONIAL

mid-Aug. The biggest annual event in Gallup, the ceremonial was established in 1922 and now attracts members from more than 30 tribes from across North America for dance competitions and performances, parades, rodeos, and other sporting events. Marketplaces are filled with Navajo rugs, Hopi kachinas, jewelry, pottery, basketry and beadwork, paintings, sculpture, and other American Indian arts and crafts. There is also a competition held for Miss Indian America.

For many, the biggest attractions are the ceremonial dances, resplendent with the most beautiful costumes and offering greater variety than you can expect to see anywhere else in the world. In addition, afternoon performances give the amateur photographer a better chance to record the dances and the costumes by natural light. Most of the activities take place at Red Rock State Park. From I-40 exit 26, go east 2 miles on the frontage road, and then follow signs to the park. **Gallup Inter-Tribal Indian Ceremonial Association, 226 W. Coal Ave., Gallup, 87301; 888-685-2564; 505-863-3896.**

RED ROCK BALLOON RALLY

early Dec. Hot air balloonists come from around the country for this event, filling the skies above Red Rock State Park with colorful balloons. **505-722-0463; 505-722-6274.**

Outdoor Activities

Fishing

The sprawling Navajo Indian Reservation ends just 9 miles north of Gallup, and the southern part of the reservation holds some of its most scenic areas. In addition, there is good fishing for trout and other species on several waters of the reservation. Follow US Hwy. 491 north past Yah-tah-hey and you'll find several fishing lakes that offer good rainbow trout fishing, including Chuska, Asaayi, and Whiskey. The waters of the Navajo Reservation remain well stocked with trout from federal fish hatcheries.

One-day, two-day, and season-long permits are available from the Navajo. The Navajos also put out a regular fishing report, which gives an accurate picture of the current fishing chances. And they tell it like it is: if fishing is slow at a particular lake or if the lake level is too low, they'll tell you so. For more information, contact the **Navajo Fish and Wildlife Department, P.O. Box 1480, Window Rock, AZ 86515; 928- 871-6451; 928-871-6452; www.navajofishandwildlife.org**. Remember, you'll also need a New Mexico fishing license.

There are also fishing opportunities at Zuni Pueblo; see the Major Attraction section.

Golf

GALLUP MUNICIPAL GOLF COURSE

You won't be traveling to Gallup specifically to golf, but if you feel like a round or two while here, head to this inexpensive public course, with all the usual amenities, in a desert setting. Open year-round, weather permitting. **1109 Susan Ave., Gallup; 505-863-9224.**

Seeing and Doing

Museums and Historic Buildings

GALLUP CULTURAL CENTER
Located in the handsomely restored Santa Fe Railroad Depot, built in 1923, this multipurpose community facility contains a museum with exhibits on the history of American Indians of the Southwest, a film about Indian cultures, art exhibits, a cafe, gift shop, and visitor center. Open Mon.–Sat. 8 A.M.–4 P.M. **201 E. Historic Route 66, Gallup, 87301; 505-863-4131.**

HISTORIC WALKING TOUR
Gallup has a number of historic buildings, and you can see many of them on a walk through the 12-block downtown area bordered by Main St./Historic Route 66 on the north, 1st St. on the east, Hill Ave. on the south, and 4th St. on the west. You'll find many buildings from the late 1800s and early 1900s and many of the area's best art galleries and Indian trading posts. Especially noteworthy are the McKinley County Court House (201 W. Hill Ave.), built in 1938 in the pueblo revival style; the 1928 El Morro Theater (207 W. Coal Ave.), a good example of Spanish colonial revival style; and the Rex Museum, formerly the Rex Hotel (discussed below). This is also where you'll find the Gallup Cultural Center, discussed above. Stop at the Gallup Cultural Center or the other Gallup visitor centers for maps and additional information.

RED ROCK MUSEUM
A good introduction to the American Indians of northwest New Mexico, this city-run museum, located in Red Rock State Park, explores the Indian culture of the region from the prehistoric Ancestral

There is good fishing for trout and other species throughout northern New Mexico.

Puebloans to today's Zuni, Hopi, and Navajo. Included are excellent examples of the local tribes' pottery, baskets, and weavings, and a gallery offers changing exhibits of regional art. Open Mon.–Fri. 8:30 A.M.–6 P.M. in summer, with shorter hours the rest of the year. Small admission fee. From I-40 take exit 26, go east 2 miles on the frontage road, and follow signs to the park. **P.O. Box 328, Church Rock, 87311; 505-722-3839; www.ci.gallup.nm.us.**

REX MUSEUM

Located in the historic Rex Hotel, built in 1900, this museum is operated by the Gallup Historical Society, with exhibits on the community's history from 1880 to modern times, including railroad and mining artifacts, tools, household items, historic photos, and an especially good display of vintage clothing. Call for current hours; donations welcome. **300 W. Historic Route 66, Gallup, 87301; 505-863-1363.**

Shopping

INDIAN MARKETS

Despite what the dealers in Santa Fe may say, Gallup is the undisputed center for southwestern American Indian arts and crafts. Here you buy from the Indians themselves—we highly recommend a trip to Zuni Pueblo (see Major Attraction, above)—or from the too-numerous-to-count trading posts that seem to be everywhere in the Gallup area. You'll find many of the more established trading posts along Main St. (Historic Route 66) and Coal Ave., which parallels Main to the south. The genuine Old Pawn turquoise and silver is the most valuable. It was made for and by the Navajos. It usually features larger pieces and heavier silver mountings and got its name from the fact that the Navajos pawned their

jewelry when they were short of cash. When it wasn't redeemed, it was put up for sale. Thus Old Pawn means the most authentic. The modern stuff, made to sell to tourists, may be even more beautiful, but it lacks the collector's value of Old Pawn. Remember that a piece of jewelry doesn't become Old Pawn just because some trader says it is. Ask to see the original tag from when it was pawned, and be sure to keep it if you buy the piece; it makes it more valuable.

Throughout the United States you'll find fake Indian crafts, and unfortunately Gallup is not immune. You're best bet is to buy directly from an Indian or at a well-established trading post or gallery. You can get a list of traders from the Convention and Visitors Bureau. Among the oldest is **Richardson's Trading Co., 222 W. Hwy. 66, 505-722-4762; www.richardsontrading.com.** They've been there since 1913!

Where to Stay

Accommodations

HISTORIC HOTEL
El Rancho Hotel and Motel—$$

A historic hotel, built in 1937 by the brother of movie producer and director D. W. Griffith, El Rancho simply oozes with historic charm, as well as providing a hit of Hollywood nostalgia. Numerous films were made in the Gallup area, and many famous movie stars have signed the register here, including Spencer Tracy, Katharine Hepburn, Humphrey Bogart, James Stewart, John Wayne, Mae West, Rosalind Russell, Ronald Reagan, and Kirk Douglas. Rooms are named for the actors who stayed in them, and photos of the celebrities and stills from films are everywhere. Each room is different, but most are average size with dark-stained pine furnishings. As is typical with hotels of the era, bathrooms are small; some have showers only, while others have shower/tub combos. The hotel has 75 rooms. A standard motel next door, under the same management, has an additional 24 rooms. There's an outdoor heated swimming pool and a restaurant with bar. Pets are accepted. **1000 E. Hwy. 66, 87301; 800-543-6351; 505-863-9311; www.elranchohotel.com.**

MOTELS
Best Western Inn & Suites—$$$
This handsome Best Western has everything you expect in a full-service hotel, including spacious, attractive rooms, a heated indoor swimming pool, sauna, whirlpool, game room, gift shop, self-serve laundry, restaurant and bar, and more. Small pets accepted. There are 126 units. **3009 W. Hwy. 66, Gallup, 87301; 800-722-6399; 505-722-2221.**

Comfort Inn—$$
An indoor heated pool and all the usual amenities expected in a well-respected chain in this price range. Pets are accepted with a fee. **3208 W. Hwy. 66, Gallup, 87301; 888-722-0982; 505-722-0982.**

Days Inn—$$
There are two Days Inns in Gallup, both with heated swimming pools and open pet policies with a fee. One has 74 rooms; the other has 78 rooms. **3201 W. Hwy. 66, Gallup, 87301; 800-329-7466; 505-863-6889** (indoor pool) and **1603 W. Hwy. 66, Gallup, 87301; 800-329-7466; 505-863-3891** (outdoor pool).

Holiday Inn—$$$
An attractive, full-service hotel with all the usual amenities, including a heated

indoor pool and even its own putting green. Offers 212 units and two restaurants. **2915 W. Hwy. 66, Gallup, 87301; 800-432-2211; 505-722-2201.**

Roadrunner Motel—$–$$
A well-maintained independent motel with 31 basic rooms and an outdoor heated pool. Small pets accepted. **3012 E. Hwy. 66, Gallup, 87301; 505-863-3804.**

Travelodge—$$
Inexpensive, well-maintained, basic motel, with a heated indoor pool and whirlpool. There are 50 rooms; pets are accepted with a fee. **3275 W. Hwy. 66, Gallup, 87301; 800-578-7878; 505-722-2100.**

Campgrounds

RED ROCK STATE PARK
Not part of the New Mexico State Park system, this City of Gallup park is a good camping spot, set among the region's beautiful red rock country, but it is not the place to go for peace and quiet, especially in summer. The campground, with about 140 sites, has RV hookups, restrooms, showers, picnic areas, a dump station, laundry facilities, general store, and post office. It is extremely busy during the Inter-Tribal Indian Ceremonial, which is held at the park in Aug., and spaces are at a premium. Also, all summer long, Memorial Day–Labor Day, there are American Indian dances each night at this park (fee charged). From I-40 take exit 26, go east 2 miles on the frontage road, and follow signs to the park. **P.O. Box 10, Church Rock, 87311; 505-722-3839; www.ci.gallup.nm.us.**

USA RV PARK
Located just south of Historic Route 66,

this former KOA is more than a regular campground. It's a happening place that includes pancake breakfasts and cowboy cookouts in summer, a large outdoor heated pool, a TV and movie lounge, game room, playground, convenience store and gift shop, and laundry facilities. The grounds are nicely landscaped and well maintained. Our only complaint is that their restrictions for dog owners are pretty stiff, but then it is one of the cleanest RV parks around and it seems they want to keep it that way. It has 117 sites, and there are camping cabins that share the campground's bathhouse. From I-40 take exit 16 and go 1 mile east on Historic Route 66. **2925 W. Highway 66, Gallup, 87301; 505-863-5021; www.usarvpark.com.**

Where to Eat

Earl's Restaurant—$$

Since it opened in 1947, everyone in Gallup has been coming to Earl's, which serves an extensive menu of American and southwestern/Mexican items. It's a bustling family restaurant where you can also buy genuine American Indian crafts from your table. The Mexican items are especially good, and if you feel like mixing your cultures, try the popular enchiladas and steak. No alcohol is served. Open Mon.–Sat. 6 A.M.–9:30 P.M., Sun. 7 A.M.–9 P.M.; closed major holidays. **1400 E. Hwy. 66, Gallup; 505-863-4201.**

El Sombrero—$$–$$$

Good Mexican dishes plus some American items make this a locally popular spot, with a southwestern atmosphere. Open daily 9 A.M.–10:30 P.M.; closed

New Year's Day, Thanksgiving, and Christmas. **1201 W. Hwy. 66, Gallup; 505-863-4554.**

Ranch Kitchen—$$–$$$

Southwestern-style Mexican food and American basics are the fare here, where there are two large, attractive dining rooms with southwestern decor. Recommended are the Navajo tacos (taco fixings on Navajo fry bread), the smoked barbecue, and the steaks. Open daily 7 A.M.–10 P.M. Apr.–Sept., 7 A.M.–9 P.M. the rest of the year; closed Easter and Christmas. **3001 W. Hwy. 66, Gallup; 505-722-2537; www.ranchkitchen.com.**

Virgie's Restaurant & Lounge—$$–$$$

A local favorite, Virgie's serves generous portions Mexican food items and is especially well known for its enchiladas. Open Mon.–Sat. 7 A.M.–11 P.M.; closed major holidays. **2720 W. Hwy. 66, Gallup; 505-863-5152.**

Services

Visitor Information

Gallup Convention & Visitors Bureau, 701 Montoya Blvd., P.O. Box 600, Gallup 87305; 800-242-4282; 505-863-3841; www.gallupnm.org.

Gallup-McKinley County Chamber of Commerce, 103 W. Historic Route 66, Gallup, 87301; 505-722-2228; www.gallupchamber.com. Both places operate visitor centers, and information is available at the Gallup Cultural Center.

GRANTS

Located along I-40 roughly halfway between Albuquerque and Gallup, the town of Grants at first glance looks like just another stop for the night along the highway, and indeed, the motels and restaurants of Grants do get a lot of business from people just passing through. To our way of thinking, though, those people are just missing out. There's a lot to see and do in this part of New Mexico—including two national monuments and two American Indian Pueblos—and the community of Grants makes a good, economical place to use as a home base while exploring the area. The town even has a worthwhile little museum of its own. Elevation is 6,520 feet above sea level.

History

The first known European settlement in this area was the homestead of Don Jesus Blea (1872) on the south side of San Jose Creek. But historians tell us that a certain Don Diego Antonio Chavez lived there at the time of the Civil War. Chavez controlled access to the only spring in the area and charged 10 cents to water a horse at "his" spring.

From then on, it was pretty much boom and bust for Grants. The railroad was building west, and the Grant brothers—Angus, Lewis, and John—obtained the contract to build track to this point. The area was known as Grants Camp, then Grants Station, and finally just Grants. After the railroad boom, Grants threw its energies into the logging boom, and millions of board feet of lumber from the Zuni Mountains went to Albuquerque via Grants for milling.

Grants evolved into a farming center as well as a stop along Route 66 for the many travelers motoring west to California. In 1950, rancher Paddy Martinez, who called himself "75 cents Navajo and 25 cents Mexican," discovered uranium. The uranium boom was on, and Grants grew until, by 1980, it had 11,800 people, an all-time high. Then the uranium market crashed, and by 1983, Grants looked like a ghost town, with many stores and homes standing empty. But the community refused to die, and with tourism and some other factors, things have gotten a bit better. The population now approaches 9,000.

Getting There

Grants is on I-40, about 75 miles west of Albuquerque.

Major Attractions

El Malpais National Monument and Conservation Area
Malpais means "badlands," from the Spanish *mal* (bad) and *país* (region), and this national monument and adjacent national conservation area are certainly that—an exceedingly rugged 114,000-acre valley filled with razor-sharp, flesh-ripping black rocks, under a burning sun with no shade or water for miles.

But there is an eerie beauty to this land of lava, created by volcanic eruptions from as recently as 2,000 to 3,000 years ago. There are fascinating lava flows and cinder cones and towering sandstone cliffs and arches. It also enchants us with its strange lava tubes, oases of green among the barren, black landscape, and the ruins left by prehistoric American Indians. There are scenic drives, opportunities for hiking, backpacking, and caving, plus a surprising amount of wildlife.

There is evidence that prehistoric peoples spent time here as early as 10,000 years ago, and from about A.D. 950 to 1350 El Malpais was an outlying community of the vast Chacoan culture, centered some 80 miles to the north at what is now called Chaco Culture National Historical Park. In the mid-1300s, these people left El Malpais and are believed to have established the area's pueblos, where their descendents live today.

EXPLORING THE MONUMENT AND CONSERVATION AREA

The area is jointly managed by the National Park Service and Bureau of Land Management, and both have visitor centers with exhibits, maps, and information.

Many of the main attractions at El Malpais can be seen fairly easily from roadside viewpoints. To begin, take NM 117 off I-40, drive a couple of hundred yards on this slightly uphill road, and stop to look back at the lava flows. Then continue south on NM 117 to the truly spectacular Sandstone Bluffs lookout.

Continue on to the La Ventana Natural Arch, which can be seen from a viewpoint along NM 117 or from a short and easy walk. This spectacular arch, among the largest in New Mexico, was sculpted by the forces of erosion from sandstone deposited during the time of the dinosaurs. La Ventana is Spanish for "the window." Still continuing south on NM 117 you'll reach the narrows. Here the highway is squeezed

between a black lava flow that looks to be about 12 feet high and the pastel sandstone bluffs. This is a good place for close-up views of the convoluted black lava. Continuing south you reach the Lava Falls Area, with an easy-to-moderate 1 mile loop trail that provides a good view of this striking lava formation.

There are also good views along NM 53, but these two state roads are not connected. El Malpais also has backcountry dirt roads, although they often become mud bogs when it rains, so it is best to check with either visitor center before attempting them.

One of the most popular hikes in El Malpais is the relatively level but challenging Zuni-Acoma Trail, which runs 7.5 miles one-way, following a historic trade route between Zuni and Acoma Pueblos. A strenuous hike that crosses four of the area's five lava flows, the trail is over jagged chunks of unstable lava, and although marked by cairns

La Ventana Natural Arch, among the largest arches in New Mexico.

and trail posts, is difficult to follow in spots. Arranging a shuttle and hiking from west to east is recommended, and sturdy hiking boots with good ankle support are mandatory. Hikers should carry plenty of drinking water, and heavy gloves will protect your hands from the sharp rocks and cactus.

The Big Tubes Trail offers a relatively easy way to see a variety of volcanic features up close, including a system of fascinating lava tubes, which are formed from a river of molten lava when the surface cools faster than the core. The outer edges harden into solid rock and the molten lava pours out, leaving a tunnel. At 17 miles long, this is among the largest lava tube systems in North America. The trail is easy, but the dirt road to it, CR 42, is rough and rutted when dry and completely impassable when wet. The trail follows rock cairns about 0.5 mile to a junction, where it branches into three sections that lead to a variety of lava tubes and collapsed tubes, including 1,200-foot-long Four Windows Cave. A trail guide is available at the information centers and at the trailhead.

There are several other developed trails, and a section of the national Continental Divide Trail crosses El Malpais; check at the information center or ranger station for directions. Backcountry hiking is permitted, although overnight trips require a free backcountry permit, available at information centers.

The remains of an early Ancestral Puebloan village can be seen at the Dittert Site in Armijo Canyon, on the edge of the Cebolla Wilderness off CR 41. This L-shaped sandstone structure was originally two stories high and had 30 to 35 large rooms. Nine rooms and a kiva have been excavated.

This seemingly desolate land supports a surprising amount of wildlife, some of which has adapted its colors to blend in with the dark volcanic rocks. Among the lava flows watch for lizards, rodents, and rabbits; in the few forested areas and among the sandstone bluffs look for mule deer, coyotes, bobcats, and even black bear. Pronghorn are sometimes seen in the West Malpais Wilderness.

About 200 bird species have been spotted here, with the Narrows Picnic Area an especially good bird-watching location. Resident species include red-tailed hawks, American kestrels, common ravens, northern harriers, killdeer, western bluebirds, mountain bluebirds, mountain chickadees, white-breasted nuthatches, and dark-eyed juncos. Watch for a variety of hummingbirds in summer, along with white-throated swifts and cliff swallows.

On summer weekends, rangers lead hikes and cave trips plus offer evening bat flight programs and other activities.

VISITOR INFORMATION, DIRECTIONS, AND FACTS

El Malpais National Monument and Conservation Area are located south of Grants off I-40, with access from I-40 exits 89 and 81. The national monument visitor center, located 23 miles south of I-40 exit 81 via NM 53, is open daily 8:30 A.M.–4:30 P.M. The national conservation area ranger station/visitor center, open the same hours, is 9 miles south of I-40 exit 89 via NM 117. Both visitor centers are closed New Year's Day, Thanksgiving, and Christmas. The monument and conservation area are open daily 24 hours, except the Sandstone Bluffs Overlook, which is open from dawn to dusk only. **El Malpais National Monument, 123 E. Roosevelt Ave., Grants, 87020; 505-783-4774; 505-876-2783; 505-285-4641; www.nps.gov/elma. El Malpais National Conservation Area, Bureau of Land**

Management, P.O. Box 846, Grants, 87020-0846; 505-287-7911; www.nm.blm.gov.

El Morro National Monument

Among New Mexico's top attractions, El Morro provides a fascinating look into the history of this region, and some of that history is signed personally by the people who made it happen. Here you'll see Inscription Rock, long a stopping point where weary and thirsty travelers inscribed messages, plus pre-Columbian American Indian ruins and a variety of petroglyphs.

The key to the importance of this particular spot is a permanent water hole at the base of a 200-foot high sandstone bluff. Since the first humans arrived on the scene, this water hole has drawn travelers like a shopping mall draws teenagers.

The first people likely to drop by were prehistoric hunter-gatherers. By about 1275, Ancestral Puebloans had constructed two multistoried stone villages on the mesa above the bluff. One of these has been excavated and can be explored by visitors today. It contained almost 900 living, work, and storage rooms surrounding an open courtyard, and probably housed from 1,000 to 1,500 people. There are also several kivas, grinding bins, and fire pits. In addition, a series of hand and toe steps lead

---

Bandera Volcano and the Ice Cave

Two interesting sites at El Malpais are not actually part of the national monument and conservation area, but on a section of private land within the federal property boundaries. These are the Bandera Volcano and the Ice Cave, both under the same ownership.

We suggest doing the volcano first, especially if you arrive fairly early in the morning—the ice cave is especially refreshing later, in the heat of the day. The cinder trail to the volcano overlook is about 0.5 mile each way, and gains about 150 feet. Upon reaching the caldera (the open cone from which the volcanic lava once blew out) you are treated to a wonderful look into the mechanics of an extinct volcano. Millions of tons of molten rock spewed out of this crater, probably many times in the past million years. Some of the lava was hurled out, flying miles before smashing to the ground. Most of the lava flowed out just like water, only slower. It's fun to try to imagine the tremendous heat of that eruption!

The easy trail to the ice cave is 400 yards (one-way), although to get to the ice cave viewing platform you will need to descend about 70 steps on a stairway. Here's where you feel the cooling effect of nature's icebox. This is a small volcanic sink, formed when lava tubes collapsed as they cooled. Water flowing down into the tubes froze in the wintertime—remember, you are nearly 8,500 feet above sea level—and the perfect insulation of the lava walls kept it frozen. Many hundreds, perhaps thousands, of tons of ice are still locked in blue-green brilliance down at the bottom of the solid stairway. The ice has remained frozen over millions of summers. Its temperature is 31° F, and you'll find the Ice Cave a pleasant surprise and a comfortable spot to rest and cool off.

Take NM 53 southwest from Grants for about 25 miles to the well-marked entrance. Daily 8 A.M.–1 hour before dusk (usually about 7 P.M. in summer). Fee charged. **888-423-2283; 505-783-4303; www.icecaves.com.**

from the mesa top down to the water hole at the base, of the bluff. By about 1350, the pueblo's residents were gone, and it's believed that the people of nearby Zuni Pueblo are their descendents.

Although no one has lived here since the Ancestral Puebloans left, El Morro's reliable year-round water source guaranteed that this would be a popular spot.

Spanish explorers arrived in the area in the 1500s, and at least some are believed to have stopped at the base of this bluff for water and a night's rest. In 1605, Don Juan de Oñate, who established the first Spanish colony in what is now New Mexico, left his mark. Perhaps inspired by petroglyphs left by American Indians, Oñate became the first European to etch his name in the soft sandstone when he wrote in Spanish, *"Paso por aquí el adelantado Don Juan de Oñate del descubrimiento de la mar del sur 16 de Abril de 1605,"* which translates to "Here passed the governor Don Juan de Oñate from the discovery of the Sea of the South Apr. 16, 1605." The Sea of the South refers to the Gulf of California.

Numerous other Spanish travelers also left their names on the rock, including Diego de Vargas, who stopped by in 1692 during his mission to retake New Mexico for Spain following the Pueblo Revolt of 1680.

After New Mexico became a U.S. territory in 1848, English-speaking people continued the tradition. The first Americans to add their signatures were U.S. Army cartographer Lt. J. H. Simpson and artist R. H. Kern, on Sept. 18, 1849. Kern made drawings of the inscriptions, and Simpson is credited with coining the name "Inscription Rock."

Several inscriptions from the late 1850s were left by members of a unique U.S. Army caravan—a short-lived experiment in using camels to travel through the Southwest's deserts. The Union Pacific Railroad surveyed the area in 1868, and many of its workers added their names, usually followed by the initials U.P.R. Use of the El Morro water hole and Inscription Rock, however, essentially ended when the Santa Fe Railroad laid its tracks 11 miles to the north.

EXPLORING THE MONUMENT
Inscription Rock and the Ancestral Puebloan ruins can be seen via two interconnecting self-guiding trails, totaling about 2.3 miles, with trail guides available at the visitor center.

The remains of these multistoried stone structures can be seen at El Morro National Monument.

The easy, paved Inscription Trail leads from the visitor center past the water hole to Inscription Rock, and then loops back to the visitor center, a total distance of 0.5 mile.

Instead of heading back from Inscription Rock, though, most visitors continue on the moderate 2-mile round-trip Mesa Top Trail, which follows the base of the cliff through an open wood of ponderosa pines before climbing about 200 feet to the top of the bluff. The trail leads past the unexcavated pueblo site to the excavated pueblo, and along the way offers panoramic views of the surrounding mountains and canyons. It then climbs back down from the mesa, among juniper and piñon trees, and ends back at the visitor center.

The monument's visitor center/museum has exhibits on the various people who have lived here or visited El Morro, a 15-minute introductory video program, plus a small bookstore. Rangers present talks and other programs during the summer. A pleasant but small primitive campground has 9 sites, on a first-come, first-served basis, less than a mile from the visitor center. Water is available at the campground from May through Oct., and there are fire grills and vault toilets.

VISITOR INFORMATION, DIRECTIONS, AND FACTS
Located 42 miles southwest of Grants via NM 53. Trails open 9 A.M.–4 P.M.; visitor center open daily 9 A.M.–5 P.M. Monument closed New Year's Day and Christmas. Entrance fee charged year-round; camping fee charged May–Oct. **HC 61, Box 43, Ramah, 87321-9603; 505-783-4226; www.nps.gov/elmo.**

Festivals and Events

Contact the Grants Chamber of Commerce at 800-748-2142 for information on all of the following.

GOVERNOR'S FEAST DAY
Feb. A celebration at Acoma Pueblo honoring the incoming Pueblo governor, with traditional dances.

MOUNT TAYLOR WINTER QUADRATHLON
President's Day Weekend, Feb. On the slopes of Mount Taylor, an extremely challenging test of endurance that includes bicycling, running, cross-country skiing, and snowshoeing. **www.mttaylorquad.org.**

LA FIESTA DE COLORES
first weekend in May. This Hispanic celebration includes an art show, car show, live entertainment, parade, hot air balloon rally, and traditional Hispanic foods.

WILD WEST DAYS AND RODEO
Fourth of July weekend. A weekend-long Independence Day celebration in Grants with rodeos for both adults and kids, a parade, a street dance, food, entertainment, and fireworks.

FESTIVAL OF ST. ANNE
late July. A celebration at Laguna Pueblo that honors the pueblo's patron saint.

SAN LORENZO FESTIVAL
mid-Aug. Celebration at many pueblos, including Laguna and Acoma, in which people named Lorenzo or Lawrence throw gifts to visitors from pueblo rooftops.

HARVEST FESTIVAL ON THE FEAST DAY OF SAN ESTEBAN DEL REY
early Sept. A celebration and feast day with dances honoring San Esteban (Saint Stephen). Takes place at Acoma Pueblo,

with a Roman Catholic mass, procession, corn dance, and an arts and crafts fair.

Outdoor Activities

Boating and Fishing

BLUEWATER LAKE STATE PARK

A delightful, large lake set among low hills covered with piñon and juniper trees, this deep lake is especially popular with anglers, but the state park is also great for boaters and campers and offers a bit of hiking. Located at 7,400 feet elevation in the Zuni Mountains just east of the Continental Divide, the lake freezes hard in winter, making it among the state's best ice fishing destinations. It also attracts an occasional ice skater.

The site of an inland sea some 200 million years ago, the plains of what would eventually become western New Mexico emerged when the sea retreated, and eventually Bluewater Creek carved the canyon and provided life-giving water. Pioneers built a series of earthen dams to store irrigation water, but they were all washed away. Then, in the 1920s, an 80-foot-tall concrete dam was built, and Bluewater Lake was born.

The 65-foot-deep lake is stocked several times each year by the New Mexico Department of Game and Fish. Rainbow trout weighing up to 9 pounds have been taken from the lake, and anglers catch cutthroat trout, German browns, and catfish. The best lakeshore fishing is in spring and fall, and boat fishing is usually preferred in June and July. Ice fishing through foot-thick ice is popular in winter, usually Dec. through Mar. Anglers also find good fishing in Bluewater Creek mid-Apr. through Sept.

Most of the boats on the lake are fishing boats with trolling motors, but water-skiers with high-powered speedboats and personal watercraft also use the lake, mostly on summer weekends, and occasionally a sailboat or canoe will be seen. Swimming is permitted everywhere but is best on the north end of the lake, which is a no-wake area and where the beach gradually drops off into the lake. Scuba divers also sometimes enjoy the clear but often chilly water.

Short trails lead to several scenic overlooks, including views of the lake and its impressive concrete dam.

Wildlife seen in the park includes ground squirrels, cottontail rabbits, ringtail cats, foxes, and coyotes. There are also tarantulas, though contrary to popular belief they're not poisonous (at least the ones in New Mexico). The park is home to an abundance of piñon jays, recognized by their bright blue color and love of the nuts of piñon trees. Also watch for pelicans in the spring, bald eagles along the west side of the lake in the winter, and great blue herons along the lakeshore year-round. Other species you might see include American coots, mountain bluebirds, mourning doves, red-tailed hawks, dark-eyed juncos, red-headed woodpeckers, and meadowlarks.

There are plenty of camping possibilities, including 149 developed sites—14 with electric hookups—plus you can camp anywhere you want along much of the lakeshore. There's an RV dump station and restrooms with showers. The park also has a visitor center with exhibits on the park's flora and fauna and a playground.

The park is located 28 miles west of Grants via I-40 and NM 412. **P.O. Box 3419, Prewitt, 87045; 505-876-2391; www.nmparks.com.**

Golf

COYOTE DEL MALPAIS GOLF COURSE

This attractive and somewhat challenging 18-hole public course, set at the foot of 11,300-foot Mount Taylor, is wide open—no trees—with only its 16 ponds to get in your way! Open year-round, weather permitting 2001 Camino del Coyote; 505-285-5544.

Seeing and Doing

The list of things to see in the Grants area is a long one. There are some short jaunts from your base in Grants, and one rather long loop drive that will take you to Gallup, which would be a good place to spend the night. From Grants, go south and west on NM 53 through part of El Malpais National Monument, and then to Bandera Volcano and the Ice Cave. Then continue on to El Morro National Monument, through the beautiful Ramah Valley, which is Navajo, and onto the Zuni Pueblo lands. Take some time at Zuni Pueblo to visit the historic pueblo area, with its cross-filled churchyard, and compare that with the modern hospital and the thriving gift shops in the newer parts of town. From Zuni, drive north on NM 602 to Gallup, and you're back on I-40. See the individual descriptions of most of these attractions elsewhere in this section; Zuni Pueblo is described in the **Gallup** chapter.

American Indian Villages

ACOMA-SKY CITY

Believed to be the oldest continuously occupied community in North America, Acoma Pueblo, situated on top of a virtually impregnable stone mesa 367 feet above the valley floor, has been home to these American Indians since at least 1150. Acoma was visited by Spanish conquistadors in 1540, when Francisco Vasquez de Coronado commented that as a fort the pueblo's location atop the mesa made it one of the strongest he had ever seen. In 1598, the pueblo was almost destroyed by Spanish troops under Juan de Oñate, the governor of New Spain, in retaliation for the killing of 13 Spanish soldiers by the Acomas, who claim to have caught the soldiers attempting to steal grain from the pueblo's storehouses. Today only 13 or 14 families live full time at what has come to be called Sky City; most live in communities in the reservation's lower levels. Life on top is fairly primitive, with no running water or electricity.

Your first stop will be at the visitor center, where there is a restaurant featuring traditional American Indian foods and a good museum that provides an introduction to the pueblo and its people. This is also where you'll register for a guided tour—you must be on a guided tour to see the pueblo, except during certain festivities and other special events that the public is allowed to watch.

From the visitor center you'll ride to the top of the mesa in a small, modern bus. The walking tour takes about an hour. Your guide will show you the terraced three-story adobe buildings with mica windows and handmade wooden ladders and will tell you about the construction of the beautiful Spanish-style church, built in 1629 in honor of San Esteban del Rey, the patron saint of the Acomas since the first missionaries arrived. Note the huge vigas, the logs forming the roof of the church. The vigas, 40 feet in length and more than 14 inches in diameter, were carried some 40 miles from the slopes of Mount Taylor on the shoulders of Acoma workers. The church, built under the supervision of Franciscan missionaries, also has two massive bell towers and tall walls, similar to the fort-like churches of the era in Old Mexico.

Acoma pottery patterns are recognized as some of the very best in New Mexico. White with brown and black designs, the pottery is offered for sale on top of the mesa and can be purchased at the visitor center.

There are several festivals open to the public that are celebrated on Acoma's high mesa during the year (see Festivals and Events). If you are lucky enough to be able to participate in one of the ceremonies, be sure to check the rules about photography and respect these rules.

Open daily 8 A.M.–7 P.M. Apr.–Oct. and 8 A.M.–4:30 P.M. Nov.–Mar. Last tour begins one hour before closing. Closed July 10–13 and the first or second weekend in Oct. Tour fee charged, and there is an extra fee to take in a still camera; movie and video cameras are not permitted. To get to Acoma, take I-40 east from Grants and turn south at exit 108, where there is a well-marked turnoff and a blacktopped road leading to the visitor center. The pueblo also operates Sky City Casino, at I-40 exit 102. **Acoma Tourist Visitor Center, P.O. Box 309, Acoma Pueblo, 87034; 800-747-0181; 505-552-6604; www.puebloofacoma.org.**

LAGUNA PUEBLO

Founded by refugees from other New Mexico pueblos after the 1680 Pueblo Revolt, Laguna Pueblo is actually spread out among six major villages, with a total of about 8,000 members. The main village and the seat of tribal government is Laguna—the original pueblo, also called Old Laguna—and this is the best place to visit. The main attraction here is the whitewashed adobe and stone church, San Jose de Laguna (St. Joseph's at Laguna). This impressive church, with a handsome interior and two bells near the top of its tall front façade, was built in about 1700 under the direction of the Franciscans. Laguna artisans re-established the traditional craft of pottery-making in the 1970s—much of it decorated with geometric designs in red, yellow, and orange—and also make jewelry and other arts and crafts, which are sold locally. The pueblo is open daily during daylight hours, with free admission. Closed to the public during certain ceremonies. The pueblo is located along I-40, 32 miles east of Grants at exit 114. Laguna Pueblo also operates two casinos: Dancing Eagle Casino and Travel Center is at I-40 exit 108, and Laguna Casino and Travel Center is at I-40 exit 140. **Tribal Governor's Office, P.O. Box 194, Laguna Pueblo, 87026; 505-552-6654.**

Art Gallery

DOUBLE SIX GALLERY

While the city of Grants may not be at the top of our list of major art centers, there are a surprising number of artists living and working in the area, attracted in large part by the stark, rugged beauty of this part of New Mexico. The Double Six Gallery (named for Historic Route 66), is run by the nonprofit Cibola Arts Council and displays and sells work by close to 100 regional artists, representing all of the area's cultures—from American Indian to Hispanic to Anglo, and even cowboy! Open Tues.–Fri. 10 A.M.–4 P.M. **117 N. 1st St., Grants, 87020; 505-287-7311; www.double6gallery.org.**

Museum

NEW MEXICO MUSEUM OF MINING

This fascinating museum, which bills

itself as the "only uranium mining museum in the world," is well worth a visit. Start by exploring the museum itself, on the ground floor, with exhibits not only on the 1950 discovery of uranium in Grants and uranium mining in general, but also exhibits on geology, including minerals and gems from around the world, and the history of the Grants area. Displays include prehistoric baskets, pottery, and other artifacts from as far back as 700, plus exhibits on the region's ranching and railroading past and the community's role in Historic Route 66.

Then head underground for a self-guided tour of a uranium mine, accurately portrayed from the "cage" elevator that takes you below ground to the eerie tunnels carved into rock, where you see the mining equipment and facilities, if you can call them that, where the miners worked. You can see and even feel what it must have been like in this spooky, dark underground world, where workers risked their lives to bring out the yellowcake that became uranium, which would became the key ingredient in atomic bombs and atomic power plants.

Open Mon.–Sat. 9 A.M.–4 P.M. Closed New Year's Day, Thanksgiving, and Christmas. A small admission fee is charged; guided tours available by appointment. **100 N. Iron Ave., Grants, 87020; 800-748-2142; 505-287-4802; www.grants.org.**

Where to Stay

Accommodations

MOTELS AND HOTELS
Best Western Inn & Suites—$$–$$$
An upscale property with spacious,

attractive rooms and an indoor heated pool, sauna, whirlpool, and exercise room. Small pets accepted; 126 units. **1501 E. Santa Fe Ave., Grants, 87020; 800-937-8376; 505-287-7901.**

Comfort Inn—$$
A good small hotel, with an indoor heated pool and whirlpool. Accepts pets for a fee; 51 rooms. **1551 E. Santa Fe Ave., Grants, 87020; 800-424-6423; 505-287-8700.**

Days Inn—$$
A typical and quite acceptable example of this respected chain. No pool but small pets accepted; 55 units. **1504 E. Santa Fe Ave., P.O. Box 29, Grants, 87020; 800-329-7466; 505-287-8883.**

Sands Motel—$–$$
This throwback to the glory days of Route 66 is our favorite lodging in Grants. Not nearly as fancy or as spiffy as its much newer competitors from the national chains, this mom-and-pop motel is simply decorated, with spacious and extremely well-maintained rooms. Pets are accepted for a fee and rates are very reasonable. No swimming pool; 24 rooms. **112 McArthur St., Grants, 87020; 800-424-7679; 505-287-2996.**

The neon at the Sands Motel in Grants beckons weary travelers for a night's stay.

Super 8—$$

A good choice for families, with reasonable rates and an indoor heated pool and whirlpool. Pets accepted for a fee; 69 rooms. **1604 E. Santa Fe Ave., Grants 87020; 800-800-8000; 505-287-8811.**

Campgrounds

In addition to the commercial campgrounds listed here, there is camping at El Morro National Monument and Bluewater Lake State Park, which are discussed earlier in this chapter.

GRANTS/CIBOLA SANDS KOA

A well-designed, well-kept RV park with the usual commercial campground amenities except a pool, this KOA is quiet and friendly, with 44 RV sites and a few tent sites. Open year-round. From I-40 take exit 81, go south 0.5 mile on NM 53. **P.O. Box 179, Grants, 87020; 888-562-5608 (reservations only); 505-287-4376.**

LAVALAND RV PARK

Well-spaced sites and some shade trees make this a pleasant place to set up camp, although the vast majority of its 56 sites are for RVs. No pool. From I-40 take exit 85. **1901 E. Santa Fe Ave., Grants, 87020; 505-287-8665.**

Where to Eat

La Ventana—$$–$$$$

Excellent steaks and specialty salads make this dimly lit restaurant with southwestern decor a local favorite. The menu also includes seafood and a few spicy Mexican dishes. The slow-roasted prime rib is especially good. Full bar. Reservations recommended. Open Mon.–Sat. 11 A.M.–11 P.M.; bar open until 2 A.M. In **Hillcrest Shopping Center, 110 ¹/₂ Geis St.; 505-287-9393.**

Monte Carlo Restaurant—$$–$$$

A historical landmark on old Route 66, the Monte Carlo opened in 1947. The menu is varied, and we especially recommend the New Mexico–style Mexican dishes such as the huevos rancheros, burritos, and chile rellenos. There's a full bar and a children's menu. Open daily 7 A.M.–10 P.M. **721 W. Santa Fe Ave., Grants; 505-287-9250.**

Services

Visitor Information

Grants/Cibola County Chamber of Commerce, 100 N. Iron Ave., P.O. Box 297, Grants, 87020; 800-748-2142; 505-287-4802; www.grants.org. The chamber operates a visitor center in the New Mexico Mining Museum, at the same address. For information on outdoor recreation and other activities on public lands in the area, stop at the multi-agency **Northwest New Mexico Visitor Center, 1900 E. Santa Fe Ave., Grants (just southeast of I-40 exit 85); 505-876-2783.**

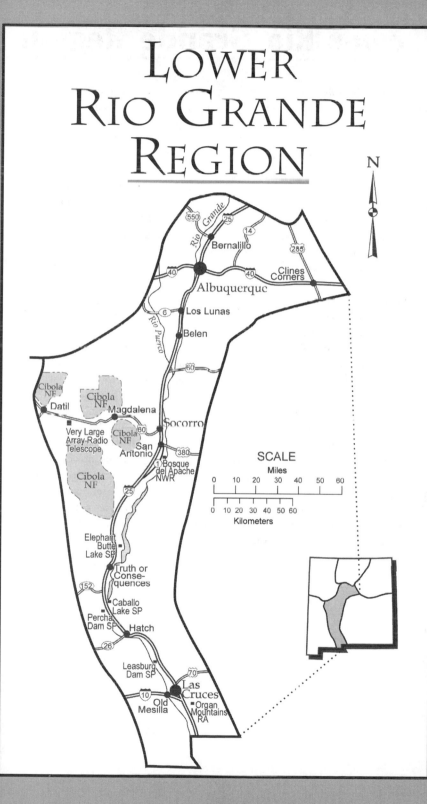

LOWER RIO GRANDE REGION

Lower Rio Grande Region

The first Spanish explorers noted that when the Rio Grande dropped down through the gorge, it became a much more placid stream. Leaving the Rocky Mountains behind, the river entered a broad plain. The Spanish word *bajo* is important here. The explorers called the upper river Rio Arriba and the lower river Rio Abajo. There's a big hill dropping down off the mesa top between Santa Fe and Albuquerque called La Bajada, the "coming down" or the "descent" in Spanish.

Where the river slowed, it became more useful for agriculture. It watered wide, flat areas that were home to the pre-Columbian pueblos, places like Isleta on the south edge of Albuquerque and San Felipe to the north. Following the river was the easiest form of travel, and it still is. Interstate 25 closely parallels the Rio Grande from just south of Santa Fe, through Albuquerque and Socorro, on down to Las Cruces and into foreign land—El Paso, Texas. *El paso* is Spanish for "the passage," but it refers to the passage to the north ... to Santa Fe!

The earliest conquistadors followed the Rio Grande from El Paso to Santa Fe, then they left the river and went to Taos and on into Colorado. The rio never flowed in a straight north-south line, though. Hoping to shorten the trip by at least a day, early travelers turned north, away from the river, at Rincon and made a straight line all the way up to San Marcial. It was a 91-mile stretch without any water that became know as the *Jornada del Muerto* ("journey of death") because of all the travelers who died along the route.

Today this central strip of the Land of Enchantment is far from a journey of death. It boasts three great state universities—in Albuquerque, Socorro, and Las Cruces—has the biggest concentration of wintering waterfowl in the state, and has fascinating historic sites, museums, art galleries, and a slew of great restaurants. You'll find opportunities for outdoor recreation in its reservoirs and in the nearby mountains and also a look into space travel and distant worlds.

But enough of this introductory stuff. Let's get busy and retrace the steps of the conquistadors, backward, traveling the lower Rio Grande corridor from north to south, with our first stop in Albuquerque.

ALBUQUERQUE

New Mexico's largest city, with about 500,000 people within its city limits, Albuquerque is home to about one-third of the state's inhabitants, along with most of its major industries. Although Albuquerque is the most metropolitan that New Mexico can do, it isn't very "citified"—it feels more like an overgrown western town than a real city like Chicago, Phoenix, or Denver. Albuquerque straddles the Rio Grande, sitting just west of the 10,628-foot-high Sandia Mountains. (*Sandia* is Spanish for "watermelon"—the late afternoon sun on the mountains reminded the Spanish settlers of the flesh of the ripe watermelon.) Residents claim that Albuquerque, at an elevation of 5,326 feet, has one of the best climates to be found anywhere. In winter, there's snow on the mountains to look at, but rarely any on the city streets to walk through. In summer, daytime temperatures have been known to top 100° F, but the humidity is low and it always cools down at night.

History

A relative newcomer, compared to New Mexico cities such as Santa Fe or Taos, Albuquerque wasn't established until 1706, and it was named to honor Don Francisco Fernandez de la Cueva Enriquez, duke of Alburquerque and the viceroy of New Spain, who had his headquarters in Mexico City. You'll notice the extra "r" in Albuquerque, which survived for more than a century before it disappeared after the arrival of English-speaking people in the 1800s. The original site of Albuquerque was founded by 35 families—a total of about 250 people—in what is now Old Town.

Nothing much happened for almost 200 years until in 1880 the railroad came to town, picking a location on higher ground about 2 miles to the east, where the present business district of Albuquerque now stands. For a while, the original settlement languished, but eventually the new city grew around it and absorbed it.

Throughout its history the city has been a hub of trade, with an extension of the Santa Fe Trail connecting it with the Spanish trails into old Mexico. In the mid-1900s it became a major stop along the fabled Route 66. Today Albuquerque remains a crossroads of trade and is also the state's economic center, with a variety of high-tech industries. The city is home to the University of New Mexico and Kirtland Air Force Base, and its historic Old Town attracts throngs of tourists.

Getting There

Albuquerque is at the junction of I-25 and I-40, two of America's busiest interstate highways. It also has an international airport served by most major airlines, has transcontinental bus service, and is a stop on a major east-west Amtrak rail route.

Major Attractions

Old Town
The spot where Albuquerque began in 1706, Old Town is a delightful and

ALBUQUERQUE

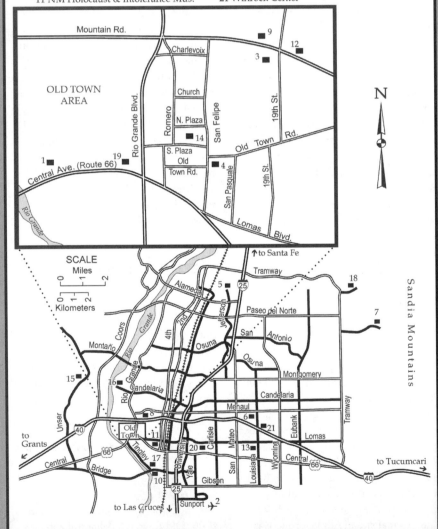

■ KEY to POINTS of INTEREST

1 Alb. Aquarium & Botanic Gardens
2 Alb. Int'l. Sunport
3 Alb. Museum of Art & History
4 American Int'l. Rattlesnake Mus.
5 Balloon Fiesta Park
6 Coronado Center
7 Elena Gallegos Picnic Area
8 Indian Pueblo Cultural Center
9 Nat'l. Atomic Mus.
10 Nat'l. Hispanic Cultural Center
11 NM Holocaust & Intolerance Mus.

12 NM Mus. of Natural HIstory
13 NM State Fairgrounds
14 Old Town Plaza
15 Petroglyph Nat'l. Mon.
16 Rio Grande Nature Center SP
17 Rio Grande Zoo
18 Sandia Peak Aerial Tramway
19 Turquoise Mus.
20 Univ. of NM - Art Museum; Maxwell
   Mus. of Anthropology
21 Winrock Center

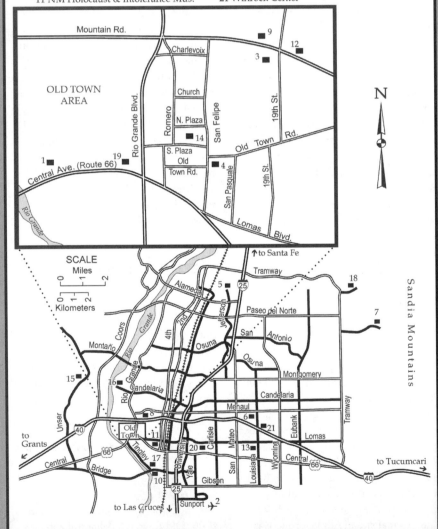

bustling area of historical buildings—many now housing art galleries, shops, and restaurants—that offers easy access to many of the city's best museums. The tree-shaded Old Town Plaza, built in 1780, is the center of activity and a good spot to take a breather while trying to explore the 150 or so galleries, shops, and other retail businesses. There are numerous historic buildings in Old Town; you can get details at the Old Town visitors center (see Services, page 170).

Facing the plaza on its north side is the impressive San Felipe de Neri Church, still in use as a Roman Catholic church. This is the second building, which replaced the original in about 1790, and boasts 4-foot-thick walls (so it could also serve as a fort if necessary), stained-glass windows, and hand-carved woodwork. **2005 N. Plaza NW, Albuquerque; 505-243-4628; www.sanfelipedeneri.org.**

Petroglyph National Monument

Some 25,000 petroglyphs are preserved at this national monument, where several hiking trails make it easy to experience a glimpse into the region's past while also getting a good look at the volcanos that created this rugged badlands and providing opportunities for wildlife viewing and bird-watching.

Petroglyphs, from the Greek words *petra* (rock) and *glyph* (carving) are simply images carved or chipped into the surfaces of rocks, in this case by scratching away the black desert varnish to expose the light gray below.

Most of the petroglyphs here were created between 1300 and 1600, but there are some abstract images believed to have been made by nomadic hunter-gatherers at least 2,000 years ago and some slightly more recent depictions of wolves, mountain lions, humans, masks, and some curious animal bodies with human heads. In addition to petroglyphs created by prehistoric American Indians, there are images left by Spanish settlers, created in the 17th and 18th centuries, that depict livestock brands and Christian crosses. There is also evidence of later images, usually initials, left by Anglo settlers in the late 19th and early 20th centuries. Anything much newer than that is considered graffiti.

SEEING THE MONUMENT

A fantastic variety of images can be easily seen along three short, paved trails, each with interpretive signs, in Boca Negra Canyon. In addition, a guide to the three trails is available at the visitor center. Among our favorite image is a macaw—a Mexican parrot—that you can't miss seeing on the Macaw Trail. On this and the other trails you'll also see four-pointed stars, wildlife, handprints, and masked figures.

Hundreds of petroglyphs can also be seen along the 3-mile round-trip Rinconada Trail in Rinconada Canyon. The trail follows a path created by wildlife and used by Spanish sheepherders, and images here include roadrunners and lizards, handprints, and human and godlike figures. There are also images left by Spanish settlers of livestock brands, crosses, and sheep and the names of two young Anglo men—Milton Thorpe and Victor Buday—who

An ancient petroglyph found at Petroglyph National Monument.

were hunting rabbits and rattlesnakes in the canyon on Feb. 22, 1919. You'll also discover a variety of petroglyphs along the Piedras Marcada Canyon Trail. The sandy, 3-mile round-trip hike is also a good setting for observing wildlife.

A variety of desert wildlife live in the monument, such as desert cottontail and black-tailed jackrabbits, white-tailed antelope squirrels, coyotes, and numerous lizards, including the colorful collared lizard. There are also snakes, including poisonous rattlesnakes. Birds here include horned larks, rock and canyon wrens, northern mockingbirds, white-crowned sparrows, western meadowlarks, loggerhead shrikes, barn swallows, mourning doves, American kestrels, turkey vultures, and great horned owls.

There's a visitor center with exhibits on the people who lived here and created the petroglyphs. Outside the visitor center is a short paved nature trail. During summer and early fall rangers present occasional talks and lead hikes and walks.

VISITOR INFORMATION AND DIRECTIONS

The monument is open daily 8 A.M.–5 P.M.; closed New Year's, Thanksgiving, and Christmas. A small admission fee is charged. The monument stretches 17 miles along Albuquerque's West Mesa; the visitor center is 3 miles north of I-40 via Unser Blvd. **6001 Unser Blvd. NW, Albuquerque; 505-899-0205; www.nps.gov/petr.**

Festivals and Events

FIERY FOODS & BARBECUE SHOW

early Mar. Every super-spicy food product imaginable as well as related fiery food and barbecue items are displayed at this event, which fills the Albuquerque Convention Center with about 200 exhibitors. There are demonstrations, samples, and sales. **505-873-8680; www.fiery-foods.com/ffshow.**

SPRING ARTS & CRAFTS SHOW

early Mar. This juried fine arts and crafts festival features more than 200 national artists with works in a variety of mediums, plus demonstrations, entertainment, and food. Presented by Rio Grande Arts & Crafts Festival, which also has shows in Albuquerque in early Oct. and early Dec. Takes place at the state fairgrounds. **505-292-7457; www.riograndefestivals.com.**

GATHERING OF NATIONS POWWOW

late Apr. The name says it all—tribes from across the country come together for this event. Up to 3,000 Indian dancers perform and compete, there's a singing competition, a trade fair, and the crowning of Miss Indian World. **505-836-2810; www.gatheringofnations.com.**

NEW MEXICO ARTS & CRAFTS FAIR

late June. Featuring only New Mexico artists, this outdoor fair, which has been an annual event since 1962, showcases the work of more than 200 of the state's artists and craftspeople, working in a wide range of mediums. It takes place at the state fairgrounds. **505-884-9043; www.nmartsandcraftsfair.org.**

SUMMER WINGS FESTIVAL

early Aug. A celebration of hummingbirds—the only birds known to fly backward—plus butterflies, dragonflies, and bees. The daylong event includes guided walks, hands-on dragonfly capture and release, children's craft-making, talks, and demonstrations of bird-banding and identification. Held at the Rio Grande Nature Center. **505-344-7240; www.nmparks.com.**

NEW MEXICO WINE FESTIVAL AT BERNALILLO

first weekend in Sept. The state's largest wine festival takes over the town of Bernalillo, north of Albuquerque, with music, arts and crafts, and the star attraction: practically all of New Mexico's more than two dozen wineries offering samples and sales of genuine New Mexico wines. **505-867-3311; www.nmwine.com.**

NEW MEXICO STATE FAIR

early to mid-Sept. New Mexico's cowboy heritage, along with a whole lot of other stuff, is on display at the annual state fair, which takes over the city for two weeks every Sept. Activities include a Professional Rodeo Cowboy Association rodeo, a midway carnival, nationally famous country singers, livestock shows, craft demonstrations, numerous exhibits, sales of New Mexico–made products, and Indian and Spanish villages. Wonderful food of all kinds. **505-265-1791; www.exponm.com.**

RIO RANCHO OKTOBERFEST

late Sept. Lots of beer, lots of food, lots of music, and fun at this traditional German-American festival. **505-891-0411.**

ALBUQUERQUE INTERNATIONAL BALLOON FIESTA

early Oct. The biggest event of the year in Albuquerque, with more than a week of activities when the sky is filled with more than 750 colorful hot air balloons. Balloonists come from across the United States and a few foreign countries to take part in the festival, which features mass ascensions at dawn, evening

balloon glows, special shapes contests, hare and hounds competitions, and grab-the-brass-ring contests. There are also opportunities for spectators to take balloon rides or to help on a chase crew. **888-422-7277; 505-821-1000; www.balloonfiesta.com.**

WEEMS ARTFEST

mid-Nov. This top-rated fine arts and crafts fair at Weems Gallery raises money for charities, with help from celebrity guests—Lauren Bacall was delightful. **2801-M Eubank Blvd. NE, Albuquerque; 505-293-6133; www.weemsgallery.com.**

RIVER OF LIGHTS

month of Dec. Spectacular light sculptures, including animated figures, illuminate the Rio Grande Botanic Garden. There are also fireworks, a miniature garden railroad, hot food and beverages, and live music. The light sculptures, constructed of steel and flexible light tubing in various colors, depict all sorts of things, from zebras to fish to trains to Santa. One of the most popular sculptures is of two elephants—one squirting the other with water. **505-764-6200; www.cabq.gov/biopark.**

LUMINARIA DISPLAY

Christmas season. This event dates from the days when Spanish settlers and local American Indians lighted signal fires to guide the coming of the Christ child. We now have pathways, buildings, walls, and sidewalks lined in luminarias (also called *farolitos*), which are brown paper bags partially filled with sand to stabilize them, with a candle or electric light burning inside. You'll see these lighting displays during the Christmas season throughout New Mexico, and it is especially beautiful in Albuquerque's Old Town.

Outdoor Activities

Bird-Watching

RIO GRANDE
NATURE CENTER STATE PARK

Located on the east bank of the Rio Grande, this delightful oasis is an excellent place for bird-watchers, as well as anyone who would enjoy a hike along the river or through a peaceful woods. Nestled among the cottonwoods and willows along the Rio Grande, the nature center offers two interpretative nature trails, demonstration gardens, numerous exhibits on the area's natural environment, guided walks, and an abundance of birds and other wildlife.

The park is located in what is called a *bosque*, a Spanish word for forest that in New Mexico is often used to describe the wetlands along rivers, particularly along the Rio Grande. The nature center covers some 270 acres of woods and meadows, with native grasses, wildflowers, willows, Russian olives, and cottonwoods. It also has a 3-acre pond, which helps attract more than 260 species of birds.

Seeing the Nature Center

Start at the visitor center, where there are exhibits describing the bosque's flora and fauna, including a large turtle skeleton and a series of river photos by well-known New Mexico photographer Laura Gilpin. The visitor center also has an observation room, complete with a sound system, that overlooks the pond and lets you see the birds (and usually turtles) fairly close up while also bringing the sounds of the pond into the room. There are also blinds just outside the visitor center that allow people to observe the numerous birds and other wildlife without scaring them off.

Trails here are easy and relatively short. Two interpretive nature trails, the Riverwalk Trail and Bosque Loop Trail, meander through the bosque, and a 1.25-mile paved loop runs along a flood-control ditch between the visitor center and river.

Numerous birds make their homes in the park, although the greatest number of species can be seen from Nov. through Feb. Among birds likely to be observed in winter are waterfowl such as ring-necked ducks, American wigeons, and cinnamon teal, plus northern harriers, ruby-crowned kinglets, hermit thrushes, chipping sparrows, song sparrows, dark-eyed juncos, western meadowlarks, sandhill cranes, and occasionally a bald eagle. Summer visitors include various species of warblers plus western meadowlarks, black-chinned hummingbirds, black phoebes, and western kingbirds. Year-round residents include Cooper's hawks, great horned owls, American coots, Canada geese, Gambel's quail, ring-necked pheasants, Mandarin ducks, mallards, wood ducks, black-capped chickadees, great blue herons, northern flickers, and both downy and hairy woodpeckers.

Also in the park are turtles—look for them sunning themselves on logs in the pond—plus toads, lizards, bull snakes, dragonflies, beavers, muskrats, cottontail rabbits, pocket gophers, rock squirrels, and coyotes. Demonstration gardens grow herbs and a variety of drought-tolerant plants, and a viewing platform provides a look at the nature center's farm where corn is grown for bird feed.

The nature center offers a variety of guided walks, classes, programs, and special events, and back in the visitor center the Discovery Room has hands-on exhibits for children, including a "Please Touch" display that lets kids feel the scaly skin of a bull snake. Also at the visitor center are park trail guides, available either in printed or recorded form, plus players, binoculars, birding books, and similar items that can be borrowed.

Visitor Information and Directions

Trails are open 24 hours year round; visitor center open daily 10 A.M.–5 P.M. The parking lot is open daily 8 A.M.–5 P.M. and is padlocked shut when the visitor center closes. The visitor center and parking lot are closed Thanksgiving, Christmas, and New Year's Day. A small admission fee is charged. The park is located at the west end of Candelaria Rd. NW. From I-40 take exit 157A take Rio Grande Blvd. north 3 blocks, and turn left onto Candelaria Rd.; from I-25 take exit 227 (frontage road) and turn right onto Candelaria Rd. **2901 Candelaria Rd. NW, Albuquerque; 505-344-7240; www.nmparks.com.**

Boating and Fishing

COCHITI LAKE

Less than an hour's drive north of Albuquerque, Cochiti Lake is a popular swimming, fishing, and boating destination on the Rio Grande. The lake was created by the construction of one of the 10 largest earth-filled dams in the United States—251 feet high and 5.5 miles long—which took 10 years to build at a cost of $94.4 million dollars by the time it was completed in 1975.

There are recreation areas on each side of the lake, with boat ramps, picnic areas, restrooms with showers, RV dump stations, and campgrounds with both electric hookup and non–electric hookup sites. Fishing is good for trout, northern pike, catfish, bluegill, and crappie. It's a no-wake lake, so although motorboats are permitted, they have to be kept at low speeds. Swimming is good, although a bit chilly most of the

time—the Rio Grande is fed from northern New Mexico's snowpack—and the fairly common winds make the lake a prime spot for sailing and sailboarding.

There's a visitor center with exhibits on construction of the dam and the natural resources of the area, plus a short nature trail. The lake can be reached from I-25, exits 259 or 264, follow the signs. Fees are charged for boat launching and camping; other use of the recreation area is free. It is managed by the **U.S. Army Corps of Engineers, Albuquerque District Office, 4101 Jefferson Plaza NE, Albuquerque, 87109-3435; 505-342-3262; www.spa.usace.army.mil. Cochiti Lake office direct, 505-465-0307. Campsite reservations, 877-444-6777; www.reserveusa.com.**

SANDIA LAKES RECREATION AREA

Located just north of Albuquerque along the Rio Grande on Sandia Pueblo land, this multiuse park has three small, stocked fishing lakes, covering a total of 18 acres, and a bait and tackle shop. There are also picnic tables, a playground, and hiking and bird-watching opportunities. Open in summer from 6:30 A.M.–9 P.M., shorter hours the rest of the year. Fees charged. Located off I-25 exit 234, west and then north 1 mile on NM 313. **505-897-3971; www. sandiapueblo.nsn.us/lakes.html.**

Golf

The following are among the top golf courses in the Albuquerque area; all are open year-round, weather permitting.

CHAMPIONSHIP GOLF COURSE AT THE UNIVERSITY OF NEW MEXICO

Known locally as the UNM South Course or simply "the Monster," this public 18-hole course is challenging and can be surprising, with elevated greens, rolling fairways, gullies, ridges, and water hazards. There's also a 3-hole beginner course. **3601 University Blvd. SE, Albuquerque; 505-277-4546; www.unm.edu/~golf.**

ISLETA EAGLE GOLF COURSE
One of the state's top courses, Isleta Eagle offers great views and 27 challenging holes designed around three lakes. Located just south of Albuquerque. **4001 NM 47 SE, Albuquerque; 888-293-9146; 505-869-0950; www.isletaeagle.com.**

PAA-KO RIDGE GOLF CLUB
Among America's and New Mexico's top public golf courses, this 27-hole mountain course at 6,500 feet elevation is both challenging and scenic. Located east of Albuquerque via I-40 and NM 14. **1 Clubhouse Dr., Sandia Park; 866-898-5987; 505-281-6000; www.paakoridge.com.**

PUEBLO DE COCHITI GOLF COURSE
This challenging 18-hole public course, designed by Robert Trent Jones Jr., has lush greens set in the high desert away from the city and is considered one of the best affordable courses in the state. Located between Albuquerque and Santa Fe off I-25, exit 264. **5200 Cochiti Hwy., Cochiti Lake; 505-465-2239.**

SANTA ANA GOLF CLUB
This challenging 27-hole links-style course is set in desert terrain along the Rio Grande, with native grasses, lakes, and waterfalls. Located north of Albuquerque (via I-25, exit 242). **288 Prairie Star Rd., Santa Ana Pueblo; 505-867-9464; www.santaanagolf.com.**

TWIN WARRIORS GOLF CLUB
This fine 18-hole public course is in a desert setting with wonderful views of the Sandia Mountains. Located north of Albuquerque (via I-25, exit 242) at Hyatt Regency Tamaya Resort & Spa. **1301 Tuyuna Tr., Santa Ana Pueblo; 505-771-6155; www.twinwarriorsgolf.com.**

UNIVERSITY OF NEW MEXICO NORTH GOLF COURSE
This 9-hole public course is well maintained and a good spot for a few hours of golf. **2201 Tucker Rd. NE (at Yale Blvd.), Albuquerque; 505-277-4146; www.unm.edu/~golf.**

Hiking
There are hiking opportunities at Petroglyph National Monument, Rio Grande Nature Center State Park, and Sandia Lakes Recreation Area, which are discussed elsewhere in this section, and there are numerous trails in the Cibola National Forest, in the mountains just east of the city. For information contact **Cibola National Forest, 2113 Osuna Rd. NE, Ste. A, Albuquerque; 505-346-3900; www.fs.fed.us/r3.**

ELENA GALLEGOS PICNIC AREA, ALBERT G. SIMMS PARK
This city park, which covers 640 acres at the northeast edge of Albuquerque, offers trails for hikers, mountain bikers, and horseback riders, as well as picnicking and some splendid mountain scenery. Among recommended hikes are the Domingo Baca Trail, which goes northeast from the park's picnic area. It's well marked, about 2 miles one-way, and considered easy to moderate as it meanders across piñon-dotted hillsides to Domingo Baca Canyon and a picturesque stream. From Apr.–Oct.

the park is open daily 6 A.M.–9 P.M., from Nov.–Mar. daily 7 A.M.–7 P.M. Small per car admission fee is charged. Take Tramway Blvd. (I-40 exit 167) north to Simms Park Rd. and go east. **7100 Tramway Blvd. NE, Albuquerque; 505-857-8334; 505-452-5200; www.cabq.gov/openspace.**

Skiing

SANDIA PEAK SKI AREA
A fun family ski and snowboard area geared to beginners and intermediates, with 30 named trails on 200 skiable acres. With a vertical drop of 1,700 feet from its peak elevation of 10,378 feet, Sandia Peak has six lifts and trails rated 35 percent beginner, 55 percent intermediate, and 10 percent advanced. Located atop Sandia Peak, accessible by the Sandia Peak Aerial Tramway (see Scenic Ride, below) or by road via I-40, exit 175, then north on NM 14 and northwest on NM 536. **10 Tramway Loop NE, Albuquerque; 800-473-1000; 505-242-9052; 505-857-8977 (snow report); www.sandiapeak.com.**

Seeing and Doing

Archeological Site

CORONADO STATE MONUMENT
Named for Spanish explorer Francisco Vásquez de Coronado, who camped here with his soldiers in 1540 while searching for the Seven Cities of Gold, this monument preserves the ruins of a prehistoric pueblo, settled in about A.D. 1300. A highlight is the reconstructed kiva—an underground ceremonial chamber with a mural depicting prehistoric figures and ceremonies. Several of the original

murals—there were actually many layers of murals—are displayed in the monument's visitor center/museum, where other exhibits trace the effect the arrival of Spanish explorers had on the Pueblo people. Open Wed.–Mon. 8:30 A.M. 4:30 P.M. Small admission fee. The monument is located 1 mile west of the town of Bernalillo, which is north of Albuquerque off I 25, exit 242. **485 Kuaua Rd., Bernalillo, 87004; 505-867-5351; www.newmexicoculture.org.**

Auto Racing

SANDIA MOTOR SPEEDWAY
Fans of fast cars head to this race track, which offers a variety of racing on two flat ovals and a 1.65-mile road course. Admission fee. Located about 4 miles west of I-40, exit 149. **100 Speedway Blvd. SW, Albuquerque; 505-352-8888; www.sandiamotorsports.com.**

Children and Families

CLIFF'S AMUSEMENT PARK
A first-class family amusement park with everything you would expect plus more, including the New Mexico Rattler, a super–roller coaster 2,750 feet long and 800 feet high. There's also a log flume and other water activities, numerous other rides, a kiddieland, an arcade, and family-oriented games. Open Apr.–Sept. only. Hours vary considerably; call for the current schedule. Admission fee charged. Located off I-25, exit 230. **4800 Osuna Rd. NE, Albuquerque; 505-881-9373; www.cliffsamusementpark.com.**

EXPLORA
This state-of-the-art science center and museum has some 250 different exhibits geared to children of all ages. Visitors are

encouraged to touch every one of them. The center features interactive exhibits focusing on science, technology, and art, such as the kinetic sculpture and ball run, which involve motion, force, and energy. Especially popular is the robot-making room, where kids use a computer to design a robot and then build it out of sophisticated LEGO pieces. Then there's the high-wire bike, strung on a cable 17 feet up, which demonstrates gravity. There are also exhibits in which participants use math to discover scientific facts, plus exhibits on optics and light as well as electricity. A section for babies and toddlers includes a mirror maze, experiments that demonstrate cause and effect, a construction area, and a tarantula house. Open Mon.–Sat. 10 A.M.–6 P.M., Sun. noon–6 P.M. Admission fee charged. Located near Old Town. **1701 Mountain Rd. NW, Albuquerque; 505-224-8300; www.explora.mus.nm.us.**

TINKERTOWN MUSEUM

A 22-room museum, Tinkertown is a massive collection of fun stuff—a miniature animated western town and circus, intricately carved from wood, an automated one-man band, Esmeralda the fortune teller, a not-so-miniature antique wooden sailboat, and all sorts of Americana. Open Apr.–Oct. only, daily 9 A.M.–6 P.M. Admission fee charged. Located northeast of Albuquerque: from I-40 take exit 175, go north on NM 14, and then west on NM 536. **121 Sandia Crest Rd., Sandia Park; 505-281-5233; www.tinkertown.com.**

Geologic Wonder

KASHA-KATUWE TENT ROCKS NATIONAL MONUMENT

Created by the powerful forces of volcanic action and then erosion, the cone-shaped rock formation at this national monument provides a fascinating look at the geologic history of this area. Volcanic eruptions some 6 to 7 million years ago left deposits of pumice, ash, and tuff topped by harder rock. As erosion wore down these deposits, the harder cap protected some of the softer rock below, creating the odd cones—or tents—that dominate this landscape today. The formations are quite uniform in shape—many look as though they had been turned out on a lathe—but vary in height from just a few feet to about 90 feet. The rock layers vary in color, with gray bands highlighting the beige- and pink-colored layers.

This is a relatively new national monument, designated in 2001, and facilities remain limited. There are restrooms, a picnic area, and a kiosk with information at the trailhead. Trails here are open to foot travel only (no mountain bikes) and are sandy in spots. The easy-to-moderate 1.2-mile Cave Loop Trail meanders among the formations before heading back to its starting point; the moderate Canyon Trail, with one steep climb, branches off the Cave Loop Trail and goes 1 mile (one-way) to a scenic overlook. Depending on the season, watch for various birds such as western bluebirds, violet-green swallows, American kestrels, red-tailed hawks, and maybe even a golden eagle. Mammals you might see include rabbits, ground squirrels, chipmunks, and coyotes.

The monument is open for day use only: Apr.–Oct. daily 7 A.M.–6 P.M., Nov.–Mar. 8 A.M.–5 P.M. Small per vehicle admission fee charged. Located 50 miles north of Albuquerque. From I-25 take exit 259, go northwest on NM 22, following signs to Cochiti Pueblo, and turn right (west) at the pueblo water tank (painted like a drum) onto Tribal Route 92 (which connects with Forest Service Road 266), and follow this route to the monument. **Bureau of Land**

Management, Albuquerque Field Office, 435 Montaño Rd. NE, Albuquerque; 505-761-8700; www.nm.blm.gov.

Museums and Historic Sites

ALBUQUERQUE MUSEUM OF ART & HISTORY

Features exhibits of the area's history going back more than 400 years, as well as changing exhibits of artwork from the past and the present. There's also an outdoor sculpture garden with four dozen works of art and a theater showing a film on how Albuquerque has changed over the years. Open Tues.–Sun. 9 A.M.–5 P.M. Closed major holidays. Admission fee charged. Located just north of Old Town Plaza. **2000 Mountain Rd. NW, Albuquerque; 505-243-7255; 505-242-4600 (recorded exhibit information); www.cabq.gov/museum.**

AMERICAN INTERNATIONAL RATTLESNAKE MUSEUM

So you want to go eyeball-to-eyeball with a rattlesnake? This is the place! The rattlesnake museum contains the world's largest collection of different species of live rattlesnakes, plus exhibits about rattlesnakes, including the various myths and mysteries about these creatures and rattlesnakes in art and advertising. There's also a short film on rattlesnakes. Open daily 10 A.M.–6 P.M. Closed major holidays. Admission fee charged. Located off the southeast corner of Old Town Plaza. **202 San Felipe NW, Ste. A, Albuquerque; 505-242-6569; www.rattlesnakes.com.**

INDIAN PUEBLO CULTURAL CENTER

Showcasing the history of New Mexico's 19 Indian pueblos, this fine museum's exhibits include artifacts dating from the pre-Columbian era. There are also exhibits on what the Pueblos are doing today, including their arts and crafts, and a theater shows films about the Pueblo people. There are traditional Indian dances and artists demonstrations each weekend, and this is a good place to get current information on visiting the individual pueblos. The museum shop offers high-quality, authentic arts and crafts, including paintings, sculptures, pottery, and jewelry, plus recordings of American Indian music. There is also a cafe, open daily 8 A.M.–3 P.M., that serves traditional Indian foods plus some southwestern favorites. Open daily 9 A.M.–5:30 P.M. Closed New Year's Day, Memorial Day, Labor Day, Thanksgiving, and Christmas. Located just north of I-40. **2401 12th St. NW, Albuquerque; 800-766-4405; 505-843-7270; www.indianpueblo.com.**

ISLETA PUEBLO

Established around the 1300s, Isleta Pueblo didn't get its current name for about three centuries, when the Spanish arrived— *isleta* is Spanish for "little island." Isleta, with a population of more than 3,000 people, operates a large casino and a golf course, discussed elsewhere in this section. The biggest attraction for us, though, is the historic St. Augustine Church, located on the pueblo's main plaza. The original church, built in 1613, was partly destroyed in the Pueblo Revolt of 1680. When Isleta was reconquered by the Spanish in 1692 the church was rebuilt, using the same walls and foundations. Today it stands much as it did 300 years ago and remains in use by the pueblo. Isleta Pueblo is located south of Albuquerque via I-25, exit 215 and NM 47. **505-869-3111; www.isletapueblo.com.**

J&R VINTAGE AUTO MUSEUM

Dozens of beautifully restored classic cars and trucks are displayed at this fine museum, which also has a well-stocked auto-related gift shop and large windows that provide a good view of the restoration shop. The cars are for sale—you did remember to bring some extra spending money, didn't you?—so the collection changes, but you can be assured that you'll see a variety of fine classics, from the exotic cars the movie stars of the 1930s drove to the muscle cars of the 1960s. The collection includes vehicles from the beginning of the 20th century—lots of brass and wooden wheels—along with some heavy duty trucks. On display during one visit were a 1917 Marmon, Lasalles from the 1920s and 1930s, and some big Buicks and Packards. You're also likely to see a Ford Model A V-8 sedan or two, supposedly the favorite getaway car of outlaws Bonnie and Clyde. Open in summer Mon.–Sat. 10 A.M.–6 P.M., Sun. 1–5 P.M. and the rest of the year Mon.–Sat. 10 A.M.–5 P.M. (closed Sun. Nov.–Apr.). Admission fee charged. Located north of Albuquerque via I-25, exit 242, 0.5 mile south of the intersection of NM 550 and NM 528. **3650 NM 528, Rio Rancho; 87124; 888-298-1885; 505-867-2882; www.jrvintageautos.com.**

MAXWELL MUSEUM OF ANTHROPOLOGY

This excellent museum explores the history of humans around the world, going back 4 million years, with permanent and changing exhibits. It also focuses on the Southwest, with one of the best collections in the country of Navajo rugs and Indian pottery on display, plus artifacts excavated from Chaco Canyon since the early 1920s. A reconstruction of a room at Chaco and other exhibits tell the story of humans during the 11,000 years that we know they were in this area. A variety of demonstrations, lectures, and workshops are offered, and the museum store—offering splendid textiles, pottery, jewelry, folk art, and the like—is among the best in Albuquerque. Open Tues.–Fri. 9 A.M.–4 P.M., Sat. 10 A.M.–4 P.M. Closed major holidays. Located on the University of New Mexico campus, one block north of Martin Luther King Blvd. on University Blvd. **505-277-4405; www.unm.edu/~maxwell.**

NATIONAL ATOMIC MUSEUM

This excellent museum traces the history of atomic energy, with a large exhibit about the creation of the atomic bomb and the first use of the bomb when it was dropped on Hiroshima and Nagasaki, Japan, in 1945. The exhibits here don't just dish out the government line—you'll learn about all the controversies of the times in both the United States and Japan. The museum also continues the story of atomic power from post–World War II up to present day, with a look at nuclear medicine, such as the development of X-rays, and the many other things that have evolved from the study of nuclear energy. A variety of video presentations are given in the museum theater, and there's a fascinating gift shop with a number of items you're not likely to find anywhere else. Open daily 9 A.M.–5 P.M. Admission fee charged. Located just north of Old Town Plaza. **1905 Mountain Rd. NW, Albuquerque; 505-245-2137; www.atomicmuseum.com.**

NATIONAL HISPANIC CULTURAL CENTER

A growing collection of works by Hispanic artists are displayed in an art museum and a sculpture courtyard. The library (call for hours) collects and preserves Hispanic literature and family histories, and the center presents traditional and contemporary Hispanic theatrical, musical, and dance productions. Open Tues.–Sun. 10 A.M.–5 P.M. Admission fee charged. **1701 4th St. NW, Albuquerque; 505-246-2261; www.nhccnm.org.**

NEW MEXICO HOLOCAUST & INTOLERANCE MUSEUM AND STUDY CENTER

This unique and sobering museum has as its goal the prevention of hatred and intolerance and the persecution, suffering, and death it produces. Visitors to the museum learn about the history of intolerance and what people can do to promote understanding and mutual respect. There are exhibits on some of the most atrocious examples of intolerance, including the genocide committed by the Nazis, the Bataan Death March, and the inhumane treatment and cultural genocide of American Indians. There are also displays on how people have fought against this intolerance, including the story of how during World War II the Danes smuggled out over 90 percent of the Danish Jews under the noses of the Nazis. Open Tues.–Sat. 11 A.M.–3:30 P.M. **415 Central Ave. NW, Albuquerque; 505-247-0606; www.nmholocaustmuseum.org.**

NEW MEXICO MUSEUM OF NATURAL HISTORY

This museum does a wonderful job of bringing the prehistoric past to life in the minds of young and old alike. Walk into the middle of the volcano? Sure. Why not? Travel back 70 million years to the land of dinosaurs and meet life-size sculptures Spike and Alberta and check out the fossil laboratory. Also be sure to take in a show at the Dynamax Theater, which has the largest screen in New Mexico—five stories tall—and visit the Lodestar Astronomy Center, which has a planetarium, a motion simulation theater, astronomy exhibits, and an observatory. Open daily 9 A.M.–5 P.M.; closed Thanksgiving and Christmas and non-holiday Mondays in Jan. and Sept. Admission fee charged. Located several blocks northwest of Old Town Plaza. **1801 Mountain Rd. NW, Albuquerque; 505-841-2800; 505-841-5958 (Lodestar Astronomy Center); www.museums.state.nm.us/nmmnh.**

TURQUOISE MUSEUM

Just what is that gorgeous bluish stone you see in almost every piece of New Mexico jewelry? It's turquoise! To find out all about it, come to this museum where you'll discover rare turquoise specimens, see lapidary and silversmithing demonstrations, and learn about the history of turquoise and how and where it's mined. There are also hands-on exhibits for kids. Open Mon.–Sat. 9:30 A.M.–5:30 P.M. Admission fee charged. Located southwest of Old Town Plaza. **2107 Central Ave. NW, Albuquerque; 505-247-8650.**

UNIVERSITY OF NEW MEXICO ART MUSEUM

Founded in 1963, this museum contains the largest collection of fine art in New Mexico—with more than 27,000 pieces in its permanent collection—including Old Master paintings and sculptures, Spanish colonial works, as well as pieces from the 19th and 20th centuries. The museum has an excellent photography and print collection, and periodic lectures and gallery tours are offered. Open Tues.–Fri. 9 A.M.–4 P.M., Tues. 5–8 P.M., Sun. 1–5 P.M. Closed major holidays. Located on the University of New Mexico campus. **Cornell St. and**

Redondo Dr. NE, Albuquerque;
505-277-4001;
http://unmartmuseum.unm.edu.

Nightlife and Gambling

Much of the live entertainment in New
Mexico, including national and regional
performers, as well as gambling, takes
place at the American Indian casinos,
which are spread across the state. The
state's largest newspaper, the *Albuquerque
Journal*, has a nightlife section each Fri.
and there are often newspaper ads
throughout the week for major performers. There are also no lack of billboards
promoting the casinos and their
entertainment. We suggest you check
before going, since these casinos are relatively new and are still feeling their way
in this competitive business.

Casinos near Albuquerque include
**Isleta Casino & Resort (11000
Broadway SE, just south of
Albuquerque; 877-747-5382;
www.isleta-casino.com); San
Felipe's Casino Hollywood (I-25,
exit 252 at San Felipe Pueblo,
north of Albuquerque; 877-529-
2946; 505-867-6700;
www.sanfelipecasino.com); Sandia
Casino (30 Rainbow Rd., via I-25,
exit 234; 800-526-9366; 505-796-
7500; www.sandiacasino.com);
Santa Ana Star Hotel Casino (54
Jemez Canyon Dam Rd., Santa Ana
Pueblo; 505-867-0000;
www.santaanastar.com); and Route
66 Casino (I-40 exit 140, at Laguna
Pueblo, west of Albuquerque; 505-
352-7866; www.rt66casino.com).**
You'll also find an abundance of slot
machines at **The Downs of Albuquerque Racetrack & Casino,** which is
discussed below under Spectator Sports.

In addition to the casinos, a number of
well-established clubs and bars in
Albuquerque offer entertainment. It
varies, and you'll find the most choices
Fri. and Sat. nights. Among places worth
checking out, all in Albuquerque: **The
Atomic Cantina (315 Gold Ave. SW;
505-242-2200); BackStreet Bar &
Grill (5210 San Mateo Blvd. NE; 505-
888-3688); Charlie's Back Door (8224
Menaul Blvd. NE; 505-294-3130);
Club Rhythm & Blues (3523 Central
Ave. NE; 505-256-0849); El Rey/Puc-
cini's Golden West (620 Central Ave.
SW; 505-242-2353); Graham Central
Station (4770 Montgomery Blvd.
NE; 505-883-3041; www.graham
centralstation.com); Le Cafe Miche
Wine Bar (1431 Wyoming Blvd. NE;
505-299-6088); Little Anita's (1105
Juan Tabo Blvd. NE; 505-292-4111);
Martini Grill (4200 Central Ave. SE;
505-255-4111); O'Niell's Pub (3211
Central Ave. NE; 505-256-0564;
www.oniells.com); and O'Niell's
Uptown (6601 Uptown Blvd. NE;
505-884-4714; www.oniells.com).**

Many of Albuquerque's major hotels
also have live entertainment in their
lounges—usually jazz or piano. Among
those listed below under Where to Stay
that often have live music are the Hyatt
Regency Tamaya Resort and Spa, Sheraton Old Town, and La Posada. The
Rancher's Club of New Mexico,
discussed under Where to Eat, is also a
good spot for live music.

Performing Arts

You can get tickets to many of the
following at **Tickets.com** outlets in
Raley's Supermarkets, and at **800-
905-3315; www.tickets.com.** Another
source for tickets is **Ticketmaster** at
505-883-7800; www.ticketmaster.com.

ALBUQUERQUE LITTLE THEATRE

Dating to 1930, this amateur theater
company produces a variety of
comedies, dramas, and musicals—recent

productions included *Our Town* and *Driving Miss Daisy*. It also has a children's theater program. **224 San Pasquale Ave. SW, Albuquerque; 505-242-4750; www.swcp.com/~alt.**

KIMO THEATRE

This beautifully restored pueblo–art deco style theater hosts a wide range of events year-round. **423 Central Ave. NW, Albuquerque; 505-768-3522; www.cabq.gov/kimo.**

MUSICAL THEATRE SOUTHWEST

This theater company, based at the historic Hiland Theater, has been presenting Broadway musicals using local talent since the 1960s. Recent productions have included *Annie, Kiss Me Kate,* and *South Pacific.* **4804 Central Ave. SE, Albuquerque; 505-265-9119; 505-262-9301 (box office); www.musicaltheatresw.com.**

NEW MEXICO SYMPHONY ORCHESTRA

This fine orchestra, which sometimes performs with a chorus, presents classical music programs, Broadway musicals, and pops concerts in various venues. **4407 Menaul Blvd. NE, Albuquerque; 505-881-8999 (box office); www.nmso.org.**

OPERA SOUTHWEST

This well-established opera company presents such standards as *Falstaff, Tosca, The Mikado,* and *Carmen* at the historic KiMo Theatre (see above). **505-243-0591; www.operasouthwest.org.**

POPEJOY HALL

Presents a wide variety of performing arts events throughout the year on the University of New Mexico campus. **505-277-4569; www.popejoyhall.com.**

Scenic Ride

The following tramway ride is great, but if you don't cotton to hanging by a steel cable in a gondola that's swaying in the breeze, you can also drive to Sandia Crest and get the same great views. From I-40 take exit 175, then NM 14 north to NM 536, the Sandia Crest National Scenic Rd., which you follow west to Sandia Crest. Several good picnic spots dot the road up through the ponderosa pine forest. Take caution during the wintertime, as the road may be snow-packed.

SANDIA PEAK AERIAL TRAMWAY

A fantastic view awaits on this trip by aerial tram to 10,378-foot Sandia Peak. The ride up and down the mountainside is fun, too. Billed as the world's longest aerial tramway, it travels 2.7 miles each way. Go for the ride, the views, or to spend time on the top where you can take your pick from 24 miles of hiking and mountain biking trails before heading back down. During winter you can access Sandia Peak Ski Area by tram, and anytime you can take the tram to High Finance Restaurant and Tavern (discussed below under Where to Eat). Especially nice are the views of sunsets and the lights coming on in the city below. Open during the summer daily 9 A.M.–9 P.M., with shorter hours at other times; closed for maintenance for about 10 days during spring and fall. Admission fee charged. Located at the east edge of Albuquerque. **10 Tramway Loop NE, Albuquerque; 505-856-7325; www.sandiapeak.com.**

Spectator Sports

BASEBALL

Professional baseball is king each Apr. through Sept. with the Albuquerque Isotopes of the Pacific Coast League.

1601 Avenida Cesar Chavez SE, Albuquerque; 505-924-2255; www.albuquerquebaseball.com.

HOCKEY

The professional New Mexico Scorpions play an Oct. to Apr. season. **6300 San Mateo Blvd. NE, Albuquerque; 505-881-7825; www.scorpionshockey.com.**

HORSE RACING

Horse racing in the spring and during the state fair in Sept., plus simulcasting year-round at The Downs of Albuquerque Racetrack & Casino, at the state fairgrounds, where you'll also find hundreds of slot machines begging to be fed. **201 California St., Albuquerque; 505-266-5555; www.abqdowns.com.**

UNM BASKETBALL & FOOTBALL

Albuquerque goes absolutely ape over its University of New Mexico basketball and football teams, called the Lobos. The 17,000-seat arena, commonly called the Pit, sells out for almost every basketball game, even the exhibitions. The football team plays at University Stadium. **1414 University Blvd. NE, Albuquerque; 800-955-4695; 505-925-5626; 505-925-5858; www.golobos.com.**

Wineries

Several Albuquerque wineries offer tastings, tours, and sales. These include **Anderson Valley Vineyards (4920 Rio Grande Blvd. NW, Albuquerque; 505-344-7266)**, which produces many of the usual wines plus a chile wine. In the same general area is **Casa Rondeña Winery (733 Chavez Rd. NW, Los Ranchos de Albuquerque; 800-706-1699; 505-344-5911; www.casarondena.com)**, which produces Bordeaux-style wines. Those who

enjoy sparkling wines should definitely pay a visit to **Gruet Winery,** which has won so many national and international awards they must be having trouble finding shelf space for them. The tasting room is at **8400 Pan American Freeway NE, Albuquerque; 888-857-9463; 505-821-0055; www.gruetwinery.com.**

Zoological Parks and Nature Centers

The Albuquerque Aquarium, Rio Grande Botanic Garden, and Rio Grande Zoo are all part of the city of Albuquerque's Biopark, and a combination admission ticket for all three entities is available. In addition to the following, see the write-up on the Rio Grande Nature Center State Park, under Outdoor Activities.

ALBUQUERQUE AQUARIUM

The marine habitats of the Gulf of Mexico are the focus of this aquarium, where large tanks contains sea creatures of all sorts, from stingrays to eels to sharks. A short orientation film is shown. Open daily 9 A.M.–5 P.M. (until 6 P.M. Sat.–Sun. June–Aug.); closed New Year's Day, Thanksgiving, Christmas. Admission fee charged. **2601 Central Ave. NW, Albuquerque; 505-764-6200; www.cabq.gov/biopark.**

RIO GRANDE BOTANIC GARDEN

Plants of the world, and especially the Southwest deserts, are highlighted at this facility, which contains formal Old World–style gardens, a wonderful larger-than-life kids fantasy garden, a butterfly pavilion, a butterfly and hummingbird garden, and numerous other plant exhibits. Open daily 9 A.M.–5 P.M. (until 6 P.M. Sat.–Sun. June–Aug.); closed New Year's Day, Thanksgiving, Christmas. Admission fee charged. **2601 Central**

Ave. NW, Albuquerque; 505-764-6200; www.cabq.gov/biopark.

RIO GRANDE ZOO

This fine city-run zoo has some 1,200 animals representing about 250 species displayed in natural appearing habitats in a cottonwood-shaded oasis. There are polar bears, Bengal tigers, the always-popular elephants, gorillas, sea lions, and a number of southwestern species. Public feedings of the sea lions and seals are held daily, usually about 10:30 A.M. and 3:30 P.M. Open daily 9 A.M.–5 P.M. (until 6 P.M. Sat.–Sun. June–Aug.); closed New Year's Day, Thanksgiving, and Christmas. Admission fee charged. **903 10th St. SW, Albuquerque; 505-764-6200; www.cabq.gov/biopark.**

WILDLIFE WEST NATURE PARK

You'll see cougars, wolves, deer, elk, pronghorn, javelina, hawks, and other wildlife native to the Southwest, along with native plants, at this 122-acre nature park and environmental education center. A project of the non-profit New Mexico Wildlife Association, all the wildlife here has been rescued and cannot be released back into the wild. The nature park offers a variety of festivals, classes, and other events (call

See the lions and about 1,200 other animals at the Rio Grande Zoo.

or check the Web site for the current schedule), and Sat. nights from July Fourth through Labor Day weekend the center has a chuckwagon supper and western show. In summer, the center is open daily 10 A.M.–6 P.M., the rest of the year open daily noon–4 P.M. Admission fee charged. Located 19 miles east of Albuquerque off I-40, exit 187. **87 N. Frontage Rd., Edgewood; 877-981-9453; 505-281-7655; www.wildlifewest.org.**

163

Where to Stay

Accommodations

Every chain motel imaginable plus some interesting bed-and-breakfasts and historic properties provide a wide variety of lodging choices. Albuquerque is a fairly easy city for driving and parking, but it is spread out, so it's a good idea to choose your lodging based at least somewhat on where you plan to spend most of your time. When we're visiting museums and historic sites we like to stay in the Old Town area, where we can leave the car at the hotel and walk to most of what we want to see. Lodging rates are usually higher—sometimes downright obscene—during special events, especially the balloon rally in early Oct.

BED-AND-BREAKFAST INNS
Böttger Mansion Bed & Breakfast in Old Town—$$$$

Among Albuquerque's most luxurious bed-and-breakfast inns, this elegant Victorian mansion, built in 1897, has eight exquisite units, all individually decorated with Victorian charm. Rooms have tall ceilings—some with ornate pressed tin—and some have whirlpool tubs. One unit, which can sleep up to 6, has a small kitchen. Smoking is not permitted. Located in Old Town. **110 San Felipe NW, Albuquerque 87104; 800-758-3639; 505-243-3639; www.bottger.com.**

Brittania & W.E. Mauger Estate B&B— $$$–$$$$

This restored Queen Anne home, built in 1897, offers a delightful place to relax within easy walking distance of Old Town. It is noted for its rich woodwork, etched glass, and high ceilings, and all rooms are decorated with period furnishings. Bathrooms have showers only—the mini-suite has a double-headed shower for two—and one ground-floor room is especially designed for those with small or medium-sized dogs, with a dog door that opens onto a fenced side yard. Rates include full breakfast; smoking is not permitted. **701 Roma Ave. NW, Albuquerque, 87102; 800-719-9189; 505-242-8755; www.maugerbb.com.**

Casas de Suenos Bed & Breakfast— $$$–$$$$

An amazingly authentic Old Mexico–style bed-and-breakfast, Casas de Suenos offers 17 large and luxuriously appointed units, with private entrances, beautiful gardens, and inviting patios. Some suites have private hot tubs; some have full kitchens or kitchenettes; some have fireplaces. Rates include full breakfast. Although only three blocks from the crowds of Old Town, it is truly quiet. **310 Rio Grande Blvd. SW, Albuquerque, 87104; 505-247-4560; www.casasdesuenos.com.**

Hacienda Antigua Bed & Breakfast— $$$–$$$$

Built in the late 1700s, this delightful bed-and-breakfast inn offers eight units that ooze New Mexico charm. Each is furnished with antiques and each has a fireplace or woodstove. There is a hot tub open year-round and an outdoor pool open during warmer months. Small, well-behaved dogs are welcome (for a fee), and a full breakfast is included in the rates. Smoking is not permitted. **6708 Tierra Dr. NW, Albuquerque, 87107; 800-201-2986; 505-345-5399; www.haciendantigua.com.**

Hacienda Vargas Bed and Breakfast Inn—$$$–$$$$

A quietly elegant bed-and-breakfast lodging, located conveniently to Albuquerque and Santa Fe along the historic Camino Real, which linked Mexico City and Santa Fe in the 16th century. All eight of the rooms in this historic adobe house, which dates from the 1700s, are decorated with New Mexico antiques and have traditional kiva fireplaces and private outside entrances. Some units have whirlpool tubs. A full breakfast is included in the price; smoking is not permitted in the rooms. Take I-25 north of Albuquerque to exit 248 and go west about 0.5 mile. **1431 NM 313, Algodones, 87001; 800-261-0006; 505-867-9115; www.haciendavargas.com.**

HOTELS AND MOTELS
Best Western InnSuites Hotel & Suites—$$–$$$

Attractive hotel close to the airport, with an indoor/outdoor heated pool and whirlpool; 102 units. Pets accepted (for a fee). **2400 Yale Blvd. SE, Albuquerque, 87106; 877-771-7810; 505-242-7022.**

Best Western Rio Grande Inn—$$$

Near Old Town, this Best Western does a good job of capturing the ambiance of the Southwest in the guest rooms and public areas. It offers 173 rooms and has a heated outdoor pool plus a whirlpool and exercise room, as well as a restaurant and lounge. **1015 Rio Grande Blvd. NW, Albuquerque, 87104; 800-959-4726; 505-843-9500.**

Best Western Winrock Inn—$$$
Beautiful landscaping and a convenient location for shoppers—it's in one mall and close to another—are pluses for this well-maintained Best Western. There's a heated outdoor pool and an exercise room; 173 units. **18 Winrock Center NE, Albuquerque, 87110; 800-866-5252; 505-883-5252.**

Comfort Inn Midtown—$$
An outdoor heated pool, central location, and 147 rooms. **2015 Menual Blvd. NE, Albuquerque, 87107; 505-881-3210.**

Econo Lodge Old Town—$$
An indoor heated swimming pool and a good location close to Old Town make this a good choice. Pets are accepted (fee). There are 51 units. **2321 Central Ave. NW, Albuquerque, 87104; 888-811-4477; 505-243-8475.**

El Vado Motel—$-$$
Close to Old Town on old Route 66, you'll get a kick of nostalgia at this throwback to Route 66's glory days. It offers 33 rooms and 5 suites; basic, clean, and well maintained. **2500 Central Ave. SW, Albuquerque, 87104; 505-243-4594.**

Howard Johnson Express Inn—$$
An economical, well-kept small hotel close to I-25, with a heated outdoor, an exercise room, and a playground. There are 85 rooms and pets are accepted (for a fee). **7630 Pan American Fwy. NE, Albuquerque, 87109; 505-828-1600.**

Hyatt Regency Albuquerque—$$$-$$$$
Adjacent to the convention center, this top-notch full-service hotel has 395 rooms and 14 suites, a restaurant and two bars, a golf course, heated outdoor pool plus sauna, whirlpool, and exercise room. **330 Tijeras Ave. NW, Albuquerque, 87102; 800-233-1234; 505-842-1234.**

Hyatt Regency Tamaya Resort and Spa—$$$$
This very upscale resort, located about 20 minutes north of Albuquerque, has an excellent spa offering massages, skin treatments, and the like, plus a well-equipped fitness center, yoga instruction, an 18-hole golf course, three outdoor heated pools, two tennis courts, horseback riding, and kids programs. The 350 units are spectacular, decorated in southwestern style with everything you would expect in a first-class resort, including in-room mini-refrigerators and safes. There are four restaurants on the property and 24-hour room service is available. Located at Santa Ana Pueblo near the town of Bernalillo, north of Albuquerque. Take I-25 to exit 242, then west on NM 550, north on Tamaya Rd., and follow signs. **1300 Tuyuna Tr., Santa Ana Pueblo, 87004; 800-532-1496; 505-867-1234.**

La Posada—$$$
Built in 1939 by New Mexico native Conrad Hilton—perhaps you've heard of some of his other hotels—La Posada offers abundant Southwest charm with all the modern conveniences, including two-line phones with data ports and voice mail. There are 114 units, a nice restaurant, and bar. **125 2nd St. NW, Albuquerque, 87102; 800-777-5732; 505-242-9090; www.laposada-abq.com.**

165

La Quinta Inn North—$$–$$$

A heated outdoor pool and available video games makes this a good choice for travelers with teenagers. Small pets accepted; 130 rooms. **5241 San Antonio Dr. NE, Albuquerque, 87109; 505-821-9000.**

Quality Inn & Suites Old Town—$$

An economical choice for a well-maintained chain motel with easy access to the many sites in Old Town. There's an indoor heated pool and an exercise room; 70 units. **2411 Central Ave. NW, Albuquerque, 87104; 505-247-2751.**

Sheraton Old Town—$$$–$$$$

This 11-story full-service hotel is a popular conference site, and its Old Town location makes it a good choice for those who want to see the city's museums and other sites. It has 188 units and all the usual amenities you would expect in a Sheraton, including a heated outdoor pool, whirlpool, exercise room, and video games. **800 Rio Grande Blvd. NW, Albuquerque, 87104; 800-237-2133; 505-843-6300.**

HOSTEL

Route 66 Hostel

Twelve rooms offer low-cost dormitory accommodations, or rent an entire room for privacy. Kitchen privileges, and there is often free food available; within walking distance of the bus and train stations. Office hours daily 7:30–10:30 A.M.; 4–11 P.M. **1012 Central Ave. SW, Albuquerque, 87102; 505-247-1813; www.members.aol.com/route66hos/htmlRT66/index.htm.**

Campgrounds

PUBLIC

Coronado Campground

This city-owned campground along the Rio Grande offers good views of the river and mountains, with 35 RV sites either with or without water and electric hookups, plus a separate, pleasant tent area with space for about 15 tents. It has restrooms with showers and an RV dump station, but no other facilities. North of Albuquerque in Bernalillo. From I-25, take exit 242 and go west on NM 550; **505-980-8256.**

PRIVATE

Albuquerque Central KOA

This in-town RV park and campground has all the usual amenities, including a heated outdoor swimming pool and an indoor hot tub. Good views of the mountains, but little shade; more than 200 sites. Open year-round. Located just off I-40, exit 166. **12400 Skyline Rd. NE, Albuquerque, 87123; 800-562-7781 (reservations); 505-296-2729.**

Albuquerque North KOA

A quiet, tree-shaded RV park and campground with easy access to the sites of Albuquerque. It has all the usual commercial campground amenities, including a heated outdoor pool, and 60 sites. Open year-round. Located north of Albuquerque between I-25, exits 240 and 242. **55 Hill Rd., Bernalillo, 87004; 800-562-3616 (reservations); 505-867-5227.**

American RV Park

An extremely clean and well-maintained RV park with a paved road system. Offers 186 spaces with all hookups, a heated outdoor swimming pool, laundry, propane sales, video room, game room, and more. Located at I-40, exit 149. **13500 Central Ave. SW, Albuquerque, 87121; 800-282-8885; 505-831-3545; www.americanrvpark.com.**

Where to Eat

Cervantes Restaurant—$$–$$$

Tasty and authentic New Mexican cuisine with judicious use of chile peppers are what you'll find in this casual family restaurant. Especially recommended are the chile rellenos, tamales, and carne adovada. Open Mon.–Sat. 11 A.M.–2 P.M. and 4:30–10 P.M., Sun. noon–10 P.M. Closed Easter and Christmas. **5801 Gibson Blvd. SE (at the corner of San Mateo Blvd.), Albuquerque; 505-262-2253.**

Chama River Brewing Company—$$–$$$

This upscale brewpub, with a hunting lodge feel, is the spot to come for well-prepared American grill cuisine and a variety of microbrewed beers. The menu includes lots of steaks, seafood, and pasta, plus Rio Chama Chile—a hearty dish of spicy chile with beans and steak. Among appetizers, try the Rio Fondue—a blend of cheeses with wine and amber ale served in a fondue pot with cubes of bread, fresh vegetables, and apples. The half-pound green chile cheeseburger is one of the best in the state, and the fish and chips go especially well with the brewery's selections. There are usually 10 beers on tap—six standards and four seasonal brews. We especially like the hoppy Jackrabbit IPA and the Rio Chama Amber Ale. Open Mon.–Thurs. 11 A.M.–10 P.M., Fri.–Sat. 11 A.M.–11 P.M., Sun. 11 A.M.–10 P.M. Closed Thanksgiving and Christmas. **4939 Pan American Freeway, Albuquerque; 505-342-1800; www.riochamabrewery.com.**

The County Line of Albuquerque—$$$

Looking for Texas barbecue? This is the spot. Part of a small, regional chain based in Austin, The County Line serves extremely tender brisket, smoked chicken, smoked prime rib, and huge pork ribs that require two hands and a whole pile of napkins. The sauce is thick and spicy, and among the many side dishes available, the pinto beans are perfect. Among non-barbecue items, we recommend the grilled salmon. The restaurant is made up to look like a Texas roadhouse, with longhorns, guns, wagon wheels, and the like, and it offers terrific views of the city lights. Open Mon.–Thurs. 5–8:30 P.M., Fri.–Sat. 5–9:30 P.M., Sun. noon–8:30 P.M. **9600 Tramway Blvd. NE, Albuquerque; 505-856-7477; www.countyline.com.**

Dion's—$–$$

A giant step above all the national pizza chains, this local operation has 10 restaurants (eat in or take-out) in the Albuquerque area, all with a lively family-friendly atmosphere—no alcohol is served and there are viewing stands to enable kids to see the pizzas being made. You'll find all the usual toppings and then some, spicy sauce, and a nice chewy crust. A variety of salads are available, as are submarine sandwiches. Open Sun.–Thurs. 10:30 A.M.–10 P.M., Fri.–Sat. 10:30 A.M.–11 P.M. Locations include **Montgomery Blvd. at Morris St., Albuquerque; 505-293-7183 and Academy Blvd. at Wyoming Blvd.; 505-821-3911; www.dionspizza.com.**

Duran Central Pharmacy—$–$$

It's not often we get the opportunity to recommend a drug store for its food, but we have no hesitation about sending you to Duran's, which has been here since 1945. You'll walk through the pharmacy section to get to the dining area, which consists of a counter and a few tables, with an unpretentious decor. The menu is fairly short, featuring New Mexico–style Mexican dishes, including excellent blue corn enchiladas and green chile stew. Open Mon.–Fri. 9 A.M.–6:30 P.M., Sat. 9 A.M.–2 P.M. Closed major holidays. **1815 Central Ave. NW, Albuquerque; 505-247-4141.**

Fratelli Italian Deli—$–$$

Overstuffed Italian-style sandwiches, plus pasta, pizza, calzones, and salads are the fare at this deli, which offers eat-in or take-out food and limited delivery. Begun in 2002 by two brothers—*fratelli* is Italian for brother—the deli is in a simple storefront with a mural of an Italian street scene along one wall. Subs are the specialty here, served on submarine rolls that are baked daily in-house. A variety of cold subs are available, using Italian meats and cheeses, and hot sandwiches include a fantastic spicy meatball sub with marinara sauce and melted mozzarella cheese. Open Mon.–Wed. 11 A.M.–8:30 P.M., Thurs.–Sat. 11 A.M.–9 P.M. Closed major holidays. **11110 Lomas Blvd. NE (in the Target Shopping Center), Albuquerque; 505-242-7146.**

Garduño's—$$

Okay, it's a chain, but a small chain with barely more than a dozen restaurants in three states, and its headquarters are in Albuquerque. Garduño's—all seven Albuquerque locations—also happens to be a favorite of Albuquerque residents, and with good reasons: generous portions of well-prepared New Mexico–style Mexican standards such as burritos, tacos, chimichangas and enchiladas, plus a festive Mexican cantina atmosphere with live mariachi music. There's also a full bar that specializes in tequila drinks. Open Mon.–Thurs. 11 A.M.–10 P.M., Fri.–Sat. 11 A.M.–10:30 P.M., Sun. 10:30 A.M.–10 P.M. Closed Thanksgiving and Christmas. **5400 Academy Rd. NE, Albuquerque; 505-821-3030 (this location); for** information on other locations 888-666-5514; 505-298-5514; www.gardunosrestaurants.com.

Gin Mill Restaurant & Tavern—$$–$$$

Among our favorite Albuquerque restaurants, the Gin Mill is spacious and dark, with rich wood and comfortable seating—a neighborhood bar with a touch of class. There are daily specials, happy hours, and a lot of regulars who have been coming here since it opened in 1982. The menu offers a mix of American and Mexican standards. At any time you can get really good half-pound burgers, excellent turkey enchiladas, huevos rancheros, burritos, various sandwiches, and plates including chicken-fried steak with gravy and roast turkey with bread stuffing and gravy. Available after 5 P.M. are dinners such as a 16-ounce T-bone steak with mushrooms, a platter of charbroiled baby back ribs, or the rib eye steak and swordfish filet combo. Open Mon.–Fri. 11 A.M.–midnight, Sat. 9 A.M.–midnight, Sun. 9 A.M.–11 P.M. Closed major holidays. Located in the Far North Shopping Center. **6300 San Mateo Blvd. NE, Albuquerque; 505-821-6300; www.ginmill.com.**

High Finance Restaurant and Tavern— $$$–$$$$

Located atop Sandia Peak and reached only by riding the Sandia Peak Tramway, this elegant restaurant offers a wonderful, romantic atmosphere with a splendid view of the city a full mile below. The dinner menu includes slow-roasted Black Angus prime rib, steaks such as grilled filet mignon and New York strip, seafood including the skillet-roasted ahi tuna and pan-seared mahi-mahi, and several pasta and vegetarian dishes. Burgers, innovative sandwiches, pasta, and salads comprise the lunch menu.

Dinner reservations recommended. Open daily 11 A.M.–3 P.M., 4:30–9 P.M. Closed Christmas. **40 Tramway Rd. NE, Albuquerque; 505-243-9742; www.highfinancerestaurant.com.**

M & J Restaurant—$$

For authentic, home-cooked New Mexico food, this is the place to come. The atmosphere is casual, sort of like sitting down at a friend's kitchen table in the 1950s. Like the decor, the food isn't fancy, but it's well prepared and the prices are reasonable. The homemade tortillas—served with practically everything—are great, and we especially recommend the chicken enchiladas and carne adovada. There are also salads and a soup of the day, and be sure to save room for a sopaipilla with honey for dessert. Open Mon.–Fri. 9 A.M.–4 P.M. Closed major holidays. **403 Second St. SW, Albuquerque; 505-243-2444.**

Mario's Pizza & Ristorante Italiano—$$–$$$

This unpretentious storefront restaurant, just west of Coronado Shopping Center, offers delicious Italian standards and New York–style pizza. A locals' favorite for years, Mario's pizzas have a fat, chewy crust and tasty marinara sauce, and you can get a variety of toppings, from traditional pepperoni to more trendy sun-dried tomatoes or artichoke hearts. Among the full-scale dinners, spaghetti and meatballs are especially popular—the meatballs are huge—as is the chicken parmigiana. Open Mon.–Thurs. 11 A.M.–9 P.M., Fri.–Sat. 11 A.M.–10 P.M., Sun. 11 A.M.–9 P.M. **2401 San Pedro Dr. NE, Albuquerque; 505-883-4414.**

Padilla's Mexican Kitchen—$–$$

A busy, noisy neighborhood restaurant, Padilla's serves good home-style Mexican food in a casual storefront setting. Decor here is simple—a few pieces of artwork and a dozen or so carved, ceramic, and whatever elephants (a favorite of owner Mary Padilla). The food is authentic and relatively simple, made by hand with fresh ingredients. Especially recommended are the carne adovada (available Mon., Tues., and Wed. only), the blue corn chicken enchiladas, and the tamales. It's open Mon.–Sat. 11 A.M.–7:45 P.M. **1510 Girard Blvd. NE, Albuquerque; 505-262-0115.**

Rancher's Club of New Mexico—$$$–$$$$

Quite possibly Albuquerque's best and most luxurious restaurant, the Rancher's Club boasts superb service in an elegant dining room with a refined ranch decor—lots of polished wood and a handsome stone fireplace. Cuisine is primarily steak and seafood, and meals include prime aged beef, seafood, and chicken cooked on a wood grill using mesquite and hickory and other aromatic woods. Reservations recommended. Open Mon.–Fri. 11:30 A.M.–2 P.M., Mon.–Thurs. 5:30–10 P.M., Fri.–Sat. 5:30–10:30 P.M., Sun. 5:30–9 P.M. **1901 University Blvd. NE (in the Hilton Hotel), Albuquerque; 505-889-8071.**

Seagull Street Fish Market—$$–$$$$

A fine place for fresh seafood—and we do mean *fresh*—the specialty here is mesquite-grilled fish such as Pacific snapper Vera Cruz and blackened mahi mahi. There's patio dining in warm weather. Reservations recommended. Open Mon.–Sat. 11:30 A.M.–2:30 P.M. and 4:30–10 P.M. (Fri.–Sat. until 11 P.M.), Sun. noon–9 P.M. Closed Christmas. **5410 Academy Rd. NE, Albuquerque; 505-821-0020.**

Scalo's Italian Restaurant—$$$

A good choice for Italian food in the Duke City, Scalo's offers what many Albuquerqueans consider the city's best wood-oven pizza and interesting variations on traditional Italian fare. The menu changes periodically but likely will include calamari in a spicy marinara sauce, a house favorite. The wine list is exceptional and includes more than 30 wines by the glass. Reservations are recommended. Open Mon.–Sat. 11:30 A.M.–2:30 P.M., Mon.–Thurs. 5–10 P.M., Fri.–Sat. 5–11 P.M., Sun. 5–9 P.M. Closed Independence Day, Thanksgiving, Christmas. **3500 Central Ave. SE, Albuquerque; 505-255-8782.**

66 Diner—$–$$

This 1950s-style diner wasn't actually around during the heyday of Route 66, but it certainly does a good job of capturing the spirit of those times, or at least our rose-colored recollections of that era. There's plenty of neon and chrome, photos of Elvis and Marilyn, and even the servers dress the part. The food is exactly what you would expect—good burgers, including an excellent green chile cheeseburger, sandwiches, and meals such as grilled liver and onions, green chile chicken enchiladas, and meat loaf with mashed potatoes and gravy. There are daily blue-plate specials, including chicken pot pie on Tuesdays and fried catfish on Fridays, and an old-fashioned soda fountain creates wonderful malts and milkshakes. Open Mon.–Thurs. 11 A.M.–11 P.M., Fri. 11 A.M.–midnight, Sat. 8 A.M.–midnight, Sun. 8 A.M.–10 P.M. **1405 Central Ave. NE, Albuquerque; 505-247-1421; www.66diner.com.**

Services

Visitor Information

Albuquerque Convention & Visitors Bureau, 800-284-2282; 505-842-9918; www.itsatrip.org, operates three visitor information centers: **Albuquerque International Sunport (the airport), Baggage Claim, 2200 Sunport SE, Albuquerque; downtown in the Albuquerque Convention Center, 401 2nd St. NW, Albuquerque;** and **Old Town, Plaza Don Luis, 303 Romero NW, Albuquerque.**

There is a State Visitor Information Center in the **Indian Pueblo Cultural Center, 2401 12th St. NW, Albuquerque; 505-843-6950.** The University of New Mexico operates a visitor center at **1700 Las Lomas Blvd. NE, Albuquerque; 505-277-1989.**

SOCORRO

This town of about 8,900 people has a lot to offer to the traveler. It's a quiet overnight spot along north-south I-25 or the last area of civilization for those heading into the "wilds" to the west or east. Socorro has an impressive historic church, a historic bar on its historic plaza, a good golf course, some museums, and modern motels and restaurants. Socorro makes a good home base while exploring one of the best wildlife refuges in the country, just southeast of here, or the historic mining towns to the west. It sits at 4,585 feet elevation. Nearby, the tiny community of San Antonio—there's no chance of getting it confused with its namesake down in Texas—is the birthplace and childhood home of Conrad Hilton, who rented out a couple of rooms in his parents' house to railroad travelers. From that start he opened a hotel in Cisco, Texas, and then went on to build one of the greatest hotel chains the world has ever seen. Ask one of the locals to point out the Hilton home to you.

History

Socorro is the Spanish word for help. The town received the name through helpfulness, although it wasn't the people of present-day Socorro who provided it. The name was coined by Juan de Oñate in 1598 when the people of the nearby pueblo—Pilabo—provided help to his expedition, which was headed for Santa Fe to establish a colony. The Indians of the pueblo provided corn to the near-starving travelers, the name was coined, and it lasted. But Socorro described only a locality until after the

Pueblo Revolt in 1680. The Indians of the Pueblo del Pilabo did not join in the Pueblo Revolt but instead retreated southward with the Spanish. They never returned to their Pilabo and still live in Socorro Del Sur ("Socorro of the South") near El Paso. After the Spanish reconquered New Mexico, Socorro was formally established as an outpost on the Camino Real—the "Royal Road"—which led all the way from Mexico City to Santa Fe.

After the reconquest, Socorro remained a tiny, relatively unimportant village until the coming of the railroad in 1880, when it absolutely boomed. The town was officially founded in 1816. A silver smelter was soon going strong, and when the rails were extended westward to Magdalena, things really exploded. Ore from mines all over that country was hauled to Magdalena by horses and mules, then railroaded into Socorro. Lumbering operations in the Magdalena Mountains brought logs to the railhead—known as Trails End—to load onto trains. Livestock was driven from western New Mexico and eastern Arizona pastures to reach the railhead in Magdalena for its journey east.

The mining, past and present, is still evident in Socorro, the home of the New Mexico Institute of Mining and Technology—better known as Tech—with more than 1,500 students, many majoring in computer science or engineering, and a very active research program. Today Socorro is the center of a thriving agricultural area and the shopping center for a large area of rural New Mexico, but you can still get a sense of the frontier days by exploring historic Socorro Plaza.

Getting There

Socorro is located 75 miles south of Albuquerque on I-25, at the junction with US Hwy. 60.

Major Attractions

Bosque del Apache National Wildlife Refuge

The swallows may head for Capistrano, but sandhill cranes prefer the Bosque del Apache. Among America's top national wildlife refuges, this 57,000-acre preserve is located along the Rio Grande at the northern edge of the Chihuahuan Desert and is home to tens of thousands of birds—more than 340 species—and a variety of mammals and other wildlife. The name, Bosque del Apache, is Spanish for "woods of the Apaches," and the area received the name from Spanish settlers who saw that Apache Indians frequently camped here.

Some birds are year-round residents, including red-winged blackbirds, Gambel's quail, American coots, western meadowlarks, American kestrels, ring-necked pheasants, and wild turkeys. Others, however, make the bosque their winter home, arriving during the fall and departing in spring. These winter residents include thousands of greater sandhill cranes, which usually make their annual appearance in late Sept. or early Oct., with late Dec. and Jan. being the peak time to see these spectacular birds. Also watch for a variety of ducks, Canada geese, golden eagles, and several species of sparrows.

There are several dozen species of mammals at the refuge, including coyotes (probably in search of a snow goose dinner) and possibly mule deer and elk.

A good first stop is the visitor center, where you can examine the exhibits, pick up a free refuge newspaper with a map of the 12-mile auto tour loop, rent binoculars if you neglected to bring your own, and check on recent bird and wildlife sightings.

Out on the loop drive you will often get closer to the birds and animals by staying in your vehicle, which acts as a blind, but there are some observation decks along the route. A 1,500-foot boardwalk into a marshy area helps you

The sandhill cranes of Bosque del Apache National Wildlife Refuge.

see waterfowl and some mammals up close. There are also several nature trails, which are described in the refuge newspaper. Early and late in the day are often the best times to see the birds and other wildlife.

The refuge grounds are open daily one hour before sunrise to one hour after sunset; the visitor center is open weekdays from 7:30 A.M. to 4 P.M. and weekends from 8 A.M. to 4:30 P.M. A small entry fee is charged. Bosque del Apache is located 18 miles south of Socorro; go south on I-25 to exit 139 at San Antonio and follow signs south on US Hwy. 380 and NM 1. **P.O. Box 1246, Socorro, 87801; 505-835-1828; http://southwest.fws.gov/refuges/newmex/bosque/index.html.**

The Very Large Array Radio Telescope

West of Socorro, out in the middle of nowhere, we come across the amazing spectacle of 27 huge, gleaming white satellite dishes. This is the Very Large Array Radio Telescope, usually called the VLA. Each satellite dish measures 82 feet across and 94 feet tall and weighs 230 tons. They're pointed at various celestial bodies in space, and the signals received by each of the antennae are combined electronically, resulting in a resolution that would enable us to see a golf ball 100 miles away.

Each of the satellite dishes is mounted on a railroad car, which sits on a Y-shaped system of tracks. By traveling the 13-mile legs of the rail system, the dishes can take on many different formations. Concentrating the dishes close together, radio astronomers have the equivalent of a wide-angle lens. But stretching out the dishes into longer arrangements gives the equivalent of a telescopic lens.

What they're seeing, however, is not the usual visual image we're used to. These antennae "see" radio waves, which are long-wavelength electromagnetic waves, produced by the energy emitted by the celestial objects. Visual light—what we see—is also produced by electromagnetic waves, but with a wavelength far smaller than radio waves.

So while radio telescopes produce vivid images of objects that we can see, such as the sun and stars, they also give us images of distant galaxies that are invisible to conventional telescopes.

The antennae, as well as some of the buildings at the VLA, were prominently featured in the 1997 sci-fi movie *Contact*. The film, based on a novel by the late scientist Carl Sagan, stars Jodie Foster as a scientist who is ridiculed by her colleagues for believing that there must be life in outer space, until … Well, you get the idea.

Visitors to the VLA should start at the visitor center to see the 9 minute video presentation, which provides an easy-to-understand overview of radio astronomy and the Very Large Array itself, plus various exhibits. From the visitor center a self-guided walking tour (free brochure available) wanders among some of the VLA buildings and gives you a close-up view of one of the giant dish antennae. Photography is permitted, but cell phones must be turned off—their electronic signals interfere with the radio telescopes!

Free guided tours are offered periodically; call or check the Web site for the current schedule. The VLA is open daily 8:30 A.M.–dusk. Located about 50 miles west of Socorro via US Hwy. 60 and NM 52. **505-835-7000; www.vla.nrao.edu.**

Festivals and Events

Unless otherwise noted, obtain information from the Socorro County Chamber of Commerce (see Services).

CIVIL WAR BATTLE REENACTMENTS

late Feb. The battle reenactment, demonstrations of camp life, contests, and a dance mark the anniversary of a battle that took place Feb. 21, 1862, in which Confederate troops defeated Union forces and took the city of Socorro for the Confederacy.

WOMEN OF THE WEST HISTORY TRAIL

mid-May. This two-day event, organized by a local elementary school, honors pioneer women of the Socorro area with a short play, a parade, and other activities.

CONRAD HILTON OPEN GOLF TOURNAMENT

early June. Getting its name from the famous hotelier born in nearby San Antonio, this weeklong tournament attracts not only professional golfers from across the country but also amateurs who compete in the Pro-Am. What is considered the world's longest—and strangest—golf hole is the Elfago Baca Shoot, which takes place on the tournament's last day and goes from the top of nearby M Mountain, dropping some 2,500 feet and covering about 2 miles.

MAGDALENA OLD TIMERS CELEBRATION

mid-July. Begun as a reunion of Magdalena families, this annual event has grown into a celebration of the town's history and tricultural heritage. There's a parade, complete with a cattle drive down Main St., traditional foods, and dancing and music by members of the

Alamo band of the Navajo Nation, as well as a Spanish village with food, arts, and crafts. The event also includes a fiddling contest, street dances, tours of the area's historic mines, lots of food, and a rodeo.

SOCORRO COUNTY FAIR & RODEO

early Sept. This fun-filled event includes agricultural exhibits, arts and crafts, food booths, a livestock show, a fiddling contest, children's games, and a parade.

SAN MIGUEL FIESTA

late Sept. Held at the historic San Miguel Mission, this event includes a variety of entertainment as well as religious services, with the crowning of the fiesta queen and her court plus a procession around the Socorro Plaza. **505-835-1620.**

ALAMO INDIAN DAYS

early Oct. The Alamo band of the Navajo Nation, with a reservation along the northwestern edge of Socorro County, northwest of Magdalena via NM 169, may be isolated from their Navajo kin, but they work hard to maintain their cultural heritage. This annual event features a parade, native foods, arts and crafts, and athletic contests. **505-854-2686.**

OCTOBERFEST

first Sat. in Oct. Take your choice between bratwurst and sauerkraut or chile cheeseburgers at this annual fund-raiser for the Hammel Museum, located in Socorro's first brewery. The event also includes live music, plant and bake sales, and arts and crafts booths. **505-835-3440.**

NEW MEXICO MINERAL SYMPOSIUM

early Nov. Like rocks? This annual

event, open to both professional geologists and enthusiastic amateurs, offers presentations and demonstrations on the geology of New Mexico and surrounding areas, including some rare and exotic minerals. **505-835-5140; www.geoinfo.nmt.edu.**

FESTIVAL OF THE CRANES

mid-Nov. The top annual event in this area, this five-day festival at El Bosque del Apache National Wildlife Refuge and locations in Socorro is timed to coincide with the yearly return of the refuge's most famous winter residents—sandhill cranes—as well as the arrival of myriad other species of migrating birds, including snow geese and a variety of ducks. The festival includes guided tours of the refuge and workshops on subjects ranging from bird photography to identifying duck rumps, as well as talks and demonstrations. Walking tours of historical Socorro are also offered, and there are usually arts and crafts fairs, live entertainment, and general merriment in nearby communities. **505-835-2077; www.friendsofthebosque.org/crane.**

BALLOON RALLY, POSOLE COOK-OFF, AND CHRISTMAS ELECTRIC LIGHT PARADE

weekend before Christmas. Combines a hot air balloon rally with mass ascensions, night glows, and contests, including a posole cooking contest, live music, and a Christmas parade.

Outdoor Activities

Golf

NEW MEXICO TECH GOLF COURSE

This challenging 18-hole public course has small greens and well-manicured tree-lined fairways, with water hazards on more than half the holes. Open year-round. Located at the university. **801 Leroy Place, Socorro; 505-835-5335; www.nmt.edu/nmtgolf.**

Seeing and Doing

Historic Walking Tour

Socorro was an especially wild place in the late 1800s when extensive mining in the surrounding hills made it the biggest town in New Mexico. A number of historic buildings on and near the plaza date from that period or earlier. These include the Juan Nepomoceno Garcia House, a good example of the Spanish-Mexican period, with sections that may have been built in 1816. On the south side of the plaza is the Capitol Bar, which opened in 1896 and has been serving demon rum and related beverages nonstop since then—no, it didn't let a little thing like Prohibition interfere with business, and it was said that it had the best moonshine in town. Nearby you'll also find an old stone brewery that was operating even earlier, so at least we know what the people of 1890s Socorro liked to do. For a free historic walking tour brochure stop at the chamber of commerce office (see Services).

While exploring historic Socorro be sure to walk several blocks north of the plaza to the San Miguel Mission Church. The original was built in the early 1600s but was destroyed during the Pueblo Revolt in 1680. The current church was built on the original site between 1819 and 1821 and was probably flat roofed. The handsome twin towers and peaked roof are believed to have been added later. **403 El Camino Real, Socorro; 505-835-1620.**

Museums

HAMMEL MUSEUM

This handsome old stone brewery and icehouse, which dates from about the 1880s, is open occasionally (usually the first and last Sat. of the month 9 A.M.–1 P.M.; call to check), with tours offered by members of the Socorro Historical Society. It contains some of the old brewing equipment and artifacts and photographs on the history of Socorro, and there is a model railroad display. **600 6th St., P.O. Box 923, Socorro; 505-835-3437.**

THE MINERAL MUSEUM

Home to the largest collection of minerals in New Mexico, the museum shows off spectacular minerals and rocks from around the state, as well as from other states and around the world. There are also displays of mining memorabilia, a small exhibit of fossils, and a spectacular ultraviolet exhibit of minerals. Open Mon.–Fri. 8 A.M.–5 P.M. and Sat.–Sun. 10 A.M.–3 P.M. **New Mexico Institute of Mining and Technology, Workman Addition, 801 Leroy Pl., Socorro; 505-835-5140; www.geoinfo.nmt.edu.**

The original San Miguel Mission Church was destroyed by fire in the Pueblo Revolt of 1680, but was rebuilt on the same site in the early 1800s.

Nearby

MAGDALENA

Twenty-seven miles west of Socorro on US Hwy. 60, the picturesque community of Magdalena, with a population of about 1,000, was named for Mary Magdalene of biblical fame, because an early Spanish priest thought that a rock formation near the town resembled her head. Although it got its start as a mining center, it boomed after 1885, when the Atchison, Topeka and Santa Fe Railroad Company built a spur line to Magdalena from Socorro. The rail line not only made it possible to get the ore to smelters, but also made Magdalena a shipping point for livestock. Cattle and sheep were taken by trail to Magdalena, then were herded into railroad cars.

There was a U.S. Army post at Pueblo Springs, just north of the present town of Magdalena. Idle soldiers got to prospecting and found rich veins of silver. In 1886, Col. J. S. Hutchason of the U.S. Army opened the first mines, and in the next 60 years more than $60 million of ore was mined here. After gold and silver, the miners also found lead, zinc, and copper. Ores are finite and always play out in the end. But cattle and sheep are renewable resources, and they kept coming, some of them trailed as far as 120 miles to reach Magdalena. At one time, Magdalena was the biggest livestock shipping point west of Chicago, and it continued as a livestock shipping point until 1971 when the A, T & SF discontinued the line.

Today visitors can explore the historic downtown area, which includes the restored 100-year-old railroad depot—where the Magdalena Village Hall and Library are located—a hotel, bank, and the old stock pens, which held the cattle and sheep before they were shipped east by rail. The Box Car Museum, located on Main St. next to the railroad depot, contains memorabilia of the town's Wild West days, mining, and cattle drives. For hours and other information, call the **Village Hall, 505-854-2261**.

You can also gaze up at Magdalena Peak, due south of town, to see the profile of Mary Magdalene. The mountain is said to have been a sacred place for American Indians, and The Lady on the Mountain, as the rock formation is also called, is said to have protected area miners and even led them to the mountain's riches.

The ghost town of Kelly is about 3 miles southeast of Magdalena via Forest Rd. 505, and it definitely is a ghost town, with no occupants, no ticket takers, no commercialism. What it does have is a cemetery and some ruins, opportunities for rockhounding and imagining what Kelly must have been like during its heyday when it had two churches and seven saloons.

For additional information, contact the **Magdalena Chamber of Commerce, P.O. Box 281, Magdalena, 87825; 866-854-3217; www.magdalena-nm.com.**

Where to Stay

Accommodations

MOTELS

Days Inn—$$

Offers 41 rooms and a heated outdoor pool. **507 N. California Ave., Socorro, 87801; 800-329-7466; 505-835-0230.**

Econo Lodge—$–$$

An especially good value, this Econo Lodge has 64 rooms, a heated outdoor

Hot Stuff!

New Mexico's official state question, approved by the legislature and signed into law by the governor, is "Red or green?" Being able to understand and answer this extremely important question is essential to your enjoyment and appreciation of New Mexico. The question, of course, refers to the choice you will get when ordering burritos and other dishes in New Mexico restaurants—do you want your chile sauce, usually just called salsa, made from red or green chile peppers?

The best chile peppers in the world are grown in the Mesilla Valley of southern New Mexico. Hatch chile—grown near the small community of Hatch—draws raves from chile lovers all over the world, and New Mexican cuisine features these savory chiles in many dishes.

There are chiles for every taste and occasion, from mild and sweet to outrageously hot. The peppers come in red, orange, yellow, and various shades of green, but usually we talk about them being either red or green. Some chiles are long and skinny, others short and plump, still others are quite tiny. There are smooth ones and wrinkled ones and some that curl. And since they cross-pollinate wherever they grow, chiles are continually evolving and changing.

Our personal favorite is *chile verde*, or green chile, which are medium-sized, often about 6 inches long, plump but not fat. Although hot, they are also sweet so the heat doesn't bite, and they are very tasty. They are the basis of delicious chile rellenos, one of New Mexico's premier dishes. The chile is first roasted and peeled, the seeds are removed, and then it's stuffed, usually with cheese, and the best ones, we think, are lightly breaded and pan-fried. Green chiles are also used to make a luscious sauce, which can be poured over burritos, *frijoles refritos* (refried beans), scrambled eggs, burgers, and almost anything that takes your fancy. We put green chile in just about everything, from mashed potatoes to white rice to apple pie! (Try it, you'll like it.)

Jalapeño chiles are also green, but smaller and generally hotter than the verde. The heat seems to depend on the soil in which they have been grown and how much water the plant received while the fruit was developing. Some people pop them down like candy, others run in terror at their mere sight, because their first taste wasn't a taste at all, but a fireball that caused blisters! So approach your first jalapeño with caution, remembering that heat can build slowly. But they do add wonderful flavors to strong dishes such as beef stew and chile con carne. Chopped small, they are tasty additions to a tossed salad.

The serrano chile is close in size to the jalapeño, but even hotter. Whatever you do, don't pick one up to nibble—you'll regret it. But they are used to advantage in making salsa picante, along with onions, tomatoes, and cilantro. Many New Mexican restaurants serve this with tortilla chips, often while you're waiting for your meal. Every chef makes it a bit differently, so be sure to try some whenever you get the chance.

You may have noticed chile *ristras* in your meanderings around our state: long strings of dark red peppers—almost dried-blood color—hanging on adobe walls

continued next page

pool, sauna, and whirlpool; pets accepted (for a fee). **713 N. California Ave., Socorro, 87801; 800-424-6423; 505-835-1500.**

Holiday Inn Express—$$$

The largest, fanciest, and most expensive motel in Socorro, this property offers 120 well-equipped rooms, decorated in a pleasant southwestern style, all with mini-refrigerators and microwaves. There's an indoor heated pool, a whirlpool, exercise facilities, and video games. Small pets are accepted

(for a fee). **1100 N. California Ave., Socorro, 87801; 888-526-4567; 505-838-0556.**

Motel 6—$$

Has 97 rooms with showers only (no tubs) and a heated outdoor pool. Pets accepted. **807 S. US Hwy. 85, Socorro, 87801; 800-466-8356; 505-835-4300.**

Super 8—$$

An attractive member of this chain, it has 88 rooms, a heated outdoor pool,

---

Hot Stuff! continued

next to a door, archway, or window. Traditionally, New Mexicans tie the red chiles into these strings, or *ristras*, to air-dry. Once thoroughly dry they are practically dust and can be easily crushed and put into shakers for use in spicy stews and meat dishes. In recent years, they have also become a popular decorative item and are frequently formed into a variety of shapes and combined with dried grasses, gourds, berries, and greens. When intended for decor only, they are generally sprayed with a semigloss finish to help preserve them.

Chile piquins, sometimes called *chile pequeños*, are diminutive copies of the big chiles verdes. They are 2 to 3 inches long, slender, and picked when red. Used in many authentic Mexican dishes, they can be hot or mild, again depending on the variety, the amount of water they receive, and the nature of the soil in which they grow.

So what causes all this heat? The active ingredient in chile is capsaicin. Technically, it's measured by Scoville units, on a scale from 0 to 500,000. But a scale of 0 to 10 is more commonly used, with sweet peppers rating 0 and the fiery habañeros topping out at 10. It is said that capsaicin also releases endorphins in the brain, inducing a sense of well-being or euphoria. Some claim it is also an aphrodisiac.

If you do overdo a bite of a fiery member of the chile family, here's a tip: *don't* reach for your water glass, as it only spreads the pain. The best thing for cutting the heat is a dairy product, which is one reason many recipes include cheese or sour cream on top. Or try chewing fresh bread to absorb the fire. Beer also is cooling, rinsing away the volatile oils; the alcohol helps dissolve the oils besides deadening the pain. Neutral spirits such as vodka, tequila, or gin are equally effective.

Chiles are tasty and versatile, but don't rush into anything. Ask your restaurant server about the heat in the food you're considering, and even then taste cautiously. Soon you'll enjoy the fiery New Mexico cuisine as much as we do.

and whirlpool. **1121 Frontage Rd. NW, Socorro, 87801; 800-800-8000; 505-835-4626.**

Campground

BOSQUE BIRDWATCHERS RV PARK

Conveniently located for those visiting Bosque del Apache National Wildlife Refuge, this quiet campground has 30 RV sites with full hookups plus 10 tent sites. There are restrooms with showers and an RV dump station. Located 13 miles south of Socorro near San Antonio, on the road (NM 1) between San Antonio and the wildlife refuge. From I-25 take exit 139, then follow NM 1. **505-835-1366.**

Where to Eat

El Camino Restaurant & Lounge— $$–$$$

This casual restaurant offers generous portions of well-prepared American and Mexican standards at attractive prices. Open 24 hours. **707 N. California Ave., Socorro; 505-835-1180.**

El Sombrero Cafe—$$

A locals' favorite, El Sombrero offers genuine New Mexico–style Mexican dishes including enchiladas and fajitas, with assertive red or green chile. Decor is Mexican cantina. Open daily 11 A.M.–9 P.M. Closed major holidays. **210 Mesquite St., Socorro; 505-835-3945.**

Owl Bar—$$

Green chile cheeseburgers are the specialty at this dark, funky bar, which is a good place to stop on the way to or

from the Bosque del Apache National Wildlife Refuge. Located about 10 miles south of Socorro via I-25. Open Mon.–Sat. 8 A.M.–9:30 P.M. **NM 1 and US Hwy. 380, San Antonio; 505-835-9946.**

Socorro Springs Brewing Company—$$

Fresh-brewed beer plus good pizzas, sandwiches, and burgers make this a good choice for lunch or dinner. The menu is a little more interesting than the standard brewpub fare, with what seems like a California influence. Located in a historic adobe building dating from the late 1800s. Open daily 11 A.M.–10 P.M. **115 Abeyta Ave., Socorro; 505-838-0650.**

Val Verde Steak House—$$–$$$$

Socorro's finest restaurant, this steak house is located in a stately historic hotel built in 1919. Although the hotel is not open to the public, the restaurant serves excellent beef—try the pepper steak in a wine sauce or the beef Stroganoff— plus enchiladas and other southwestern specialties. There's a full bar with live entertainment most weekends. Open Mon.–Fri. 11 A.M.–2 P.M. and 5–9:30 P.M., Fri.–Sat. 5–10 P.M., Sun. noon–9 P.M. **203 E. Manzanares Ave., Socorro; 505-835-3380.**

Services

Visitor Information

The **Socorro County Chamber of Commerce** operates a visitor center at the northeast corner of the historic plaza; **101 Plaza, P.O. Box 743, Socorro, 87801-0743; 505-835-0424; www.socorro-nm.com.**

TRUTH OR CONSEQUENCES

Once called Hot Springs, an appropriate name for a community that boasted numerous hot mineral springs, one fine day in 1950 the townspeople voted to change Hot Springs's name to Truth or Consequences (usually shortened to T or C). Now, why on earth would a relatively sane town do that?

Ralph Edwards, a famous game-show master of ceremonies, hosted a popular radio (and then TV) program called *Truth or Consequences*. On this show, the contestants were given a question that was nearly impossible to answer. When they failed to "tell the truth," they were forced to face the consequences, which were usually undignified but safe enough.

Edwards advertised to find a town that would be willing to change its name to Truth or Consequences to commemorate the 10th anniversary of that program. The folks in Hot Springs thought it over and decided that they had nothing to lose. Several other towns vied for the honor to become T or C, but Ralph Edwards's staff chose Hot Springs because of the mineral hot springs found here and because of the Carrie Tingley Orthopedic Hospital, which helped so many children.

The decision started a unique relationship that has provided publicity for the town and the program. T or C changed the name of a street to Ralph Edwards. It built Ralph Edwards Park. And several times after the name change the residents were asked to vote on changing the name back to Hot Springs. The loyal residents stuck to their new name, and Ralph Edwards is revered in Truth or Consequences.

History

True, the town was put on the map in 1950 when it changed its name, but it had actually been there for many years before that. Spanish conquistador Juan de Oñate came through here on his famed 1598 trip to establish Santa Fe. The discovery of copper, silver, and gold in the surrounding mountains helped Hot Springs grow. The discovery was an added attraction to the mineral springs and lured new settlers. Hot Springs soon became the biggest and most influential city in Sierra County.

Getting There

Truth or Consequences is located between I-25 exits 75 and 79. It is about 150 miles south of Albuquerque and 75 miles north of Las Cruces.

Festivals and Events

For information on the following, contact the Truth or Consequences/Sierra County Chamber of Commerce (see Services).

TRUTH OR CONSEQUENCES FIESTA

early May. Every year since the town changed its name in 1950 it has staged an annual fiesta to celebrate. Radio and TV celebrity Ralph Edwards joined the festivities each year from 1950 until 2000. The fiesta includes an old-time fiddlers contest and other music, the Miss Fiesta contest, a parade, food, games, arts and crafts, and a whole lot of partying.

GERONIMO DAYS
PEACE GATHERING

mid-Oct. T or C remembers that the town was once the location of the sacred hot springs of the Apache people and celebrates with Apache dancers, mariachi bands, bluegrass music, and Spanish folk music.

VETERANS DAY CAR SHOW

early Nov. Held the Sat. closest to Veterans Day, this event is one of the biggest car shows in the state, attracting more than 150 antique and classic cars, motorcycles, and tractors to the New Mexico Veterans Center in Truth or Consequences.

Outdoor Activities

Boating and Fishing

The main outdoor attractions here are three state parks produced by dams on the Rio Grande. They're all easily reached from T or C via I-25.

CABALLO LAKE STATE PARK

A pleasant family-oriented park, Caballo Lake provides ample opportunities for fishing and water sports and offers several hiking trails and good bird-watching possibilities. The lake was created in the late 1930s with the construction of an earth-filled dam 96 feet high by 4,558 feet long. When full the skinny lake is 18 miles long, but even in good years it shrinks considerably after a spring and summer of providing water for irrigation. Elevation is 4,100 feet.

Fishing is the main activity here, primarily for white bass and walleye, although anglers also catch black bass, crappie, catfish, northern pike, and sunfish. Close by are several fishing supply stores. Most boats on the lake are of the fishing variety, but you'll also see small sailboats and windsurfers, especially in spring. Canoeists often put into the Rio Grande just south of Elephant Butte Dam near the town of Williamsburg and paddle down to Caballo Lake, a distance of about 10 miles. There is no designated swimming beach; the best swimming is usually just west of the dam and in the Upper Flats, which are on the north edge of the main park campgrounds.

The bulk of the park's facilities are in this main section, on the west side of the lake, just north of the dam. There are developed campsites on a bluff overlooking the lake, where there are even a few trees, and another campground, more secluded and with more trees, is along the Rio Grande just south of the dam. Of the 135 developed sites, 63 have electric hookups. There is also an undeveloped camping area to the north of the main section, which has picnic tables, grills, and chemical toilets, and where campers can set up their tents or park their RVs wherever they want.

Both bald and golden eagles nest at the lake during the winter. Also seen are double-crested cormorants, common loons, snowy egrets, scaled quail, sandhill cranes, American white pelicans, and roadrunners. There are also dozens of songbirds, several species of hummingbirds, and numerous geese and ducks. Other wildlife include numerous rock squirrels and cottontail rabbits, plus coyotes, wolves, foxes, raccoons, mule deer, and rattlesnakes.

The 5.5 miles of sandy trails here are more for getting from place to place than for serious hiking, and all are considered easy. The 0.25-mile Overlook Trail is a loop over a grassy and cactus-studded knoll that offers good views out across the lake. Another trail heads north from the campgrounds about 3 miles to a point, and a branch of this trail also goes south of the visitor center to the lake. The park also has several well tended cactus gardens, with yucca, agave, ocotillo, prickly pear, mesquite, and other desert plants.

A small visitor center has displays on archeology of the area and historic photos from the construction of the dam, plus photos to help visitors identify the park's birds, fish, and plants. The park is located 16 miles south of Truth or Consequences via I-25 exit 59 and NM 187. Entrance and camping fees are charged. **P.O. Box 32, Caballo, 87931; 877-664-7787 (camping reservations); 505-743-3942; www.nmparks.com.**

ELEPHANT BUTTE LAKE STATE PARK

New Mexico's largest body of water, Elephant Butte Lake was created by construction of a dam by the Federal Bureau of Reclamation in 1916. It holds back the waters of the Rio Grande and forms a lake that varies in length from 20 to 45 miles, depending on the snowpack in Colorado and northern New Mexico and on the needs of irrigation

farming downstream. Of more importance to the visitor, however, the lake provides opportunities for just about every form of water-based recreation, from waterskiing to scuba diving to canoeing. It has sandy beaches, quiet little coves, full service marinas, and enough open water for cabin cruisers and houseboats.

Elephant Butte Lake is named for a rock formation that resembles an elephant, at least to some observers who see the left side of its head, with a prominent ear, and its trunk curled by a foot. The formation—the eroded core of an ancient volcano—is an island in the lake, just northeast of the dam. Although it is not known when the formation and lake were named, this area once had real elephants. Fossils of a primitive ancestor of today's elephants, the stegomastodon, have been found just west of the lake. The animal was about 7 feet tall, stocky, with long upper tusks.

The primary activity here is boating, with every imaginable type of watercraft represented, from the tiniest inflatable to the largest and most luxurious cabin

Elephant Butte Lake was formed when the Rio Grande was dammed in 1916.

cruiser. No-wake areas make canoeing and kayaking fun and safe, personal watercraft and ski boats are popular, and colorful sailboats and sailboards are seen on the lake. Boat rentals are available. Fishing from both shore and boat is popular, with anglers catching largemouth, smallmouth, striped, and white bass, plus catfish, sunfish, walleye, crappie, and bluegill. Trout fishing is good in the Rio Grande south of the dam.

There are several short hiking trails. The Luchini Trail is an easy, flat 1.6-mile sandy loop that winds through desert grasses and cactus, with signs identifying plants such as honey mesquite, soaptree yucca, and desert Christmas cactus along one leg of the trail. The Old Butte Nature Trail is a 0.5-mile loop, steep and rocky, with signs identifying a variety of desert plants. It leads to a high overlook that provides wonderful panoramic views of the lake and its namesake rock formation.

Bird-watching is especially good in winter, when you are apt to see bald eagles—Jan. is the best time—plus numerous species of ducks, ring-billed gulls, and an occasional American white pelican. Bird-watchers also have a good chance of seeing red-tailed hawks, black-chinned hummingbirds, great blue herons, Gambel's quail, mourning doves, western grebes, rufous-crowned sparrows, western bluebirds, and double-crested cormorants. The park is also home to cottontail rabbits, black-tailed jackrabbits, a few deer, plus rattlesnakes and countless lizards.

The park's visitor center has exhibits on the geology, fish, and birds of the area, plus historic photos of the dam construction.

A variety of options are available for campers. There are 250 developed campsites, including 150 with electricity hookups. Those who want to rough it can camp along the beach but should be careful to avoid getting their vehicles stuck in the soft sand. The park has restrooms with showers and RV dump stations.

Unbelievable crowds jam into the state park on Memorial Day, the Fourth of July, and Labor Day. Outside of those three times, you'll not find it too crowded. Park headquarters are 5 miles north of Truth or Consequences via I-25, exit 83 or NM 51 (3rd Ave.). Entrance and camping fees are charged. **P.O. Box 13, Elephant Butte, 87935; 877-664-7787 (camping reservations); 505-744-5421; www.nmparks.com.**

PERCHA DAM STATE PARK

A hidden treasure in the New Mexico State Park system, this relatively unknown but delightful little park is a quiet getaway, with excellent fishing and bird-watching and an especially nice campground. Under the shade of tall cottonwoods, Russian olives, and green ash, the park hugs the Rio Grande in a rich riparian area that seems a bit out of place in the southern New Mexico desert. Percha Dam was built in 1917 to provide water for local farms. The name comes from Percha Creek, which enters the Rio Grande above the dam. The word *percha* is Spanish for "bird roost."

Fishing for walleye is very good, especially just below the dam, and anglers also catch white bass and catfish. The shady river is also a prime spot for canoeing. Among the area's best bird-watching locales, the park has most of the same species that are seen at nearby Caballo Lake State Park, but often in greater numbers, and it is easier to see them because it's usually less crowded here. Migratory species include numerous ducks and geese plus American white pelicans, trumpeter swans, sandhill cranes, great blue herons, golden eagles, bald eagles, scaled quail, red-winged blackbirds, western bluebirds, dark-eyed juncos, and yellow-breasted chats. Also seen scurrying through the underbrush and in the grassy fields are rock squirrels and cottontail rabbits, and there are also coyotes, foxes, and mule deer.

The 50 developed campsites—including 30 with electric hookups—are spacious and shady, and most are close enough to hear the river, even when its view is blocked by trees. An open, grassy area at the south end of the park is available for primitive camping. Nearby is a playground. Both Percha Dam and Caballo Lake State Parks are managed from one office. Percha Dam State Park is located 21 miles south of Truth or Consequences via I-25, exit 59. Entrance and camping fees are charged. **P.O. Box 32, Caballo, 87931; 877-664-7787 (camping reservations); 505-743-3942; www.nmparks.com.**

Seeing and Doing

Hot Springs

Soaking in the waters here goes back at least to Geronimo's time, when the famous Apache brought his warriors to the hot mineral springs to relieve the pains of battle. It was also these springs that gave the community the name of Hot Springs, which it had from at least the 1870s until that fateful day in 1950 when the townspeople cast their ballots to change it. And the hot springs are still a major attraction here, regardless of the town's name. Truth or Consequences sits atop a huge aquifer of 100° F mineral water that makes its way to the surface through numerous springs, ending up in

various pools and wells. The water is odorless, has a pH of 7 (neutral), and contains traces of 38 different minerals, including sodium chloride, bicarbonate, calcium chloride, potassium chloride, calcium sulfate, magnesium sulfate, and silicate.

The first recorded bathhouse was a small adobe structure, built in 1882 by cowboys from a nearby ranch. Today more than a half-dozen choices of commercial bathhouses are available for those who want to soak in the soothing mineral water. Temperatures at the bathhouses range from about 98° F to about 115° F. Hourly rates are charged, and facilities are located both indoors and outdoors, ranging from small private tubs for one or two to fairly spacious pools. Massage therapists are usually available, and some facilities also offer lodging.

For a list of bathhouses with facilities and current rates and hours, check with the Truth or Consequences/Sierra County Chamber of Commerce or stop at the Geronimo Trail Visitors Center (see Services).

185

Museums

CALLAHAN'S AUTO MUSEUM

New Mexico's first automobile museum, Callahan's has some beautifully restored classic cars—a 1936 Desoto Airflow, a 1936 Pierce Arrow limousine, a 1967 Lincoln Continental convertible, and a dozen or so others, mostly from the 1920s through the 1960s. Numerous items of automotive memorabilia are on display, as well as historic maps and road signs, and a variety of auto-related books are for sale. Call for current hours. Admission fee charged. **410 Cedar St., Truth or Consequences; 505-894-6900.**

GERONIMO SPRINGS MUSEUM

Definitely one of the better small-town museums in New Mexico, this facility has excellent exhibits on the region's history from prehistoric times to modern times—starting with the skull of a hairy mammoth that was found in the area and an excellent collection of Mimbres and other prehistoric pottery. There is also a life-size wax statue of the famous Apache chief Geronimo and information about the Apache's resistance to the coming of white settlers. There's an authentic miner's log cabin, relocated from the Gila National Forest, plus information on Hispanic settlers and other early farmers and ranchers. Not to be left out, the Ralph Edwards Room details the town's change of name from Hot Springs to Truth or Consequences, and a TV plays videotapes of the now long-gone *Truth or Consequences* TV show. There is also a visitor center at the museum. Open Mon.–Sat. 9 A.M.–5 P.M. A small admission fee is charged. **211 Main St., Truth or Consequences; 505-894-6600.**

Where to Stay

Accommodations

Best Western Hot Springs Inn—$$

This attractive motel has all the amenities you would expect in a first-class Best Western, including in-room mini-refrigerators and microwaves. There are 41 spacious units and a heated outdoor pool. Small pets are accepted. Located 3 miles from Elephant Butte Lake, just off I-25, exit 79. **2270 N. Date St., Truth or Consequences, 87901; 505-894-6665.**

Holiday Inn—$$–$$$

This handsome hotel, which opened in 2000, offers a slew of amenities, including in-room mini-refrigerators and

24-hour room service, along with a heated indoor pool, whirlpool, and exercise room. There are 50 units, including a whirlpool suite, and pets are accepted. Located about 3 miles from Elephant Butte Lake, just off I-25, exit 79. **2250 N. Date St., Truth or Consequences, 87901; 505-894-1660.**

Quality Inn—$$–$$$

Overlooking Elephant Butte Lake, this resort motel offers some of the best views in the area, and the rooms are pretty nice too. It has a very attractive outdoor pool, tennis courts, and a good restaurant and lounge. Mini-refrigerators and microwave ovens are available. Pets are accepted (for a fee); 48 units. Take I-25, exit 83, and follow the signs to Elephant Butte Dam. **401 NM 195, Elephant Butte, 87935; 505-744-5431.**

Super 8 Motel—$$

Among the lower priced chains in the area, this 40-room motel offers well-maintained basic rooms and accepts pets. There is no pool. Off I-25, exit 79. **2151 N. Date St., Truth or Consequences, 87901; 505-894-7888.**

Campgrounds

The best camping in this area, to our way of thinking, will be found at the three state parks: Elephant Butte, Caballo Lake, and Percha Dam. But for those who want the greater number of amenities found at commercial campgrounds, the area offers those as well. All of the following are open year-round.

CIELO VISTA RV PARK

Overlooking Truth of Consequences from a quiet hilltop, but still within walking distance of downtown, this RV park (no tents allowed) has 73 sites with full hookups including cable TV. It has a recreation room, horseshoes, and shuffleboard, but no pool. It's located between I-25 exits 75 and 79, but use exit 79 to avoid making a U-turn. **501 S. Broadway, Truth or Consequences, 87901; 888-414-8478 (reservations); 505-894-3738.**

LAKESIDE RV PARK

Close to Elephant Butte Lake, this RV park (no tents) is off the main road so it's nice and quiet. It has 50 sites, all the usual amenities except a pool, and offers a variety of planned activities including bingo and crafts. Take I-25, exit 83. **107 Country Club Blvd., P.O. Drawer 981, Elephant Butte Lake, 87935; 800-808-5848 (reservations); 505-744-5996; www.lakesiderv.com.**

R.J. RV PARK

All the usual commercial campground amenities except a pool, and rates include cable TV. There are 47 sites. Take I-25 exit 75. **2103 S. Broadway, Truth or Consequences, 87901; 505-894-9777.**

Where to Eat

In addition to the restaurants mentioned below, the restaurant at the Quality Inn, discussed under Accommodations, offers good food for three meals daily, including fine dining at dinner and a great view.

Hodge's Corner Restaurant—$–$$$

Generous portions of home-style American and Mexican dishes are what you'll find at this casual family restaurant. Try the half-pound burgers, served with curly fries, or the locally popular fried chicken. Breakfast is served all day—the huevos rancheros are especially good—and there are lunch and dinner buffets. Open Mon. 6:30 A.M.–2 P.M.; Tues.–Sun. 6:30 A.M.–8 P.M. **915 NM 195, Elephant Butte; 505-744-5626.**

La Cocina—$$–$$$

Excellent Mexican and American food in a festive, southwestern atmosphere. Especially recommended are the enchiladas and burgers, plus the giant sopaipillas. Open daily 10:30 A.M.–10 P.M. (closes 9 P.M. weekdays in winter). **1 Lakeway Dr., Truth or Consequences; 505-894-6499.**

Los Arcos Steak & Lobster—$$–$$$$

The decor may be Mexican, but this is a great place for steak, seafood, and other American dishes, and it has a good salad bar. Open daily 5 P.M.–10:30 P.M.; closed Thanksgiving and Christmas. **1400 N. Date St., Truth or Consequences; 505-894-6200.**

Services

Visitor Information

Truth or Consequences/Sierra County Chamber of Commerce, 400 W. 4th St., P.O. Drawer 31, Truth or Consequences, 87901; 505-894-3536; www.truthorconsequencesnm.net.

Elephant Butte Chamber of Commerce, 419 Warm Springs Blvd., Elephant Butte, 87935; 877-744-4900; 505-744-4708; www.elephantbuttecoc.com.

Once you get there, stop at the **Geronimo Trail Visitors Center** located at the **Geronimo Springs Museum, 211 Main St., Truth or Consequences; 800-831-9487; 505-894-1968; www.geronimotrail.com.**

187

LAS CRUCES

With about 75,000 people, Las Cruces is New Mexico's second largest city—no matter how much Santa Fe, with a mere 62,000, might protest. It's located at the crossroads—*las cruces*—of Interstate 25, Interstate 10, US Hwy. 70, and railroad lines. But it wasn't that kind of crossing that gave this lovely city its name. One legend says that the *cruces* were crosses erected over Spanish settlers who had been buried after an Indian massacre in 1848. Another story says that the *cruces* were crosses erected over the graves of Spanish settlers who were ambushed and massacred on their way back from Taos in 1830. In any event, Las Cruces is a relative newcomer among New Mexico cities, and most of the truly historic sites here are located in the adjacent community of Mesilla, with a population of just more than 2,000.

Both Mesilla and Las Cruces owe their existence to the waters of the Rio Grande, which, along with a very mild climate, have made the Mesilla Valley an ideal spot to grow pecans, alfalfa, cotton, chile peppers, corn, onions, lettuce, and grapes. Las Cruces is the home of New Mexico State University, the state's second largest university. While we wouldn't say that Las Cruces and Mesilla are a major tourist destination like Santa Fe and Taos, there are quite a few things here to see and do, and it would be very easy to spend an enjoyable two to four days exploring the area. The mild winter weather here—daytime temperatures in the 60s and 70s in Jan. are not uncommon—has been attracting increasing numbers of "snowbirds," those residents of northern areas who point their RVs south as winter snows begin to fall. Elevation of Las Cruces is 3,909 feet, and in Mesilla it's 3,896 feet.

Old Mesilla Plaza bears a historic marker commemorating Cura Ramón Ortiz, who was commissioned by the Mexican government to establish Mesilla. Ortiz brought residents from New Mexico and Juarez to populate the new town.

History

There's archeological evidence that this area was occupied by prehistoric Indians as far back as 200 B.C., but in relatively recent times Las Cruces figured into the story of Alvar Nuñez Cabeza de Vaca, who survived a shipwreck somewhere in the Gulf of Mexico and got ashore in the 1530s. With three companions he traveled on foot across the entire length of present-day Louisiana and Texas in search of Spanish settlements. He finally found his way to the Mesilla Valley in 1535 and thus has the distinction of being the first European to see this land. Five years after Cabeza de Vaca's arrival, the Coronado expedition passed through the Mesilla Valley on its way to search for the fabled (and nonexistent) Seven Cities of Gold.

Sixty-three years after the arrival of Cabeza de Vaca, Don Juan de Oñate led colonists all the way from Chihuahua, Mexico, to Santa Fe. Some colonists stopped in this area and thus avoided traveling the 90 miles of hell that came to be known as the Jornada del Muerto (journey of death).

In Mesilla, the Gadsden Treaty was signed in 1854, establishing the border between the United States and Mexico. Here, too, was the Butterfield Stage route stopover, and it was said that this was the only place along the route between San Antonio and the West Coast where you could rent a bed.

Lots of things happened here. The notorious William Bonney, otherwise known as Billy the Kid, was tried for murder in a building that still stands on the Mesilla Plaza. The "Kid" was sentenced to hang, but he escaped and was the subject of quite a manhunt. Famed sheriff Pat Garrett finally tracked him down and shot him. Garrett was himself shot and killed just outside of Las Cruces under mysterious circumstances and is buried in a local cemetery.

Getting There

Las Cruces, 223 miles south of Albuquerque, is located along I-10 where it meets the southern terminus of I-25. Service from most major airlines is available at El Paso International Airport, about 45 miles south of Las Cruces.

Major Attractions

Fort Selden State Monument
Once an impressive and busy frontier fort, today Fort Selden is a collection of crumbling adobe walls built around a military quadrangle, where we as visitors listen to the wind and imagine what life was like here more than 100 years ago. The fort was established along the banks of the Rio Grande in 1865 to protect settlers from Apaches and outlaws, but by 1890, the Apache were no longer a threat and at least some sense of law and order was arriving in the West. In 1891, Fort Selden was declared obsolete by the army and abandoned.

Today it features an interpretive trail through its ruins, with explanatory signposts describing life at the fort. The visitor center/museum has exhibits on frontier military life in the late 19th century, and living history demonstrations are scheduled on most summer weekends. The monument is open Wed.–Mon. 8:30 A.M.–5 P.M. Small admission fee. Located about 15 miles north of Las Cruces off I-25, exit 19. **P.O. Box 58, Radium Springs, 88054; 505-526-8911; www.newmexicoculture.org.**

Old Mesilla Plaza
A step back into the mid-1800s, Old Mesilla Plaza contains numerous beautifully restored historic buildings, many containing charming restaurants, galleries, and shops. This is where Billy the Kid was tried and sentenced to hang—it never happened—and was a major stop for the Butterfield stage line. In fact, at one time Mesilla—with some 3,000 residents—was the largest community between San Antonio, Texas, and San Diego, California. Mesilla was the seat of Doña Ana County until 1881 when the railroad arrived 4 miles to the northeast in Las Cruces. The county seat was then moved to Las Cruces, causing that community to begin its growth to eventually become New Mexico's second largest city, leaving Mesilla literally in the dust.

Among the historical buildings on Old Mesilla Plaza is the handsome San Albino Church. The original church was built about 1850, and the current structure was constructed in 1906. It's named for St. Albin, a medieval English Bishop; the three church bells in the church's two bell towers date from the 1870s. The church offers mass in English and Spanish, and is open to visitors Mon.–Sat. 1–3 P.M. Call **505-526-9349** for times of masses and other information. For additional information on Old Mesilla Plaza contact the **Las Cruces Convention & Visitors Bureau** or the **Old Mesilla Association** (listed under Services) and pick up a copy of the map and guide to the plaza's historic buildings from one of the local businesses or at a visitor center.

Festivals and Events

FARMER'S & CRAFTS MARKET
Wed. and Sat. 8 A.M.–noon year-round. More than 200 area farmers, artists, and craftsworkers participate in this open-air market, selling numerous items ranging from fresh produce to home baked goods to pottery, stained glass, fine art, jewelry, and clothing. It takes place at the Downtown Mall on Main St., just south of Picacho Ave. **505-541-2554.**

BRITISH CAR DAYS
last Sat. in Apr. British car buffs from New Mexico and surrounding states show off their shiny automobiles each year on Old Mesilla Plaza. The event is limited to 88 vehicles, and recent shows have included cars from the 1930s to recent years, ranging from Bentleys to Jags to Triumphs to classic MGs, and even a three-wheeled Morgan. **505-524-8887.**

CINCO DE MAYO
early May. Similar to festivities in many Hispanic communities, this event celebrates Mexico's independence day, with lots of bands, parades, and food. Takes place on Old Mesilla Plaza. **505-525-1965.**

SOUTHERN NEW MEXICO WINE FESTIVAL
Memorial Day weekend. Wine and chile—what could be better? There are tastings from wineries across the state, arts and crafts booths, kids pony rides, and plenty of spicy southwestern food. Takes place at the Southern New Mexico State Fairgrounds, west of Las Cruces at I-10, exit 132. **505-646-4543.**

MESILLA VALLEY ANTIQUE AND COLLECTIBLE SHOW
early June. A vast variety of antiques are available for admiring and buying. At St. Genevieve's Parish Hall, Las Cruces. **505-526-8624.**

WHOLE ENCHILADA FIESTA
late Sept. or early Oct. Three fun-filled

days of celebrating the local chile harvest, with street dancing, entertainment, and plenty of food, including the world's largest enchilada! Takes place at the Downtown Mall in Las Cruces. **505-526-1938; www.twefie.com.**

RENAISSANCE CRAFTFAIRE

mid-Nov. Exhibition and sale of works by southwestern artists and craftspeople Lots of extra entertainment. Takes place at Young Park in Las Cruces. **505-523-6403.**

CHRISTMAS CAROLS AND LUMINARIAS ON THE PLAZA

Christmas Eve. Traditional Christmas Eve festivities on the Old Mesilla Plaza.

Outdoor Activities

Fishing, Hiking, and More

LEASBURG DAM STATE PARK

Built in 1908 to divert water from the Rio Grande to irrigate the upper Mesilla Valley, one of the most productive agricultural areas in the state, Leasburg Dam is also the parent of an attractive state park and a great spot for fishing, kayaking, canoeing, and camping. It also boasts beautiful cactus gardens, several short trails, and a pleasant campground. It sits at 4,200 feet elevation.

The Rio Grande here is mostly calm, with little white water, and the park makes a good put-in or take-out point for canoeing the Rio Grande, coming downriver about 45 miles from Percha Dam State Park or going downriver from Leasburg Dam about 10 miles to Las Cruces. There's good fishing in spring and summer, when the river is at its highest, and anglers catch channel catfish, white bass, and some walleye.

A highlight of the park is its large, well-tended Cactus Patch botanical garden, where you'll see numerous species of cactus and other desert plants, with identifying labels, such as yucca and agave, cholla, cow's tongue, prickly pear, mesquite, creosote bush, and

One of the beautiful cactus gardens at Leasburg Dam State Park.

ocotillo. In addition to the Cactus Patch, there are a number of smaller cactus gardens throughout the park, which look spectacular in spring when the cactus burst into bloom with flowers of red, purple, and yellow.

Hiking trails here are short and easy, great for an after-dinner walk. The Apache Trail runs 0.33 mile (one-way) from the west end of Cactus Patch Campground to the park's playground, meandering through a sandy desert of prickly pear, Christmas cactus, cholla, and ocotillo. Benches along the way offer good views out over the Rio Grande and distant mountains. Branching off Apache Trail near its west end, the Buffalo Soldier Trail goes through an arroyo for about 0.2 mile (one-way) to connect Cactus Patch Campground with Grease-wood Road Campground. The 0.25-mile (one-way) River Trail connects the two day-use areas along the Rio Grande, following the river through a riparian area of willows, tamarisk, and mesquite.

Water always means wildlife, and animals sometimes seen in the park include cottontail rabbits, black-tailed jack-rabbits, rock squirrels, coyotes, and an occasional deer. Birds known to frequent the park include sandhill cranes, Gambel's quail, ladder-backed woodpeckers, road-runners, and pyrrhuloxias (also called desert cardinals).

The campground has 31 developed campsites, with water and electric hookups at about two-thirds of them, plus some primitive camping. There are also restrooms with showers and an RV dump station. Day-use and camping fees are charged. Located about 15 miles north of Las Cruces via I-25; from exit 19 take NM 157 west to the park entrance. **P.O. Box 6, Radium Springs, 88054; 877-664-7787 (camping reservations); 505-524-4068; www.nmparks.com.**

ORGAN MOUNTAINS RECREATION AREA

Among southern New Mexico's most scenic regions, the Organ Mountains dominate the skyline to the east of Las Cruces. This Bureau of Land Management recreation area offers hiking, mountain biking, and horseback riding trails, as well as picnicking and camping. The area also provides great views of the city lights after the sun sets. An especially good hike is the Baylor Pass Trail, 6 miles each way, but just hiking the firsts few miles will take you to the pass, which has wonderful views. You can access the trailhead at the Aguirre Spring Campground, which has about 55 sites at an elevation of 6,400 feet, with picnic tables and vault toilets, but no showers or drinking water. Dispersed camping is also permitted. There are a number of other trails and sites worth visiting; stop at the BLM office in Las Cruces for information and detailed directions before you set out. A small use fee is charged for all activities in the recreation area. To get to the campground from Las Cruces, go east 20 miles on US Hwy. 70 and then south 5 miles on a signed BLM access road. **Bureau of Land Management, 1800 Marquess St., Las Cruces, 88005; 505-525-4300; www.nm.blm.gov.**

Golf

LAS CRUCES COUNTRY CLUB

Dating to 1928, this 18-hole semiprivate course offers auxiliary memberships. It has small, bent-grass greens and flat, open bent-grass fairways. **2700 N. Main St., Las Cruces; 505-526-9723.**

NEW MEXICO STATE UNIVERSITY GOLF COURSE

One of the most challenging courses in the Southwest, this 18-hole public course also offers spectacular views of the Organ Mountains. It includes two driving ranges and three putting greens. **2990 E. University Ave., Las Cruces; 505-646-3219.**

PICACHO HILLS COUNTRY CLUB
This 18-hole private course, set in a desert setting, is one of the state's top courses. It has bluegrass fairways and bent-grass greens and tees and offers reciprocal agreements with other clubs. **6861 Via Campestre, Las Cruces; 505-523-2556.**

SONOMA RANCH GOLF COURSE
A natural desert landscape, breathtaking views of the Organ Mountains, and perfectly laid-out greens over rolling hills make this 18-hole public course a favorite. **1274 Golf Club Rd., Las Cruces; 505-521-1818; www.sonomaranchgolf.com.**

Seeing and Doing

Auto Racing

SOUTHERN NEW MEXICO SPEEDWAY
Fans of dirt track racing head to this oval clay track for races Fri. and Sat. evenings from May through Sept., featuring street stocks, super stocks, trucks, modifieds, wing sprints, and others. The track is located 11 miles west of Las Cruces, off I-10, exit 132. **Southern New Mexico State Fairgrounds; 800-658-9650; 505-524-7913; www.snmspeedway.com.**

Historic Sites

BICENTENNIAL LOG CABIN
Dating to the late 1870s, this well-preserved pioneer cabin was originally in the mining town of Grafton, New Mexico, located in the mountains northwest of Las Cruces, and was disassembled and brought to Las Cruces in 1976 for America's Bicentennial. It was built of hand-hewn logs in a German style of pegged and notched construction, and chinked with a mixture of clay, mud, ashes, and sawdust. The small cabin has four doors—one on each wall—that presumably served as alternate escape routes in case of fire or attack. The cabin is furnished with period antiques. You can see the outside anytime, and you can get inside by appointment. **671 N. Main St. (at Lucero St.), Las Cruces; 505-541-2155; www.lascruces-culture.org.**

NEW MEXICO RAILROAD & TRANSPORTATION MUSEUM
The newest of the Las Cruces city museums—it opened in 2003 in the historic Las Cruces railroad depot after a major renovation of the 1910 building—this museum contains exhibits and memorabilia depicting transportation in Las Cruces from the late 1800s into the 1900s. It's worth stopping by just to see the beautifully restored depot; exhibits also include a model train display depicting the early train routes through this region. Call for current hours. **351 N. Mesilla St., Las Cruces; 505-541-2155; www.lascruces-culture.org.**

Horse Racing and Gambling

SUNLAND PARK RACE TRACK AND CASINO
A favorite horse racing spot, Sunland Park has live horse racing each Tues., Fri., Sat., and Sun. from mid-Nov. to mid.-Apr. and year-round simulcast racing from tracks worldwide. There's also a

casino open year-round with more than 700 slot machines and several restaurants and bars. Located 40 miles south of Las Cruces via I-10. **505-589-1131.**

Museums

BRANIGAN CULTURAL CENTER/LAS CRUCES MUSEUM OF FINE ARTS & CULTURE

This excellent city-owned complex contains the Branigan Cultural Center, with permanent and changing exhibits on the history of the region, both traveling exhibits and displays from the center's permanent collection, which dates from the 1850s. Also in the complex, the Museum of Fine Arts & Culture offers changing exhibits of contemporary art. The Branigan Cultural Complex is open Mon.–Fri. 9 A.M.–5 P.M. and Sat. 9 A.M.–3 P.M.; the museum is open Wed.–Fri. 10 A.M.–2 P.M. and Sat. 9 A.M.–2 P.M. **500 N. Water St., Las Cruces; 505-541-2155; www.lascruces-culture.org.**

BRUCE KING FARM & RANCH HERITAGE MUSEUM

A day on the farm and then some are what this excellent museum offers, tracing the 3,000-year history of agriculture in this region with exhibits—both interactive and visual—plus demonstrations of cow milking, blacksmithing, cooking, and various other farm and ranch activities. There are a variety of changing exhibits plus a native plant garden, an orchard with five varieties of apple trees, lots of farm equipment, and churro sheep and longhorn cattle. One large room is set aside for hands-on activities for kids ages 3 to 10, and films and videos about different aspects of farming and ranching are shown daily. Open Mon.–Sat. 9 A.M.–5 P.M. and Sun. noon–5 P.M. Admission fee charged.

Located 1.5 miles east of I-25, exit 1. **4100 Dripping Springs Rd., Las Cruces; 505-522-4100; www.frhm.org.**

GADSDEN MUSEUM

This worthwhile historical museum contains an interesting collection of memorabilia on this area, including jail cell bars that held famed outlaw Billy the Kid during his murder trial in Mesilla. It also has little-known information on the Gadsden Purchase, in which the United States in 1854 purchased from Mexico some 30,000 square miles of land west of the Rio Grande for $10 million, as well as details about the history of the town of Mesilla. The museum curator is the great-granddaughter of Col. Albert Jennings Fountain, a prominent and controversial New Mexico lawyer in the late 1800s, and there is some information in the museum about Fountain, who along with his 8-year-old son, Henry, mysteriously disappeared near White Sands on Feb. 1, 1896. Although their bodies were never found, there was evidence that their wagon had been forced off the roadway and there was blood on the ground. Several area men were tried for what everyone believed was a double murder, but they were acquitted. Open Mon.–Sat. 9–11 A.M. and 1–5 P.M. and Sun. 1–5 P.M. Closed major holidays. A small admission fee is charged. **Boutz Rd., just east of NM 28 (also known as Avenida de Mesilla), Mesilla; 505-526-6293.**

HISTORICAL MUSEUM OF LAWMEN

A peek into the area's wild and wicked past is promised at this small museum maintained by the county sheriff's department. There are historical photos, some rare guns, sheriff's badges, handcuffs, law enforcement ledgers, and other memorabilia from the late 1800s to modern times, plus some buggies used by past sheriffs and a 1949 police car. (Note: A move was scheduled in 2005; call for current location.) **Doña Ana County Sheriff's Office, 750 Motel Blvd., Las Cruces; 505-525-1911.**

LAS CRUCES MUSEUM OF NATURAL HISTORY

Natural history and science exhibits, including hands-on exhibits for kids, are the focus of this museum, operated by the city of Las Cruces. Permanent displays include live animals and plants of the Chihuahuan Desert, along with several rare species from other areas. There are also traveling exhibits. Open Mon.–Thurs. and Sat. 10 A.M.–5 P.M., Fri. 10 A.M.–8 P.M., and Sun. 1–5 P.M. Mesilla Valley Mall, **700 S. Telshor Blvd. #1608, Las Cruces; 505-522-3120; www.lascruces.org/museums/natural-history/index.html.**

NEW MEXICO STATE UNIVERSITY

Established in 1888, NMSU began as an agricultural college and still remains true to its origins—its sports teams remain the Aggies—although it now offers more than 70 bachelor's degree programs in six undergraduate colleges, plus about 50 master's programs and two dozen doctoral programs. The school is especially known for its agricultural and engineering programs. It has an enrollment more than 15,000 students, representing all 50 states and almost 90 foreign countries. The university is home to the Solar Energy Institute, the Water Resources Institute of New Mexico, and the Clyde Tombaugh Observatory, named for the

astronomer who discovered Pluto—no, not the cartoon character, the planet!

The University Museum (505-646-3739), located in Kent Hall at the corner of University Ave. and Solano Dr., has exhibits on anthropology as well as the history and culture of the area from the university's permanent collection; it's open to the public Tues.–Sat. noon–4 P.M. **The University Art Gallery (505-646-2545),** just east of the museum, presents eight to 10 exhibits of contemporary and historical art. During the school year it's open Tues.–Fri. 10 A.M.–5 P.M., plus Thurs. evenings until 7 P.M.; in summer it's open Mon.–Wed. 11 A.M.–4 P.M., Sat.–Sun. 1–5 P.M. **University Ave. and Locust St., Las Cruces; 505-646-0111; www.nmsu.edu.**

SPACE MURALS, INC. MUSEUM & GIFT SHOP

The history of space exploration is the focus of this museum, which also contains actual missiles, a replica of the space shuttle, plus hands-on exhibits for kids, and air and space models and photos. The gift shop has an extensive selection of space-related items. Open in summer Mon.–Sat. 9 A.M.–6 P.M. and Sun. 10 A.M.–6 P.M. **12450 US Hwy. 70 E., Organ; 505-382-0977; www.zianet.com/spacemurals.**

WAR EAGLES AIR MUSEUM

Beautifully restored airplanes from World War II, the Korean Conflict, and later are displayed in a large building, chronicling military aircraft from these eras. Many of the planes are in flying condition, and occasional demonstrations are presented. Among planes on display are a P-51 Mustang, P-38 Lightning, P-40 Warhawk, a DC-3 Transport, a German Fieseler-Storch, Soviet MIG-15s, and an F-86 Sabre. There are also some classic automobiles on display and exhibits on women aviators. Open Tues.–Sun. 10 A.M.–4 P.M. Located about 30 miles southeast of Las Cruces off I-10, exit 8. **Santa Teresa Airport, 8012 Airport Rd., Santa Teresa; 505-589-2000; www.war-eagles-air-museum.com.**

WHITE SANDS MISSILE RANGE MUSEUM

Located on White Sands Missile Range, a U.S. Army installation, this museum includes "Missile Park," an outdoor display of more than 50 rockets and missiles—some of them gigantic and some dating back more than 50 years. The museum tells the history of the missile range, which was established in 1945, but starts a bit earlier—back to prehistoric times when hunter-gatherers roamed this area in search of now extinct mammoths and camel-like animals. Exhibits continue through the arrival of Spanish explorers and the Apache wars to relatively modern times when the missile range was established to test some of the most significant weapons of the nuclear age and rockets used in space exploration. There's also a gift shop. Note: visitors are required to show their driver's license, vehicle registration, and proof of vehicle insurance. Open Mon.–Fri. 8 A.M.–4 P.M.; Sat.–Sun. 10 A.M.–3 P.M.; closed major holidays. Located 22 miles east of Las Cruces via US Hwy. 70, between mile markers 169 and 170. **505-678-8824; www.wsmr-history.org.**

Performing Arts

Concerts by famed artists from all over the world are held in the **Pan American Center** on the New Mexico State University campus, which is also home to the "Aggie" basketball team. For information and tickets: **505-646-4413; http://panam.nmsu.edu.**

NMSU's Music Department (http://nmsu.edu/~music) produces a number of programs annually. Its Doña Ana Lyric Opera **(505-646-1993)** presents four shows a year, including a Broadway musical each summer, at the NMSU Music Center Recital Hall. The music department's choral department **(505-646-1306)** presents concerts and recitals, also at the recital hall; and the Mesilla Valley Concert Band **(505-646-1920)** performs six times each school year. Also at NMSU, the American Southwest Theatre Company **(505-646-4515)** produces a variety of programs, ranging from Shakespeare to musical theater, between Sept. and May.

The Las Cruces Symphony (505-646-3709; www.lascrucessymphony.com/frame.htm) presents nationally known artists at six concerts between Oct. and May each year, and the **Las Cruces Chamber Ballet (505-523-1654)** stages two major productions each year, including a Christmas season performance of *The Nutcracker.* The **No Strings Theatre Company** presents an eclectic mix of a half-dozen plays each year, primarily little-known works, at the **Black Box Theatre, 430 N. Downtown Mall, Las Cruces; 505-523-1223; www.zianet.com/nstcbbt.** Fans of swing music will want to check the schedule for the Big Band on the Rio Grande, a 16-piece group that presents a dance concert once a month. Check with the **Las Cruces Convention & Visitors Bureau or call 505-526-5772.**

Wineries and Other Agricultural Stops

A splendid year-round climate for grape growing has made southern New Mexico a popular location for vineyards and wineries, and most wineries offer free

A Day Trip to Hatch

About 36 miles north of Las Cruces, I-25 brings you to the turnoff for the small town of Hatch, a town that lives, eats, and breathes chile peppers. Shortly after Juan de Oñate began to settle New Mexico in 1598, small Spanish towns sprang up in the fertile valley of the Rio Grande. The people brought chile peppers with them, and what they started some 400 years ago has grown to the point where Hatch is the undisputed chile capital of the world (see the sidebar on New Mexican chile on page 178).

Hatch produces many varieties of chiles, and Hatch residents love them all. Stop in at one of the local chile emporiums, such as **Flores Farms** or **Hatch Chile Express**, both located on **Franklin St.,** the road into town from I-25 exit 41. See all the various kinds of fresh chiles and the numerous products made from the locally grown peppers—salsas, of course, plus chile jelly, chile honey, chile candy, decorations of chile, and on—as well as all sorts of chile-related products including just about every type of clothing produced with the image of a chile prominently displayed on it. Both of the above-mentioned stores also sell mail order: **Flores Farms, 616 Franklin St., P.O. Box 715, Hatch, 87937; 505-267-1988,** and **Hatch Chile Express, 657 Franklin St., P.O. Box 350, Hatch 87937; 505-267-3226; www.hatch-chile.com.**

It's fun to drop in on Hatch at any time, but the best time to visit is over the Labor Day weekend, when the residents celebrate the annual chile harvest with the **Hatch Chile Festival.** A chile festival queen reigns over the two-day event, which includes chile cooking and chile *ristra* contests. A *ristra* is a bunch of red chiles strung on cords and used as a wall decoration, and in many parts of New Mexico *ristras* are the preferred Christmas ornament. There's also a fiddlers contest, chile and watermelon eating contests, a chile throwing contest, tractor pulls, a parade, live music, and a dance.

Just to be fair, even though Hatch is the self-proclaimed chile capital of the world, it does occasionally think of other things. In addition to chile, local farms grow pecans, onions, lettuce, cabbage, sweet potatoes, alfalfa, wheat, and cotton. There are several dairies and a flour mill.

The **Hatch Museum** in the town of Hatch, with a variety of pioneer memorabilia and photos, is open Mon.–Fri. 9 A.M.–3 P.M. at **149 W. Hall St.,** and is a distribution center for information on the chile festival and everything else going on in Hatch. For more information contact the **Hatch Chamber of Commerce, P.O. Box 38, Hatch, 87937; 505-267-5050; www.villageofhatch.org.**

samples—they call them tastings in hopes that after you've tried their wines you'll buy a case or two. New Mexico's oldest winery is **La Viña,** located about 25 miles south of Las Cruces off I-10, exit 2, at **4201 S. NM 28, Anthony; 505-882-7632.** Another good local winery is **Blue Teal Vineyards, 1710 Avenida de Mesilla, Las Cruces; 877-669-4637; 505-524-0390; www.blueteal.com.** A tasting room for two other local wineries, **Mademoiselle Vineyards** and **Santa Rita Cellars,** is **Wines of the Southwest,** located southeast of the Old Mesilla Plaza at **2641 Calle de Guadalupe, Mesilla; 877-NMWINES; 505-524-2408; www.mademoisellevineyards.com; www.santaritacellars.com.** Call for current hours.

Drive south from Las Cruces on NM 28 and you'll see rows and rows of pecan trees. These are part of **Stahmann Farms,** one of the world's largest pecan growers, harvesting several million pounds of pecans each year. A country store at the farm offers a wide variety of pecan delicacies, including pecan candy and brittle, and during the summer visitors can tour the candy-making facility. The store is open Mon.–Sat. 9 A.M.–6 P.M., Sun. 11 A.M.–5 P.M. Located 7 miles south of Las Cruces on NM 28. **505-526-8974; www.stahmanns.com.**

Where to Stay

Accommodations

You'll find no lack of places to stay in Las Cruces, with a wide range of prices. However, keep in mind that this a college town—New Mexico State University is here—and rooms can be hard

to find, and more expensive when you do find one, during graduation and other major collegiate events.

INNS AND BED-AND-BREAKFASTS

Lundeen's Inn of the Arts—$$–$$$

This historic and elegantly furnished inn, with some delightful artwork, has 22 comfortable rooms in a late 19th-century territorial-style adobe. Rooms are named for and decorated in the style of a New Mexico artist, including Georgia O'Keeffe, R. C. Gorman, and Maria Martinez. Rates include a full breakfast, and pets are accepted (for a fee). A fine art gallery is also on the premises. The entire inn is non-smoking. **618 S. Alameda Blvd., Las Cruces, 88005; 888-526-3326; 505-526-3326; www.innofthearts.com.**

T.R.H. Smith Mansion Bed & Breakfast—$$$–$$$$

This stately mansion, built in 1914, offers a wonderful combination of historic charm and modern amenities, with stained-glass windows and handsome hardwood floors, plus computers with high-speed Internet access in each of the inn's four rooms. One unit has a fireplace. A full German-style breakfast is included in the rates, and small pets are welcome. The property is non-smoking. **909 N. Alameda Blvd., Las Cruces, 88001; 800-526-1914; 505-525-2525; www.smithmansion.com.**

HOTELS AND MOTELS

Best Western Mesilla Valley Inn—$$–$$$

A well-equipped full-service hotel, this Best Western offers 160 units with all the amenities you would expect, and a large outdoor heated pool and whirlpool, video games, and a popular restaurant and bar. Pets accepted. **901 Avenida de Mesilla, Las Cruces, 88005; 800-327-3314; 505-524-8603.**

Comfort Inn—$$–$$$

This small, attractive Comfort Inn, with 38 rooms, has an outdoor heated pool, and mini-refrigerators and microwaves are available. **2585 S. Valley Dr., Las Cruces, 88005; 505-527-2000.**

Hampton Inn—$$

Hampton Inns are generally attractive, well maintained, and offer one of the best continental breakfasts you'll find, and this one is no exception. The 118 rooms are decorated in a tasteful southwestern style and all have mini-refrigerators. There's an outdoor pool and exercise room, and pets are welcome. **755 Avenida de Mesilla, Las Cruces, 88005; 505-526-8311.**

One of the features at White Sands Missile Range Museum is the more than 50 rockets and missiles displayed at "Missile Park."

Hilton Las Cruces—$$$

This seven story full service hotel, with 203 units, offers all the facilities and amenities expected in this well-respected chain, including an attractive heated outdoor swimming pool, whirlpool, exercise room, and video games. There's also a very good restaurant and bar. Pets are accepted. **705 S. Telshor Blvd., Las Cruces, 88011; 800-445-8667; 505-522-4300.**

La Quinta Inn—$$

A comfortable, modern motel with 139 rooms, this La Quinta has a heated outdoor pool and a fitness center. Pets are accepted. **790 Avenida de Mesilla, Las Cruces, 88005; 505-524-0331.**

Mesón de Mesilla—$$–$$$$

This small hotel, built in the 1980s, has 15 units attractively decorated in southwestern style. Most units open onto a balcony, and several have kiva fireplaces and small refrigerators. There's an attractive outdoor pool with great views of the Organ Mountains. Rates include a full breakfast, and pets are accepted. There's also a very good restaurant on the premises (see Where to Eat). **1803 Avenida de Mesilla, Mesilla, 88046; 800-732-6025; 505-525-9212; www.mesondemesilla.com.**

Royal Host Motel—$–$$

Basic, well-maintained rooms at a bargain rate are what you'll find here, along with an outdoor heated pool. There are 26 rooms and pets are accepted (for a fee). **2146 W. Picacho Ave., Las Cruces, 88007; 505-524-8536.**

Sleep Inn—$$–$$$

An attractive, small three-story hotel, this property has an indoor heated swimming pool and whirlpool. Mini-refrigerators and microwaves are available. There are 63 units. Pets accepted (for a fee). 2121 S. Triviz, Las Cruces, 88001; 505-522-1700.

Super 8—$$

Basic lodging at attractive rates and located near New Mexico State University. Small pets accepted; 60 rooms. **245 La Posada Ln., Las Cruces, 88005; 505-523-8695.**

Teakwood Inn & Suites—$$–$$$

This attractive property, located next to the university, has 130 basic but spacious and well-maintained motel-type units, all with mini-refrigerators and microwave ovens. There's also an indoor heated swimming pool and dry sauna, restaurant with bar, and a 24-hour business center with high-speed Internet access. Pets accepted (for a fee). **2600 S. Valley Dr., Las Cruces, 88005; 505-526-4441.**

Campgrounds

BEST VIEW RV PARK

All the usual amenities of a first-class commercial campground, with 92 RV sites and 14 tent sites. There are some shade trees, good views of the Organ Mountains, an outdoor pool, and a playground. Located off I-10, exit 135. **814 Weinrich Rd., Las Cruces, 88005; 800-526-6555 (reservations); 505-526-6555; www.bestviewrvpark.com.**

DALMONT'S RV PARK

A basic RV park (no tents) with full hookups, clean restrooms with showers, and a coin-op laundry, but no swimming pool. There are 26 sites. Located about 0.5 mile from I-10, exit 142. **2224 S. Valley Dr., Las Cruces, 88005; 505-523-2992.**

HACIENDA RV RESORT

Don't come to Hacienda RV Resort to rough it; this is no campground. This is a full-service luxury resort for recreational vehicles (no tents), with 113 sites with full hookups, a clubhouse, hydrotherapy pool (but no swimming pool), a putting green, exercise room, and a large covered patio with a fireplace. Located off I-10, exit 140. **740 Stern Dr., Las Cruces, 88005; 888-686-9090; 505-528-5800; www.haciendarv.com.**

RV DOC'S RV PARK

Mainly an RV park, with 70 large pull-through RV sites, there are also a few tent sites. The park is well-maintained and has all the usual amenities and then some, including a whirlpool but not a swimming pool. An RV service center is on the premises. Located off I-10, exit 140. **1475 Avenida de Mesilla, Las Cruces, 88005; 888-278-3627; 505-526-8401.**

SIESTA RV PARK

No pool, but everything else you expect from a basic RV park, with 54 RV sites and 1 tent site. There are shade trees and horseshoes. Located about 0.5 mile south of I-10, exit 140. **1551 Avenida de Mesilla, Las Cruces, 88005; 800-414-6816; 505-523-6816.**

Where to Eat

Cattle Baron—$$–$$$$

This regional chain—there are also Cattle Barons in Ruidoso, Portales, Hobbs, and Roswell in New Mexico, plus El Paso, Lubbock, and Midland in Texas—offers wonderful prime rib (the house specialty), hand-cut steaks, and fresh seafood in a ranch house–style atmosphere. All the beef is aged USDA

Choice, and a variety of beef and seafood combos are available. The salad bar is one of the best and biggest in the area. **790 S. Telshor, Las Cruces; 505-522-7533; www.cattlebaron.com.**

Double Eagle—$$$–$$$$

Located in a historic building with a gold leaf ceiling and decorated with Victorian antiques, this elegant restaurant serves excellent filet mignon and other steaks plus seafood, often with a southwestern touch. The Sun. champagne brunch is fabulous. Reservations recommended for dinner. Open Mon.–Sat. 11 A.M.–10 P.M. and Sun. 11 A.M.–9 P.M. On Old Mesilla Plaza. **308 Calle de Guadalupe, Mesilla; 505-523-6700; www.doubleeagledining.com.**

Farley's—$$

A casual, noisy, fun spot where the food is good and reasonably priced, and the beer is cold and plentiful. Pizzas from the wood-fired stone hearth oven are especially good, as are the half-pound burgers—try the Farley's Favorite: a USDA Choice burger topped with guacamole, grilled mushrooms, onions, and Swiss cheese. There are also numerous sandwiches and entrées such as chicken-fried steak and fried catfish. There is also a Farley's in Ruidoso; the restaurants are owned by the same company that owns the Cattle Baron restaurants (see page 200). Open Mon.–Sat. 11 A.M.–1:30 A.M. and Sun. 11 A.M.–midnight. **3499 Foothills Blvd., Las Cruces; 505-522-0466; www.farleyspub.com.**

La Posta de Mesilla—$$–$$$

Housed in a historic adobe building dating to the mid-1800s, this popular landmark serves New Mexico–style Mexican food and charbroiled steaks. Especially good are the enchiladas and the tostadas compuestas—a toasted corn tortilla cup filled with chile con carne and beans and topped with lettuce, tomato, and cheese. La Posta also has excellent margaritas. Open Tues.–Thurs. and Sun. 11 A.M.–9 P.M., Fri. Sat. 11 A.M.–9:30 P.M. Closed Thanksgiving and Christmas. On Old Mesilla Plaza. **2410 Calle de San Albino, Mesilla; 505-524-3524; www.laposta-de-mesilla.com.**

Lorenzo's—$$–$$$

Sicilian-style Italian cuisine with imported pastas and a variety of sauces are the specialties in this pleasant, casual restaurant. Offerings include eggplant parmigiana, linguini and clams, calamari, and hand-tossed pizzas. Open Tues.–Fri. 11 A.M.–2 P.M., Tues.–Thurs. 5–8:30 P.M., Fri. 5–9:30 P.M., Sat. 11 A.M.–9:30 P.M. and Sun. 4–8:30 P.M. **1753 E. University Ave., Las Cruces; 505-521-3505.** There is also a Lorenzo's in Mesilla at **1750 Calle de Mercado; 505-525-3170.**

Mesón de Mesilla—$$$$

This fine restaurant, decorated in southwestern style, is a delightful spot for a romantic evening. The menu changes periodically, but might include fresh Atlantic salmon baked on a cedar plank with a dill cream sauce, an 8-ounce Black Angus filet mignon in a portobella mushroom brandied cream sauce, or the perennial favorite, chateaubriand for two, flamed tableside in a cognac cream sauce. There is also a very good wine list. Reservations are recommended. Open Tues.–Thurs. and Sun. 5:30–9:30 P.M. and Fri.–Sat. 5:30–10:30 P.M. Closed Christmas. **1803 Avenida de Mesilla, Mesilla; 800-732-6025; 505-525-9212; www.mesondemesilla.com.**

Nellie's—$$–$$$

Homemade Mexican food at very reasonable prices make this small, unassuming restaurant a locals' favorite. For a bit of everything try the combo plate, but all the Mexican standards served here are good. Open Tues.–Wed. and Sat. 8 A.M.–4 P.M.; Thurs.–Fri. 8 A.M.– 8 P.M. **1226 W. Hadley Ave., Las Cruces; 505-524-9982.**

Peppers—$$–$$$

Under the same ownership and in the same building as the Double Eagle (see page 201), Peppers is a fun place serving innovative variations of southwestern fare, such as green chile, cheese wontons with pineapple-jalapeño salsa and grilled chicken topped with sautéed sweet onions, roasted green chile, and cheese, and served with guacamole. The chile rellenos are a dinner treat; lunches are simpler fare, including burgers and sandwiches. Extremely popular for dessert are the banana enchiladas. Open Mon.–Sat. 11 A.M.–10 P.M. and Sun. noon–9 P.M. Located on Old Mesilla Plaza. **306 Calle de Guadalupe, Mesilla; 505-523-4999.**

Tatsu—$$$–$$$$

For a break from the steaks and Mexican food that dominate in this area, head to Tatsu, an upscale restaurant that specializes in Japanese and Oriental cuisine, with fresh seafood, sushi, chicken, and beef dishes. One suggestion is the sesame tempura-seared tuna, served rare with a sauce of chile and garlic. There is an extensive selection of Japanese beer and wine; dinner reservations are recommended. Open Sun.–Fri. 11 A.M.–2 P.M. and 5–9 P.M.; Sat. 5–9 P.M. **930 El Paseo Rd., Las Cruces; 505-526-7144.**

Services

Visitor Information

Las Cruces Convention & Visitors Bureau, 211 N. Water St., Las Cruces, 88001; 800-343-7827; 505-541-2444; www.lascrucescvb.org.

The Old Mesilla Association, P.O. Box 1005, Mesilla, 88046; 505-647-9668; www.oldmesilla.org, operates a visitor center in the Old Mesilla Plaza area; call or check the Web site for current location.

202

SOUTHEAST REGION

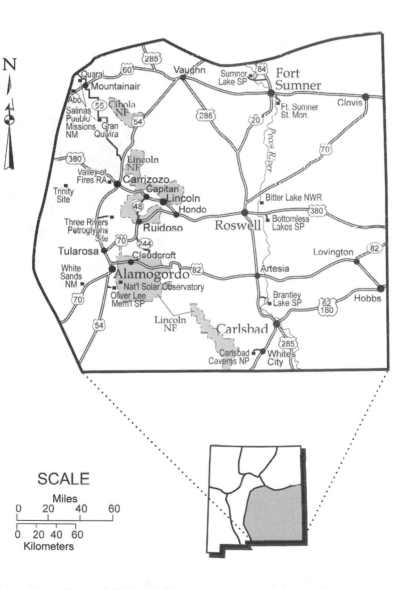

Southeast Region

This large, wide open corner of New Mexico is a region of contrasts. It contains some of the state's flattest and most boring scenery practically side by side with some of the very best New Mexico has to offer—in particular, Carlsbad Caverns National Park and White Sands National Monument. The region is rich in history and the lore of the gunmen of the pioneer days; it was the home of famed outlaw Billy the Kid and sheriff Pat Garrett and a place where unsolved murders of long ago are still controversial. This is where the world's first atomic bomb was tested in a dramatic explosion on July 16, 1945, and long-range missiles continue to be tested at White Sands Missile Range.

The area contains large stretches of nothing, where the only thing to break the monotonous sameness is an occasional oil well or lone steer, searching for some grass among the sagebrush and cactus. But along with the cruel deserts are delightful alpine meadows, lakes, trout streams, and some of the state's best agricultural areas. The Pecos River runs south through this region and has helped turn the city of Carlsbad into a relatively lush oasis. The region offers excellent museums, ancient ruins and rock art, a variety of special events, and, of course, those space aliens you'll meet in Roswell.

Javalinas are well suited to the arid climate of southern New Mexico.

CARLSBAD

Originally called Eddy, Carlsbad was renamed in 1899 because the city fathers decided that the minerals in their spring water reminded them of Karlsbad in Bohemia. The attractive small city of 26,000, at an elevation of 3,120 feet, provides goods and services for the surrounding farms, where alfalfa, cotton, and vegetables grow, and for the nearby oil and gas fields and potash mines. But Carlsbad's main claim to fame is that it is just 30 miles from world-famous Carlsbad Caverns, one of the world's most spectacular natural wonders. Even without the caverns, Carlsbad has a lot going for it, including the Pecos River, which flows right through the middle of town.

History

A couple hundred million years ago, Carlsbad was on the shore of the Permian Sea and the Gulf of Mexico. At that time, potash was being laid down in huge quantities and oil was being formed. The first Europeans to visit this area were Cabeza de Vaca, in 1536; Coronado, who came close in 1541; and Espejo, who followed the Pecos River through this area in 1583. The first railroad tracks came from Pecos, Texas, in 1891. Oil was discovered in 1913, and all of Eddy County is a big producer today. Fertilizer is important in Carlsbad. First of all, bat guano from the Carlsbad Caverns was used in 100,000 tons of fertilizer that went to California orange groves from 1903 to 1923. Now, mineral potash, one of the best fertilizers in the world, is mined in greater tonnage in this area than anywhere else in the United States.

The Waste Isolation Pilot Project (WIPP), a storage center for radioactive waste from research and production of nuclear weapons, began operations in the late 1990s, and even before construction began it was one of the most controversial projects that has ever occurred in this area. Many Carlsbad residents are happy with the new jobs created and say they believe the U.S. Department of Energy assertions that the project is safe. People on the other side—many from the more liberal northern sections of the state—shout the slogan "Don't Waste New Mexico." These opponents are often morally opposed to nuclear weapons generally and also believe it is not wise to accept the nuclear waste problems of other states, hiding it underground for an indefinite amount of time.

Getting There

Carlsbad is in extreme southeastern New Mexico, at the junction of US Hwys. 62/180 and US Hwy. 285.

Major Attractions

Carlsbad Caverns National Park
A definite must-see for visitors to southern New Mexico, Carlsbad Caverns is one of the most beautiful and fantastic cave systems in the world. Those venturing into these underground chambers discover weird and lovely sculptures created by the slow work of minerals and tiny drops of water over thousands

of years. There are frozen waterfalls, strands of pearls, soda straws, miniature castles, draperies, and ice-cream cones.

Creation of the caverns began about 250 million years ago, when a huge inland sea covered this area. A reef was created, but then the sea disappeared, leaving the reef covered with deposits of salts and gypsum. Uplifting and erosion eventually brought the reef back to the surface. Rainwater, seeping down through cracks in the earth's surface, dissolved the limestone and left passageways and rooms. Then nature became artistic, creating the stalactites, stalagmites, and other cave formations that make complete this journey into a fantasyland.

SEEING THE CAVERNS

Self-guided and guided tours over paved, lighted trails take you through some of the caves here, and there are opportunities to see other caves in their more natural state by crawling through tight passages by the

A cave formation at Carlsbad Caverns National Park.

light of flashlights. Practically all visitors head first to the park's main cave, called Carlsbad Cavern, to see the Big Room, one of the largest and most easily accessible of the caverns. The ceiling is 25 stories high and its floor could easily hold 14 football fields. A 1.25-mile paved trail meanders through a massive chamber—it isn't called the Big Room for nothing—where you'll see some of the park's most spectacular formations and likely be overwhelmed by the enormity of it all. You can hike in (an extra 1.25 miles) or take an elevator from the visitor center, and there are restrooms and even a restaurant deep underground.

After seeing the main section of the Big Room, there are other parts of the main cave to see, and then you might want to sign up for one of the guided tours to one of the other caves for a more genuine caving adventure. These caving tours vary in difficulty, but all include a period of absolute darkness, which makes some people uncomfortable. Because some tours involve walking or crawling through tight spaces, people who suffer from claustrophobia or who have other health concerns should discuss specifics with rangers before purchasing tickets.

Among our favorite of these caving tours is the excursion to Slaughter Canyon Cave. It is 1.25 miles round-trip, plus an extra 1-mile round-trip hike to and from the cave entrance. No crawling is involved, although the smooth flowstone and old bat guano on the floor can be slippery, so good hiking boots are recommended. You'll see a number of wonderful cave formations, including the crystal-decorated Christmas Tree, the 89-foot-high Monarch, and the menacing Klansman. It is open only to those 6 and older, and participants must take D-battery flashlights.

OTHER ACTIVITIES

Carlsbad Caverns is the summer home to about a million Mexican free-tailed bats, which hang from the ceiling of Bat Cave during the day but put on a spectacular show each evening as they leave the cave in search of food and again in the morning when they return for a good day's sleep. Each evening during the summer, rangers give an interesting talk about the bat flight at the walking entrance to the cave just before it begins. Times vary (you'll have to ask the bats why), so check at the visitor center for the current schedule.

The park also has a 9.5-mile scenic loop drive that offers dramatic views of the surrounding Chihuahuan Desert, backcountry hiking trails for exploring that desert, and an interpretative nature trail. The excellent visitor center has all sorts of exhibits that explain how these caves were created, has the schedules for guided hikes, and sells tickets.

VISITOR INFORMATION AND DIRECTIONS

There is no camping at the park, but there are campgrounds in nearby White's City and the city of Carlsbad. From Memorial Day weekend through Labor Day open daily 8 A.M.–7 P.M., the rest of the year daily 8 A.M.–5 P.M. Closed Christmas. Fees charged for admission and guided tours. Located 30 miles southwest of Carlsbad via US Hwys. 62/180 and NM 7. **3225 National Parks Hwy., Carlsbad, 88220; 505-785-2232; 505-885-8884; www.nps.gov/cave.**

Living Desert Zoo & Gardens State Park

Leave the city behind and step into the wilds of New Mexico, and especially the Chihuahuan Desert, for an intimate view of the region's numerous animals and plants. A 1.3-mile trail meanders through the various habitats that make up the Chihuahuan Desert, from the sand hills like those that can be found along the nearby Pecos River to the gypsum rock formations of the desert uplands and on through a dry desert streambed to the mountainous piñon-juniper zone.

The Chihuahuan Desert covers more than 200,000 square miles, from central Mexico into west Texas and southern New Mexico. Although it at first appears to be an arid wasteland, with little rain and temperatures into the triple digits, this land is actually home to a vast number of animals, birds, and plants, which have adapted to survive in this unforgiving environment.

Among the several hundred species of animals you'll see here are elk, mule deer, pronghorn, black bear, bison, bobcat, mountain lion, badger, kit fox, and porcupine. There's a small herd of

Stalagmites grow up from the floor of the cave from a buildup of minerals deposited by the constant dripping of mineral-rich water.

javelina, named for their short, javelin-sharp tusks, that seem to enjoy a meal of tasty prickly pear cactus, spines and all. You can also see the endangered Mexican wolf, once common in the Southwest, and the prairie dog village, with its ever-vigilant residents standing guard, is always entertaining.

Like snakes? The Reptile House provides a good opportunity to see snakes up close and learn which are poisonous and which are not from behind a protective wall of glass. In addition to the various rattlesnakes and their brethren, you'll also see the Gila monster, one of the desert's few poisonous lizards. There's an aviary—a screened-in oasis of trees and bushes—where you'll see numerous birds, including broad-winged hawks, golden eagles, white-winged doves, owls, and roadrunners. The park also has a pond, which attracts migrating ducks and geese.

The desert wildlife you see as you explore the park was not captured or even bred for their zoo careers; rather, they have been injured or orphaned and are brought to Living Desert because they cannot survive in the wild.

In addition to wildlife, the park is alive with plants of the Chihuahuan Desert and an amazing collection of cacti and succulents from around the world—those hardy species that can endure extreme heat and cold, sandy soil, and a decided lack of moisture.

The park's large visitor center offers exhibits on the region's plants and animals, as well as geology and history, including a hands-on discovery area. There is also a restaurant, gift shop, and bookstore. A docent program presents guided tours, storytelling, and other activities. Open in summer daily 8 A.M.–8 P.M., the rest of the year daily 9 A.M.–5 P.M. Closed Christmas. Admission fee charged. Located on the northwest edge of Carlsbad off US Hwy. 285. **P.O. Box 100, Carlsbad, 88221; 505-887-5516; www.nmparks.com.**

Festivals and Events

GO-FLY-A-KITE RALLY
mid-Mar. Exactly what the name says, this big get-together at Brantley Lake State Park takes advantage of southern New Mexico's strong spring winds. **505-457-2384; www.nmparks.com.**

MESCAL ROAST
mid-May. This four-day event includes demonstrations of harvesting and preparation of spike-leaf agave, also known as the century plant, by the Mescalero Apache people, plus dances, a show of American Indian art, and tasting of mescal, which is the cooked heart of the agave. Takes place at the Living Desert Zoo and Gardens State Park. **505-887-5516; www.nmparks.com.**

BAT FLIGHT BREAKFAST
second Thurs. in Aug. Carlsbad National Park rangers prepare breakfast for early morning park visitors and then join them to watch the bats return to the cavern after a night of insect hunting. **505-785-2232; www.nps.gov/cave.**

CHRISTMAS ON THE PECOS
nightly Thanksgiving through New Year's Eve (except Christmas Eve). Boat tours along the Pecos River through residential areas of Carlsbad where riverfront property owners have decorated their backyards with millions of Christmas lights and decorations, with displays that range from the absurdly whimsical to deeply religious. **505-887-6516; 505-628-0952; www.christmasonthepecos.com.**

Outdoor Activities

Boating, Fishing, and More

BRANTLEY LAKE STATE PARK

An oasis in southern New Mexico's hot, desolate desert, Brantley Lake was created in 1988 by the completion of a 1 mile-long dam across the Pecos River. Although its primary purpose is to protect downstream areas from floods while providing a reliable source of irrigation water for local farmers and ranchers, the lake also offers a variety of recreational uses as well as fish and wildlife habitat. Terrain here is mostly flat and sandy, with creosote bush, desert grasses, mesquite, grease-wood, cacti, and other Chihuahuan Desert plants that can survive in the semiarid climate.

Activities include boating—no speed or horsepower restrictions—swimming, and fishing on the 4,000-acre lake. Having the largest body of water in the area has made the park a prime location for bird-watching. Oct. through mid-Feb. is a particularly good time to see waterbirds, including mallards, northern pintails, pelicans, loons, teals, and Canada and snow geese. Others to watch for include red-tailed hawks, great horned owls, cactus wrens, western meadowlarks, white-crowned sparrows, scaled quail, rufous hummingbirds, and mourning doves. Texas horned lizards also make their home in the park.

The hot summers here bring out water-skiers and other recreational boaters, but spring and fall belong mostly to anglers, who catch large crappie and largemouth bass, plus bluegills, white bass, channel catfish, and walleye. Spring is pretty, with wildflowers and cacti in bloom, but winds can get ferocious.

A visitor center contains exhibits on the area's plants and wildlife plus the 19th-century community of Seven Rivers, which now lies at the bottom of the lake. While many tales of the Wild West have been greatly exaggerated, historians have proof that Seven Rivers really was a wild place. When Brantley Dam was being built, graves in the old Seven Rivers cemetery were relocated to Artesia, about 24 miles north. Forensic scientists and anthropologists discovered that of the 14 bodies of men between 18 and 45 years old, 10 contained fragments of bullets or knives, including two with knives still in place.

There are 51 developed RV campsites, all with RV hookups, plus primitive camping along the lakeshore. The park has restrooms with showers, an RV dump station, boat ramps, picnic tables, and two playgrounds. Rangers present programs in the campground Sat. evenings during the summer. Admission and camping fees are charged. Located 12 miles north of the

A pair of pronghorns from the Living Desert Zoo & Gardens State Park.

city of Carlsbad via US Hwy. 285, and then 4.5 miles northeast on Eddy CR 30. **P.O. Box 2288, Carlsbad, 88221; 505-457-2384; www.nmparks.com.**

PECOS RIVER

Carlsbad may be in the desert, but that certainly doesn't mean there isn't any water. The Pecos River, which begins in northern New Mexico and then runs south to Texas to join the Rio Grande, winds through downtown Carlsbad (where it's also called Lake Carlsbad). It provides area farmers with irrigation water and provides a delightful oasis and plenty of opportunities for recreation.

The 4.5-mile paved Riverwalk is a great place for a leisurely stroll or brisk walk, and it has benches and picnic tables, as well as numerous ducks. The walk runs from the railroad bridge at the north end of Riverside Dr. to the Bataan Bridge at Greene St. Nearby, the Lake Carlsbad Beach Park has more than 1,000 feet of beach, with a bathhouse and lifeguards on duty daily during the summer.

The Municipal Beach Park has paddle boats and canoes for rent, picnic tables, and lots of shade trees, and nearby are a variety of children's rides, including a merry-go-round. Boat rides on the Pecos are available on the George Washington paddlewheel boat, built in 1858, and several other boats, and there are also sunset dinner cruises.

The parks and Riverwalk are open daily year-round. The rentals and boat tours take place from spring through early Sept., and tours are offered again for Christmas on the Pecos (see Festivals and Events). **City of Carlsbad Recreation Dept.; 800-658-2713; 505-887-1191; www.cityofcarlsbadnm.com/parks _and_recreation (parks and Riverwalk). Carlsbad Cruise Lines, 505-885-4993;** **www.carlsbadcruiselines.com (rentals and tours).**

Seeing and Doing

Museums

CARLSBAD MUSEUM AND ART CENTER

Prehistoric bones of mastodons and camels, Apache Indian relics, Indian pottery, and pioneer artifacts help explain the history of the area. There are also exhibits of southwestern and contemporary art, and the McAdoo Collection contains works from the early 20th century by founders of the Taos Society of Artists. Open Mon.–Sat. 10 A.M.–5 P.M. (closes at 6 P.M. during summer); closed major holidays. Located one block west of Canal St. (US Hwy. 285) in Halagueno Park. **418 W. Fox St., Carlsbad; 505-887-0276.**

WHITE'S CITY MILLION DOLLAR MUSEUM

A vast collection of neat stuff—more than 50,000 items—from the Old West are crammed into the 11 large rooms of this museum, with exhibits that range from guns to dolls to classic vehicles. Under the same management, Granny's Opera House presents original melodramas. Open daily 7 A.M.–6 P.M.; closed Christmas. Admission fee charged. **17 Carlsbad Cavern Hwy. at NM 7, Carlsbad; 800-228-3767; 505-785-2291; www.whitescity.com.**

Where to Stay

Accommodations

Best Western Cavern Inn—$$$

The Cavern Inn and its associated properties (all the facilities in White's City discussed in this section are under the same management) are the most convenient places to stay while visiting Carlsbad Caverns. The 105 rooms are spacious, with southwestern decor, and many have whirlpool tubs. Between the Cavern Inn and its neighbor properties, there are two outdoor heated pools, two hot tubs, and a tennis court. Pets are accepted (for a fee). **17 Carlsbad Cavern Hwy. at NM 7, White's City, 88268; 800-228-3767; 505-785-2291; www.whitescity.com.**

Best Western Stevens Inn—$$–$$$

Well-landscaped gardens surround this attractive downtown property, which has 202 units, an outdoor pool, an exercise room, and a playground. There's also a good restaurant, The Flume, open for three meals daily, that does especially good prime rib. Pets accepted. **1829 S. Canal St., Carlsbad, 88220; 800-730-2851; 505-887-2851.**

Days Inn—$$–$$$

Located on the southwest edge of Carlsbad, on the road to Carlsbad Caverns. Has 50 rooms, a small indoor heated pool, and accepts pets (for a fee). **3910 National Parks Hwy., Carlsbad, 88220; 505-887-7800.**

Holiday Inn—$$$

This handsome New Mexico territorial-style building in downtown Carlsbad houses 100 units in a first-rate full-service hotel, with an outdoor heated swimming pool, sauna, whirlpool, exercise room, and playground. Pets accepted. **601 S. Canal St., Carlsbad, 88220; 800-742-9586; 505-885-8500.**

Quality Inn—$$

This attractive, reasonably priced motel, with 123 units, has an outdoor pool, a whirlpool, a game room, restaurant, and bar. Pets accepted. Located on the road to Carlsbad Caverns. **3706 National Parks Hwy., Carlsbad, 88220; 505-887-2861.**

Campgrounds

There's very pleasant camping at Brantley Lake State Park (see Outdoor Activities).

The closest camping to Carlsbad Caverns National Park is at **White's City RV Park.** In addition to RV sites with hookups and shade shelters, the campground has practically unlimited tent camping in a grassy area with picnic tables and some trees. Because the campground is part of the White's City complex, with its motels, restaurants, and other services, campers have access to the pools, an ATM, a convenience store, a liquor store, and a gift shop. **17 Carlsbad Cavern Hwy. at NM 7, P.O. Box 128, White's City, 88268; 800-228-3767; 505-785-2291; www.whitescity.com.**

A good choice in the city of Carlsbad is **Carlsbad RV Park & Campground,** a tree-shaded campground that offers pull-through sites large enough to accommodate big rigs with slide-outs, as well as tent sites and sites for everything in between. Some sites have cable TV hookups and there's an indoor heated pool, a game room, and a playground. **4301 National Parks Hwy., Carlsbad, 88220; 888-878-7275; 505-885-6333; www.carlsbadrvpark.com.**

Where to Eat

In addition to the restaurants discussed below, there are also good restaurants at the Best Western Stevens Inn and Quality Inn, and two restaurants (one above-ground, one below) at Carlsbad Caverns National Park.

The Firehouse Grill & Club—$$–$$$

This popular restaurant and nightclub—there's music nightly—is located in the town's original fire station, built in 1922. Now it's a steak house, offering excellent aged Black Angus beef and some seafood. There are also fancy salads, barbecue, and various sandwiches, plus a great half-pound burger. Open Mon.–Fri. 11 A.M.–2 P.M., and daily 5–9 P.M. Located at the corner of Canal St. and Fox St. **222 W. Fox St., Carlsbad; 505-234-1546.**

Larez Restaurant—$–$$

Our choice for home-style Mexican food in Carlsbad, Larez Restaurant also serves American favorites, all prepared from scratch by restaurant owner Dora Larez. The food is tasty and not excessively spicy; we especially like the chile rellenos and, for a little bit of everything, the Larez deluxe plate—an enchilada, tamale, asado, taco, rice, beans, chile relleno, green chile, and guacamole salad. Open Mon.–Fri. 11 A.M.–1:45 P.M. and 4:30–8:30 P.M. **1524 S. Canal St., Carlsbad; 505-885-5113.**

Velvet Garter Saloon and Restaurant and Fast Jack's—$–$$$

Part of the White's City complex (discussed under Accommodations), there are two eateries here—a comfort-able family-style restaurant that opens at 5 P.M. and serves steaks, chicken, and fish, and a fast-food joint that offers various breakfast items, burgers, sandwiches, and a few full meals. Open daily 8 A.M.–9 P.M. **26 Carlsbad Hwy., White's City; 505-785-2291; www.whitescity.com.**

Services

Visitor Information

Carlsbad Chamber of Commerce, 302 S. Canal St., Carlsbad; 800-221-1224; 505-887-6516; www.carlsbadchamber.com.

ALAMOGORDO

The name Alamogordo is Spanish, and roughly translated means "fat cottonwood tree," which seems an odd name for a thriving city of 36,000 people. At an elevation of 4,350 feet, Alamogordo is nestled against the towering Sacramento Mountains on the west edge of the flat Tularosa Basin. The Sacramentos are real mountains with peaks reaching higher than 10,000 feet. As a result, they are covered with tall, cool pine forests and get lots of snow, providing enjoyable skiing.

The city is also the home of Holloman Air Force Base—a major component in its economy—plus the White Sands Missile Range. For visitors it offers the spectacular White Sands National Monument, the New Mexico Museum of Space History, Alameda Park Zoo (the oldest zoo in the Southwest), Oliver Lee Memorial State Park, and a fascinating little museum of toy trains.

Nearby are the lovely little town of Tularosa ("reddish reeds" in Spanish) and the historic mountain community of Cloudcroft, with its majestic old lodge. Alamogordo also makes a good home base for visiting the mountain resort town of Ruidoso and the historic town of Lincoln, among the wildest of New Mexico's Wild West towns in the late 1800s.

Getting There

Alamogordo sits at the base of the Sacramento Mountains along US Hwy. 54, just south of its intersection with US Hwy. 82.

Major Attractions

Oliver Lee Memorial State Park

Among New Mexico's top state parks, Oliver Lee Memorial offers a glimpse of the Wild West, plants and birds not often seen in this area, good hiking trails, and a pleasant campground with spectacular views. Situated along the western slope of the Sacramento Mountains in what is known as Dog Canyon, the park looks out across the arid Tularosa Basin to White Sands National Monument and Missile Range. Within feet of the barren desert are year-round springs that feed a lush forest of ash and cottonwood trees, maidenhair ferns, and wild orchids.

Although prehistoric Indians were here more than 1,000 years ago, it was the Apaches that put Dog Canyon on the map and inspired the canyon's name. It's believed that the Apaches arrived in the area in the 16th century, taking advantage of the reliable water source. When Europeans began moving into the region in the mid-1800s, the Apaches raided their farms and ranches and then escaped back into the canyon. Sometimes they deliberately left a trail for soldiers or settlers to follow, and then attacked from above, sending rocks, arrows, and bullets down from the hillsides. In about 1850, a posse of settlers followed a band of Apaches into the canyon, but, according to legend, found only a dog that the Apaches had abandoned, and thus gave the canyon its name. By the 1880s, the Apaches had been subdued and wide-scale settlement of the area began.

213

French immigrant Francois-Jean "Frenchy" Rochas began homesteading at the mouth of Dog Canyon in the mid-1880s. He built a rock cabin, raised cattle, and grew grapes, apples, peaches, and even olives. He also helped Texas rancher Oliver Lee to channel water from Dog Canyon to Lee's ranch, about a mile away. Frenchy mysteriously met his end just after Christmas in 1894, when he was found dead in his cabin, a bullet in the chest. Although the official cause of death was suicide, historians believe it is more likely that he was murdered. Lee, on the other hand, prospered, and by the early 1900s, he controlled the largest ranch in southern New Mexico, with almost 1 million acres.

The park's visitor center has exhibits about Lee, Frenchy, the Apaches, and U.S. Cavalry soldiers. West of the visitor center is Frenchy's two-room cabin, which has been partially reconstructed. Lee's ranch house has been rebuilt and authentically furnished as it would have been when Lee and his family lived there

from 1893 to 1907. It's located about 1 mile south of the visitor center and can be seen only on guided tours; check with the park office for a current schedule.

The park has several trails, including an easy, short interpretive trail that follows a spring-fed stream through a rich riparian area. There's also a fairly strenuous trail that climbs 5 miles (one-way) straight up into the mountains, following nearly the same path used by prehistoric Indians and then Apaches. Along the way views of the Tularosa Basin and the glistening white gypsum of White Sands National Monument get progressively better.

A reliable water source in the desert always attracts wildlife, and here you're likely to see mule deer in winter, plus black-tailed jackrabbits, raccoons, and skunks. Birds that frequent the park include black-throated and black-chinned sparrows, cactus and canyon wrens, Gambel's quail, blue-gray gnatcatchers, ladder-backed woodpeckers, mourning doves, and roadrunners.

Frenchy's cabin at Oliver Lee Memorial State Park.

The campground, just southwest of the mouth of Dog Canyon, is in a desert environment, and although campsites have little shade they offer great views across the desert into the Tularosa Basin, with Dog Canyon and the Sacramento Mountains at your back. There are 48 campsites, including about 18 with electric and water hookups. There are also restrooms with showers and an RV dump station. Located 12 miles south of Alamogordo via US Hwy. 54. **409 Dog Canyon, Alamogordo, 88310; 505-437-8284; www.nmparks.com.**

Three Rivers Petroglyph Site

Sitting at the base of the Sacramento Mountains, with a beautiful view over the Tularosa Basin, this relatively unknown site operated by the Bureau of Land Management contains more than 21,000 petroglyphs. They are believed to have been created at least 1,000 years ago by the Mogollon, a prehistoric people who lived in an area that extended from here west into southeast Arizona and south into Mexico. This was their home until the early 1400s. It's not known for sure what happened to them then, although some archeologists theorize that they joined existing pueblos to the north.

A relatively easy 1-mile round-trip hike on a well-marked but rocky trail meanders among the petroglyphs. A free brochure includes a trail guide keyed to numbers along the route. Petroglyph images range from handprints to geometric patterns, animal tracks, bighorn sheep, lizards, mountain lions, bears, and humans. There are also stylized images of birds, which some archeologists theorize may have had religious significance, and animal images that are pierced by arrows or spears, which may have been a report of a successful hunt or possibly a plea to the gods for a good hunt.

A covered visitor contact station at the base of the hill is usually staffed by volunteers, who set up a spotting scope aimed up at the petroglyphs. A short trail leads from the picnic/camping area to the partially excavated remains of a prehistoric village, which includes the foundations of a pit house, a multiroom adobe building, and a rock structure. A campground has eight sites, including two with electric and water hookups, and restrooms (no showers). Small entrance and camping fees. Located 38 miles north of Alamogordo via US Hwy. 54 and CR B30. **Las Cruces Field Office, 1800 Marquess St., Las Cruces, 88005; 505-525-4300.**

White Sands National Monument

This surreal spot, a seemingly unending sea of pure-white sand, is part of the largest area of gypsum sands in the world. The sparkling white dunes were formed over thousands of years as rain and snow brought minerals down from the surrounding mountains. As the water evaporated, gypsum crystallized into minute grains of sand, and the prevailing southwest winds piled the white granules into rows of intricately shaped and constantly shifting dunes, a process that continues today.

The 16-mile (round-trip) Dunes Drive goes from the visitor center into the dunes, with pullouts along the route where exhibits help explain the geology and ecology of the dunes. The Dunes Drive also provides access to the monument's four designated hiking trails, plus parking areas where you can leave your vehicle to take off on foot among the dunes. The road is paved for 5 miles and is packed gypsum the last 3 miles. It's suitable for all vehicles.

The first three trails are relatively easy—the longest is a 1-mile loop—and the Interdune Boardwalk Trail is accessible to wheelchairs and strollers. This boardwalk is also the best trail for seeing the monument's wildflowers.

The longest hike here is at the end of the Dunes Drive in the Heart of the Dunes. The moderately rated Alkali Flat Trail is 4.6 miles round-trip, but it isn't necessary to hike the whole thing to appreciate the wide panoramic views across a seemingly endless parade of pure sand dunes, with practically no vegetation in sight. The trail is marked by white posts topped with orange reflective tape, and hikers are warned to turn back if blowing sand obscures the next post. Hikers on this trail are required to sign in and out at the register at the trailhead.

The Heart of the Dunes is the monument's playground, where you can run up and down these huge piles of sand or lie in the warm sun with your toes buried in the cool subsurface sand. Although hiking is permitted anywhere in the monument, rangers warn that it is

Yucca in bloom at White Sands National Monument.

easy to become lost among the constantly shifting dunes, where the wind sometimes sweeps away footprints in a matter of minutes. Therefore, before hikers set out they should orient themselves to the more permanent landmarks, such as mountain ranges and water towers.

Guided walks and a variety of interpretive programs are offered, with the greatest number and variety during the summer. Especially popular are the Sunset Stroll Nature Walks, leisurely one-hour guided walks in which rangers discuss the monument's plants and animals as the sun is setting. From May through Sept., the monument holds Full Moon programs on or near the evenings of the full moon, with talks on a variety of subjects. Also in summer, evening stargazing programs are scheduled several times each month.

Once each month, usually on a Sat., rangers give tours of Lake Lucero, the lowest point in the Tularosa Basin, where sand dunes begin to form. Because access to Lake Lucero crosses White Sands Missile Range, it is only open to the public during these monthly tours, in which rangers lead an auto caravan to the lake. Advance registration is required.

A visitor center has exhibits explaining the formation of the dunes and provides the only supply of drinking water in the monument. The monument does not have a drive-in campground, but backcountry hikers can make in-person requests for permits to camp in a small backcountry camping area.

Occasionally the Dunes Drive and even US Hwys. 70/82 are closed for an hour or two during missile testing on the adjacent White Sands Missile Range, at which times you must stay wherever you are until the testing is completed. Check with monument offices a day in advance for information on possible closures. From Memorial Day through Labor Day the Dunes Drive is open daily 7 A.M. 9 P.M., visitor center 8 A.M.–7 P.M.; the rest of the year, Dunes Drive 7 A.M.–sunset, visitor center 8 A.M.–5 P.M. Open later during full moon in summer; closed Christmas. Small admission fee. Located 15 miles southwest of Alamogordo via US Hwys. 70/82. **P.O. Box 1086, Holloman AFB, 88330; 505-679-2599; 505-479-6124; www.nps.gov/whsa.**

Outdoor Activities

There are good hiking trails at Oliver Lee Memorial State Park, Three Rivers Petroglyph Site, and White Sands National Monument (see Major Attractions). Also, the Lincoln National Forest, which covers much of the Sacramento Mountains to the east of Alamogordo, offers practically unlimited opportunities for hiking, mountain biking, fishing, picnicking, and camping. **Supervisor's Office, Federal Building, 1101 New York Ave., Alamogordo; 505-434-7200; www.fs.fed.us/r3.**

Golf

DESERT LAKES GOLF COURSE

With a desert environment at the base of the Sacramento Mountains, this city-owned public course was opened in 1950 and has plenty of mature trees and well-established greens. Open year-round. **2351 Hamilton Rd., Alamogordo; 505-437-0290.**

INN OF THE MOUNTAIN GODS GOLF COURSE

This attractive mountain course, at 7,200 feet elevation, offers spectacular views along with a challenging game—many of the holes are uphill. It's open year-round, weather permitting. Located next to the Mescalero Apaches' Inn of the Mountain Gods northeast of Alamogordo off US Hwy. 70. **Carrizo Canyon Rd., Mescalero; 800-446-2963; 505-464-7445; www.innofthemountaingods.com.**

THE LODGE AT CLOUDCROFT GOLF COURSE

A challenging 9-hole mountain course at 9,000 feet elevation, this course is governed by the Scottish tradition of playing different tees and separate flags on each hole. Open Apr.–Oct. Located at The Lodge resort. **1 Corona Pl., Cloudcroft; 866-595-6343; 505-682-2098; www.thelodgeresort.com.**

Skiing

SKI APACHE

Operated by the Mescalero Apache Indian tribe, Ski Apache is located on the slopes of 12,000-foot Sierra Blanca and is the state's third highest-elevation ski resort, behind Taos and Santa Fe. It has a peak elevation of 11,500 feet with a vertical drop of 1,900 feet and 55 runs rated 20 percent beginner, 35 percent intermediate, and 45 percent expert. With 750 skiable acres, it is the state's second biggest ski area, behind Taos. From Alamogordo it's about 65 miles to Ski Apache. Take US Hwy. 54 to Tularosa and go east to NM 48, which you take north through Ruidoso to NM 532, and follow it northwest to the ski area. **505-336-4356; 505-257-9001 (snow conditions); www.skiapache.com.**

SKI CLOUDCROFT

New Mexico's smallest ski area, 2 miles east of the community of Cloudcroft, is a good spot for beginner and intermediate skiers, with its 21 runs divided equally among beginner, intermediate, and expert. It has 68 skiable acres and a vertical drop of 700 feet from its peak elevation of 9,050 feet. From Alamogordo, go north on US Hwys. 54/70 and east on US Hwy. 82 for 18 miles to Cloudcroft, then continue east another 2 miles to the ski area. **800-333-7542; 505-682-2333.**

Seeing and Doing

Museums, Observatories, and Historic Sites

NEW MEXICO MUSEUM OF SPACE HISTORY

Among the state's most popular museums, and for good reason, here you will learn all about efforts to conquer space, from early rockets to sophisticated space stations. All of the pioneers of space travel

Just one of the missiles on display at the New Mexico Museum of Space History.

are honored here, Russian as well as American, along with the rockets and satellites that have been lofted into the heavens by humankind. The museum also has exhibits on New Mexico's role in space research. Ride the elevator to the fourth floor, then journey slowly downward on sloping ramps that lead you past the exhibits, which range from a moon rock to a Russian space suit to a lunar exploration vehicle. A state-of-the-art IMAX theater and planetarium offer a variety of movies and programs, and outside is an air and space park where you can see a collection of historic missiles, rockets, and other large space-related items. Open daily 9 A.M.–5 P.M.; closed Thanksgiving and Christmas. Admission fee charged. Located on Scenic Dr. and Indian Wells Rd., about 2 miles east of White Sands Blvd. (look for the gleaming gold building and the 90-foot-tall white rocket). **877-333-6589; 505-437-2840; www.spacefame.org.**

NATIONAL SOLAR OBSERVATORY

Atop the Sacramento Mountains at 9,200 feet above sea level, in a place chosen for the purity of its air, this observatory's main purpose is to monitor the sun and particularly sunspots, which have a direct effect upon our weather. You can tour the grounds and see some of the equipment on your own during daylight hours, but the best way to learn about the observatory is on a guided tour, which usually includes a slide show and a walk around the observatory, including a close-up view of the largest telescope. There are also some very good exhibits at the visitor center. A gift shop sells astronomy-related items. Self-guided tours daily dawn to dusk; guided tours June–Aug., Fri.–Sun. at 2 P.M. Visitor center open in summer daily 10 A.M.–6 P.M., the rest of the year

A replica of the Fat Man atomic bomb that was dropped on Nagasaki at the end of World War II.

Fri.–Sun. 10 A.M.–4 P.M. Small fee for guided tours. The 38-mile drive to the solar observatory is an attraction in itself, although the upper elevations of the road may be closed by snow in winter. From Alamogordo, drive north on US Hwys. 54/70 and east on US Hwy. 82 for 18 miles to Cloudcroft, then 20 miles south on NM 6563 to Sunspot. **P.O. Box 62, Sunspot, 88349-0062; 505-434-7000; www.sunspot.noao.edu.**

TOY TRAIN DEPOT

Anyone who enjoys toy trains can easily spend an hour here, and devoted train aficionados should schedule at least two hours. Housed in an 1898 railroad depot, this overstuffed little museum contains more than 1,200 feet of model train track and numerous operating electric trains. Some date to the 1800s, although most are from the 1930s through 1950s, including the Lionel company's big marketing flop: a pink train just for girls. Rides through the grounds on 12- and 16-gauge trains are also available, and a good little shop sells model train supplies and railroad

memorabilia. Open Wed.–Sun. noon 5 P.M. Admission and train ride fees, Located in Alameda Park (near the zoo and chamber of commerce visitor center). **1991 N. White Sands Blvd., Alamogordo; 505-437-2855; www. toytraindepot.homestead.com.**

TRINITY SITE

This is the exact spot where the world's first atomic bomb was detonated, to see if it would really work, on July 16, 1945. Although it's off-limits to the public most of the year, the military allows visitors on two days—the first Sat. in Apr. and Oct. There's something both eerie and almost sacred about Trinity Site, where a small monument commemorates the event and trinitite—green rock created by the atomic blast—is scattered on the ground. Nearby, the McDonald House, where the plutonium core of the bomb was assembled, can also be visited, and during the two days a year that the site is open the military sets up exhibits about the test explosion. Regardless of your feelings about nuclear weapons, there's no denying that the development of the atomic bomb was a significant chapter in the modern history of the world and that this spot, in a very remote place in the desert some 60 miles northwest of Alamogordo, played an important role in the bomb's development. The site is located on the White Sands Missile Range. Directions, regulations, times, and other information is available from the range's public affairs office. **White Sands Missile Range, White Sands, 88002; 505-678-1134; www.wsmr.army.mil (then click on Visitors, Public Affairs, Trinity Site).**

TULAROSA BASIN HISTORICAL MUSEUM

Artifacts and photos on the history of the area, from prehistoric times to pioneer days and into the 20th century. Open Mon.–Fri. 10 A.M.–4 P.M., Sat. 10 A.M.–3 P.M. and Sun. noon–3 P.M. Located next door to the Alamogordo Chamber of Commerce Visitor Center.

Trinity Site, the exact spot where the world's first atomic bomb was detonated on July 16, 1945, to see if it would really work.

1301 N. White Sands Blvd., Alamogordo; 505-434-4438; www.alamogordomuseum.org.

Scenic Drive

THE RUIDOSO-LINCOLN LOOP

This 200-mile tour offers beautiful scenery, hiking and fishing opportunities, and a glimpse into the Wild West. It could be done in one long day, but would be better if broken into several days, possibly spending the night in Ruidoso or Capitan. From Alamogordo, go north on US Hwy. 54 to Tularosa, where you might visit Tularosa Vineyards (see page 221) to pick up a bottle of the local wine. Then head east on US Hwy. 70 into the Sacramento Mountains to the resort community of Ruidoso **(800-253-2255; 505-257-7395; www.ruidoso.net),** whose name, Spanish for "noisy," comes from the babbling Ruidoso Creek. Surrounded by the Lincoln National Forest, this picturesque town is a good base for hiking and fishing. Just east of Ruidoso is the village of Ruidoso Downs, home of Ruidoso Downs Race Track **(505-378-4431),** which offers quarter horse and thoroughbred racing, and the Hubbard Museum of the American West **(505-378-4142),** with displays on horses, horse racing, and related items. From here continue east to Hondo, then turn back northwest on US Hwy. 380, which takes you to Lincoln. This genuine Wild West town, which is preserved as a state monument, was the site of a jailbreak by famed outlaw Billy the Kid. It's also known for the notorious Lincoln County War, in which ranchers and merchants staged a lengthy and bloody battle, all in the name of business (see sidebar on page 224).

From Lincoln continue west on US Hwy. 380 to the town of Capitan **(505-354-2247)** for a visit to Smokey Bear

Historical Park **(505-354-2748).** Here you'll see exhibits and the grave of the orphaned bear cub, who was rescued from a forest fire near here and became a national symbol of forest fire prevention. Leaving Capitan, drive west on US Hwy. 380 to the town of Carrizozo **(505-648-2732).** Cross US Hwy. 54 and go 4 miles to Valley of Fires Recreation Area, administered by the Bureau of Land Management **(505-648-2241).** A trail provides close-up views of numerous jet black lava formations, and this is also a good spot for a picnic or to camp for the night. Return to Carrizozo and head south on US Hwy. 54 to the turnoff to Three Rivers Petroglyph Site, which is described under Major Attractions. From Three Rivers, return to US Hwy. 54 and continue south through Tularosa back to Alamogordo.

Wineries and other Agricultural Stops

EAGLE RANCH PISTACHIO GROVES

More than 12,000 pistachio trees grow on this farm, which has the state's first and largest-producing pistachio groves. The trees are cultivated and harvested, and the crop is processed on-site, where there is a salting and roasting facility. A shop sells all sorts of pistachio products, including raw or roasted nuts and pistachio cookies, candy, and popcorn. Tours of the farm and facilities are also offered. Shop open Mon.–Sat. 8 A.M.–6 P.M., Sun. 9 A.M.–6 P.M. Tours June–Aug. Mon.–Fri. 10 A.M., 1:30 P.M., the rest of the year Mon.–Fri. 1:30 P.M. Located a few miles north of Alamogordo via US Hwys. 54/70. **7288 US Hwys. 54/70, Alamogordo; 800-432-0999; 505-434-0035; www.eagleranchpistachios.com.**

Capitan, New Mexico, is the home to Smokey Bear Historical Park.

TULAROSA VINEYARDS & WINERY

This family-owned and operated winery produces good quality wines, including Cabernet Sauvignon, Merlot, Sauvignon Blanc, and Chardonnay, using only New Mexico grapes. There's a shady picnic area and tours, tastings, and sales are usually offered daily noon–5 P.M., although calling before you go is recommended. Located 12 miles north of Alamogordo via US Hwys. 54/70 to Tularosa and then 2 miles north via US Hwy. 54 to the turnoff. **23 Coyote Canyon Rd., Tularosa; 800-687-4467; 505-585-2260; www.tularosavineyards.com.**

Zoo

ALAMEDA PARK ZOO

Established in 1898 as a diversion for railroad passengers while the steam locomotives refueled and took on water, the Alameda Park Zoo is the Southwest's oldest zoo. It now contains more than 300 animals representing about 90 species, displayed in a well-shaded environment covering 7 acres. Among animals here are monkeys, lions, bears, wolves, a playful otter, and numerous colorful birds. There's also a duck pond, picnic area, and a children's playground. Open daily 9 A.M.–5 P.M.; closed Christmas and New Year's Day. Admission fee charged. The zoo entrance is on White Sands Blvd. at 10th St. **1321 White Sands Blvd., Alamogordo; 505-439-4290.**

Where to Stay

Accommodations

Best Western Desert Aire Hotel—$$
This attractive Best Western has 99 rooms, a heated outdoor swimming pool, whirlpool, sauna, and game room. Pets accepted. **1021 S. White Sands Blvd., Alamogordo, 88310; 505-437-2110.**

Hampton Inn—$$–$$$
A member of one of our favorite motel chains, this Hampton Inn has all the usual amenities—including one of the best continental breakfasts offered—with 71 rooms, a self-serve laundry, heated outdoor pool, whirlpool, and an exercise room. **1295 Hamilton Rd., Alamogordo, 88310; 505-439-1782.**

Holiday Inn Express—$$
Attractive rooms, with a southwesern style, at reasonable prices make this motel a good choice. It has 106 rooms, a self-serve laundry, and a heated outdoor swimming pool. Pets accepted. **1401 S. White Sands Blvd., Alamogordo, 88310; 505-437-7100.**

The Lodge—$$$$
For our money, this is the best place to stay in this part of the state. The handsome historic lodge, built in 1909 after a fire destroyed the original 1899 lodge, has 61 units, all decorated with antiques and oozing historic charm. Even if you can't afford the price to stay, take the time to stop in, sit in the lobby, and pretend you're rich. Perhaps get lunch at Rebecca's, the lodge's restaurant (see Where to Eat), named for its resident ghost, a beautiful red-haired chambermaid at The Lodge in the 1930s who mysteriously disappeared after her lumberjack lover discovered her in the arms of another. Some units have refrigerators and microwaves; there's a heated outdoor pool, whirlpool, sauna, and 9-hole golf course. Pets accepted (for a fee). Located 18 miles east of Alamogordo. **1 Corona Pl., P.O. Box 497, Cloudcroft, 88317; 800-395-6343; 505-682-2566; www.thelodgeresort.com.**

Satellite Inn—$–$$
An inexpensive alternative to the chain motels, the Satellite Inn offers well-maintained basic rooms with microwaves and small refrigerators, including rooms with three double beds. It also has efficiency apartments. There's an outdoor swimming pool and self-serve laundry. **2224 N. White Sands Blvd., Alamogordo, 88310; 800-221-7690 (reservations); 505-437-8454; www.satelliteinn.com.**

Super 8—$$
Pleasant rooms—we especially like the ones with a king-size bed and a relaxing recliner—and an outdoor pool are the hallmarks of this 57-unit motel, which also has a coin-op laundry and accepts pets. **3204 N. White Sands Blvd., Alamogordo, 88310; 505-434-4205.**

Western Motel—$$

Clean, basic lodging at reasonable prices is what you'll find at this independent motel, which has 25 rooms. No pool. **1101 S. White Sands Blvd., Alamogordo, 88310; 505-437-2922.**

Campgrounds

In addition to the commercial campground discussed here, there are numerous places to camp in the Lincoln National Forest. We especially like the campground at Oliver Lee Memorial State Park. Also see the Outdoor Activities and Major Attractions sections.

ALAMOGORDO ROADRUNNER CAMPGROUND

Lots of shade trees, a swimming pool, and large, level sites make this a good choice. A former KOA, this campground has all the usual hookups and other amenities, 65 RV sites, and 11 tent sites. Located 1 block east of White Sands Blvd. **412 24th St., Alamogordo, 88310; 877-437-3003 (reservations); 505-437-3003; www. roadrunnercampground.com.**

Where to Eat

Brown Bag Deli—$

Great deli sandwiches at very reasonable prices are the fare here, with more than 30 choices—just about every type of meat, cheese, bread, and condiment you can imagine. Order at the counter and eat in the simple storefront dining room or get your sandwich to go. Open Mon.–Sat. 9 A.M.–9 P.M., Sun. 10 A.M.–9 P.M. **1504 E. 10th St., Alamogordo; 505-437-9751.**

Memories—$$–$$$

This upscale restaurant has lots of class, from its location in a handsome Victorian home dating from the early 1900s to its innovative American cuisine. The lunch menu includes burgers, sandwiches on a variety of breads and croissants, lasagna, and interesting

Three Rivers Petroglyph Site contains more than 21,000 petroglyphs. They are believed to have been created at least 1,000 years ago by the Mogollon prehistoric people who lived in an area that extended from here west into southeast Arizona and south into Mexico.

Lincoln and the Lincoln County War

Lincoln County was one wild place during the last half of the 19th century, and the tiny town of Lincoln, in a pretty mountain valley watered by the Rio Hondo, was the scene of a real Wild West shoot 'em-up more dramatic than anything you'll see in the movies.

First let's look at the cast of characters. Start with a skinny teenager named Henry McCarty, who traveled with his oft-married mother around the southern half of the state and came to Lincoln County. He started using the name of William H. Bonney, not as an alias but just because he liked the sound of it. Enter retired army officer L. G. Murphy, who built a merchandising empire in the tiny town by supplying the needs of nearby Fort Stanton and by overcharging farmers and ranchers, who were forced to deal with him as the only source of most everything. He also controlled the law in Lincoln County, including the local sheriff. Sounds like the plot for a B Western movie, but it's all true.

A wealthy young Englishman named John Tunstall came on the scene with his pockets full of family money to invest. He started a mercantile business in competition with the retired army officer, which earned him no gratitude. Tunstall teamed up with Alexander McSween, an attorney, to promote the business, and they worked with John Chisum, a pioneer cattleman, in trying to get the supply contract from Fort Stanton.

Tunstall, realizing that he wasn't getting a fair shake from the law, created his own law enforcement organization called the Regulators. One of the Regulators was young William Bonney, also known as Billy the Kid. It seems that Billy worshipped the suave, urbane Tunstall, who liked Billy because he needed the Kid's ability with the gun.

Then the real trouble started. On Feb. 18, 1878, Tunstall was ambushed and murdered in cold blood by a group of gunmen hired by Murphy's supporters. Billy and others in the McSween faction swore to kill everyone guilty of the foul deed, and in Apr. they murdered the corrupt sheriff and one of his deputies. More gunfights and more killings followed, and the culmination occurred in mid-July with a five-day gunfight at the McSween home in Lincoln, resulting in the death of McSween and two of his gunmen. Billy and the other supporters of McSween escaped.

Sheriff Pat Garrett got on the trail of Billy and his partners and two days before Christmas 1880 killed one of the McSween men and captured Billy in the tiny community of Stinking Springs, roughly 100 miles northeast of Lincoln. Billy was tried and sentenced to hang, and returned to Lincoln to await his execution. Apparently someone supplied Billy with a gun, and he escaped, killing two deputies.

The story goes that Sheriff Garrett surprised the Kid in the town of Fort Sumner and shot him dead, and that Billy now lies in the Fort Sumner cemetery. But like many stories from the Wild West, not everyone agrees, and over the years several men have claimed to be Billy the Kid. There's one story that Garrett and the Kid were actually friends and that Billy's death was staged—using a proxy

continued next page

Lincoln and the Lincoln County War continued

corpse—so Billy could escape to Mexico without fear of being tracked down. At least one man stated that as a boy he was told this in confidence by Garrett's widow.

The story of Billy the Kid and the Lincoln County War comes alive in the pioneer setting of the town of Lincoln, which is now a state monument. You can walk where the Kid walked, visit the big store that was the first mercantile business in Lincoln County, see other stores and homes, and explore the Lincoln County Courthouse. Wandering through this one-street town is free, but if you want to get inside seven of the buildings, which we highly recommend, there is an admission charge. The street is accessible all the time, but the buildings are open daily 8:30 A.M.–5 P.M.; closed major holidays. Located on US Hwy. 380, about 90 miles northeast of Alamogordo and 55 miles west of Roswell. **505-653-4372; www.newmexicoculture.org.**

salads such as the crab-stuffed avocado salad. Many of these items (except the sandwiches) are also offered at dinner, plus chicken and steak, including an 8-ounce Black Angus filet mignon, hand-cut, lightly seasoned, and charbroiled. There is also a good selection of seafood, including salmon and charbroiled mahi mahi. Reservations recommended. Open Mon.–Sat. 11 A.M.–9 P.M. **1223 N. New York Ave., Alamogordo; 505-437-0077.**

Rebecca's—$$–$$$$

Worth coming here just to soak up some of the atmosphere of this delightful historic hotel (see Accommodations), Rebecca's is an excellent restaurant offering a variety of sandwiches and pasta at lunch and steaks and seafood at dinner. The specialty dessert is fruit cobbler. Lunch prices are quite reasonable; the elegant dinners, with live piano music, are a bit pricey. Open daily 7–10:30 A.M., 11:30 A.M.–2:30 P.M., 5:30–10 P.M. Located 18 miles east of Alamogordo at The Lodge resort. **1 Corona Pl., Cloudcroft; 800-395-6343; 505-682-2566; www.thelodgeresort.com.**

Services

Visitor Information

Alamogordo Chamber of Commerce, 1301 N. White Sands Blvd., Alamogordo, 88310; 800-826-0294; 505-437-6120; www.alamogordo.com.

FORT SUMNER

Fort Sumner, a small town of about 1,200 people on the high, dry eastern plains of New Mexico at 4,025 feet, stakes its chief claim to fame on the story of Billy the Kid, aka William H. Bonney, whose real name was Henry McCarty. Even the top athletic event of the area is a tombstone race. Believe it or not, contestants go over an obstacle course while carrying tombstones! (By the way, tombstones are provided so you don't have to bring one.) The event, which takes place in early June, is based on the history of Billy the Kid's tombstone, which has been stolen three times, one time spending 27 years under a boxcar in Texas before its rescue and return to the Old Fort Sumner Military Cemetery.

History

Fort Sumner was built in 1862 to house American soldiers fighting the Apache, who once called all of southeastern New Mexico their own. During the Civil War and shortly thereafter, the soldiers won the battle with the Apache and the Navajo. It was decided to move all of the Indians to Fort Sumner and keep them on a long stretch of woods, watered by the Pecos River, known as the Bosque Redondo. The 400-mile journey of defeated Navajos from Fort Defiance, Arizona, to Fort Sumner, led by Kit Carson, went down in history as the Long Walk. During their time at Fort Sumner, hundreds of Indians died of disease, malnutrition, and exposure to the elements.

In 1868, Gen. William Sherman, upon inspecting the Bosque Redondo situation, determined that the relocation reservation was a failure and sent the Indians back to their tribal lands. In 1870, the buildings were sold to Lucien Bonaparte Maxwell, one of the country's largest private landowners, with holdings of more than 2 million acres in northern New Mexico. When Maxwell retired, he came to Fort Sumner and remodeled the old officers' quarters as his own home. It is in this home where in 1881 Sheriff Pat Garrett reportedly gunned down Billy the Kid.

Getting There

Fort Sumner is located at the junction of US Hwy. 84, US Hwy. 60, and NM 20.

Outdoor Activities

Sumner Lake State Park

Primarily a destination for anglers and boaters, Sumner Lake offers a refreshing change from the flat grasslands of New Mexico's eastern plains. It was created by damming the Pecos River to provide irrigation water for area farmers, and therefore the lake level fluctuates greatly. Both power boats and sailboats use the lake, and windsurfers take advantage of the spring winds. The most frequently caught fish are walleye, crappie, and white bass, and there are also some channel catfish, black bass, and bluegill. There are boat ramps and a courtesy dock, but no boat rentals.

The lake attracts migrating waterfowl in winter, such as geese, pelicans, and various ducks. Also watch for raptors such as osprey, a variety of hawks, and golden and bald eagles. Also seen in the park are raccoons, squirrels, skunks, rabbits, fox, and lizards. Almost everyone visiting in the fall sees deer.

The park has some trees, including junipers and cottonwoods, plus prairie grasses and several varieties of cactus. Wildflowers are often seen in spring. Unfortunately there are also unpleasant little sand burrs that can be very painful to pets and people going barefoot.

Camping ranges from developed sites with RV hookups to practically unlimited primitive lakeshore camping. The 50 developed campsites (18 with electric and water hookups) are mostly well spaced, with good views of the lake. There are restrooms with showers and an RV dump station. There are admission and camping fees. From Fort Sumner take US Hwy. 84 northwest 10 miles, then head west on NM 203 for 6 miles to the park entrance. **HC 64, Box 125, Fort Sumner, 88119; 505-355-2541; www.nmparks.com.**

Seeing and Doing

Museums and Historic Sites

BILLY THE KID'S GRAVE
The grave of Billy the Kid, including his tombstone securely held in place with a metal cage, is in the Old Fort Sumner Military Cemetery, which also contains the graves of other notables including land baron Lucien Bonaparte Maxwell. The cemetery is open around the clock and is located behind the Old Fort Sumner Museum (see page 228).

BILLY THE KID MUSEUM
This well-stuffed museum contains some 60,000 items from this area's wild days from the mid-1800s to the early 1900s,

including a rifle that belonged to Billy the Kid, ranch implements, a horse-drawn hearse, and antique automobiles. There are also mementos of the original fort and lots of Indian artifacts. Open Mon.–Sat. 8:30 A.M.–5:00 P.M., Sun. 11 A.M.–5 P.M.; closed Jan. 1–15, Thanksgiving, Christmas. Admission fee charged. Located at E. Sumner Ave. and US Hwy. 60. **1601 E. Sumner Ave., Fort Sumner; 505-355-2380.**

FORT SUMNER STATE MONUMENT
This fort housed troops that guarded thousands of Navajos and Apaches who were captured and forced onto a reservation near here. Although the buildings are gone, there is a marker on the site and a museum tells the story of this sad chapter of American history. Open Wed.–Mon. 8:30 A.M.–5 P.M.; closed

Billy the Kid's grave can be found at the Old Fort Sumner Military Cemetery.

winter holidays. Admission fee charged. Located 4 miles east of Fort Sumner via US Hwy. 60, then about 3 miles south on Billy the Kid Rd.; about 0.25 mile west of Old Fort Sumner Museum. **505-355-2573; www. newmexicoculture.org.**

OLD FORT SUMNER MUSEUM

This museum contains displays of memorabilia and photographs on the history of the fort and life in general in these parts beginning in 1865. Open Mon.–Tues. 9 A.M.–4 P.M., Wed.–Thurs. 12:30–4:30 P.M., Fri.–Sun. 8:30 A.M.–4:30 P.M. Admission fee charged. Located 4 miles east of Fort Sumner via US Hwy. 60, then 3 miles south on Billy the Kid Rd. **505-355-2942.**

Where to Stay and Eat

Motels in Fort Sumner include a **Super 8** ($$), **1707 Ft. Sumner Ave., Fort Sumner, 88119; 505-355-7888,** which has 44 rooms, and the independent **Coronado Motel** ($$), **309 W. Sumner Ave., Fort Sumner, 88119; 505-355-2466,** with 15 rooms. There is camping at **Sumner Lake State Park,** discussed under Outdoor Activities. Of the several restaurants in town, we suggest **Fred's Restaurant & Lounge** ($$–$$$), **1408 E. Sumner Ave., Fort Sumner; 505-355-7500,** which offers good American and Mexican items, including burgers, steaks, grilled chicken breast, enchiladas, burritos, and fajitas.

Services

Visitor Information

Fort Sumner/De Baca County Chamber of Commerce, 707 N. 4th St., P.O. Box 28, Fort Sumner, 88119; 505-355-7705; www.ftsumnerchamber.com.

A quack-mire at Sumner Lake State Park.

ROSWELL

The largest city in the southeastern part of the state, lying at an elevation of 3,669 feet with more than 45,000 people, Roswell provides goods and services for a large area of ranches, farms, and oil and gas production. It is home to New Mexico Military Institute, which turns out military leaders, and also has a branch college of Eastern New Mexico University. Its famous citizens include artist Peter Hurd and pro golfer Nancy Lopez, who became the youngest inductee into the LPGA Hall of Fame in 1987 at the age of 30.

In recent years, however, Roswell's fame has come mostly from space aliens, and the community's efforts to capitalize on the crash landing of what some people believe was an alien spaceship in 1947. Although the city has a few too many shops hawking T-shirts and souvenirs depicting space aliens, there is some fascinating information at the UFO Museum and fun times during the annual UFO Festival. And Roswell is more than UFOs—there's art and military history, wildlife viewing, and a pleasant state park.

History

In its early days the area that would become Roswell was a stopping point—for Indian hunting parties, Spanish explorers, and then cowboys taking cattle to market. The community began in 1869, when gambler Van C. Smith built two adobe buildings and named the town Roswell in honor of his father, Roswell Smith. Eight years later Capt. Joseph C. Lea bought him out, and when artesian water was discovered in

1890, Roswell really began to grow as a center of irrigated agriculture. The discovery of oil in the area brought more people. In the 1930s, scientist Robert Goddard experimented with rockets near Roswell, work that is credited with making space flight possible today.

In the summer of 1947, a local rancher discovered some strange wreckage while checking on his sheep. He showed some of the metal debris to friends, then notified the sheriff, who notified the Air Force. At first the Air Force said it was the wreckage of a flying saucer, but within hours changed their tune, claiming that it was actually parts from a military weather balloon. What has come to be called the Roswell Incident continues to live, with claims that alien beings were actually taken from the crashed "spacecraft" and charges of a government cover-up.

Getting There

Roswell is at the junction of US Hwys. 285, 70, and 380.

Festivals and Events

UFO FESTIVAL
early July. The main event on the Roswellian calendar, this festival commemorates the alleged crash of a UFO here in 1947, often referred to as the "Roswell Incident." The multiday event mixes the serious with the festive. There are lectures on space aliens in general as well as new information about the Roswell Incident, plus a

parade and alien costume contest, showings of science fiction films, music, and games. Contact either of the agencies under Visitor Information, or **www.uforoswell.com.**

PIÑATAFEST

mid-Sept. Mexican culture is celebrated with mariachi music, traditional foods, games, arts and crafts, and a Mexican-style rodeo. **888-616-0889.**

EASTERN NEW MEXICO STATE FAIR

early Oct. The oldest fair in New Mexico, with a parade, midway, carnival, rodeo, and lots of exhibits. **505-623-9411.**

Outdoor Activities

Bird-Watching

BITTER LAKE NATIONAL WILDLIFE REFUGE

This is the place to come to see a variety of migrating waterfowl and sandhill cranes, as well as more than four dozen species of dragonflies and rare barking frogs. Thousands of lesser sandhill cranes, ducks, and snow geese stop at the refuge during their fall migrations each year, and many stay through Feb. In summer interior least terns, snowy plovers, killdeer, avocets, and black-necked stilts breed here. Year-round watch for sparrows, scaled quail, and roadrunners, among others. There are four short hiking trails and two longer trails, plus an 8-mile round-trip auto tour. The refuge is open daily dawn to dusk; office open Mon.–Fri. 7:30 A.M.–4:30 P.M. Located about 9 miles northeast of Roswell. Take US Hwy. 380 east from Roswell, turn left (north) onto Red Bridge Rd., then right (east) onto East Pine Lodge Rd.,

which leads into the refuge. **P.O. Box 7, Roswell, 88202; 505-622-6755; http://southwest.fws.gov/refuges/newmex/bitterlake.**

Fishing, Hiking, and Swimming

BOTTOMLESS LAKES STATE PARK

A favorite stop for 19th-century cowboys herding cattle between Texas and Wyoming, they called the lakes "bottomless" because their ropes failed to touch bottom. In reality, of course, the cowboys' ropes probably were simply not long enough, and the park's eight lakes, which are actually water-filled sinkholes, range in depth from 17 to 90 feet. Attractions here are swimming, scuba diving, a short hiking trail, camping, boating and paddleboarding, fishing, wildlife and bird viewing, and spectacular views of red rock cliffs.

Swimming is permitted only at Lea Lake, the park's largest lake with 15 surface acres and a depth of 90 feet. The water here is clear, fed by an underground spring that delivers an average of 2.5 million gallons of water into the lake each day, making Lea Lake particularly popular with scuba divers. Water temperatures in summer rarely rise over 75° F, even when air temperatures are over 100° F. Along the beach is a handsome stone building, constructed in the mid-1930s by the Civilian Conservation Corps, which in summer houses a gift shop, boat rental station, and vending machines for refreshments.

Lifeguards are on duty only during the summer, but swimming is permitted year-round for those hardy enough. Lea Lake is also the only one of the Bottomless Lakes where boating is permitted. During the summer paddleboards and pedal boats are available for rent. Sailboards, inflatables, canoes, and other boats with motors up to three horsepower are also permitted, but not available for rent at the park. There is no boat ramp.

A hiking trail of a little less than 1 mile goes north from the Lea Lake parking lot, with a cutoff to Lost Lake—smallest of the park's lakes—before connecting with a paved park road that leads to the park's five other lakes and the visitor center. It is well worth the short hike to a vantage point above Devil's Inkwell, a small lake with steep banks and very dark water. Just north of Devil's Inkwell is Mirror Lake, named for its picture-perfect reflection of the surrounding red cliffs.

Wildlife here—most easily seen in the cooler months—includes jackrabbits, roadrunners, lizards, rattlesnakes, mule deer, raccoons, and coyotes. There are also coots—small black birds with white beaks that are members of the chicken family—plus snow geese, mallards, peregrine falcons, and red-tailed hawks. Anglers have the best luck in winter, when several lakes are stocked with rainbow trout.

The Lea Lake Campground has 32 RV campsites with hookups, plus 12 designated tent sites with little shade. It also has restrooms with showers and an RV dump station. There are also less-developed camping areas, with a bit more shade but no showers, along the rock bluffs near the other lakes. These offer pit toilets and centralized water. Those visiting during the hot summer months will find the best cooling breezes at Lea Lake.

Located 12 miles east of Roswell via US Hwy. 380, then south 3 miles on NM 409. **HC 12, Box 1200, Roswell, 88201; 505-624-6058; www.nmparks.com.**

Golf

There are several public golf courses here, including the 18-hole **Spring River Golf Course, 1612 W. 8th St., Roswell; 505-622-9505;** and the 18-hole **New Mexico Military Institute Golf Course, 201 W. 19th St., Roswell; 505-622-6033.**

Bottomless Lakes State Park. Eight lakes are home to all types of wildlife.

Seeing and Doing

Museums

GENERAL DOUGLAS L. MCBRIDE MUSEUM

The history of the U.S. military, and in particular New Mexicans and graduates of New Mexico Military Institute, is documented here with a variety of exhibits. Open Tues.–Fri. 8:30 A.M.–11:30 A.M. and 1–3 P.M. Closed major holidays. Located on the campus of New Mexico Military Institute. **101 W. College Blvd., Roswell; 505-624-8220.**

HISTORICAL CENTER OF SOUTHEAST NEW MEXICO

An impressive collection of the area's historical artifacts is housed in this stately home, built in 1912 by James Phelps White, a wealthy and influential

The International UFO Museum & Research Center attracts a lot of visitors—those who believe an alien craft crashed nearby or those who are simply amused by the controversy.

rancher who came to this area from Texas in 1881. The home shows how wealthy families of the late 1800s and early 1900s lived in southeastern New Mexico, and it also contains a vast array of antiques and curiosities from the era. Open daily 1–4 P.M. and by appointment. **200 N. Lea Ave., Roswell; 505-622-8333.**

INTERNATIONAL UFO MUSEUM & RESEARCH CENTER

An impressive museum, this facility is dedicated to the mysteries of unidentified flying objects and aliens from outer space, in particular the alleged crash landing of a space vehicle in the Roswell area in 1947. It presents an enormous amount of information—too much to be absorbed in just one visit—about the purported UFO crash, as well as mysterious sightings and incidents in other areas. It also has information on the government's explanations of these events and views from skeptical scientists. There's a lot of fun stuff, such as the simulated "alien examination room," alien related paintings, and the sculpture of RALF—Roswell Alien Life Form—the museum mascot. Open daily 9 A.M.–5 P.M. Closed New Year's Day, Thanksgiving, and Christmas. **114 N. Main St., Roswell; 800-822-3545; 505-625-9495; www.iufomrc.org.**

ROSWELL MUSEUM AND ART CENTER

This excellent facility features the works of prominent southwestern artists, such as Peter Hurd (born in Roswell), Henriette Wyeth, Victor Higgins, Georgia O'Keeffe, and Andrew Dasburg. It also houses historical items relating to space, including the memorabilia of Robert H. Goddard, the first person to test liquid rocket fuels and a pioneer in the U.S. space program. Adjacent is the Robert

Goddard Planetarium, which offers multimedia shows and programs on astronomy. Open Mon.–Sat. 9 A.M.–5 P.M., Sun. and holidays 1–5 P.M. Free admission to the museum and art center; fees for planetarium shows. Located in Civic Center Plaza and 11th and Main Sts. **100 W. 11th St., Roswell; 505-624-6744; www.roswellmuseum.org.**

Zoo and Fish Hatchery

DEXTER NATIONAL FISH HATCHERY
A center for the study of threatened and endangered fish species, the hatchery has a visitors center, exhibits, and an aquarium containing endangered fish. Open Mon.–Fri. 7 A.M.–4 P.M. Located on NM 190 (Shawnee Rd.) 1 mile east of Dexter, about 16 miles southeast of Roswell via NM 2. **505-734-5910.**

SPRING RIVER PARK AND ZOO
This small, well-run zoo is a fun place for children. It has more than 100 animals, ranging from prairie dogs to longhorn cattle, plus an old-fashioned carousel, rides on a miniature train, a kids' fishing pond, and a picnic area. Open daily 10 A.M.–dusk; closed Christmas. Located at College Blvd. and Atkinson St. **1306 E. College Blvd.; 505-624-6760.**

Where to Stay

Accommodations
Best Western El Rancho Palacio—$$
Good, basic lodging at reasonable prices. This Best Western has 44 rooms, a small outdoor heated pool, and whirlpool. Mini-refrigerators and microwaves are available. Pets accepted.

2205 N. Main St., Roswell, 88201; 505-622-2721.

Best Western Sally Port Inn & Suites— $$$
This very attractive hotel has 124 rooms, a heated indoor pool, whirlpool, and sauna. There's also an exercise room and game room, plus a beauty salon, restaurant, and lounge. Refrigerators and microwaves available. Pets accepted (fee). 2000 N. Main St., Roswell, 88201; 505-622-6430.

Budget Inn North—$–$$
There are 42 rooms, a small outdoor pool, and whirlpool. Mini-refrigerators and microwaves are available. Pets accepted (for a fee). 2101 N. Main St., Roswell, 88201; 505-623-6050.

Budget Inn West—$–$$
There's a small outdoor pool and whirlpool and 29 standard rooms. Mini-refrigerators and microwaves available. Pets accepted (for a fee). 2200 W. 2nd St., Roswell, 88201; 505-623-3811.

Comfort Inn—$$$
There are 55 attractive rooms, including some with whirlpool tubs, and all units have two phones, a mini-refrigerator, and microwave. There's an indoor heated pool, whirlpool, and exercise equipment. Pets accepted. 3595 N. Main St., Roswell, 88201; 505-623-4567.

Days Inn—$$
There's a small outdoor pool and whirlpool; 62 standard rooms. Pets accepted. 1310 N. Main St., 88201; 505-623-4021.

Frontier Motel—$–$$
This attractive independent motel offers 38 spacious rooms on one ground floor, all with mini-refrigerators, plus a small

outdoor pool. Pets accepted. **3010 N. Main St. Roswell, 88201; 800-678-1401; 505-622-1400; www.frontiermotelroswell.com.**

Leisure Inn—$$

Offers 90 large, well-maintained rooms, some with mini-refrigerators and microwaves. There's an outdoor heated pool and exercise equipment. Pets accepted (for a fee). **2700 W. 2nd St., Roswell, 88201; 505-622-2575.**

Super 8—$$

There are 63 units, an indoor pool, and a whirlpool. **3575 N. Main St., Roswell, 88201; 505-622-8886.**

Campgrounds

Camping possibilities here include the campground at Bottomless Lakes State Park (see Outdoor Activities).

TOWN AND COUNTRY RV PARK

This well-run facility, with all the amenities you would expect in a first-class commercial campground, has 75 sites, including 5 tent sites. There are shade trees, an outdoor heated pool, a recreation room, self-serve laundry, and sites for big RVs. Cable TV is included with hookup sites and daily phone service is available. **331 W. Brasher Rd., Roswell, 88203; 800-499-4364 (reservations); 505-624-1833; www.roswell-usa.com/tandcrv.**

TRAILER VILLAGE CAMPGROUND

This pleasant RV park (no tents) has 53 sites with full hookups, including cable TV, laundry facilities, clean showers, and all the other usual amenities except a pool. **1706 E. 2nd St., Roswell, 88201; 505-623-6040.**

Where to Eat

Cattle Baron Steak and Seafood Restaurant—$$–$$$

Slow-roasted prime rib—the house specialty—plus hand-cut steaks, chicken, and seafood, make this Old West–style restaurant a local favorite. There is also a huge salad bar. It's part of a regional chain, and there are also Cattle Barons in Ruidoso, Portales, Hobbs, and Las Cruces in New Mexico, plus El Paso, Lubbock, and Midland in Texas. Open Sun.–Thurs. 11 A.M.–9:30 P.M., Fri.–Sat. 11 A.M.–10 P.M. Closed Thanksgiving and Christmas. **1113 N. Main St., Roswell; 505-622-2465; www.cattlebaron.com.**

Nuthin' Fancy Cafe—$$

Just as the name implies, this is the place to come for good, basic American food—burgers, sandwiches, meatloaf, grilled chicken, and salads—in a cafe-type setting. Open Sun.–Thurs. 6 A.M.–9 P.M., Fri.–Sat. 6 A.M.–9:30 P.M. **2103 N. Main St., Roswell; 505-623-4098.**

Services

Visitor Information

Roswell Chamber of Commerce, 131 W. 2nd St., P.O. Box 70, Roswell, 88202; 877-849-7679; 505-623-5695; www.roswellnm.org.

Roswell Visitors Center, 426 N. Main St., Roswell, 88201; 888-767-9355; 505-624-7704; www.roswellcvb.com.

SALINAS PUEBLO MISSIONS NATIONAL MONUMENT

Made up of three separate sites, this isolated national monument preserves the ruins of three large American Indian pueblos and some of the best remaining 17th-century Franciscan mission churches in the United States. Each site offers a slightly different perspective on the history of this region, but they all explain the conflict of cultures that occurred between the Pueblo people and the Spanish colonists who arrived in the 1700s.

The pueblos of Abó, Gran Quivira (also called Las Humanas), and Quarai were constructed by people of the Ancestral Puebloan and Mogollon cultures beginning in the 1300s and were thriving communities when Spanish conquistadors first saw them in the late 1500s. The pueblos were ideally situated for trade, and residents traded with the Plains tribes to the east and the Rio Grande pueblos to the west and north. Collectively, these pueblos are now known as the *Salinas*, the Spanish word for salt, which was abundant in the area and an important trading commodity.

One of the goals of Spain in exploring the new world was economic—the search for gold and other riches—but converting the local people to Christianity was almost equally important. The Franciscan missionaries were partly successful in their conversion efforts, but they also brought a great deal of bitterness plus European diseases, to which the Indians had little immunity.

The Spanish missionaries considered the Indians' native religion to be idolatry, and tried to prevent the Pueblo people from practicing their kachina dances

The Quarai site of Salinas Pueblo Missions National Monument.

236

and other rituals. At first, the Pueblo religious leaders thought they could incorporate this new Christian god into their rituals, but after some of the Franciscans destroyed kivas and kachina masks, it became obvious that there could be no middle ground. Adding to the animosity of the Pueblo people, some Spanish colonists were allowed to demand tribute from the Indians, often in the form of grain or cloth.

Drought, European diseases, and the resulting famine in the 1660s and 1670s decimated the Pueblo people, and the remaining residents abandoned their villages in the 1670s, mostly joining other pueblos. In 1680, the pueblos to the north revolted against the Spanish, driving them back into Mexico, where they stayed until the reconquest of New Mexico in 1692.

Seeing the Pueblos

Start your visit at the national monument visitor center in Mountainair, which has exhibits on the three pueblos and the missions. Then head out to the individual sites, where you'll find impressive ruins that can be seen on short, easy paths.

Quarai has the most impressive mission—the Nuestra Señora de la Purísima Concepción de Cuarac Church—where a 0.5-mile gravel loop trail leads from the contact station/museum into the church and past some partially excavated pueblo ruins. An easy side trip off the main trail takes you onto the 1-mile round-trip Spanish Corral Trail, which follows a hillside to the remains of what historians believe was a pen for sheep

used by Hispanic settlers in the 19th century. Also from this trail are views east into the Estancia Valley and its salt lakes, where since prehistoric times people obtained salt.

At Abó, a paved 0.25-mile trail leads to the towering walls of San Gregorio de Abó Church and continues for another 0.5 mile among the unexcavated ruins, with a number of visible walls, from the Abó Pueblo. Gran Quivira's 0.5-mile gravel trail winds among the ruins of two churches—the Mission of San Buenaventura and the Church of San Isidro—plus the excavated and stabilized ruins of the Pueblo de Las Humanas, the largest of the Salinas pueblos. Also at the Gran Quivira site visitors can see a one-hour video on the excavation of a section of the pueblo.

Visitor Information and Directions

The visitor center and sites are open in summer daily 9 A.M.–6 P.M., and the rest of the year daily 9 A.M.–5 P.M. The monument visitor center is in the small community of Mountainair, along US Hwy. 60 about 36 miles east of I-25, exit 175 (Bernardo), or about 40 miles southwest of I-40, exit 196 (Moriarty) via NM 41 and US Hwy. 60. From Mountainair, Quarai is 8 miles north on NM 55 and 1 mile west on an access road, Abó is 9 miles west on US Hwy. 60 and 0.5 mile north on NM 513, and Gran Quivira is 25 miles south on NM 55. **Corner of Ripley St. and Broadway, P.O. Box 517, Mountainair, 87036; 505-847-2585; www.nps.gov/sapu.**

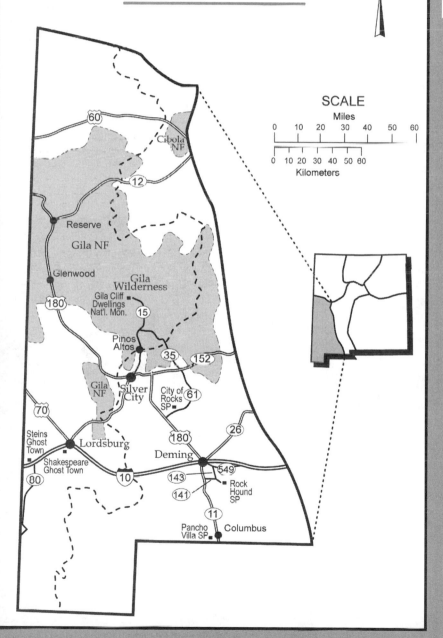

SOUTHWEST REGION

N

SCALE

Miles

0 10 20 30 40 50 60

0 10 20 30 40 50 60
Kilometers

60

Cibola NF

12

Reserve

Gila NF

Glenwood

Gila Wilderness

Gila Cliff Dwellings Nat'l. Mon.

15

180

Pinos Altos

35 152

Gila NF

Silver City

City of Rocks SP 61

70

Steins Ghost Town

Lordsburg

Shakespeare Ghost Town

26

180

80

10

Deming

143

141

549

Rock Hound SP

11

Pancho Villa SP

Columbus

Southwest Region

Southwestern New Mexico is a land of extreme contrasts, from vast, bone-dry deserts to expanses of cool, pine-clad mountains. You'll find some of the oldest Ancestral Puebloan ruins at Gila Cliff Dwellings National Monument and more recent marks of humankind's passing at the huge copper mines near Silver City. Some of the largest wilderness areas in America are in this region of New Mexico, including the first-ever established U.S. wilderness area, and at Pancho Villa State Park you'll learn about the day in 1916 when the small town of Columbus was raided by Mexi-can troops. This corner boasts several ghost towns from the state's mining era, when millions of dollars came out of these mountains and deserts.

In the late 1800s, the railroads came through, bringing settlers from around the country, and when Interstate 10 was built in the late 1960s, more people poured into the area. Then tourists started coming, and "snowbirds," people fleeing the cold of northern climes for several months each winter, discovered the warmth of Deming and Lordsburg.

This is a land of diversity. Come along. Let's take a look.

These boulders from the City of Rocks State Park were formed from volcanic ash that was hardened into rock and sculpted by wind, water, and blowing desert sand.

DEMING

Deming straddles I-10 exactly halfway between Las Cruces and Lordsburg and bills itself as the city of "pure water and fast ducks." The water sustains fields of cotton, chile, and other produce, and the ducks take over for the annual Deming Duck Race. The town is also the jumping off place for three great state parks: City of Rocks, 28 miles northwest of town; Rockhound, about 14 miles southeast; and Pancho Villa, 35 miles south. Deming has about 14,000 people and lies at an elevation of 4,300 feet.

History

Deming sprang up as a small tent and wooden shanty settlement when the Southern Pacific and Atchison, Topeka and Santa Fe Railroads were ceremonially joined to complete the route through southern New Mexico. On Mar. 8, 1881, Dick Coleman of the A, T & SF and three Southern Pacific officials drove in the silver spike at the junction of the two lines, and in Nov. of that year, the small community at the crossroads was officially christened Deming.

Eventually most of the railroad traffic was diverted away from Deming to El Paso, but Deming refused to die. It soon boasted more substantial buildings of wood and adobe and by 1900 had a population of about 1,500 with two newspapers, four churches, 25 places of business, a public school, and four hotels. They also claimed to have absolutely pure water. Early farmers found the soil good for growing a variety of produce: alfalfa, lettuce, onions, chile, and cotton. Agriculture is still the main economic base here,

and farmers have recently added grapes and pecans to their crops. Cattle ranches have proliferated and prospered here also.

Getting There

You can't miss Deming if you're driving through the state on I-10: just take exits 81, 82, or 85 and there you are. It's about 60 miles west of Las Cruces and 60 miles east of Lordsburg. US Hwy. 180 heads northwest out of town toward Silver City; NM 11 goes south to Columbus and Pancho Villa State Park; and NM 26 takes off northeast to Hatch (see the **Lower Rio Grande** chapter).

Major Attractions

City of Rocks State Park

These boulders, haphazardly tumbled around the landscape, conjure images of stone skyscrapers abandoned by some ancient race of giants, or maybe they're the result of a special effects wizard for some other-worldly Hollywood adventure. Whatever it may look like, these are the real thing—ash spewed from volcanos some 33 million years ago hardened into rock and sculpted by the forces of wind, water, and blowing desert sand into the fanciful and bizarre shapes seen today.

Most park visitors come primarily for the rocks—to climb over, photograph, camp among, or just sit and gaze at. To visitors with active imaginations, individual boulders become camels, bears, turtles, rockets, temples, people, or ice-cream cones. And even these change as the sun moves across the sky, producing ever-changing shadows.

The visitor center has exhibits on the park's geology, archeology, plants, and wildlife. Monthly campfire programs generally include music and storytelling. Each year, usually in mid-May, the park celebrates Heritage Preservation Day with guided tours, demonstrations, and other activities.

The delightful Botanical Garden has neatly labeled desert plants, and an easy 0.75-mile loop trail at the back of the garden offers some fine views of the rocks and surrounding desert. Although this is the only officially designated trail, hikers can travel for several miles, walking around and over the boulders or along the 1.5-mile dirt road that circles the park's clustered namesake "city of rocks."

More than 35 species of birds have been spotted in the park, including golden eagles, Swainson's hawks, greater roadrunners, red-tailed hawks, prairie falcons, and great horned owls. Mammals you might catch a glimpse of include cottontail rabbits, black-tailed jackrabbits, rock squirrels, kangaroo rats, porcupines, and coyotes. Also in the park are numerous lizards—mostly whiptails but some collared—plus desert box turtles and several kinds of snakes, including rattlesnakes, seen mainly in summer. Wildflowers and cactus often bloom in Apr. and May.

For a distant view of the rock formations, seen in contrast to the surrounding desert, drive the 0.25-mile (one-way) dirt road up to Observation Point, in the southeast corner of the park. From this perspective, the formations look almost surreal.

The campground, which is open year-round, has 52 sites tucked among the boulders and juniper trees of the "city" and another area with 10 RV sites containing electric and water hookups. There are picnic tables, restrooms with showers, and an RV dump station. Admission and camping fees. From Deming take US Hwy. 180 northwest 24 miles, then go northeast on NM 61 for 4 miles to the park access road. **P.O. Box**

A grease rack installed to service military vehicles for the U.S. Army. It's on display at Pancho Villa State Park. Motorized transport was used in a military operation for the first time in a mission to apprehend Pancho Villa and his troups.

50, Faywood, 88034; 505-536-2800; www.nmparks.com.

Pancho Villa State Park

No moon shone during the early morning hours of Mar. 9, 1916, when Mexican guerillas, led by famed bandit-revolutionary Francisco "Pancho" Villa, crossed the Mexico–U.S. border and attacked, looted, and set fire to the tiny New Mexico village of Columbus, killing 18 Americans and wounding another 12. A small garrison of U.S. troops on the south edge of town mounted a defense, and by dawn, the Mexicans had fled back across the border. Initial reports said there were 2,000 attackers, but later estimates put it closer to 500.

President Woodrow Wilson sent Gen. John "Black Jack" Pershing on what was called a "punitive expedition" in which thousands of U.S. troops chased Villa for 11 months, traveling some 400 miles into Mexico. Although there were a number of skirmishes with Villa's men, in which 75 to 100 Mexican guerillas were killed, Villa himself avoided capture.

Although Pershing's trek through Mexico in search of Villa didn't attain its goal, it was successful in another way— as a training ground for World War I. Industrialization had brought changes to the world and to war. Pershing's punitive expedition was the last time the United States used mounted cavalry and the first time a U.S. military operation used motorized trucks and planes. Park visitors today can see the ruins of the military camp, including the adobe shell of the judge advocate's office and jail, the first grease rack installed to service military vehicles, and the camp's airstrip, used by the Army's First Aero Squadron, which consisted of eight biplanes. The old U.S. Customs Service building, constructed in 1902, serves as the park's visitor center, with artifacts, historic photos, and exhibits describing the attack on Columbus and the U.S. military's incursion into Mexico.

Each year on Mar. 9, the park hosts "Raid Day," which includes a commemorative program to remember those Americans killed in the raid plus a barbecue.

Another side to the park is natural rather than historical: the botanical garden boasts more than 30 varieties of cacti and their drought-resistant brethren, and late spring is usually the best time to see them in bloom. Birders have catalogued more than 50 species in the park, mostly from fall through early spring. The park also has jackrabbits, coyotes, javelina, rattlesnakes, bull snakes, and the occasional bobcat.

Trails here are short and easy. A 130-yard nature trail has identifying signs on cacti and other desert plants. The paved Coote's Hill Trail, named for a soldier who was stationed here, is actually a series of interconnecting trails that takes you to the top of Coote's Hill for a good view of the surrounding countryside all the way to Mexico. There's also a 1-mile exercise loop trail, convenient for getting to and from the campground and other park facilities.

Those who want to find out more about Villa's raid on Columbus, or other aspects of the village's history, can walk across the street from the park to the Columbus Historical Museum, housed in an old Southern Pacific Railroad depot. It contains exhibits and artifacts from Villa's raid, plus exhibits from the community's early railroad days.

The campground, open year-round, doesn't have an abundance of shade, although there are a few trees. There are 56 RV sites, and a few of the large sites have multiple hookups, plus there's a small tenting area, restrooms with showers, dump station, recreation hall, picnic tables, group shelters, and playground. Admission and camping fees are charged. The park is in the village of Columbus, 35 miles south of Deming via NM 11. **P.O. Box 450, Columbus, 88029; 505-531-2711; www.nmparks.com.**

Rockhound State Park

This is one of the few public places in the country where visitors are actively encouraged to attack the land with shovels and carry off the fruits of their labors. Established in 1966, Rockhound State Park sits on the rugged western slope of the Little Florida Mountains, in an area of volcanic origins rich in color-ful agates, quartz crystals, and other rocks and minerals. For those who can take their eyes off the ground, the scenery is fine too, and there are opportunities for hiking and bird-watching.

Individuals are permitted to take up to 15 pounds of rock, and you can use rock hammers and small shovels but no power equipment. Remember: more interesting specimens can be found off the beaten track, farther from the camp-ground and visitor center.

The moderately rated 1.2-mile loop trail provides access to rock collecting areas, plus adjacent public state and

Some of the rocks found in Rockhound State Park, where visitors are encouraged to hunt and take home rock treasures that they find.

federal lands. The trail has a few steep sections, and if you continue higher into the mountains you'll have wonderful panoramic views southwest to the Sierra Madre Mountains of Mexico and west to the Victorio Mountains, named for the famous Apache chief.

Stop at the visitor center to see rocks and minerals found in the park, first how they look in the ground and again, after they have been cut and polished. Some of the more fascinating ones to us are the variegated nodules—called thunder eggs and geodes—which often contain intriguing patterns of agate, common opal, manganese oxide minerals, or quartz crystals. During the park's busiest times—from Oct. through Mar.—several geology talks and rockhounding tours are offered each week; about one per month is offered the rest of the year.

Spring Canyon is a seasonal day-use area about 3 miles south of Rockhound. Far more rugged than the main section of the park, it's open from Easter through Nov. and offers excellent oppor-tunities to see wildlife, particularly Persian ibex, a type of wild goat imported into this area in 1976. Mountain lions are present but seldom seen. There are no designated hiking trails, but there are miles of trails left by cattle and other animals. In addition, the area has picnic tables, a group shelter, and solar energy–powered vault toilets.

Sunsets can be spellbinding from the southwest-facing campground, especially from the higher-elevation sites. Juniper, mesquite, and other low bushes and trees produce little shade, but sites are spacious. Of the 32 campsites, 29 have electric hookups. A botanical garden contains numerous species of cacti and other desert plants. There's also a play-ground, restrooms with showers, and a dump station. Admission and camping fees are charged. From Deming take NM

11 south 5 miles, then head east on NM 141 for about 9 miles. **P.O. Box 1064, Deming, 88030; 505-546-6182; www.nmparks.com.**

Festivals and Events

ROCKHOUND ROUNDUP
first weekend in Mar. For rock lovers, this grand display of magnificent rocks is sponsored by the Deming Gem and Mineral Society. Gems and minerals are bought, sold, and swapped, and there are guided field trips led by local experts. Southwest New Mexico State Fairgrounds. **Deming Gem and Mineral Society, P.O. Box 1459, Deming, 88031; 505-546-0348.**

GREAT AMERICAN DUCK RACES
fourth weekend in Aug. This unusual event draws notice from across the country and around the world. First held in 1980, the races have expanded to include both a dry run and wet paddle, both over a 16-foot distance. The first and most important rule of the race is that mistreatment of a duck, even touching them in any way during the race, calls for immediate disqualification. Other events—such as choosing the Darling Duckling of the year, crowning the Duck Queen, a golf tournament, a Duck Queen Ball, a hot air balloon rally, softball tournaments, chili cook-offs, and the annual outhouse race—are also scheduled. It's a fun time for the entire family. The climax, of course, is the duck race itself, when the world's fastest ducks compete for a purse of several thousand dollars. Bring your duck! **Deming-Luna County Chamber of Commerce; 800-848-4955; 505-546-2674.**

SOUTHWESTERN NEW MEXICO STATE FAIR
second week in Oct. Events, food, crafts, and all the usual state fair fun. **Southwest New Mexico State Fairgrounds, Deming, 505-546-0177.**

TIN STREET LUMINARIA DISPLAY
Christmas Eve. The soft glow of candles in sand-weighted paper bags light the way for the Christ child. Christmas tradition in Deming since 1990. **505-546-9535.**

Seeing and Doing

Museum

DEMING LUNA MIMBRES MUSEUM
One wall of this museum has a 53-foot mural depicting the history of Luna County. There's also a restored 1853 customs house and displays of early railroad equipment, military items from the cavalry era through World War II, a cowboy display, and an excellent collection of basketry and Mimbres Indian pottery. It offers a good introduction to this part of New Mexico. Donations welcome. Open Mon.–Sat. 9 A.M.–4 P.M.; Sun. 1:30–4 P.M.; closed major holidays. **301 S. Silver St., Deming, 88031; 505-546-2382.**

Winery

ST. CLAIR VINEYARDS
The 4,500 foot elevation in the Mimbres Valley produces warm days and cool nights, making it possible to grow some of the best grapes in New Mexico. Begun in 1984, St. Clair is now one of New Mexico's largest wineries, with a

Luminarias, also called farolitos, decorate homes and other buildings statewide during the Christmas season.

capacity of 500,000 gallons. In 2003, they had 70 acres planted with a variety of grapes including Zinfandel, Cabernet Sauvignon, Chardonnay, and Sauvignon Blanc, and plan to have 100 acres planted by 2005. Stop in and taste some of their wines and take some with you. Their tasting room is open Mon.–Sat. 9 A.M.–6 P.M. and Sun. noon–5 P.M.; free tours available Sat. at 11 A.M. and 3 P.M. From I-10 take exit 85 and head east on NM 549 about 3 miles. **1325 De Baca Rd., Deming, 88030; 866-336-7357; 505-546-1179; www.stclairvineyards.com.**

Where to Stay

Accommodations

Lodging in Deming is pretty basic, and most motels can be found along Pine St. and Spruce St. between I-10 exits 81 and 85.

Best Western Mimbres Valley Inn—$$

This typical Best Western has 40 rooms, all on the ground floor, plus a pool and restaurant. Pets accepted. **1500 W. Pine St., Deming, 88030; 800-937-8376; 505-546-4544.**

Days Inn—$$

Has 57 basic rooms, free continental breakfast, heated outdoor pool, and an on-site restaurant serves lunch and dinner. Pets accepted (for a fee). A golf course is located about 0.25 mile away. **1601 E. Pine St., Deming, 88030; 505-546-8813.**

Grand Motor Inn—$$

Attractive independent motel offers 62 units, outdoor heated pool, restaurant (see below), and coin-operated laundry room; small pets accepted. **1801 E. Pine St., P.O. Box 309, Deming, 88031; 505-546-2631.**

Holiday Inn—$$–$$$

Has 116 standard units, outdoor heated pool, exercise room, restaurant (see below), pets accepted. **4600 Motel Dr., P.O. Box 1138, Deming, 88031; 505-546-2661.**

Wagon Wheel Motel—$–$$

Small independent motel with 15 rooms, some with shower only. Small pets accepted, restaurants nearby, coin-operated laundry, some rooms have mini-refrigerators. **1109 W. Pine St., Deming, 88030; 505-546-2681.**

Campgrounds

All three of the state parks discussed in Major Attractions have nice campgrounds.

DEMING ROADRUNNER RV PARK

There are 83 gravel RV sites (many of which are pull-throughs and can accommodate slide outs) and 26 grassy tent sites on 7 acres. Restrooms with showers, 24-hour coin-operated laundry, small store, propane available. Large heated indoor pool plus hut tub, exercise equipment, playground, and dump station. **2849 E. Pine St., Deming, 88030; 800-226-9937 (reservations); 505-546-6960; www.zianet.com/roadrunnerrv.**

LITTLE VINEYARD RV PARK

This well-maintained campground has 150 RV sites on 15 acres but only 2 tent sites. There are lots of long and wide pull-through sites suitable for large RVs and a beautiful indoor heated pool and hot tub. There's also exercise equipment, picnic tables, and BBQ grills, restrooms with showers, cable TV, dump station. **2901 E. Motel Dr., Deming, 88030; 800-413-0312 (reservations); 505-546-3560; www.littlevinyard.com.**

STARLIGHT VILLAGE RESORT

The Starlight Village offers 40 spacious pull-through sites with full hookups, phone service available at 25 sites. There are 11 tent sites, an outdoor pool, walking trails meandering over 85 acres, restrooms with hot showers, and a coin-operated laundry. Also, there are some casitas with one and two bedrooms and full kitchens. **2020 Hatch Hwy. NE, Deming, 88030; 505-546-9550.**

Where to Eat

Fat Eddie's at the Inn—$$–$$$

This local favorite offers casual dining featuring daily buffets, with home-style American food and very nice pies and cobblers for dessert. Open Sun.–Fri. 6:30 A.M.–1:30 P.M. and 5–9:30 P.M.; Sat. 7–11 A.M. and 5–9:30 P.M. **Holiday Inn, 4600 Motel Dr., Deming; 505-546-2661.**

Grand Restaurant—$$–$$$

This casual family-style restaurant offers steak and seafood, a salad bar, good homemade soups and pies, and real Mexican food. Open daily 6 A.M.–9 P.M. **Grand Motor Inn, 1801 E. Pine St., Deming; 505-546-2632.**

Services

Deming-Luna County Chamber of Commerce, 800 E. Pine St., P.O. Box 8, Deming, 88030; 800-848-4955; 505-546-2674; www.demingchamber.com.

245

LORDSBURG

Sitting in the southeast corner of New Mexico at an elevation of 4,250 is the small town of Lordsburg, with a population of about 3,400. It's a quiet place, representing a blending of three cultures—American Indian, Mexican, and Anglo—that caters to travelers along I-10 with motels, restaurants, campgrounds, and gasoline stations. This is the place to stay when exploring the ghost towns of Steins and Shakespeare.

History

Apaches once lived in what is now Lordsburg and the surrounding area, and the natural springs found here made it an important watering stop for anyone traveling between what later became Tucson and El Paso. Generations of Mexicans and, in 1846, the Mormon Battalion stopped for water. Once the area became a U.S. territory—after the Gadsden Purchase established the border between the United States and Mexico in 1853—the Butterfield Stagecoach Co. brought their route to the West Coast through here, followed by the Pony Express in the late 1850s.

The town of Lordsburg was finally established by the Southern Pacific Railroad in 1880. Originally a smattering of tents with little authority, it evolved into a more stable town of brick and adobe as settlers moved in and mining, ranching, and farming took the place of gambling and shooting. In the 1920s, the first airport in New Mexico was built here, with celebrities such as Charles A. Lindbergh, Amelia Earhart, and Tom Mix dropping by.

Getting There

Lordsburg is along I-10, 60 miles west of Deming and 20 miles from the state line. You can't miss it.

Major Attractions

Ghost Towns

SHAKESPEARE GHOST TOWN
Declared a National Historic Site in 1970, Shakespeare is the last name of what's left of a southwestern pioneer town. First a tiny settlement known as Grant grew up around a reliable water source along the emigrant trail to California. In 1870, it mushroomed to around 3,000 people after a silver strike and diamond swindle and was called Ralston City or the Burro Mines. Once that bubble burst, it dropped to around 50 stubborn miners. Finally, in 1879, Col. Wm. F. Boyle took control of most of the good claims, began the Shakespeare Gold and Silver Mining and Milling Co., and renamed the town for his company, hoping to obliterate any memories of the earlier swindle.

Shakespeare settled down some, with a few families moving in, but never really became the solid city Colonel Boyle hoped to establish. When the railroad bypassed Shakespeare in 1880 and instead created Lordsburg 3 miles north, it was the beginning of the end. Businesses moved out, the 1893 depression closed the mines, and people left in droves, abandoning their homes to the elements. A new copper mine a mile south of town brought some short-lived prosperity to a few remaining miners in the early 1900s. The entire town and buildings were sold in 1935 to Frank and Rita Hill to become a ranch.

The Hills maintained the buildings as best they could, and their daughter and her husband occupy the General Merchandise Building and continue to work at preservation of Shakespeare as a true example of the Old West.

You can see Shakespeare only on a guided 1.5-hour tour, which takes in the interiors of about eight buildings. Tour days are usually the second weekend of the month, and the admission fee is used for upkeep and restoration of the buildings. Take I 10, exit 22, and drive south about 2.5 miles, following the signs. **P.O Box 253, Lordsburg, 88045; 505-542-9034; www.shakespeareghostown.com.**

STEINS GHOST TOWN

This railroad ghost town also has a colorful history, although it's not as old or notorious as Shakespeare. Built in the 1880s, Steins (pronounced "Steens") was named for the first U.S. Army officer who signed a treaty with the Mimbres Apaches.

In 1858, the Butterfield Overland Stage Co. replaced the Birch stage line in servicing the area, and in Apr. 1861, shortly before the line was closed by Congress due to the outbreak of the Civil War, the stage was attacked near Steins by Cochise and his band, and all aboard were killed.

In the early 1880s, the Southern Pacific Railroad laid track through Steins Pass, and the town served as a work station to support the railroad. They hauled water from Doubtful Canyon—so

247

The arrival of the railroad in the late 1800s and the location of train stations spelled success or failure for many New Mexico communities. This scene is from Chama, in the north central mountains.

named because the Apache raids made it uncertain whether you would come through it alive—for $1 a barrel. But the town grew and had its heyday in the first half of the 20th century, with a population of about 1,300 by the outbreak of World War II. After the war the railroad switched from steam to diesel, drastically reducing the need for the support towns along its route, and people left Steins in droves, seeking a livelihood elsewhere.

Today there are two residents: Linda and Larry Link, who purchased the town and have preserved this bit of western Americana for visitors to enjoy. There are about 10 restored buildings, some with rooms in period furnishings, others crammed with memorabilia from the 1800s. Steins is just off I-10, exit 3. Open daily late May to late Oct., 9 A.M.–7 P.M., rest of year 8 A.M.–5 P.M.; closed Christmas and New Year's Day. A fee is charged. **Steins, P.O. Box 2185 Road Forks, 88045; 505-542-9791.**

Where to Stay and Eat

Most lodging in Lordsburg is along the interstate. Independents include the **American Motor Inn** ($$), with 88 standard rooms on two floors, an outdoor heated pool and wading pool, playground, and restaurant. Some rooms have a fridge and microwave, and small pets are accepted (for a fee). **944 E. Motel Dr. (I-10, exit 24), Lordsburg, 88045; 505-542-3591.**

Of the chain motels, we like the **Best Western–Western Skies Inn** ($$), with 40 ground floor rooms, a restaurant, and heated outdoor pool. Pets accepted (for a fee). **1303 S. Main**

St. **(I-10, exit 22), Lordsburg, 88045; 505-542-8807.** Other choices include the **Holiday Inn Express** ($$) with 40 rooms and a heated outdoor pool. Pets accepted (for a fee). **1408 S. Main St. (I-10, exit 22), Lordsburg, 88045; 505-542-3666;** and **Days Inn & Suites** ($$–$$$), which has 56 standard units, some with shower only, as well as a heated indoor pool, fridge and microwave in some units; pets accepted (for a fee). **1426 W. Motel Dr. (I-10, exit 20), Lordsburg, 88045; 505-542-3600.** There's also a **Super 8 Motel** ($$) with 41 standard rooms, at **110 E. Maple St., Lordsburg, 88045; 505-542-8882.**

Campgrounds include the **KOA,** with 65 graveled sites on 8 acres, a nice seasonal outdoor pool but little shade. Open year-round. **1501 Lead St. (I-10, exit 22, follow signs), Lordsburg, 88045; 800-562-5772 (reservations); 505-542-8003.**

Dining options include **Kranberry's Family Restaurant** ($–$$$), a friendly, casual restaurant with southwestern art on the walls, offering good burgers and sandwiches plus other basic American fare and Mexican foods. Baked goods are made on-site. Open daily 6 A.M.—9:30 P.M. **1405 S. Main St. (I-10, exit 22), Lordsburg, 505-542-9400.**

Services

Lordsburg-Hidalgo County Chamber of Commerce, 117 E. 2nd St., Lordsburg, 88045; 505-542-9864; www. hidalgocounty.org/lordsburgcoc.

SILVER CITY

The laid-back mountain town of Silver City is quite different from nearby Deming and Lordsburg. At 5,895 feet elevation, it's about 1,600 feet higher than either of those towns, so it's both cooler and wetter. Copper and silver have played a major role in the evolution of the area, and they still have an impact, now that Silver City's population has grown to more than 11,000.

The historic downtown district is a good place to begin your visit. It has great shops and galleries and several fine museums. Theater and musical performances take place at Western New Mexico University. Once you leave town, many outdoor opportunities await you in the surrounding countryside. North of town is America's first established wilderness, the Gila, created in 1924, and the Gila Cliff Dwellings, a fascinating spot to discover how prehistoric humans existed here.

History

The mountains and valleys around Silver City were created by huge geologic forces and water erosion over many centuries. These forces of nature left behind deposits of ore that modern humans have feverishly dug out of the ground over the last 200 years, and the ruins of old mines still exist side by side with modern operating and prosperous silver mines.

Prehistoric groups hunted and lived in the area for more than 10,000 years until around A.D. 1400. A few hundred years later, nomadic Apaches roamed about, along with Spaniards in search of the famed cities of gold. In the early 1800s,

there was a Spanish settlement here named San Vicente de la Cienaga, or St. Vincent's Marsh, but after the mining boom the name was changed to Silver City. In 1848, much of what is now New Mexico was ceded to the United States by the Treaty of Guadalupe Hidalgo. In the next 20 years, prospectors streamed in, responding to the call of gold, found in the Pinos Altos Mountains north of Silver City.

Log cabins were built in what is now downtown Silver City around 1868, and in 1870, the town was incorporated. That year saw the first silver claim to be officially filed, for the Legal Tender—about 1 mile east of the courthouse on Broadway. In 1880, the city passed an ordinance requiring that construction of all residences be of brick, stone, or adobe, to guard against fire.

Unfortunately, they didn't have anything to guard against flood, and the mining activities had left the surrounding hills naked, so when unusually heavy rains came in 1895 a 12-foot wall of water washed out Main St., leaving a 35-foot-deep gouge in its place. More flooding in 1903 dropped Main St.—now known as the Big Ditch—another 20 feet. It was stabilized by the Civilian Conservation Corps in 1936, and in 1980, the city made it into a park with shade trees and waterfalls along the river.

Getting There

Silver City is a highway hub: US Hwy. 180 heads southeast to Deming (53 miles), NM 15 winds its way north to the fabled Gila Cliff Dwellings (42 miles), NM 90 connects to Lordsburg,

112 miles southwest, and NM 152 leads east through the mountains to I-25.

Major Attraction

Gila Cliff Dwellings National Monument

Some 700 years ago the Mogollon hunted game, gathered wild plants, and planted corn, squash, and beans on the mesa tops and along the rivers in what is now the Gila National Forest. They also built homes—first simple pit houses dug into the earth, then rectangular aboveground buildings of stone or interwoven twigs. Finally, the well-protected cliff dwellings that are the namesake of this national monument appeared.

Archeologists say there may have been two groups of Mogollon people here, at different times, as evidenced by differences in pottery found during excavations. In the monument are numerous ruins of Mimbres Mogollon

pit houses dating to between A.D. 200 and 550, as well as later aboveground structures. However, the cliff dwellings, which are simply homes built into natural caves, were constructed by a different group of Mogollon, the Tularosa, who relocated from an area about 75 miles to the northwest.

This later group built their cave houses in the late 1270s and 1280s. About 40 stone rooms are spread among five caves along a southeast-facing cliff, where archeologists believe that 40 to 60 people lived. In addition to what they could grow or catch, the Mogollon traded with other tribes for cotton, shells, and obsidian (used for arrow points). They also weaved and produced striking white pottery with black designs.

Although it appears these cliff-dwellers thrived for a while, in about one generation, by 1300, their homes were abandoned. Why they left and where they went remains a mystery, although there is speculation that they joined other Indian pueblos to the north and east.

Gila Cliff Dwellings National Monument.

EXPLORING THE MONUMENT

The ruins are accessible via the unpaved Gila Cliff Dwellings Trail, a somewhat rocky 1-mile round-trip loop. This easy-to-moderate interpretive trail has a few steep sections, plus stairs and ladders, as it leads visitors about 180 feet up the side of the cliff and into the cliff dwellings. Many of the rooms can be entered, although some are off-limits because of their fragile condition. The trail becomes muddy when it rains and slick in freezing or snowy conditions, so good-traction footwear is recommended. A trail guide is available at the trailhead, and rangers are stationed at the ruins to answer questions. Guided tours are offered daily at 11 A.M. and 2 P.M.

Near the cliff dwellings, but officially in the national forest, are two small campgrounds and the Trail to the Past. This easy 0.25-mile round-trip walk provides access to a small two-room cliff dwelling, occupied about 700 years ago. There is also a Mogollon pictograph panel—a series of rock art designs created with a paint made from water and powdered hematite—and what appears to have been a Mogollon work area—a boulder worn smooth from what may have been the sharpening of stone tools.

Wildlife viewing and bird-watching opportunities are abundant in and near the national monument, as well as throughout the national forest and wilderness area. Some of the best viewing spots are along the West Fork of the Gila River.

In summer, evening campfire programs take place frequently at the amphitheater near the visitor center. Check the bulletin boards for a current schedule. The monument offers a Junior Ranger program, in which kids complete projects in an activity guide to earn badges.

The Upper and Lower Scorpion Campgrounds are little more than park-ing lots for RVs, but offer pleasant tent sites, nicely spaced among the trees, with grills and picnic tables; rest rooms have cold water sinks. Trailers are limited to 17 feet.

VISITOR INFORMATION, DIRECTIONS, AND FACTS

The visitor center, operated jointly by the U.S. Forest Service and National Park Service, has a museum with exhibits on the Mogollon culture and a small bookstore. There is also a visitor contact station at the Gila Cliff Dwellings trailhead, which also has exhibits and a small bookstore. There are self-serve dog kennels, picnic tables, an RV dump station, and horse corrals. The cliff dwelling trail is open daily 8 A.M.–6 P.M. Memorial Day through Labor Day; 9 A.M.–4 P.M. the rest of the year. Closed Christmas and New Year's Day. The Trail to the Past is open daily, 24 hours, year-round. Both admission and camping fees are charged. From Silver City travel north on NM 15 for 44 miles to the monument. **HC 68, Box 100, Silver City, 88061; 505-536-9461; www.nps.gov/gicl.**

Festivals and Events

SILVER CITY BLUES FESTIVAL
Memorial Day weekend. Blues fills the air all weekend long, outside in the parks and indoors in the clubs. Some of America's top blues bands show up for this extravaganza. In addition to artistic events, there's plenty of food and drink. **888-758-7289; 505-538-2505; www.mrac.cc.**

WILD, WILD WEST PRO RODEO
end of May. An exciting rodeo event complete with bull riding, barrel racing,

and steer roping. **800-548-9378; 505-538-3785; www.silvercity.org.**

BIG DITCH ART FAIR

Labor Day weekend. Take a self-guided art walk using a brochure provided by the San Vicente Artists of Silver City. Stop at the McCray Gallery at Western New Mexico University. **888-758-7289; 505-538-2505; www.mrac.cc.**

WEEKEND AT THE GALLERIES

Columbus Day weekend in mid-Oct. Gallery tours, a wine tasting, and live music highlight this three-day art event. See a wide range of regional art from crystal and jewelry to metal and fine paintings. **888-758-7289; 505-538-2505; www.mrac.cc.**

Outdoor Activities

Gila National Forest & Wilderness Area

There are numerous opportunities for backpacking, horseback riding, and fishing in the national forest and wilderness area, and for mountain biking in the national forest (but not in the wilderness area). In addition, there are several hot springs nearby. Stop at the Gila National Monument Visitor Center or visitor contact station for maps and recommendations.

There are some 1,500 miles of trails open to hikers and horseback riders in the Gila National Forest and Gila Wilderness. One of the most easily accessible is Forest Trail 151, a moderate hike that begins at the Gila Cliff Dwellings parking lot and follows the West Fork of the Gila River Trail into the Gila Wilderness, crossing the river a number of times. A popular turn-around point is a small cliff dwelling ruin,

located 3 miles up the trail. Several trails into the wilderness area also take off from the TJ Corral trailhead, along NM 15 about a mile and a half north of the monument's visitor center, where you can pick up a trail handout. For national forest and wilderness area information contact **Gila National Forest, 3005 E. Camino del Bosque, Silver City, 88061; 505-388-8201; www.fs.fed.us/r3.**

Golf

SCOTT PARK GOLF COURSE

This great 18-hole public course, at 6,000 feet in elevation and a championship yardage of 6,367, has a pro shop, putting green, and practice range plus carts, instruction, and clubs for rent. **720 Golf Course Rd., Silver City, 88061; 505-538-5041; www.houstonbizdir.com/scottpark.**

Seeing and Doing

Museums and Historic Sites

PINOS ALTOS

Some half-dozen miles north of Silver City on NM 15, Pinos Altos, which means "tall pines" in Spanish, cannot be called a ghost town, for too many people still live there. Gold was discovered here in 1837 and the town sprung up. But Apache Indians stayed on the warpath, and many miners lost their lives. To solve the problem, the original settlers held a powwow with the Apaches. One legend has it that Mangas Colorado, a famed chieftain of the Apache, came to town to discuss some differences of opinion with the local gentry. Although he came under a truce flag, he was subjected to a rump kicking and a horsewhipping, an insult that surely would have prolonged the Apache wars. But finally the Indians and the miners got together for another powwow. As a result of the conference, it was agreed that a big cross would be placed atop the high point of the mountains, and as long as the cross was there, no more killing would occur.

Among the buildings not to be missed are the elegant **Opera House,** built in 1869, and adjacent **Buckhorn Saloon** (see Where to Eat). A local legend at the saloon is about a prostitute called Debbie De Camp. The story is that when Debbie died in a public brawl, her sisters of the night scrawled this memorial over her room: "Shed a tear for Debbie De Camp/Born a virgin and died a tramp./For 17 years she retained her virginity/A real good record for this vicinity." Other buildings to look for include **Hearst Church,** an adobe Methodist-Episcopal church built in 1898 with money provided by publisher William Randolph Hearst, which now houses the Grant County Art Guild, and the **Pinos Altos Museum,** housed in a log cabin built as a schoolhouse about 1866.

SILVER CITY MUSEUM

Housed in the restored 1881 H. B. Ailman House, this fine small museum provides a glimpse into the early years of Silver City, especially how the founding fathers lived. There are thematic exhibits of southwestern New Mexico plus changing exhibits of local history, a local history research library, and a store stocked with numerous books on the area plus handcrafted gift items. Open Tues.–Fri. 9 A.M.–4:30 P.M. and Sat.–Sun. 10 A.M.–4 P.M. **312 W. Broadway, Silver City, 88061; 505-538-5921; www.silvercitymuseum.org.**

WESTERN NEW MEXICO UNIVERSITY MUSEUM

This fine museum houses what may be the largest permanent display of Mimbres pottery and culture in the world. Additional displays include pottery from other prehistoric southwestern cultures, more modern pottery by such well-known potters as Maria Martinez, Navajo rugs, and historic photographs of Silver City and its environs. Open Mon.–Fri. 9 A.M. 4:30 P.M., Sat.–Sun. 10 A.M.–4 P.M.; closed during university holidays. Located at the west end of 10th St. within the university. **1000 W. College Ave., P.O. Box 680, Silver City, 88062; 505-538-6386; www.wnmu.edu/univ/museum.htm.**

Performing Arts

Western New Mexico University has a fine-arts department. They have several music performances throughout the school year, plus one or two theater productions, and ongoing art exhibits. Performing arts often take place at the Fine Arts Center Theatre and exhibits are at the McCray Gallery **(505-538-6517).** For a schedule of events contact the departmental secretary **(505-538-6618)** or check the Expressive Arts Calendar online at **www.wnmu.edu.**

Where to Stay

Accommodations
Comfort Inn—$$
A small-scale hotel with 52 rooms, indoor pool and whirlpool, valet, and coin-op laundry available; restaurants nearby. **1060 E. US Hwy. 180, Silver City, 88061; 800-228-5150; 505-534-1883.**

Drifter Motel—$$
Offers 69 rooms, an outdoor heated

pool, valet laundry, and a restaurant (see below). Some rooms have refrigerators; small pets accepted. **711 E. US Hwy 180, P.O. Box 1288, Silver City, 88062; 505-538-2916.**

Econo Lodge Silver City—$$

A bit more upscale than the standard Econo Lodge, with 60 attractive rooms and three suites, in-room coffee, heated indoor pool, a whirlpool, and an exercise room. Some rooms have fridge and microwave. Restaurants are nearby. Pets accepted (for a fee). **1120 E. US Hwy. 180, Silver City, 88061; 505-534-1111.**

Holiday Inn Express—$$

Has 60 rooms, some with whirlpool tubs. There is also a small exercise room, valet, and coin-op laundry. Restaurants are nearby. Pets accepted. East of town about 3 miles on US 1 Hwy. 80 and NM 90. **1103 Superior St., Silver City, 88061; 505-538-2525.**

Campgrounds

In addition to the commercial campgrounds below, many camping opportunities are available in the **Gila National Forest,** including two campgrounds discussed above in the section on Gila Cliff Dwellings National Monument. **3005 E. Camino del Bosque, Silver City, 88061; 505-388-8201; www.fs.fed.us/r3.**

KOA SILVER CITY

Open year-round, this KOA has 75 sites, restrooms with hot showers, outdoor heated pool open mid-May to mid-Oct. Television reception is excellent without cable. LP gas is available. **11824 E. US 180, Silver City, 88061; 800-562-7623; 505-388-3351; www.koa.com.**

SILVER CITY RV PARK

There are shade trees, good security lighting, and an extra clean bathhouse and laundry room at this downtown campground. Includes 49 RV sites, 4 tent sites, and a RV dump station. **1304 N. Bennett St., Silver City, 88061; 505-538-2239; www.silvercityrv.com.**

Where to Eat

Buckhorn Saloon—$$–$$$$

This fascinating old saloon, built in the 1860s, is well worth visiting just for its historic charm—we keep expecting to see grizzled miners and ladies of the night standing at the bar tossing back a few shots of red-eye—but it also offers some of the best steaks and burgers in this part of the state. There's also seafood and homemade desserts, as well as frequent live entertainment. Open Mon.–Sat. 6–10 P.M. Reservations recommended. Located about 6 miles north of Silver City via NM 15. **32 Main St., Pinos Altos; 505-538-9911.**

Drifter Pancake House Restaurant and Lounge—$$

Offers a well-rounded menu, great for breakfast. Lounge with happy hour, pool tables, and dancing. Daily 6 A.M.–2 P.M. and 5–10 P.M. **Drifter Motel, 711 E. US Hwy 180, Silver City; 505-538-2916.**

Services

Silver City/Grant County Chamber of Commerce, 201 N. Hudson Ave., Silver City, 88061; 800-548-9378; 505-538-3785; www.silvercity.org.

254

INDEX

255

Index

Index